The Business of Baseball

The Business of Baseball

by ALBERT THEODORE POWERS

McFarland & Company, Inc., Publishers
Jefferson, North Carolina, and London

Library of Congress Cataloguing-in-Publication Data

Powers, Albert Theodore, 1953–
    The business of baseball / by Albert Theodore Powers.
        p.   cm.
    Includes bibliographical references and index.

    ISBN 0-7864-1426-X (softcover : 50# alkaline paper) ∞

    1. Baseball—Economic aspects—United States.   2. Baseball—
United States—History.   I. Title.
    GV880.P692003
    796.357'06'91—dc21   2002152442

British Library cataloguing data are available

Cover images ©2002 Photospin

Manufactured in the United States of America

McFarland & Company, Inc., Publishers
  Box 611, Jefferson, North Carolina 28640
  www.mcfarlandpub.com

CONTENTS

PREFACE

When I was a boy growing up in Kansas, a friend of mine and I went fishing and as we sat there in the warmth of a summer afternoon we talked about what we wanted to do when we grew up. I told him I wanted to be a real major league baseball player, a genuine professional like Honus Wagner. My friend said that he'd like to be President of the United States. Neither of us got our wish.
— President Dwight D. Eisenhower

Baseball is not life itself, although the resemblance keeps coming up. It's probably a good idea to keep the two sorted out, but old fans, if they're anything like me, can't help noticing how cunningly our game replicates the longer schedule, with its beguiling April optimism; the cheerful roughhouse of June; the grinding, serious, unending (surely) business of midsummer; the September settling of accounts, when hopes must be traded in for philosophies or brave smiles; and then the abrupt sunning-down of autumn, when we wish for—almost demand—a prolonged and glittering final adventure before the curtain.
— Roger Angell

You see, you spend a good piece of your life gripping a baseball, and in the end it turns out that it was the other way around all the time.
— Jim Bouton

Baseball and my love for it are among my earliest memories. I cannot recall a time when I didn't love playing the game, watching it, listening

vii

to it, thinking about it, and talking about it. For nearly half a century, I
have loved nearly everything about this sublime game—its action, its measured pace, its strategies, its players, its history, its records and statistics,
its simplicity, its complexity, its honor, its fairness, and its beauty. As I
will reveal in this book, however, there has always been a side of baseball
that is not beautiful, simple, honorable, just, or admirable. This book
clearly demonstrates that the problems of today's Major Leagues are in
most cases merely a continuation of ills that have plagued organized baseball since its inception. Much of the material in this book has been dealt
with by other writers, in many cases in a more competent, complete, and
prosaic manner. References to many of those sources are provided at the
back of this book. This book differs from other writings, however, because
it also offers a comprehensive proposal for dealing with Major League
Baseball's major shortcomings to ensure its continued success.

      In spite of the efforts of Messrs. Steinbrenner, Reinsdorf, Turner,
Murdoch, and their predecessors and Messrs. Miller, Fehr, and their predecessors to completely dominate the game, baseball is still primarily
about the players and the fans. This book will briefly look at some of Major
League Baseball's greatest players and their effects on the game and its
business. It will discuss the roles of the franchise owners, commissioners,
and players' unions in organized baseball. It will discuss Major League
Baseball's ballparks and their relevance to the game. It will look at the
fans. Finally, it will address Major League Baseball's most significant problems and offer proposals for dealing with them.

      The premise of this book is simple: There is nothing wrong with the
game of baseball, but there is plenty wrong with the business of Major
League Baseball. My proposal for remedying baseball's shortcomings is
equally simple: Don't change the game (except to eliminate some of the
bastardizations of the last 40 years), but radically alter the *business* of
Major League Baseball.

      I began to think about writing this book in the early 1990s and became
committed to doing so after the players' strike and owners' lockout in
1994 and 1995. Unfortunately, my legal practice, other commitments, and
procrastination prevented its earlier completion. I have discussed many
of the themes set forth in Chapter 16, "Baseball, Inc." over the last decade
with friends and colleagues, but the premise and proposal of Baseball,
Inc., are my own.

      I want to take this opportunity, however, to particularly acknowledge
a few individuals who have provided assistance and support in formulating
my thoughts and completing this book. First, I thank my European ancestors, who made the decision to abandon their lives in lands that would

become obsessed with soccer and move to a new land where a greater game would be played, and my Cherokee ancestors who were waiting to meet them. Second, I wish to acknowledge my father and mother, both of whom were great lovers of baseball and encouraged my early interest in the game. Next, I acknowledge my cousins, who were my first baseball teammates and opponents.

I thank the St. Louis Cardinals, and especially the great Stan Musial, who fueled my interest in the game and who have provided me with much joy, and not a little heartache, over the past half century.

I acknowledge the contributions of the late Scott Bollinger, my colleague, teammate, and friend, with whom I discussed my Baseball, Inc. premise and proposal many years ago. I must also acknowledge the research and writing contributions to early drafts of several chapters of this book by Tim Noonan, weekly sports columnist for the *South China Morning Post* and contributor to *Time* and *Forbes* magazines. I also acknowledge my friend and fellow Cardinals fan Steven Soong, who is always eager to talk about the Redbirds, and my friend and Red Sox fan Peter Schloss, with whom I discussed this book and the title of its Chapter 12 over several bottles of wine one night a number of years ago.

I also thank Bill Burdick, Laura Wentworth, and Nancy Boland of the Photograph Department of the National Baseball Hall of Fame Library and Museum in Cooperstown, New York; Bob Mayhall of the Photograph Department of the Sporting News Library in St. Louis; Clara Yim at Corbis in Hong Kong; and my friend Lawson Little, who assisted in locating and obtaining the rights to use the photographs contained in this book. I especially thank my long-time personal assistant, Elsie Mak, for her valiant efforts to decipher my handwriting and her cheerful and tireless work and many contributions to making the manuscript of this book legible, consistent, and easily publishable.

Finally, I am eternally grateful to my wife, Victoria, and our three children, Ted, Elizabeth, and Katherine, for their cheer, support, and patience during another of my time-consuming projects.

Chapter 1

THE CHURCH OF BASEBALL

I believe in the church of baseball. I've tried all the major religions and most of the minor ones. I've worshipped Buddha, Allah, Brahma, Vishnu, Siva, trees, mushrooms, and Isadora Duncan. I know things. For instance there are 108 beads in a Catholic rosary and there are 108 stitches in a baseball. When I learned that, I gave Jesus a chance. But it just didn't work out between us. The Lord laid too much guilt on me. I prefer metaphysics to theology. You see, there's no guilt in baseball. And it is never boring.... I've tried them all, I really have, and the only church that truly feeds the soul, day in and day out, is the church of baseball.

—Susan Sarandon as Annie Savoy
in *Bull Durham*

Baseball's unique possession, the real source of our strength, is the fan's memory of the times his daddy took him to the game to see the great players of his youth. Whether he remembers it or not, the excitement of those hours, the step they represented in his own growth and the part those afternoons—even one afternoon—played in his relationship with his own father is bound up in his feeling toward the ball club and toward the game. When he takes his own son to the game, as his father once took him, there is a spanning of the generations that is warm and rich and—if I may use the word—lovely.

—Bill Veeck

1

There is a war of democracy against bureaucracy. And I tell you that baseball is the very watchword of democracy. There is no other sport or business or anything under heaven which exerts the leveling influence that baseball does. Neither the public school nor the church can approach it. Baseball is unique. England is a democratic country, but it lacks the finishing touch of baseball.
—John K. Tener

It breaks your heart. It is designed to break your heart. The game begins in the spring, when everything else begins again, and it blossoms in the summer, filling the afternoons and evenings, and then as soon as the chill rains come, it stops and leaves you to face the fall alone. You count on it, rely on it to buffer the passage of time, to keep the memory of sunshine and high skies alive, and then just when the days are all twilight, when you need it most, it stops.… And summer is gone.
—Commissioner A. Bartlett Giamatti

Baseball evokes powerful and redolent memories and emotions. A multitude of recollections and sensations overtake me when I think about baseball. My father, summer, baseball's smells and sounds, and Stan Musial. I am also engulfed by emotions which are difficult to describe, feelings that are basic to my life and being an American.

My father taught me the rudiments of the game. "Elbow in!" "Follow through!" "Eye on the ball!" "Level swing!" My father and mother also took me to see games played by others—high school, American Legion, and town team baseball games, fast-pitch softball games, and on a few wonderful occasions Major League games at Sportsman's Park in St. Louis during summer driving vacations to my father's native Tennessee. My father taught me to love the game, and the Cardinals, as he did. These are the strongest and best of the limited but warm memories I have of my father, who I lost when I was ten years old. I hope I have passed on some of these feelings to my own children, Ted, Elizabeth, and Katherine, and that they also have warm memories of baseball.

As George Will emphasizes in his superb *Men at Work*,[1] baseball is a summer game. When I was a boy, summer meant freedom from school and the bitter and seemingly endless cold of winter. It also meant baseball—thousands of games every year. Not only T-shirt League and later Little League games with uniforms and nine players on each side, but countless games of catch, burn-out, work-up, 500, pitch, 5-ups, games with any ball hit to the right side of the pitcher being foul (because only five boys were playing), games where the team at bat provided the pitcher and the catcher, and a multitude of other games we learned from older boys or invented ourselves. Most of these games were played in my cousins' back yard, which was enormous when we were boys, but incredibly has shrunk over the last 40 years. Must be something to do with ozone depletion and global warming. The rosters changed daily depending upon which boys, and girls in our earliest years, were available. The numbers would decline if someone was on vacation or had been apprehended committing some childhood infraction for which indoor confinement was considered appropriate punishment. The rosters might increase if someone's relatives were visiting from out of town or a schoolmate or friend from another neighborhood was present.

My recollection of those 1950s summers is that my mother opened our back screen door after school ended the Friday before Memorial Day in late May and instructed me to return home before the Tuesday following Labor Day in early September when the succeeding school year would commence. This is more or less what I did, with baseball occupying the intervening three months. My cousins and I would play baseball from early morning until after dark. Baseball stopped only for lunch, typically Campbell's tomato or chicken noodle soup, a sandwich consisting of one slice of bologna with Miracle Whip on Wonder Bread, and a glass of milk, provided by whichever mother   often my aunt Delores—had the misfortune to have us playing nearby that day. I would return home at dark for three reasons—dinner, a place to sleep, and to listen to my beloved St. Louis Cardinals on our old, wooden upright radio. As my parents sat in their chairs reading their newspapers and listening to the game, I would assemble my baseball cards on the living room floor, arranged according to the positions of the players in the game that evening. After each half inning, I would bring the cards for the team in the field into bat and replace them with the cards for the team that had finished batting. I memorized every statistic on every one of those cards.

In those years, growing up in Nebraska and Colorado, one essentially had two choices for teams to follow—the New York Yankees, whose dynasty seemed to win the World Series every year (does this sound familiar?), or the Cardinals from St. Louis, the Major Leagues' most Western and most Southern outpost. My cousins were and remain frontrunners—Yankees fans. I was and remain a Cardinals fan. Being a Cardinals fan in the 1950s provided little joy. During that desolate decade, the Redbirds mounted a serious challenge for the National League pennant only in 1957.

Fortunately, the 1960s and 1980s brought better times. Hopefully, the new millennium will provide greater cheer.

The Yankees may have been perpetual world champions in the 1950s and early 1960s, but the Cardinals had radio station KMOX, which then boasted America's most powerful radio signal and featured the great Harry Caray and later his young sidekick, Jack Buck. I grew to love baseball not only by playing and watching games, but also by listening to Harry, who brought the game to life with his "It looks like, it could be, it is a home run!" Harry also delivered to my home and imagination the incomparable Stan Musial. Stan was not only the greatest Cardinal, but at the time he retired from baseball after the 1963 season the greatest player in the long history of the National League. Although it is now nearly half a century later, I have become an international lawyer and businessman, and I have had a number of mentors in my professional career, my only enduring hero has been not a politician, religious leader, lawyer, writer, philosopher, business executive, or my father, but Stan "The Man" Musial, who has led an exemplary life both on and off the field. One of my greatest thrills as a boy was to see Stan play in Sportsman's Park. Stan Musial was what baseball was all about. Stan was more than a great athlete who performed well on the field. He was a great man who performed admirably in life, a respected citizen of his community and his country who a boy could admire.

I have vivid memories of baseball's smells. I recall the smells I experienced as a player—grass, dirt, chalk, leather, neat's-foot oil, pine tar, resin, sweat, bubble gum, and later "Red Man" chewing tobacco. I remember the aromas I have experienced as a fan—hot dogs, peanuts, beer, Old Spice aftershave mixed with perspiration, and tobacco. I recall baseball's sounds—the chatter of undersized infielders, the jeers of bench jockeys, the crack of bat on ball, the slap of ball meeting glove, and the swell of the crowds' cheers and boos. These smells and sounds are conjured each time I think of baseball.

The deeper emotions evoked by baseball and its enduring appeal are just as powerful, but more difficult to describe. There are few inalienable truths in life, but this is one: Nothing in America inspires spiritual devotion more than baseball. Why is baseball so indelibly etched in the American psyche? Baseball has been called America's national pastime, but making money is our true national pastime. Baseball is far more important than that. Baseball is America's religion. From presidents to bricklayers, from cab drivers to poets, from laborers to scientists, and from Maine to San Diego, legions of Americans worship at the altar of baseball. Why? Like any other religion, it is difficult to describe the essence of one's baseball faith.

To begin with, in spite of its varied and primarily English origins, baseball is American. Many of our dramas as a people are played out on baseball's stage. The game of baseball is simple, fair, and for eight months of every year served up daily. Three strikes and a batter is out. Three outs for each team every inning. Each team has as many chances to bat and to score as its opponent. Nine innings except in the case of a tie. All games are played until one team wins, even if the game lasts all day and all night. Baseball, among all major American sports, is the only game not limited by a clock. Very simple, very just. Everything else about baseball is surrounded by a hazy aura where America's soul can be found.

When compared with the other two major American team sports, basketball and football, baseball is far more historically and emotionally compelling. Baseball is daily and, for better or worse, offers little respite. For many of the baseball faithful, the fortunes of their chosen teams dictate daily moods. During the season, your favorite baseball team may repeatedly disgust you, but despair may be fleeting because they can come back tomorrow and make you smile. Or lose again and provide more heartache. Poets have waxed, ad nauseam, on the daily rebirth of baseball. By the time October rolls around and more than 70 percent of Major League teams are eliminated from post season action, there is a noticeable void in the lives of many baseball fans. That nauseating, edgy, and wonderful feeling as you read the newspaper's sports page or internet website to see how your team and favorite players did last night is gone. But the playoffs and World Series provide new drama. Enthusiastic discussions of possible trades and free agent signings continue to capture fans' interest during the winter "hot stove league."

Compare baseball to football and one can appreciate baseball's intrinsic justice. In baseball, both teams have equal chances to hit and play offense. Interestingly, baseball is the only major American sport in which the team on defense has the ball. In football, stronger and more skilled teams can control the ball and the offense for extended periods of time. Greed, unbridled greed. Football, with its military metaphors of bombs, blitzes, and invading enemy territory, is played once a week. But what does a football fan do for the other six days? Read the injury list? If your football team plays abysmally, you have to wait an entire week for redemption. A National Football League team plays only 16 regular season games, eight at home and eight away. Major League baseball teams play 162 games in the regular season, giving their fans the opportunity to see them at home on 81 separate occasions. Football is far more corporate and structured. Injuries and player movements destroy a football fan's ability to experience team continuity. Football is constantly redefining itself. In any given year, there may be half a dozen significant rule changes. Quickly, can you recite the current National Football League rules on the extent to which defensive players are permitted to engage in contact with quarterbacks or wide receivers? Of course not! Neither can anyone else except a football referee, and they usually need to confer with the other referees on the field, both to understand the rules and determine whether they have been violated.

Basketball, like football, has clearly defined boundaries and time limits. The games are uniform, you can set your watch by them. Baseball? Who knows? A game can last two hours, maybe six. The recent success of basketball has more to do with the marketing acumen of the National Basketball Association and the abilities and personalities of Michael Jordan, Magic Johnson, and Larry Bird than it does with the majesty of the game. Even NBA Commissioner David Stern admits that his league is driven by its star power. Can Shaquille O'Neal, Vince Carter, Kevin Garnett, Allen Iverson, and Kobe Bryant carry the flame?

Another significant difference between baseball, on the one hand, and football and basketball, on the other, is physical. The average man has great difficulty identifying with today's football and basketball players. Football's offensive linemen today *average* well over 300 pounds; linebackers and defensive ends can weigh 300 pounds and run the 40-yard dash in 4.5 seconds! Basketball players regularly exceed seven feet in height and have incredible physical abilities. Baseball players have physiques more like ours, or at least like ours were when we were younger. Like many other American men, I still believe I could have been a power-hitting Major League outfielder, first baseman, or third baseman if I hadn't selected another profession. After all, I did lead the Little League in batting and home runs!

In spite of shortsighted and greedy ownership, labor acrimony, and obscene salaries, Major League Baseball has endured. Except for the abominable designated hitter rule in the American League and a few tweaks here and there, no significant rule changes have occurred in baseball since the 19th century. This continuity does not necessarily make baseball more exciting than football or basketball, but it does make it more enduring and mythical. Baseball resonates with all that is good in American society—our past, our joys, and our dreams. Baseball's influence on society, culture, and literature is far more pervasive than that of any other American sport. Can you remember reading one brilliant basketball or football book? All right, maybe Pete Axthelm's *The City Game*,[2] David Wolf's *Foul*,[3] one chapter of Wilt Chamberlain's *A View from Above*,[4] and Dan Jenkins's *Semi-Tough*[5] and *Life Its Ownself*[6] merit reading. But, for the most part, baseball is the only major team sport that provides any literary interest. From the King of the Beats, Jack Kerouac, to conservative commentator George Will, from Philip Roth to Ernest Hemingway, and from Bernard Malamud to F. Scott Fitzgerald baseball has attracted the literary all-stars.

Thankfully, many things about baseball defy explanation. This has not stopped the perpetually profound from weighing in with theories. The pace of baseball: patient, measured, and then, suddenly, action in several locations, lends itself to introspection. How many times have we seen the president of Yale University weigh in with a scholarly tome on the heartbreak of football or basketball? Yet, the ramblings of the late commissioner of Major League Baseball and former Yale president and classics professor, A. Bartlett Giamatti, on the beauty of baseball elicited some of the game's most elegant and esoteric prose.[7] Giamatti's writings prove that baseball exists on many levels. If you crave a deeper, more profound explanation for baseball, then armed with erudite abstractions, you can find one. But if it is a beer, a hot dog, and a warm summer day that brings you to the ball park, then have a seat and enjoy yourself!

There is also something indefinable about baseball which inspires loyalty that is absent in most marriages. In Ernest Hemingway's *The Old Man and the Sea*, in spite of "being pulled on the ocean of life by the weight of the world," Hemingway's main character Santiago was most interested in the 1941 hitting streak of "the great DiMaggio," the son of another fisherman.[8] With the advent of free agency, it is questionable whether Santiago would be so attached to DiMaggio. If he were alive and playing today, chances are Joltin' Joe would be a designated hitter for George Steinbrenner's Yankees, making about $18 million per year, after having made intermediate stops in Toronto, Anaheim, Cleveland, Arlington, and Shea Stadium. Yet, changing one's rooting allegiance even in this day and age is an unforgivable sin. The team one faithfully supports defines a baseball lover. Yankees fan? Front-runner. Red Sox or Cubs fan? Perpetually tortured.

Frank Sinatra may have possessed the richest singing voice and smoothest style of the 20th century, but he committed the unpardonable sin. As reported in Don DeLillo's *Underworld*,[9] Sinatra accompanied Jackie Gleason and Toots Shoor to that most memorable of playoff games in 1951 between the arch-rival New York Giants and Brooklyn Dodgers. Gleason, a Dodgers fan, gloated mercilessly as his team took the lead. But when Bobby Thomson hit the "Shot Heard 'Round the World," Sinatra, a Hoboken, New Jersey, native and a Giants fan, had the last laugh. Sadly, Sinatra died a Dodger's death in 1998. After relocating to Los Angeles, "Old

Blue Eyes" understandably became a little soft, culminating in the singing of duets with the likes of Liza Minnelli, Neil Diamond, and puffy saxophonist Kenny G. He also became a baseball heretic, transferring his allegiance to the Los Angeles Dodgers. No wonder Frank punched photographers in fits of rage. The man had no inner peace; he was at war with the Church of Baseball.

Compare Sinatra to film icon Jack Nicholson, another Jersey boy who migrated to Tinsel Town. As everyone knows, happy Jack is the number one fan of the Los Angeles Lakers and not just since the "showtime" era of Magic Johnson. Jack held Lakers season tickets before basketball was in vogue in southern California. But when it comes to baseball, Jack's loyalties are unwavering. He still pulls for the Yankees and is a frequent visitor to Yankee Stadium when he visits Gotham. Do you think Jack feels any guilt about not pulling for the New Jersey Nets or the New York Knicks? Do you think Jack would consider changing his baseball allegiance to the Fox Dodgers or the Disney Angels? Jack always has a smile, never punches photographers, and probably has more fun than anyone in America. His conscience is at ease; he is at peace with the Church of Baseball.

Life and baseball seemed simpler when I was a boy. The game of baseball is still simple. Thousands of variations can occur during an at-bat, an inning, or a game, but this uncertainty makes baseball interesting, exciting, sometimes frustrating, and always thought-provoking. Is there anything better than a well executed hit-and-run, a slickly fielded double play, a Randy Johnson high inside fastball to a left-handed batter, Junior Griffey pulling back an almost certain home run from over the center-field wall, a triple, a perfect sacrifice bunt, a double steal, Pedro Martinez or Greg Maddux pitching to the corners and beyond at varying speeds, or Mark McGwire launching a ball into orbit?

Why do so many Americans worship in the Church of Baseball? Because baseball is America and America is baseball. Why? Because baseball is sunshine, green grass, fathers and sons, our rural past, and summer. Why? Because baseball is our game, the American game. Why? There are some things that cannot be explained and men probably should not attempt to do so. Baseball is America's religion.

Chapter 2

PENTATEUCH

Baseball is an allegorical play about America, a poetic, complex, and subtle play of courage, fear, good luck, mistakes, patience about fate, and sober self esteem.... It is impossible to understand America without a thorough knowledge of baseball.
                    —Saul Steinberg

By and large it is the sport that a foreigner is least likely to take to. You have to grow up playing it, you have to accept the lore of the bubble gum card, and believe that if the answer to the Mays-Snider-Mantle question is found, then the universe will be a simpler and more ordered place.
                    —David Halberstam

"I loved the game," Shoeless Joe went on. "I'd have played for food money. I'd have played free and worked for food. It was the game, the parks, the smells, the sounds. Have you ever held a bat or a baseball to your face? The varnish, the leather. And it was the crowd, the excitement of them rising as one when the ball was hit deep. The sound was like a chorus. Then there was the chug-a-lug of the tin lizzies in the parking lots, and the hotels with their brass spittoons in the lobbies and brass beds in the rooms. It makes me tingle all over like a kid on his way to his first double-header, just to talk about it."
                    —W.P. Kinsella

The baseball mania has run its course. It has no future
as a professional endeavor.
                    —Cincinnati Gazette, 1879

In the beginning, Abner Doubleday created the bat, the ball, and the diamond...

Legend has it that, in 1839, Abner Doubleday was participating in a free-form game called town ball on the picturesque shores of Lake Otsego, in upper New York State. A figure of heroic improvisation, Doubleday decided to create a better game. This "new" game would be fairer, there would be rules, and it would be called "baseball." To honor baseball's founding father and the game he invented, baseball would create a pantheon of greatness and call it the Hall of Fame. This hallowed hall would be located in Cooperstown, New York, on Lake Otsego, the "birthplace" of baseball. Every year, millions of Americans would make the pilgrimage to baseball's Mecca and pay homage to their heroes. Nothing, except the Stars and Stripes, could be more symbolic of America.

There are, however, some rather serious flaws in this legend. The English games of rounders and cricket, and variations of these games such as "town ball" and "old cat," had been played in America since at least the 18th century. Recent research has unearthed newspaper articles that report on games of "base ball" being played in New York City at least as early as 1823.[10] Moreover, Abner Doubleday, a future Civil War hero, was not in Cooperstown in the summer of 1839. He was at the United States Military Academy in West Point, New York, training to be a solder. Furthermore, Doubleday claimed no role in the creation of the game. As legends go, the officially sanctioned version of Doubleday's creation of baseball is somewhat less credible than King Arthur and the Knights of the Round Table.

History is always subject to conjecture. With no microchips to store data and no 24-hour sports networks to provide video accounts, we can only view 1839 through a gauze-covered lens. Nevertheless, Major League Baseball has nominated, elevated, and propagated Abner Doubleday as the father of baseball. The truth? Perhaps we need to return to baseball's Garden of Eden where we find, not surprisingly, that the history and origins of the game are shrouded in ambiguities and half-truths.

Playing fast and loose with history is certainly not the exclusive domain of baseball or Americans. The Romans, after defeating the Greeks at Carthage, imported the Greeks' cult of mythology and made it their own. Young cultures often strive to define themselves. America in the mid–19th century was no different. Although most of the basic elements of baseball, most notably the stick, ball, and bases, could be traced back centuries to a number of diverse cultures, and most recently to the English games of cricket and rounders, Doubleday's creation was absolutely, unequivocally "Made in America."[11]

The first serious attempt to organize accomplished baseball practitioners was made by the New York Knickerbockers Baseball Club in 1845.[12] The Knickerbockers, a wholesome band of middle class merchants and clerks, met regularly to play what was then known, in its various forms, as "town ball," "goal ball," and the "New York game" in vacant lots in Manhattan. With available open space dwindling on the island, the Knickerbockers began to make regular pilgrimages to the Elysian Fields across the Hudson River in Hoboken, New Jersey. The aptly named Elysian Fields were a bucolic oasis where the game of baseball would be refined and popularized. The Knickerbockers improved their sport, enforced dress codes, and prohibited profanity. The head of the Knickerbockers' rules committee, a 25-year-old clerk and surveyor named Alexander Cartwright, codified baseball's first set of rules and established the dimensions and layout of the field.[13] In 1858, fourteen clubs from New York formed the National Association of Base Ball Players, which standardized rules and attempted to administer the sport.[14]

Although the games at Elysian Fields were still of a patrician nature and featured only Caucasian "gentlemen" born in America, usually of English or Dutch heritage, by the middle of the 19th century, in Manhattan and New York City's other boroughs, a voracious, largely recent immigrant, working class began to play baseball in every available space.[15] Like its "founding" country, baseball has long indulged the notion that it blurs social classes. To many Americans in the 19th century, the class system was uniquely and crassly British. But, like the dubious claim that Abner Doubleday invented the game, the notion of baseball being an egalitarian affair rings hollow.

During the twenty years following the establishment of the Knickerbockers, the game of baseball grew in popularity and significance. Baseball was played by both Union and Confederate soldiers during the Civil War. After the war, former soldiers returned home with the game and its popularity increased.[16] By 1866, one year after the Civil War ended, more than 200 teams were members of the National Association of Base Ball Players. These teams engaged in regularly scheduled contests in established grounds, charged admission, and attracted scores of spectators. Within five years, the membership of the National Association of Base Ball Players had increased tenfold.[17]

In 1869, baseball's first professional team, the Cincinnati Red Stockings, debuted.[18] The Red Stockings, managed by Harry Wright, the English-born son of a professional cricket player, were stocked with a

number of the greatest players of the day who signed contracts and were paid salaries between $600 and $1,400 for the season's efforts, better pay than could be achieved in most occupations.[19] The Red Stockings won all 65 of their games in 1869 and their first 27 games in 1870, before losing a tense, extra-inning affair to the Brooklyn Atlantics.[20] By various estimates, from 9,000–20,000 spectators witnessed this game and gate receipts were approximately $4,500–$6,000.[21] It is also estimated that in excess of 200,000 spectators viewed the Red Stockings in their inaugural season.[22] With ticket prices of around 25–50 cents,[23] baseball was becoming a business. Unfortunately for the Red Stockings, it was not yet big business; their net profits in their inaugural season were only $1.39.[24] Once the Red Stockings were no longer undefeated, their fan support evaporated, expenses began to exceed revenues, and the team reverted to amateur status.[25]

Recognizing the potential profit that could be achieved in professional baseball, owners of ten of the teams in the National Association of Base Ball Players decided to form a new league. Thus, on St. Patrick's Day, 1871, the National Association of *Professional* Base Ball Players was formed.[26] The National Association's original ten franchises were located in Philadelphia, Boston, Chicago, Cleveland, New York, Washington, D.C. (two teams), Fort Wayne (Indiana), Rockford (Illinois), and Troy (New York).[27] The National Association was a loose association of professional teams which did not limit themselves to playing games against one another; instead, they continued to play a portion of their games against other amateur and professional teams.[28] The league's best team, the Boston Red Stockings—which appropriated its name, manager, Harry Wright, and several key players from the now-defunct Cincinnati team—featured Albert Goodwill Spalding, the sport's greatest pitcher.[29] Spalding, who later would become a team owner and baseball's first great merchandiser, won 57 games in 1875 (including 24 in succession, pitching in every game his team played)[30] and led the Red Stockings to four of the five National Association championships.[31] After a few seasons, National Association player salaries escalated to as high as $2,000 for a season's efforts.

In the 1870s and early 1880s, baseball parks were simple affairs, with wooden grandstands that held 1,000–2,000 spectators, and were prone to destruction by fire.[32] Although attendance statistics in the 1870s are less than completely reliable, the annual attendance for the *entire* National Association was approximately 250,000.[33] Ticket prices were about 25 cents and food and other concessions, including whiskey, were sold at games. A few of the more successful teams, such as the Boston Red Stock-

Opposite: Albert Goodwill Spalding

William A. Hulbert

ings, Philadelphia Athletics, and St. Louis Browns, produced small profits for their investors.[34] The Boston Red Stockings, the league's most successful team on the field, paid its players an average salary of $1,380 for the 1874 season (from which $30 for uniforms and $.50 per day for traveling expenses was deducted).[35] In 1874, when the Red Stockings posted a 52–18 winning record, they reported a net profit of $65.20 and a net worth of $833.13.[36] The following year, after posting a 71–8 record, the Red Stockings' net worth had increased nearly fourfold, to $3,261.07.[37] Obviously baseball was not yet big business. In an effort to promote the great and unique American game to foreign audiences, a baseball tour of the United Kingdom was made in 1874 by the Boston Red Stockings and Philadelphia Athletics.[38]

The number of teams in the National Association rose and fell as weaker franchises collapsed and others took their places. New franchises were awarded in Brooklyn, Baltimore, Hartford (Connecticut), Middletown (Connecticut), New Haven (Connecticut), Elizabeth (New Jersey), Keokuk (Iowa), and St. Louis, and replacement franchises were installed in Philadelphia, Brooklyn, and Chicago. During its five-year existence, 25 different teams played in the National Association.[39] But the finances of the National Association were always weak, few team owners were experienced businessmen, gambling scandals were common,[40] no central league authority existed, and by 1875, the National Association was in serious trouble.

Sensing the imminent collapse of the National Association, on February 2, 1876, the owners of eight National Association teams met at the Grand Central Hotel in New York City and declared that they were forming a new National League of Professional Baseball Clubs.[41] The National League was conceived by William Ambrose Hulbert, a wealthy wholesale grocer, coal merchant, member of the Chicago Board of Trade, and owner of the National Association's Chicago White Stockings. Ironically, Hulbert was born in Otsego County, New York (the county in which the National Baseball Hall of Fame and Museum in Cooperstown is located).[42] The most significant difference between the National League and the earlier National Association was that the National Association was an association of "Players" and the National League was a league of "Clubs." Instead of being dominated by players or former players, the National League was dominated by its businessmen owners, most of whom possessed a range of business interests including professional baseball teams. The experience of these businessmen ensured that the National League had direction and did not suffer from the lack of centralized control that plagued the National Association. The new National League allocated exclusive territories to the participating franchises, provided for blacklisting of players who were suspended by their teams, inflicted penalties for gambling and other offenses by players, offered more reasonable (*i.e.*, lower) salaries to players, prohibited sales of alcohol at games, and banned the playing of Sunday games.[43] Importantly, each team also agreed to respect all other teams' player contracts. Original National

League franchises were located in Boston, Chicago, Cincinnati, Hartford, Louisville, New York, Philadelphia, and St. Louis.[44] The new league established ticket prices at 50 cents, with the home team receiving 70 percent of gate receipts and the visiting team 30 percent.[45] Hulbert and his cohorts now held an iron grip on the players, players' salaries, and the fans. Thus, in the year of the centennial of the Declaration of Independence, the admission of Colorado as a state, the massacre of George Armstrong Custer and his troops at the Little Big Horn, and Alexander Graham Bell's patenting of the telephone, the National League was born.

Early tests of the stability of the new National League were made in the 1876, 1877, and 1880 seasons. Near the end of the 1876 season, it became apparent that Hulbert's Chicago franchise would win the National League's inaugural pennant and that the New York and Philadelphia franchises would be distant finishers. The National League had scheduled late season road trips to St. Louis and Chicago for the New York and Philadelphia teams. In spite of pressure on the New York and Philadelphia teams to play those scheduled games, those teams elected to cancel the remaining National League games and play non-league games in their home cities. In response to those cancellations, and to protect the authority of the league and the integrity of the scheduling process, the New York and Philadelphia teams were expelled from the National League.[46] Not until 1883, the year after Hulbert's death, would National League baseball return to America's two most populous cities.

During the 1877 season, the Louisville team was leading the National League standings and appeared to be headed toward winning the pennant until it suffered an inexplicable losing streak. Upon investigation, it was discovered that four Louisville players had thrown the pennant to gamblers. To assert its moral authority and discourage further corruption, the National League banished the "Louisville Four" for life and the Louisville franchise was disbanded.[47]

In 1880, the Cincinnati club, whose operator also owned a local brewery and had defied the National League's edicts by permitting sales of beer and Sunday games, was expelled from the National League.[48]

As with the National Association, franchise stability was an issue in the new National League.[49] Weak franchises were regularly replaced by better-financed teams in other cities. Teams were established and dissolved in Providence, Rhode Island; Worcester, Massachusetts; Troy, New York; Indianapolis, Indiana; and Buffalo, New York.[50] A major problem for weaker teams was their inability to compete with stronger teams offering higher salaries to players (does this sound familiar?). By 1879, only the Chicago White Stockings—with Hulbert as its president, Albert Spalding (whom Hulbert had wooed from Boston) as its pitcher (briefly), manager, and later president, Adrian "Cap" Anson as its best player and later manager, and Mike "King" Kelly as a star player—were financially successful.[51] At the end of the 1879 season, the National League owners found a way to control player salaries, enacting a "reserve" system that would bind the top five players on each club to their team in perpetuity "to protect a loyal fan base and the integrity of the game."[52]

Although some challenge to the National League's supremacy was mounted by the International Association, a more loosely organized confederation of teams which included some of the former National Association teams, the International Association's less-regulated business practices ultimately led to team insolvencies and the failure of the association.[53] The National League entered a brief period of stability and prosperity, without outside competition from other leagues and with control over salaries. In 1882, a group of entrepreneur owners of big city teams denied membership in the National League decided to test the National League's position and formed their own American Base Ball Association.[54] With franchises in Philadelphia, Cincinnati, Louisville, Baltimore, Pittsburgh, and St. Louis, the American Association fielded teams in six cities with almost twice the population of the eight National League cities.[55] This new league charged only 25 cents for admission (one-half of the National League admission price), served alcoholic beverages, and even played on Sundays.[56] Teams in this new league easily attracted more spectators than their National League competition.[57] Among those now able to watch big league baseball on Sundays were the previously disenfranchised immigrants, whose fanatic enjoyment of the game, fueled by copious libations, not surprisingly created large and unruly crowds. The ownership, management, and American-born upper- and middle-class spectators of the National League's weekday games frowned with disdain on the "beer and whiskey league." For the American Association's fans who worked during the week and wanted to enjoy their Sundays, however, baseball was finally both accessible and enjoyable. For the American Association's ownership, large attendance and liquor sales translated into profits.[58]

The American Association also did not employ a reserve system. Although contracts of both National League and American Association players were considered binding during a season, players could sign with new American Association teams after each season.[59] Keenly aware of the benefits of monopoly power, the National League could not tolerate this challenge to player control which increased players' salaries and reduced owners' profits. In 1883, the two leagues entered into the National Agree-

ment, pledging to honor each other's contracts, reserve lists (which were expanded to cover eleven of the fourteen players on each team), and black-lists.[60] Most importantly, the National Agreement confirmed the reserve system which bound players to their teams to combat "revolving" (i.e., unrestricted movement of players). The reserve system controlled owners' costs by eliminating competition for players' services.

During the 1880s, attendance increased dramatically, with the National League drawing more than 300,000 fans in 1881 and the National League and the American Association attracting a combined 2.6 million spectators by 1889.[61]

The established leagues' order was challenged in 1884 by the new Union Association, which eschewed the reserve system and established franchises in Baltimore, Boston, Chicago, Cincinnati, Philadelphia, St. Louis, Washington, D.C., and Altoona (Pennsylvania).[62] In its sole season of play, only one-half of the Union Association's teams completed all of their schedules and a number of franchise shifts occurred, with Chicago transferring to Pittsburgh and later to St. Paul, Minnesota, Philadelphia transferring to Wilmington, Delaware and later to Milwaukee, and Altoona transferring to Kansas City. The National League and American Association blacklisted players who jumped to the Union League and refused to respect Union League contracts. The Union League quickly collapsed. This short-lived league, however, produced some lasting effects for the business of professional baseball. Unlike in the established leagues, the Union Association's teams signed players under current contracts with teams in other leagues. This practice resulted in litigation involving players who jumped leagues. In a case in St. Louis, a player who had been under contract with an American Association team and who had jumped to a Union Association team and back to an American Association team was restrained by the courts from playing in St. Louis.[63] In another case in Cincinnati, which presaged a decision of the United States Supreme Court nearly forty years later, the court refused to intervene because baseball was a sport, not a business.[64]

In 1885, a revised National Agreement was signed and the National League and American Association entered a period of peace, prosperity, and consolidation of power.[65] Newer, more permanent, ballparks such as the Polo Grounds in New York, Lakefront Park in Chicago, Sportsman's Park in St. Louis, and the Baker Bowl in Philadelphia, providing seating for 10,000–20,000 spectators each, were constructed.[66] Annual player salaries were capped at $2,000 with a $1,000 minimum.[67] Successful teams,

Opposite: Early Polo Grounds, New York

such as the Chicago White Stockings, the New York Gothams, and the Boston Beaneaters, achieved profits of more than $100,000 per season.[68] At the end of the 1884 season, the first World Series was played between the Chicago White Stockings of the National League and the New York Metropolitans of the American Association.[69]

In 1885, mirroring the labor movement sweeping America's new industrial society, a group of players, led by Columbia Law School graduate and New York Gothams shortstop and field captain John Montgomery Ward, formed the Brotherhood of Professional Base Ball Players, the game's first players' union.[70] By 1889, the Brotherhood counted among its members approximately 80 percent of all players in the National League and a majority of those in the American Association.[71] Following the 1886 season, the Chicago White Stockings became the first team to trade a player's contract, including reserve rights, to another team when they sold star outfielder Mike "King" Kelly to the Boston Red Stockings for $10,000 in a transaction approved by Kelly, who received a 60 percent raise in salary by the Boston team.[72] Other player contracts were traded in the next two seasons. Although the National League had observed an informal salary ceiling for several years, in 1889, in an effort to control expenses and increase profits, the National League set firm annual salary limits, with players being classified in five tiers of compensation from $1,500 to $2,500 based on each player's "habits, earnestness, and special qualifications."[73]

Incensed players, led by Ward and the Brotherhood of Professional Base Ball Players, formed a new Players' League which began play in 1890.[74] The Brotherhood's manifesto challenging the National League declared: "There was a time when the League stood for integrity and fair dealing. Today it stands for dollars and cents. Once it looked to the elevation of the game; today its eyes are on the turnstile.... Players have been bought, sold, and exchanged as though they were sheep, instead of American citizens."[75] The eight-team Players' League featured franchises in Brooklyn, Boston, Buffalo, Chicago, Cleveland, New York, Philadelphia, and Pittsburgh.[76] A number of players in the Players' League owned stock in their own teams and each club had its own eight-man board, with four members named by the team's players and four members named by the team's owners. The Players' League was governed by a 16-member senate comprised of one owner's representative and one players' representative from each of the eight league franchises. The Players' League had no reserve system, blacklisting was prohibited, and revenues from ticket sales were shared equally between home and visiting teams, with the home team retaining all concession revenues. All Players' League players signed three-year contracts at their 1889 salary levels and agreed to regulate themselves on alcoholism and gambling.[77] Each of the league's eight franchises contributed $25,000 to a central fund, annual profits in excess of $20,000 per team were pooled and distributed equally among all teams, $10,000 of each team's $20,000 maximum profit was distributed to the team's investors, and the remaining profits were divided among players.[78]

The National League initially challenged the Players' League in the courts. Ward's 1889 contract with the New York Giants contained the National League's typical reserve language. When Ward spurned the National League to perform in the Players' League, the Giants sought an injunction in the New York Supreme Court to prevent Ward from playing for any team except the Giants. Ward argued that the reserve clause in his Giants' contract only prevented him from playing for another National League team. The court disagreed, but found that the contract lacked mutuality because the reserve system bound a player to the team indefinitely while the team was bound for only ten days, and that Ward's 1889 Giants contract failed to specify the terms of his renewed contract for 1890 and was thus too indefinite to enforce.[79] Other legal actions followed and, in almost all cases, the players prevailed.[80]

The National League, American Association, and Players' League competed vigorously for players and fans. The renegade Players' League ultimately was able to entice approximately 80 percent of the National League's players to join it.[81] The high costs of competition, however, caused all three leagues to suffer, and the poorly capitalized Players' League folded after only one season of play.[82] In 1891, the better-financed and organized National League owners, led by Spalding, admitted four of the American Association teams to its ranks and the American Association disbanded.[83] The National League re-employed most of the players who had defected to the rival leagues, albeit at lower salaries.[84] The National League's monopoly was reinstated and control of the game and its players was reestablished.

The National League's monopoly continued virtually unfettered for a decade after the demise of the American Association and the Players' League.[85] Annual players salaries were capped at $2,400, overall team payroll limits of $30,000 were established, the reserve system applied, rosters were reduced from fifteen players to thirteen, and recalcitrant players were banished and blacklisted.[86] But, unfortunately for the National League's franchise owners, America entered the worst economic depression in its history in the 1890s, as farm prices and banks collapsed, production declined, unemployment soared, and baseball attendance plummeted.[87] Between 1889 and 1892, overall Major League annual attendance declined by almost 30 percent to 1.82 million.[88] By the middle of the 1890s, however, total Major League attendance reached 2.9 million per year[89] and, during that decade, all twelve National League teams moved into new ball parks.[90] National League owners, most of whom by now were not former players or managers but experienced businessmen, realized substantial profits. The Boston Beaneaters, Baltimore Orioles, and Brooklyn Superbas were perennial winners.[91] After the 1899 season, four weak franchises, Baltimore, Cleveland, Louisville, and Washington, D.C., were dropped from the National League.[92] The remaining eight franchises, Boston, Brooklyn, Chicago, Cincinnati, New York, Philadelphia, Pittsburgh, and St. Louis, would comprise the National League for more than half a century.

The 19th century's greatest player, Adrian "Cap" Anson, played from the National Association's first season in 1871 until 1897.[93] During his 27 Major League seasons, Anson became the first player to amass 3,000 career hits, while driving in 1,715 runs and scoring 1,719 runs, with a batting average that exceeded .300 in an incredible 25 seasons, including 20 consecutive seasons, for a career .334 batting average. Other prominent players of the 19th century included Michael Joseph "King" Kelly, who won two batting titles and maintained a batting average over .300 for his 16-year career; James Edward "Tip" O'Neill, who posted a .435 batting average in 1887, won two batting titles, and averaged .326 over 10 seasons; William Robert "Sliding Billy" Hamilton, who batted .344, scored 1,692 runs, and stole 937 bases during a 14-season career; William Henry "Wee Willie" Keeler, who won two batting titles and maintained a .345 batting average over a 19-year career beginning in 1892 and ending in 1910; and Dennis "Big Dan" Brouthers, a five-time batting champion who batted .343 and hit 106 home runs and 206 doubles during his 19-year career. Great pitchers of the day included John Clarkson, who won 326 games while posting a 2.81 earned run average in a 12-season career beginning in 1882 and ending in 1894; Timothy John "Tim" Keefe, who won 344 games and struck out 2,533 batters in a 14-year career beginning in 1880 and ending in 1893; Charles Gardner "Old Hoss" Radbourn, who won 308 games over a 12-season career, including an incredible 60 wins and an earned run average of 1.38 in 678 innings and 73 complete games in 1884; James Francis "Pud" Galvin, who won 361 games, lost 310 games, and pitched 639 complete games and nearly 6,000 innings over 14 seasons between 1879 and 1892; and Amos "The Hoosier Thunderbolt" Rusie, who won 243 games over 10 seasons, including three seasons with more than 30 victories, and who also was Major League Baseball's first holdout, when he sat

Adrian "Cap" Anson

out the entire 1896 season rather than accept a salary reduction by his team.[94]

In 1888-89, baseball pitcher, manager, franchise owner, and sporting goods impresario Albert Goodwill Spalding, who had been a member and one of the organizers of the 1874 United Kingdom tour of the Boston

Charles Comiskey

Red Stockings and Philadelphia Athletics, led a global tour of baseball stars. The players performed exhibitions in Hawaii, Australia, Ceylon, Egypt, Italy, France, England, and Ireland.[95] Perhaps the fact that Spalding's tour was an abysmal flop and failed to yield any global converts cemented the game as wholly American. In England, the British press infuriated Spalding and his colleagues by insisting that this bizarre game had its roots in cricket and rounders. Unlike cricket, baseball did not seem fair to the British. The British press was sympathetic to the plight of the hapless batsman, who they believed was at the mercy of the pitcher, who "seems to have it all his own way.... In fact, ... the odds against [the batsman] are so great that our English love of fair play is offended...."[96]

No one in 1889 thanked the British press for offering the earliest insight into the fact that a baseball batter who succeeds 30 percent of the time would someday become a multi-millionaire. Instead, the trip abroad inspired a startling fit of xenophobia back in America. Upon their return, the Spalding delegation was feted with a sumptuous banquet at Delmonico's restaurant in New York. Among those in attendance were many prominent businessmen, politicians, and public figures, including Theodore Roosevelt and Mark Twain, who gave a rousing keynote speech.[97] A number of enthusiastic orators assured the audience that baseball was irrefutably an American concept, devoid of any foreign influence.[98] History is slightly vague here, but there are no confirmed reports of the British, or anyone else, steadfastly claiming credit for the creation of baseball. Nevertheless, America declared baseball to be its own and the rest of the world shrugged with indifference. In 1905, Spalding, apparently unconvinced that previous propaganda was conclusive, urged the creation of the Mills Commission to confirm the roots of America's game.[99] The Commission's report declared that Abner Doubleday was the father of modern baseball and concluded that the Civil War veteran had indeed invented and named the game in upper New York State in the 1830s.[100] In spite of howls of protest, including some from men who had been alive to play variations of the game in the 1820s, the Mills Commission's edict stood. Baseball officially had a past; now it needed a present.

In 1901, the enterprising Byron Bancroft ("Ban") Johnson, who with Charles Comiskey controlled the old Western League, renamed that league the "American League" and proclaimed it to be a new "major league."[101] The American League, which featured franchises in Boston, Philadelphia, Washington, D.C., St. Louis, Detroit, Cleveland, Chicago, and Baltimore, promised fans cheaper ticket prices and a wholesome family atmosphere. The Baltimore franchise was transferred to New York in 1903. Johnson and his American League cohorts raided National League rosters, offering higher salaries and signing 111 of their 182 players from the established league.[102] Star shortstop Honus Wagner reportedly rejected a $20,000 offer to join the American League's Washington Senators and remained with the National League's Pittsburgh Pirates, who increased Wagner's salary

Ban Johnson

from \$2,100 to \$2,700.[103] The most significant signing by the American League was that of Philadelphia Phillies star Napoleon "Nap" Lajoie by the cross-town upstart Philadelphia Athletics.[104] In spite of a National League predilection for avoiding litigation which might expose the weakness of player contracts and particularly the reserve system, the Phillies initiated a legal proceeding in the Pennsylvania state trial court, seeking an injunction to compel Lajoie to play for the Phillies.[105] The Phillies argued that Lajoie was bound under his player contract to perform for the Phillies until they no longer wished to employ him. Citing lack of mutuality, because Lajoie was bound to the Phillies in perpetuity and the team could dismiss him on ten days' notice, the availability of legal remedies (i.e., monetary damages), and the fact that Lajoie's services were not unique, the trial court denied the Phillies' request for an injunction.[106] On appeal, the Pennsylvania Supreme Court ruled that the trial court should have granted an injunction to the Phillies, dismissing the defendant's theories of lack of mutuality and availability of adequate legal remedies.[107] After this decision was issued, the Philadelphia Athletics traded Lajoie to the American League's Cleveland franchise. In spite of the "full faith and credit" clause of the United States Constitution, the Ohio courts refused to enforce the Pennsylvania injunction. Thereafter, Lajoie played for the Cleveland team, except when they played the Athletics in Philadelphia, when he took a holiday.[108]

In 1901 and 1902, total combined National League and American League attendance was approximately 7.5 million, with American League attendance exceeding that of the National League by more than 10 percent in 1902.[109] But baseball's operating costs, particularly players' salaries, were increasing. It was clear that rival leagues were not good for franchise owners.

In 1903, a portentous National Agreement was signed between the National League and the American League.[110] There would be two "Major Leagues," separate but equal. They would honor each other's contracts and both would employ the reserve system. Thereafter, a three-member National Commission, comprised of the presidents of both leagues plus a chairman, would control baseball.[111] The two leagues pledged "to perpetuate baseball as the national game of America, and to surround it with such safeguards as to warrant absolute public confidence in its integrity and methods" and asserted that baseball "would be governed by its own decrees, enforcing them without the aid of law and answerable to no power outside of its own."[112] As the dominant member of the National Commission controlling the "Major Leagues," Ban Johnson virtually ruled baseball until the Black Sox scandal resulted in the appointment of Judge Kenesaw Mountain Landis as commissioner of Major League Baseball in 1920.[113]

In spite of acrimony among owners, shifting of franchises, and the formation of rival leagues during the first thirty years of professional baseball, the structure of organized baseball was more or less established with

the National Agreement. For half a century, from 1903 to 1953, with the exception of the short-lived Federal League, the Black Sox scandal, and a brief challenge by the Mexican League in the 1940s, organized baseball experienced peace. The Major Leagues were comprised of sixteen franchises concentrated in ten cities in the Northeastern quarter of the country, with eight franchises in the National League and eight in the American League. The distance between the Major Leagues' most Northern and Eastern city, Boston, and their most Southern and Western city, St. Louis, was approximately 1,200 miles—a 26-hour train ride. There was no movement of teams during this half century as attendance, media coverage, and profits increased sharply.[114]

Total annual Major League attendance grew gradually from 4.7 million in 1903 to 7.2 million in 1909.[115] Thereafter, attendance decreased and did not again reach the 1909 level until 1920, Babe Ruth's first season in New York. During the first two decades of the 20th century, America's urban population increased from 40 percent of the total population to 50 percent.[116] Admission prices ranged from 50 cents for bleacher seats to $2.00 for box seats. Interest in the game following the creation of the Major Leagues sparked the first of baseball's great building booms. Between 1909 and 1923, beginning with the construction of Shibe Park in Philadelphia, fourteen of the sixteen Major League teams replaced their old wooden ballparks with modern concrete and steel structures with an average seating capacity of 30,000, at costs of $500,000 to more than $2 million.[117] The ballparks were typically centrally located within Major League Baseball's home cities, close to subway or trolley lines, and often were ornately designed.[118] These ballparks increasingly became civic monuments and their permanency, when compared to earlier parks with simple wooden grandstands, was viewed as evidence of baseball's maturation and acceptance as America's national game. These ballparks continued to serve Major League Baseball until franchise shifts and expansion occurred after World War II. The Boston Red Sox, Chicago Cubs, and New York Yankees continue to occupy Fenway Park, Wrigley Field, and Yankee Stadium, respectively, which were constructed during this period. The capital investments required by the owners of such ballparks also demonstrated that Major League Baseball had clearly become big business. More profitable teams, such as the New York Giants and Chicago Cubs, earned $100,000 or more in profits per year during this period and the value of Major League franchises, as measured by selling prices, increased from less than $100,000 to approximately $2 million.[119]

Opposite: Shibe Park, Philadelphia

Honus Wagner at bat

By 1910, annual players' salaries reached $12,000 for top talent such as Pittsburgh Pirates shortstop Johannes Pieter "Honus" Wagner, baseball's first 20th century superstar.[120] Contemporary recognition of Honus Wagner's name is primarily because a baseball card bearing his likeness was purchased a few years ago for a record $1.1 million. In 21 Major League seasons beginning in 1897, however, the "Flying Dutchman" posted a career batting average of .329 with 3,430 hits, 1,732 runs batted in, 1,740 runs scored, and 722 stolen bases. Wagner won eight National League batting titles and hit at least .300 in 17 consecutive seasons.

Irrespective of the feats of Wagner and a few other offensive stars, from the beginning of organized baseball until after World War I, dominant pitching ruled the game.[121] During this so-called "Dead Ball Era," softer balls were used and new ones were rarely introduced into games. Pitchers employed a number of deliveries, as well as foreign substances, to keep hitters guessing.[122] Denton True "Cy" Young led all pitchers with 511 career wins, 815 games started, 751 complete games, 16 years with at least 20 wins, and five years with at least 30 wins, during a 22-year career beginning in 1890 and ending in 1911. Other dominant pitchers included Christy Mathewson, who posted 373 career wins, 435 complete games, 13 years with at least 20 wins, four years with at least 30 wins (including three in succession), and a career 2.13 earned run average, during a 17-year career from 1900 through 1916, and Grover Cleveland "Pete" Alexander who amassed 373 career wins, 439 complete games, 90 shutouts, nine years with at least 20 wins, and three consecutive years with at least 30 wins over a 20-year career from 1911 through 1930. During the last half of Alexander's career, he suffered from alcoholism and a variety of war injuries, including double vision, epilepsy, and deafness in one ear. Batters particularly struggled for success against the peerless Walter "The Big Train" Johnson who collected 416 career wins, a career 2.17 earned run average, and 3,508 career strikeouts. Johnson posted twelve seasons with at least 20 wins, and twice won more than 30 games in a season. Possibly the greatest pitcher who ever lived, Johnson played for the perpetually hapless Washington Senators for 21 years from 1907 through 1927. During his stellar career, Johnson collected 110 shutouts, won 38 complete game shutouts by 1–0 scores, and lost 65 games in which his team did not score at all, including 27 times by scores of 1–0.

Offensive play in the Dead Ball Era was characterized by "inside" baseball, in which teams relied heavily on singles, walks, bunts, hit-and-run tactics, and base stealing to produce a few runs. Hitting in the Dead Ball Era was scientific and calculating. Batters took short, controlled swings, sprayed their hits around the field, and put pressure on opposing teams' pitchers and fielders who were equipped only with small, lightly-padded gloves.[123] No one mastered hitting in this era as well as the Detroit Tigers' Tyrus Raymond "Ty" Cobb.[124] Cobb was the most dominant, identifiable, and reviled player of professional baseball's first fifty years. Perhaps the most ferocious competitor baseball has ever seen, Cobb completely altered the way in which the game was played. During organized

Christy Mathewson

Walter Johnson

baseball's first half-century, competition was typically amiable, and intensity was often lukewarm. For Cobb, however, baseball was war and the opposing team was the enemy. Stories of Cobb sharpening his spikes and sliding high into bases to intimidate, infuriate, and punish opponents are legendary.

In spite of an unwritten code among the media of the day to report

Ty Cobb sliding into a base spikes up

only the positive, Cobb's off-the-field transgressions were too numerous
and egregious to ignore. Growing up in the South, Cobb was an avowed
racist. Cobb once pursued and slapped a black groundskeeper who had
offered him his hand, and grabbed and choked the groundskeeper's wife.
On another occasion, Cobb assaulted a black laborer who had admonished him for stepping in new asphalt. Cobb also once stabbed a black
hotel night watchman who had the temerity to inquire as to Cobb's identity. Once, during a game, Cobb burst into the crowd to assault a heckler
who had called him a "half-nigger." Cobb pummeled and spiked the man,
who had only one hand.[125]

    Even on his own team, Cobb was openly despised. He had a number
of brawls with teammates and always reported late to spring training
because he could not stand their company. Needless to say, the opposition and their fans also despised Cobb. Late in his career, when he was a
player/manager, Detroit's own fans loudly booed Cobb when he went to
the mound to make pitching changes.

    Irrespective of Ty Cobb's misdeeds, however, his achievements as
a player were, and still are, legendary. Cobb's batting average exceeded

Connie Mack

.300 in an incredible 23 consecutive seasons. He won twelve American League batting titles, including nine in succession, and led the league in slugging average in eight seasons. After 24 seasons in Major League Baseball beginning in 1905 and ending in 1928, the "Georgia Peach" retired with a .367 career batting average with 4,191 hits, 1,961 runs batted in, 2,245 runs scored, and 892 stolen bases, all Major League career records at the time of his retirement. Although Cobb's career hits, runs batted in, runs scored, and stolen bases records have subsequently been broken, it is highly unlikely that his lifetime batting average ever will be exceeded.

Nearly as successful as Cobb was his contemporary and fellow center fielder Tris Speaker. In 22 seasons between 1907 and 1928, Speaker collected 3,515 hits, a Major League record 793 doubles, 1,559 runs batted in, 1,881 runs scored, and 433 stolen bases. Speaker maintained a batting average of over .300 in 18 seasons and posted a lifetime average of .344. Because of Cobb's consistent hitting proficiency, however, Speaker won only one batting title, in 1916, when he hit .386 and interrupted Cobb's string of twelve batting crowns. The "Grey Eagle" fielded his position with flair, grace, and precision and is considered to have been the greatest Major League center fielder to have played before Joe DiMaggio and Willie Mays came upon the scene.

The first two decades of the 20th century also featured a pair of star second basemen, Napoleon "Nap" Lajoie and Edward Trowbridge "Eddie" Collins. Lajoie posted a career batting average of .339, with 3,251 hits, 1,504 runs scored, and 1,599 runs batted in over 21 seasons beginning in 1896 and ending in 1916. Nap won three batting titles, including in 1901 when he had the highest single season batting average in American League history at .422 and also led the American League in home runs (14), runs batted in (125), runs scored (145), hits (229), doubles (48), on-base percentage (.463), slugging average (.635), fielding percentage (.960), and put-outs (395). Collins had a lifetime .333 batting average over 25 seasons, with 3,311 hits, 1,299 runs batted in, and 1,818 runs scored. Both men fielded their positions gracefully and flawlessly.

Also prominent at the end of the Dead Ball Era were Samuel Earl "Wahoo Sam" Crawford, Zachary Davis "Zack" Wheat, Frank "Home Run" Baker, and Joseph Jefferson "Shoeless Joe" Jackson. Crawford had a career batting average of .309 over 19 seasons beginning in 1899 and holds the career Major League record for triples (312). Wheat maintained a batting average of .317 over 19 seasons beginning in 1909. Baker had a lifetime batting average of .307 and hit 96 home runs in a 13-year career, including four consecutive years from 1911 through 1914 in which he led the American League in home runs, never hitting more than 12 in any single season. In the Dead Ball Era, Baker's feats were considered power hitting. Joe Jackson posted a .356 batting average, baseball's third highest career mark, over a 13-year career that was abbreviated in 1920 by his expulsion from baseball following the Black Sox scandal. Jackson's swing served as a model for the young Babe Ruth.

The leading teams of the Dead Ball Era were the American League's Philadelphia Athletics, managed by the courtly Cornelius Alexander McGillicuddy ("Connie Mack"), and Boston Red Sox, and the National League's New York Giants, managed by the pugnacious John Joseph "Little Napoleon" McGraw.[126] Mack began to manage the Athletics in their first season, 1901, and continued to do so for half a century.[127] McGraw, a former player with the Baltimore Orioles and the Giants, assumed the helm of the Giants in 1902 and occupied that role until 1932.[128] In the 15 years following the respective hirings of Mack and McGraw, the Athletics and Giants would each win half a dozen pennants.

In 1912, Major League players formed the Fraternity of Professional Baseball Players, a new players' union, in an effort to secure player pensions, eliminate the dreaded reserve system, and increase salaries.[129] In 1914, several entrepreneurs created the new Federal League, which promised to increase players' salaries, did not employ a reserve system, and fielded teams in Baltimore, Brooklyn, Buffalo, Chicago, Indianapolis, Kansas City, Pittsburgh, and St. Louis.[130] In 1915, Newark replaced Indianapolis. Unlike in the established Major Leagues, the teams in the Federal League were owned by a single corporation, the stock of which was equally owned by the operators of the various franchises.[131] All players were hired by the league, received automatic annual salary increases of five percent, and were eligible for free agency after ten years service in the Federal League.[132]

More than 80 Major League players jumped to the Federal League.[133] The dominance of the Major Leagues was challenged. In response, the more established leagues recognized the Fraternity of Professional Base Ball Players, blacklisted players who jumped to the renegade Federal League, and raised the salaries of star players who remained in the established leagues.[134] But competition resulted in increased costs, as average annual player salaries more than doubled between 1913 and 1915 from $3,200 to $7,300 and stars such as Ty Cobb earned as much as $20,000 per season.[135] Meanwhile, fan support declined, as overall attendance fell from 7.2 million in 1909 to less than 6 million in 1914.[136]

In 1915, the Federal League sought an injunction in the United States District Court in Chicago to prevent the Major Leagues from enforcing the reserve system and blacklisting players who joined the Federal League, claiming that the actions by the Major Leagues were a conspiracy in restraint of trade and violated federal antitrust laws.[137] The Major Leagues had scrupulously avoided federal litigation because of the fear that their monopoly would be found to be in violation of federal antitrust legislation. The Federal League chose this forum, at least in part, because Federal Judge Kenesaw Mountain Landis, who presided as a judge on that court, had established a reputation as a "trust buster."[138] In refusing to grant an immediate injunction, however, Landis, an avowed baseball fan, admonished the litigants: "Do you realize that a decision in this case may tear down the very foundations of this game, so loved by thousands? ... Any blows at the thing called baseball would be regarded by this court as a blow to a national institution."[139] Landis then took the case under advisement and refused to make a decision. The case ultimately was settled after the 1915 season, with the Federal League franchise owners agreeing to disband their league in exchange for $600,000 cash, stock in several Major League franchises, the proceeds from selling the contracts of players who had been signed by the Federal League's franchises, and the transfer of Major League franchises (the Chicago Cubs and the St. Louis Browns) to two of their owners.[140]

Dissatisfied with the consequences of the settlement with the Major Leagues, the owners of the Federal League's Baltimore Terrapins franchise pursued an antitrust action in the Federal courts which would become the most enduring vestige of the Federal League.[141] The Terrapins challenged the Major Leagues' "oppressive, intimidating, and coercive course of conduct" and despotic control of baseball which bound players in a "system of peonage."[142] Although the trial court agreed with the Terrapins and awarded treble damages of $240,000,[143] the United States Court of Appeals reversed that decision, agreeing with the argument of the Major Leagues' lawyer, George Wharton Pepper, that the federal antitrust laws did not apply to baseball which was "a spontaneous output of human activity.... not in its nature commerce."[144] In 1922, Justice Oliver Wendell Holmes, speaking for a unanimous United States Supreme Court in *Federal Baseball Club of Baltimore, Inc. v. National League of Professional Clubs*, affirmed the decision of the Court of Appeals, stating that Major League Baseball games were "purely state affairs" which did not involve interstate commerce and, therefore, were not an appropriate subject for Federal regulation.[145] This landmark decision established baseball's so-called "antitrust exemption." In subsequent decisions, the Supreme Court has permitted this 1922 decision to stand, insisting that it is the province of Congress to correct this "anomaly."[146]

After the demise of the Federal League, player salaries once again declined. For example, Boston Red Sox standout Tris Speaker, who had received salaries of $15,000 per year in 1914 and 1915, plus a $5,000 bonus to remain in Boston, held out for a salary of $12,000 in 1916. The Red Sox insisted they would pay Speaker no more than $9,000. Finally, just before the 1916 season began, the Red Sox sold Speaker to the Cleveland Indians for $50,000 and two players. Speaker demanded, and ultimately obtained, $10,000 of the $50,000 Cleveland paid to Boston.[147]

As baseball's Dead Ball Era drew to a close, interest in the game began to subside. During the United States' involvement in World War I (1917–1918), the United States government declared that baseball was not essential to the war effort and decreed that professional players would be required to either serve in the armed forces or otherwise engage in "employment calculated to aid in the successful prosecution of the war."[148] A number of teams lost their best performers to the war cause and attendance at baseball games plummeted from the high-water mark of 7.2 million in 1909 to only three million in 1918.[149] The combination of the owners' control over the game and slumping attendance during World War I resulted in declining player salaries. By 1917, the Major Leagues terminated their recognition of the Fraternity of Professional Base Ball Players and most players' salaries reverted to their levels of the period before the Federal League had provided competition.[150] Again, order was restored. But resentment and mistrust of ownership and management prevailed among players.

Following the 1918 season, after attendance fell below 3 million for the first time in ten years, owners voted to play an abbreviated 140-game schedule in 1919.[151] To management's surprise, however, World War I ended and Major League Baseball, in spite of a reduced schedule, reaped a windfall from 6.5 million paid spectators.[152] By the end of World War I, the World Series, which had been institutionalized in 1905 as an outgrowth of the National Agreement which formed the Major Leagues in 1903, had become baseball's most important annual event. The Boston Red Sox had won three of the four World Series between 1915 and 1918. The World Series at the end of the 1919 season promised to bring renewed excitement. Hoping to cash in on the fans' enthusiasm, and make up for lost regular-season gate receipts, Major League Baseball's owners added two games to the 1919 World Series, making it a best of nine games affair. The fans' enthusiasm and the owners' windfall was short-lived, however, as the 1919 World Series became Major League Baseball's greatest on-the-field embarrassment.

Eight players from the highly-favored American League champion Chicago White Sox, embittered over the low salaries paid to them by their parsimonious owner, Charles A. Comiskey, accepted bribes from gamblers to ensure that their team would lose the World Series to the National League champion Cincinnati Reds.[153] The fix was reportedly organized by Arnold Rothstein, a New York organized crime and gambling kingpin who had been a business partner of both John McGraw and Charles Stoneham, then manager and owner, respectively, of the New York Giants. When the "Black Sox Scandal" was made public, the reputation of an already fading game was further eroded. The eight players were indicted and tried in a Chicago court, but acquitted because of a lack of convincing evidence.[154]

As the 20th century's second decade drew to a close, baseball's attendance had declined. Its brightest star was a cruel, racist bully, reviled by fans, foes, and even his own teammates. America's national pastime, the game which had only recently been an integral part of the nation's fabric, was waning in importance and was mired in the disgrace of a gambling scandal. A savior was needed.

Chapter 3

IN THE EAST, A STAR APPEARED

He was one of the greatest pitchers of all time, and then he became a great judge of a fly ball, never threw to the wrong base when he was playing the outfield, terrific arm, good base runner, could hit the ball twice as far as any other human being. He was like an animal. He had that instinct. They know when it's going to rain. Nature, that was Ruth!
　　　　　　　　　　　　—Rube Bressler

Given the proper physical equipment—which consists solely in the strength to knock a ball 40 feet farther than the average man can do it—anybody can play big league ball today. In other words, science is out the window.
　　　　　　　　　　　　—Ty Cobb

The Roaring Twenties began, in spirit at least, with the Armistice that ended the bloodiest conflict the world had ever witnessed. World War I had exhausted America and the tired country welcomed back her doughboys with open arms. As the nation was descending from its wartime high, peace negotiations dragged along in Versailles. President Woodrow Wilson lobbied the Allies for "Peace Without Victory," which he believed would prevent history from repeating itself and avoid future, bloodier conflicts. America was in no mood, however, for Wilson's lofty moral sentiments and admonitions of its duty to the world. The war was over, the threat repelled. In 1921, Warren G. Harding became President, propelled by the promise of a "Return to Normalcy."

There was little normal about Major League Baseball as the second decade of the 20th century ended. Attendance had plummeted during

World War I. Major League Baseball had survived a challenge from the Federal League, but at a substantial cost. Scandal had rocked the game, as it became clear that eight members of the Chicago White Sox had accepted bribes from gamblers to throw the 1919 World Series against the Cincinnati Reds. Although allegations of impropriety would not surface until midway through the 1920 season, any post-war momentum Major League Baseball had built was erased by a less than stellar 1919 World Series.[155] American League and National League owners were unhappy with the National Commission that administered Major League Baseball.

The owners of most Major League teams were businessmen with diverse portfolios who used baseball as a way to enrich their fortunes and not necessarily to garner civic and public acclaim. Among Major League Baseball's entrepreneurs was Boston Red Sox owner Harry Frazee, whose business interests also included Broadway musicals. Frazee had produced a successful baseball team which won three of the four World Series between 1915 and 1918, and a string of Broadway hits. By 1919, however, his theater hits had turned into flops and his finances were hemorrhaging. Frazee's new production, *No, No Nanette*, required an immediate and substantial cash infusion.[156]

In the American League's first two decades, the Red Sox were its most successful club, winners of five World Series championships. In New York City, the hapless Yankees, which had never captured a championship, were tenants in the Polo Grounds to John McGraw's dominant Giants. Yankees owners Jacob Ruppert and Tillinghast L'Hommedieu Huston, eager to improve their team's fortunes, were prepared to pounce upon the financially vulnerable Frazee. The most valuable assets in Frazee's stable were his baseball players, and Frazee's most marketable player was his young pitcher turned slugger and outfielder, George Herman "Babe" Ruth.[157]

In his six seasons with the Red Sox, Ruth had won 89 games as a pitcher, while losing only 46. As a 20 year old, the left-handed fireballer won 18 games, posted an earned run average of 2.44, and helped the Red Sox win the World Series. The following season, he was even more successful, winning 23 games and posting an American League–leading 1.75 earned run average as his team won another World Series. That campaign was followed by a 24-win season, a 13-victory season in fewer than half as many pitching starts as the previous year, and another World Series championship in which the strapping young star pitched a record 29 consecutive scoreless innings. Although Ruth might have developed into one of the greatest pitchers in baseball history if he had continued to toil on the mound, he also could hit. In 1918, Ruth's prodigious swing forced his Red

Sox manager to halve the number of pitching starts for his left-handed ace and provide him 317 at bats playing as a regular outfielder. The following season, Ruth still pitched 133 innings and won nine games, but his 432 at bats generated previously unimagined results as he bashed a single-season Major League record 29 home runs (his teammates hit four home runs in total) and led the American League in runs batted in (114) and runs scored (103). According to sabermetrician Bill James, at the time that Ruth played in Boston (1914–19), Fenway Park was the most difficult park in the American League in which to hit home runs and largely disguised Ruth's extraordinary power.[158] During his years with the Red Sox, Ruth hit nearly three and one-half times as many home runs in road games as in home games. In 1918, Ruth hit all of his American League–leading 11 home runs on the road. In 1919, Ruth's last season as a member of the Red Sox, he hit only nine of his American League–leading 29 home runs in Fenway Park. In 1920, the first season in which New York's Polo Grounds was Ruth's home ballpark, he hit 54 home runs, 25 on the road (an increase of only five from his 1919 road total) and 29 at home (an increase of 20 from his 1919 home total in Fenway Park).[159]

Following the 1918 season, Ruth, now clearly cognizant of his value to the Red Sox, informed the team that he wanted a new two-year contract at an increase in salary from $7,000 to $15,000 per year. The team refused and Ruth held out. After posturing by both sides, Ruth signed a three-year contract at a salary of $10,000 per year.[160] Following the 1919 season, in which Ruth set his first season home run record, with 29 round-trippers, he sought to have his salary increased to $20,000, irrespective of the two years remaining on his contract.[161] Badly in need of cash, Red Sox owner Frazee sold Ruth to the Yankees for $100,000 in cash and a $300,000 loan, secured by a mortgage on Fenway Park.[162] To ensure that Ruth played for them, the Yankees paid him an immediate $1,000 transfer bonus and a total of $20,000 in bonuses over the 1920 and 1921 seasons, in addition to his $10,000 annual salary under his Red Sox contract.[163]

Over a five-year period, Frazee sent 15 players to the Yankees, including Waite Hoyt, Wally Schang, Joe Dugan, Herb Pennock, Carl Mays, Ernie Shore, Sam Jones, Dutch Leonard, Duffy Lewis, Joe Bush, and of course Babe Ruth.[164] For the Boston Red Sox, the "Curse of the Bambino" commenced. Although the Red Sox had won five of the first fifteen World Series, in the nine seasons from 1922 through 1930, they finished last in the American League standings in every season but 1924, when they finished next to last. The Red Sox did not play in another World Series until 1946 and still have not won a World Series championship since Babe Ruth was sold to the Yankees after the 1919 season.[165]

Babe Ruth as a young pitcher for the Boston Red Sox.

A number of elements are involved in the making of a legend. Among these are unique and undeniable talent, charisma, flair, determination, and timing. America, buoyed by the spirit of the Roaring Twenties, was swept up in a wave of prosperity. People were working less and spending more. Consumer affluence manifested itself in record purchases of automobiles and radios, while voracious spectators flocked to movie theaters and sporting arenas. The 1920s were an era of guiltless indulgence. America was booming. Its urban population was expanding, longing for distractions, and hungering for heroes.

Ruth's arrival in New York coincided with Major League Baseball's decisions to introduce a somewhat livelier baseball for the 1920 season, change baseballs more regularly during games, and forbid trick pitches, foreign substances, and altering baseballs.[166] The number of home runs in the Major Leagues doubled. Runs scored increased by 25 percent. Batting averages rose by more than 10 percent.[167] In 1920, playing in the Polo Grounds with its short right-field fence (257 feet from home plate down the right-field line),[168] Babe Ruth took New York, Major League Baseball, and America by storm. His 54 home runs were not only an all-time Major League single season record, they were more than any other American League *team* achieved and constituted approximately 15 percent of all home runs hit in the American League in 1920! When Mark McGwire broke Roger Maris's single season home run record in 1998, he exceeded Maris's 1961 total by nine home runs, or approximately 15 percent, and Sammy Sosa's 1998 total by only four home runs, a difference of less than seven percent. When Barry Bonds broke Mark McGwire's single season home run record in 2001, he exceeded McGwire's 1998 total by three home runs, an increase of less than five percent, and Sammy Sosa's 2001 total by nine home runs, a difference of about 12 percent. Ruth's 1920 mark of 54 nearly doubled his own previous Major League record of 29 home runs and was nearly three times the 19 hit by George Sisler, who had the second-highest individual home run total in Major League Baseball in 1920. In the Bambino's first season with the Yankees, he also posted a .376 batting average with a league-leading 158 runs scored and 137 runs batted in. He also hit nine triples and 36 doubles, received a league-leading 148 weeks, and stole 14 bases. His .847 slugging average stood as the single-season Major League record until Barry Bonds broke it in 2001. The Dead Ball Era was dead!

American adulation in the Roaring Twenties elevated the popularity of sportsmen such as boxing's heavyweight champion Jack Dempsey, football's Red Grange, golf's Bobby Jones, tennis's Bill Tilden, and horse racing's Man o' War to heights never before experienced by athletes.[169] Ruth was not only baseball's greatest and most exciting player, he became the most celebrated and venerated man in America. Ruth's prodigious feats were not limited to the ball field. In virtually no time, the Babe became a fixture in swinging Jazz Age Manhattan. His larger-than-life appetites for food, alcohol, cigars, women, and excitement made Ruth the poster boy for a generation of excess. The profligate Babe was only 25 years old and

Babe Ruth hitting a home run for the Yankees.

seemed indestructible. He could play all day on the ball field, and play all
night from speakeasy to speakeasy and bedroom to bedroom.

Baseball fans could not get enough of the Babe.[170] In Ruth's initial
season in New York, the Yankees became the first Major League team to
draw more than one million spectators.[171] Sharing the Polo Grounds with
the National League's Giants, the Yankees easily attracted more fans than

McGraw's powerhouse. There was, however, a dark side to this most prosperous campaign. Throughout the summer of 1920, damning allegations emerged about White Sox players throwing the 1919 World Series. The allegations became full-blown accusations followed by criminal charges.[172] Although the fun-loving and hard-hitting antics of Babe Ruth temporarily diverted attention from the "Black Sox" and the "Season of Guilt," owners feared irreparable damage to the game and, more importantly, their bank accounts. Fallout from the Black Sox scandal had shaken Major League Baseball.[173] Editorials of the day lampooned the game's lack of transparency and accountability. The New York Yankees, Boston Red Sox, and Chicago White Sox threatened to switch to the National League.[174] The game of baseball was idealized as a paragon of virtue that upheld the heroic ideals of sportsmanship and fair play, but the Major Leagues badly needed an infusion of credibility.

Approximately one year before the Black Sox scandal became public, Chicago Cubs shareholder and prominent businessman Albert D. Lasker formulated a plan for restructuring the administration of Major League Baseball.[175] Lasker's plan emanated from the premise that Major League Baseball's owners were incapable of governing themselves and that a commission of three eminent persons without business connections to baseball should administer the game. Although a number of owners on Major League Baseball's management committee were openly hostile to one another and prone to in-fighting, the option of permitting an outside party to run the game was unappealing. Previous efforts to introduce an independent chairman for the National Commission had been unsuccessful. In 1918, former President of the United States and future Chief Justice of the United States Supreme Court William Howard Taft rejected Major League Baseball's overture for him to serve as chairman of the Baseball Commission.[176] Other names suggested included United States Army General John J. "Black Jack" Pershing and former Secretary of the Treasury William G. McAdoo.[177] The game needed a figure of unshakable honesty and trustworthiness to restore faith in the national institution while perpetuating management's control. But, if Major League Baseball was going to be governed by a third party, the owners wanted to be certain that it would be someone who was on their side.

After considerable argument over structure, which nearly resulted in the elimination of the American League, the owners ultimately turned to Kenesaw Mountain Landis, a federal judge in the United States District Court in Chicago, whose name was derived (but misspelled) from a mountain in Georgia where his father was badly wounded in a Civil War battle. As you may recall from Chapter 2 of this book, during Major League

Babe Ruth with his other major interest.

Baseball's legal battle with the Federal League, Landis had performed a valuable service for the Major League Baseball establishment. Landis's refusal to grant an injunction to the Federal League to prevent the Major Leagues' employment of the reserve system and blacklisting had resulted in a favorable settlement for the established Major Leagues. Five years later, that invaluable service made Landis the obvious choice to be Major League Baseball's first commissioner. Landis's terms for accepting the position were, however, strict. In addition to generous financial terms, Landis insisted on being granted the absolute power, for seven years, to investigate and punish wrongdoing and arbitrate all disputes.[178] The owners also relinquished all rights to publicly complain about Landis's decisions or to seek legal redress therefrom and were forced to sign a pledge of loyalty.[179] Only Phil Ball, owner of the St. Louis Browns, refused to agree.[180]

The new commissioner's defining act was the lifetime expulsion from organized baseball of the eight Chicago "Black Sox" players who had conspired to throw the 1919 World Series.[181] The fact that these men were acquitted of cheating by a court of law did not concern Landis. He decided the eight men were guilty and banned them for life.[182] Over the next five years, Landis imposed lifetime expulsions on twelve other players for var-

Major league owners submitting to the demands of Kenesaw Mountain Landis (seated).

ious reasons, some justified and others questionable. He also forced New York Giants owner Horace Stoneham and manager John McGraw to divest themselves of their interests in a race track and casino operation in Havana, Cuba.[183] A new sheriff was in town!

Major League Baseball, ironically, now had two distinct faces. The face of the game off the field, characterized by the craggy, austere visage of Judge Landis, was authoritarian and dictatorial. On the field, the robust and joyous countenance of the swashbuckling Babe Ruth embodied America in this most optimistic decade. That these two forces of nature ultimately would collide was inevitable.

For an encore in New York in 1921, Ruth broke his one-year-old home run record by hitting 59 more, giving him a two-year Yankee total of 113, a total not exceeded until Mark McGwire surpassed it in the 1990s. Ruth also led the Major Leagues with 171 runs batted in, 177 runs scored, 144 bases on balls, and a slugging average of .846. He also paced the American League with 44 doubles and 16 triples to aggregate 119 extra base hits, 457 total bases, and 289 runs produced, while hitting for a .378 average in the greatest season for any hitter ever.

The legend of Ruth, now dubbed "the Sultan of Swat" by New York scribes, was growing to proportions never previously reached by any sportsman. The Yankees, with Ruth and other former Boston Red Sox stars purchased from Harry Frazee, were easily baseball's biggest draw, setting attendance marks both at home and on the road. In 1920, in spite of the "Season of Guilt," the Babe was largely responsible for Major League Baseball reaching new attendance records with over 9 million fans. By 1921, the Yankees accounted for 27 percent of total American League attendance. Those fortunate fans with access to Major League stadiums flocked to see Ruth. During the 1920s, Major League attendance averaged 9.3 million per year, with the Yankees averaging over 1 million per year.[184] But for the vast majority of Americans, images of the Babe were limited to black and white photographs and newsreels. Americans also visited movie theaters in record numbers to enjoy the comedy and drama of Charlie Chaplin, Mary Pickford, Buster Keaton, W.C. Fields, Gloria Swanson, and Douglas Fairbanks. Before the main features would commence, moviegoers were treated to newsreel footage of the great Babe Ruth blasting home runs and gallivanting around Manhattan accompanied by comely escorts. After the 1921 season, Ruth signed a new 5-year contract with the Yankees at an annual salary of $52,000, or $1,000 per week.[185] The team's second-highest-paid player, Home Run Baker, who had twice sat out entire seasons in salary disputes, received an annual salary of $16,000.[186] Fifteen years later, after Ruth's retirement, Lou Gehrig's salary, the highest in the Major Leagues, was $30,000.[187]

Ruth, never the most complex of characters, had a voracious appetite for life and felt no need to conceal it. With a plethora of temptations on his doorstep, Ruth made little effort at abstinence. America was indulging, so why shouldn't the country's most famous celebrity also partake? This seemed logical to most Americans, but not to the pious and devout Landis, who believed baseball players should be held to a higher standard. Landis was not pleased that the game's greatest star was as renowned for his carousing as for his hitting. Initially, the Judge was reluctant to discipline baseball's meal ticket for fear of a fan backlash. But, after having harshly and swiftly dealt with the Black Sox episode, Landis focused his sights on Ruth.

After the 1921 season, Ruth attempted to cash in on his immense popularity by barnstorming in America's nether regions with a group of other Major League players. Although the Babe received a substantial salary, in comparison to the revenue he generated for the Yankees and Major League Baseball, Ruth was woefully underpaid. Ruth had doubled his Major League salary by barnstorming after the 1919 and 1920 seasons, and

Babe Ruth with world heavyweight boxing champion Jack Dempsey.

expected to repeat that feat after the 1921 season.[188] Landis believed that Ruth's barnstorming was an affront to baseball and ordered him to stop. When Ruth publicly refused, Landis punished Ruth's insubordination by suspending him for the first 40 games of the 1922 season.[189] In spite of outrage from both fans and management (without Ruth in the lineup attendance declined dramatically), Landis stood firm. Because of his suspension,

Ruth played in only 110 games in 1922 but still managed to hit 35 home runs and tally 99 runs batted in. His slugging percentage of .672, while down significantly from the previous season's .846, was easily the highest in baseball. The Babe's return to the game after his brief sabbatical was accorded fanfare and hoopla worthy of his legendary status.

Attendance increased so dramatically after Ruth's arrival in New York that plans were launched to build a grand, new stadium with the Yankees as the sole tenant. In 1921 and 1922, the Yankees won their first two American League pennants, but also suffered the ignominy of losing both World Series to the Giants in the Polo Grounds. Perhaps no date better defines baseball's so-called "Second Golden Age" than April 18, 1923, the day Yankee Stadium opened. Dubbed "the House that Ruth Built," the massive new stadium cost the Yankees' owners approximately $2.5 million.[190] Naturally, the Babe cracked a home run on the Stadium's opening day. In his first season hitting in the new stadium, with its short right-field porch (296 feet from home plate down the right-field line),[191] the left-handed-hitting Ruth posted a .393 batting average (the highest of his career) and led the American League in home runs, runs scored, runs batted in, total bases, slugging average, and walks. He also led the Yankees to their first World Series championship.

Ruth won twelve home run titles from 1918 through 1931. In 1927, batting in the middle of the Yankees' infamous "Murderers' Row" lineup, Ruth eclipsed his earlier record and hit 60 home runs in a season. Overcoming the slow start caused by his early career as a pitcher, Ruth amassed a career total of 714 home runs, a mark that stood until Hank Aaron finally surpassed the Babe's career record in 1974. Ruth is the only player to hit at least 500 home runs and to hit more home runs after his 32nd birthday than before.[192] He also is the only player in history to have pitched in at least ten different Major League seasons and to have a winning record in every season in which he pitched. During the decade of the 1920s, Babe Ruth's *average* season was 173 hits, 86 extra-base hits, 124 bases on balls, 137 runs scored, 133 runs batted in, 47 home runs, 31 doubles, 8 triples, an on-base percentage of .485, a batting average of .355, and a slugging average of .740. During that decade, Ruth led the American League in slugging average nine times, home runs eight times, bases on balls seven times, runs scored seven times, on-base percentage six times, runs batted in five times, and won a batting title.

The Babe was larger than life, his heroic deeds magnified by performing in New York City, America's media epicenter. Ruth's explosive power led the Yankees to six pennants and three World Series titles during his first ten years in New York, and provided the foundation for the

Yankee Stadium (foreground), Bronx, with Polo Grounds (rear), Manhattan.

Yankees' dynasties that have captured 26 World Series titles. Baseball's savior transformed the game forever—in the manner in which it was played, in its compensation structure, and in its entertainment value. Baseball was big, it was an essential part of America's culture, and no one was bigger than Babe Ruth and the Yankees.[193]

Babe Ruth with U.S. Open, U.S. amateur, British Open, and British amateur champion golfer Lawson Little.

Because of Ruth's great success both on the field and at the box office, big-bang baseball became the norm throughout the Major Leagues.[194] During the 1920s, the overall Major League batting average exceeded .280, compared with approximately .255 during the first two decades of the 20th century.[195] Scoring increased nearly 40 percent from 1917 to 1925.[196] Earned-run-averages soared from about 2.95 during the 1900–1919 period to over 4.00 during the 1920s, and pitching victories declined.[197] In the 1920s, the numbers of home runs and runs scored increased dramatically. From a total of 235 home runs in both Major Leagues in 1918 (Ruth's last year as a full-time pitcher), Major League home runs increased to 630 in 1920 (54 of which were hit by Ruth), 1,169 in 1925, and 1,565 in 1930. By the mid–1950s, Major League home runs exceeded 2,000 per year. By the late 1970s, more than 3,000 Major League home runs were hit annually. This increased to more than 4,000 by the early 1990s and to more than 5,000 by 1998.[198]

Ironically, during much of the 1920s and 1930s, National League teams, led by players such as Rogers Hornsby, out-slugged their American League counterparts. Hornsby won seven National League batting titles, including six straight from 1920 through 1925. In 1922, Hornsby slugged a National League record 42 home runs to go along with a league-leading 250 hits, 46 doubles, 14 triples, 152 runs batted in, 141 runs scored, a batting average of .401, and a slugging average of .722. He also received the National League's highest salary, $30,000.[199] The "Rajah" exceeded the .400 mark in batting average three times, won two "Triple Crowns," was twice named Most Valuable Player in the National League, and retired with a career batting average of .358, the highest of any right-handed hitter in Major League Baseball history and second only to Ty Cobb overall. Hornsby also led the National League in slugging average nine times, including six consecutive seasons from 1920 through 1925, and was the career National League leader in home runs (301) at the time of his retirement. Miraculously, Hornsby's *cumulative* batting average for the five years 1921–25 was .402. He trailed only Babe Ruth in home runs and runs batted in during the 1920s.[200]

For 12 seasons, Rogers Hornsby was a fixture in St. Louis and easily the Cardinals' most popular player. While nowhere near as charismatic as Ruth, Hornsby was a potent force at the plate. Imagine, if you can, a *second baseman* who annually posts a .360 batting average with about 200 hits, 30 home runs, 70 extra-base hits, 120 runs scored, and 125 runs batted in. Imagine also that this second baseman, by far the team's greatest talent, is the manager of his team. Hornsby would seem to have had as much clout as any player, including Ruth, in baseball-related matters. But Hornsby had engaged in disputes with Cardinals owner Sam Breadon over salary, management, and other matters, and Breadon publicly maintained that Hornsby's skills were declining. Thus, the Cardinals traded Hornsby to the New York Giants for Frankie Frisch. The Cardinals' treatment of Hornsby would be a clear-cut signal for the next half century that the real power in baseball continued to belong to the game's owners. Interestingly,

Rogers Hornsby

the Cardinals' trade of Hornsby was not complete until the team repurchased from Hornsby his shareholding in the team. After a protracted dispute over the value of those shares, a settlement was reached in which the Cardinals and other National League teams paid Hornsby in excess of $100,000.[201]

That the Cardinals were even competitive during the 1920s, both on and off the field, was a testament to the vision and parsimony of St. Louis general manager Wesley Branch Rickey. Rickey, a former catcher of modest talents, went on to become baseball's greatest organizational genius. "The Mahatma" invented the modern farm system, pioneering the use of minor league clubs to develop and train young players.[202] Rickey, a former lawyer, purchased numerous minor league clubs and established working relations with others, while deploying a network of scouts who signed young players for minimal salaries. America in the 1920s was filled with starry-eyed and hungry young men with Major League baseball dreams. Rickey induced those with enough promise to sign contracts and thereafter owned the young men for the rest of their baseball lives. Players were assigned to minor league teams, instructed, scouted, graded, and advanced if their play warranted it.[203] Rickey's vertical integration ensured that the Cardinals were never short of star players and had enough surplus talent to sell to the highest bidders among baseball's other teams. From 1919 through 1946, the Cardinals did not purchase a single player, but during the same period sold a number of players to other Major League teams for a total of more than $2 million.[204] Rickey, an oddity in baseball because he knew both the game and the world of business, pocketed a neat profit for every player he sold. In signing Jackie Robinson to break baseball's color barrier some twenty years later, Rickey would become known as baseball's great emancipator. During the early part of the 20th century, however, the great emancipator was a prominent contributor to the plight of enslaved players.[205]

Players had one simple choice: to play or not to play. With which team, where, when, and for how much was not within the players' control. Unhappy with the Yankees' salary proposal one year, Babe Ruth held out and skipped spring training. When asked why he should be paid more in annual salary than President Herbert Hoover, Ruth replied, "I had a better year than Hoover." But Ruth found that his only negotiating leverage was his absence from the team.

Rogers Hornsby, like Babe Ruth, understood his value to his team in dollars and cents. Hornsby often let it be known that he was not happy with Rickey's renowned thrift in setting players' salaries. Following the 1926 season, after winning six consecutive batting titles, Hornsby "slumped" to a mere .317 batting average with 93 runs batted in and 96 runs scored. Rickey enraged Cardinals fans by trading the malcontent Hornsby to the New York Giants for Frankie Frisch. Based solely on economic criteria, Harry Frazee's sale of Babe Ruth six years earlier had a more significant impact on baseball, but Rickey's trading of Hornsby marked the first time that a Major League star and fan favorite was traded in the middle of his career because of his contentious ways. Hornsby, who

Babe Ruth (left) and Yankees owner Jacob Ruppert signing Ruth's 1930-31 contract.

was only 30 years old and still in his prime, would go on to hit .361 with 26 home runs, 125 runs batted in, and 133 runs scored for the Giants in 1926. The next season Hornsby was on the move again as he was traded to the Boston Braves where he hit a league-leading .387. The following year, the Rajah was dealt to the Chicago Cubs where he posted a .380 batting average, 39 home runs, 156 runs scored, and 149 runs batted in. In four years, Hornsby played for four different teams. Over that four-year period, he averaged 121 runs scored, 115 runs batted in, 24 home runs, and a .361 batting average. Those numbers would have made the Rajah one of Major League Baseball's most dominant offensive performers in almost any era. Hornsby's reward for his inability to conceal his displeasure with baseball's ownership and compensation structure in the 1920s was four different addresses in four years. Yet clearly at least a part of the reason for Hornsby's inability to remain with a team was the result of his own cold and irascible personality. Bill James observes, "[i]f a contest is ever held to determine the biggest horse's ass in baseball history, … I think I might choose Hornsby."[206]

While Hornsby was easily the National League's best hitter, over in New York, Ruth and strapping young first baseman Lou Gehrig led a legendary group of sluggers who were destroying both opposing pitchers and attendance records. The Yankees, easily baseball's top draw playing in America's greatest city, were emerging as a dynasty that would reshape and reposition baseball as America's national pastime. The Yankees won American League pennants in 1921, 1922, 1923, 1926, 1927, 1928, and 1929 and World Series championships in 1923, 1927, and 1928. In 1927, the Yankees' fabled "Murderers' Row" won 110 games and lost just 44. Ruth established his final single season home-run record in 1927 with 60 round trippers (the second season that the Babe hit more home runs than any other *team* in the American League and provided approximately 15 percent of all home runs in the league), while hitting .356 and driving in 164 runs. Gehrig posted a .373 batting average, added 47 home runs, and tallied 175 runs batted in as the men in pinstripes annihilated all opponents to win their fifth American League pennant in seven years and their second World Series. The 1927 Yankees hit a Major League record 158 home runs and batted .307 as a team, with their eight starting players averaging .327. Four Yankees drove in more than 100 runs, including Ruth, Gehrig, Tony Lazzeri, and Bob Meusel. Earle Combs added a league-leading 231 hits and 23 triples, batting for a .356 average. The Yankees' pitching staff included Waite Hoyt, who won 22 games and posted a 2.64 earned run average, Herb Pennock and Wilcy Moore, who each posted 19 wins, Urban Shocker, who won 18 games, Dutch Ruether, who tallied 13 wins, and George Pipgras, who added 10 wins. In 1928, the Yankees "three-peated" as American League champions and repeated as World Series champions. Like America, the Yankees were well-oiled, hard hitting, and profitable.

Major league attendance increased from 6.5 million in 1919, Ruth's last year in Boston, to 9.6 million in 1929.[707] During the decade of the 1920s, all Major League teams except the Boston Red Sox made an overall profit.[208] The Dead Ball Era was over, Babe Ruth's big ball was in, and the crowds loved it. Although purists such as Ty Cobb lamented the passing of skills like bunting and the hit and run, fans wanted to see big ball as practiced by the Babe. Baseball's boom assured that, by the end of the 1929 season, average player salaries had increased to $7,500 per season.[209] In 1927, Ruth signed a 3-year contract for 1927–1929 at an annual salary of $70,000.[210] The next-highest-paid Yankee, Herb Pennock, was paid $17,500.[211]

America was in a golden age. Peace existed throughout the world. Industrial production doubled in America during the 1920s. Everything in America was so good, so exciting, so big. The stock market and the apparent ease of making money through investments thrilled Americans. Per capita income in the United States increased. Growth in productivity and credit purchases brought hundreds of new products within the reach of average consumers. New products altered the manner in which Americans lived. The automobile, the radio, and electric appliances made life easier, more exciting, and more interesting.[212] Americans perceived business and finance as the source of a new, better life. How lucky Americans were to live in such a dynamic era! And nothing was riding as high as Babe Ruth and the Yankees except the stock market.

Chapter 4

PLAGUES

Nothing green remained on tree or plant in all the land.
—Exodus 10:15

All ballplayers should quit when it starts to feel as if all the baselines run uphill.
—Babe Ruth

It's a pretty big shadow. It gives me lots of room to spread myself.
—Lou Gehrig, on playing in the shadow of Babe Ruth

The Gashouse Gang was a group of ferocious gentlemen, willing to embrace the hazards of rational chance.
—Branch Rickey

The 1920s started with a roar and ended with a resounding thud. America got fat and so did Babe Ruth. Although Ruth's portly midsection belied his tremendous athletic ability, the Babe—along with Chicago gangster Al Capone, jazz trumpeter Louis Armstrong, heavyweight champion Jack Dempsey, and Wall Street—came to symbolize this decade of indulgence. With six World Series championships, a hefty income, and New York City as his personal playground, the 34-year-old Ruth was swinging hard in 1929, both on and off the field. "I swing big, with everything I've got. I hit big or I miss big," said Ruth. "I like to live as big as I can." Yankees management began to voice concerns to an aging Ruth about his well-known passion for non–baseball related affairs. "I'll promise to go easier on drinking and to get to bed earlier," replied the Babe, "but not for you, fifty thousand dollars, or two-hundred and fifty thousand dollars will I give up women. They're too much fun." Ruth's defiance became America's creed. Life was too much fun to compromise. Baseball participated in the fun and played a leading role in the optimistic spirit of the "Roaring Twenties." By 1929, Americans were spending nearly $5 billion annually on recreational pursuits, with a healthy portion of that amount being spent on baseball.

Many factors contributed to the Great Depression, the worst economic slump in American history and one which spread throughout the industrialized world. Causative factors included a greatly disproportionate distribution of wealth between rich and poor and between industry and agriculture, immense disparity between industry's productive capacity and purchasers' abilities to consume, extensive stock market speculation, excessive consumer credit and spending, and a European economy devastated by World War I and its aftermath. Throughout the 1920s, prices of agricultural products fell and farm debt rose. America's total income rose by 25 percent in the 1920s, but by 1929 the top one-tenth of one percent of Americans had income equal to the bottom 42 percent and controlled 34 percent of all savings, while 80 percent of Americans had no savings at all.[213] Between 1925 and 1929, consumer credit more than doubled.[214] Disparity in income was both a result and a cause of the huge gap between industry's productive capacity and purchasers' ability to consume, excessive consumer credit and spending, and stock market speculation.[215] As a result of these and other factors, on October 29, 1929, two weeks after the Philadelphia Athletics defeated the Chicago Cubs to win the 1929 World Series, America's stock markets crashed.[216] America went from fat to flat in a few hours. An unprecedented wave of panic selling of stocks led to a collapse in stock prices and the loss of many American fortunes. Between 1929 and 1933, stock prices plummeted 80 percent.[217] The stock market crash undermined consumer and investor confidence, causing spending to be curtailed, investment to be reduced, and production to fall. Capital investment declined from $10 billion in 1929 to $1 billion in 1932. Jobs were lost, factories closed, and banks failed. Between 1930 and 1933, more than 5,000 banks closed, nine million savings accounts were eliminated, and depositors lost $2.5 billion. During the same period, America's gross national product fell by nearly 50 percent.[218] Farm income fell over 60 percent and severe droughts caused much of America's agricultural land to be destroyed in a "Dust Bowl."[219] Unemployment increased from less than one million in 1929 to more than 12 million in 1933, by which time 25 percent of all Americans were unemployed.[220] Savings dropped from five percent of disposable income to minus two percent of disposable income.[221] These events cast a pall of austerity over

America for more than a decade. Not until the end of World War II would America return to prosperity.

The Wall Street crash marked the dividing line between the optimism of the Roaring Twenties and the pessimism of the Great Depression. During the 1930s, millions of workers were jobless and, for those who did work, salaries were far below pre–Depression levels. The country's economic malaise slowed population growth and greatly reduced funds available for recreational spending. From 1930 to 1945, baseball would reel first from the economic despondency gripping the nation and later from the loss of a number of star players to the armed services during World War II. Baseball was hit hard by the Great Depression. There was little money for food, and even less for baseball.[222] In 1931, with the economic crisis deepening, the American League as a whole lost money while the National League collectively barely managed to break even. In 1930, attendance had been over 10 million, a figure that would not be repeated until 1945, the year World War II ended. In 1932, attendance slipped below 7 million and, by 1933, only 6 million spectators paid to view the national pastime.[223] During the 1930s, Major League Baseball was almost completely dependent upon its live gate for revenues and this decline in attendance resulted in crippling financial losses for most teams. Minor league baseball was hit especially hard by the Great Depression, with many teams being forced to disband, although popular teams in expanding markets such as Los Angeles and San Francisco experienced some success.[224]

The principal reason for the solvency of many minor league teams was the growth of the Major League farm systems. St. Louis Cardinals general manager Branch Rickey developed the first modern farm system in the 1920s, by purchasing minor league teams and forging contractual relationships with others. As discussed in Chapter 3 of this book, Rickey and his scouts signed large numbers of young players who were trained and given experience on these minor league teams. If their skills developed to an acceptable level, they were promoted to the Major League parent. Surplus players and those that failed to satisfy the Cardinals' requirements were sold to other teams or released. By the mid–1920s, the Cardinals controlled far more young players and minor league teams than any other Major League franchise. The success of this system paid dividends to the Redbirds, both in performance and profits, for years to come. By the early 1930s, other teams were following Rickey's example. By the late 1930s, all Major League teams had adopted this method of developing talent.[225]

Although American League attendance increased slightly in the latter half of the 1930s, the improvements were uneven. Attendance for stronger teams such as the New York Yankees and Detroit Tigers improved, while weaker teams like the Philadelphia Athletics, St. Louis Browns, and Washington Senators struggled to avoid extinction. In three separate seasons during the 1930s, the Browns failed to draw 100,000 fans, with only 80,000 spectators appearing in 1935.[226] In the National League, modest recovery began in the mid–1930s for the New York Giants, Chicago Cubs, and St. Louis Cardinals, but weaker clubs like the Philadelphia Phillies barely survived. The owners of weaker teams were forced to sell their star players to teams with deeper pockets, perpetuating a pattern of inequality that continues to plague Major League Baseball and dilute fan loyalty in this new millennium.

On the field, there was no lack of excitement, but there was certainly a lack of money. Total players' salaries in the Major Leagues dropped from approximately $4 million in 1929 to $3 million in 1933 and did not return to the pre–Depression level until 1940. The average player's salary dropped from $7,500 in 1929 to $6,000 in 1933 and rose to $7,300 in 1939, still lower than a decade before.[227] After winning the American League "Triple Crown" in 1933, Jimmie Foxx was forced to accept a salary cut for 1934.[228] In spite of low salaries, however, the 1930s was not a decade of player unrest. Most Major League players realized they were lucky to be working and earning even reduced salaries when many Americans were unemployed and starving.

In 1930, Babe Ruth had signed a two-year contract with the Yankees at a salary of $80,000 per year.[229] In spite of having three consecutive seasons in 1931 through 1933 that would have been considered exceptional for anyone other than a younger Babe Ruth, the Yankees cut the Bambino's salary after each of those seasons. During that three-year period, Ruth averaged 40 home runs, 122 runs scored, and 134 runs batted in, while leading the league in bases on balls each year and maintaining a .340 batting average. Nevertheless, the Yankees cut the Babe's salary by 6.2 percent after the 1931 season, by another 30.7 percent after the 1932 season, and by another 32.5 percent after the 1933 season.[230] In those years, although the Babe's annual salary was slashed by 56.25 percent, from $80,000 to $35,000, he was still the highest-paid player in baseball.[231] Following the 1934 season, Ruth finally retired. The departure of the greatest player and personality the game had ever known could not have come at a worse time. Although his skills had waned considerably in his latter years, Ruth was still Major League Baseball's Most Valuable Player at the box office. In his last season with the Yankees in 1934, the 39-year-old Ruth played in only 125 games but still hit 22 home runs and drove in 84 runs while posting a batting average of .288. Solid numbers, but hardly Ruthian. Age and hard living had reduced the Babe to being merely human. In spite of the Babe's decline in effectiveness, however, crowds still came in record numbers to witness the legend.

Late in his career, Ruth yearned for an opportunity to manage and was openly angered when the Yankees refused to consider him as a serious managerial candidate. In spite of Ruth's flamboyance, he always possessed an innate knowledge of the game. Still, Ruth's inability to manage himself off the field foreclosed any opportunities he might have had to manage a team on the field. After the 1934 season, a disgruntled Ruth and the Yankees parted ways. The hapless Boston Braves, desperate for publicity, lured Ruth back to the city where he began his Major League career to serve as a player, vice-president, and assistant manager. It didn't take Ruth long to conclude, however, that the Braves' owners were never serious about permitting him to manage the team. After hitting six home runs in 28 games and repeatedly hearing choruses of jeers from Boston fans, the Babe hung up his spikes.[232] Ruth finished his 22-season career holding more than 50 all-time Major League records, including career records in home runs (714), runs batted in (2,174), bases on balls (2,056), slugging average (.690), extra-base hits (1,356), and home run percentage (8.5). He was second in career runs scored (2,174) only to Ty Cobb (2,245), second in career total bases (5,793) to Cobb (5,863), and had maintained a career batting average of .342. The Babe played in ten World Series, seven as the Yankees' star slugger and three as the Boston Red Sox's ace pitcher, and was on the winning squad three times with each team.

In 1936, one year after the Babe's retirement, the first election was held for the new National Baseball Hall of Fame in Cooperstown, New York. The Hall's five charter members were Ruth, Ty Cobb, Honus Wagner, Christy Mathewson, and Walter Johnson.[233] In 1939, the Hall officially opened and overflow crowds attended the induction ceremonies for baseball's pantheon. All of those elected attended the festivities except Cobb, who had no desire to socialize with any of the other inductees, particularly Ruth, who Cobb believed was half black. Even in retirement, however, Ruth was as popular as ever. Crowds besieged the Babe for a chance to see or touch the greatest baseball player of all time. No sportsman had ever made a greater impact on American society than Babe Ruth. How would baseball, reeling from the lingering effects of the Great Depression, replace its greatest player and gate attraction?

In the 1930s, a number of young sluggers began to make names for themselves. Although none would capture the public's imagination like the flamboyant Babe Ruth, a few came close to matching the Bambino's legendary feats on the field. Foremost among these young sluggers was

Top: Lou Gehrig at bat. *Bottom:* Lou Gehrig signing his Yankees contract with (left to right) Yankees owner Jacob Ruppert, Yankees manager Joe McCarthy, and a young Joe DiMaggio.

Jimmie Foxx

Ruth's teammate, Henry Louis "Lou" Gehrig, the son of German-immigrant parents. "Columbia Lou," who had been a Yankees regular since 1925, was a quiet man with a loud bat. During the ten full seasons in which Ruth and Gehrig played together, Gehrig led the American League in runs batted in five times and home runs once, during an off year for the Babe. In 1934, Ruth's last season with the Yankees, Gehrig won the "Triple

Crown," leading the American League with 49 home runs, 165 runs batted in, and a batting average of .363. In the four seasons following Ruth's retirement, Gehrig averaged 37 home runs and 136 runs batted in, as he led the Yankees to three more World Series titles. Now referred to as the "Pride of the Yankees," the quiet, family-oriented Yankees captain was the polar opposite of Ruth. "I'm not a headline guy," said Gehrig. "I know that as long as I was following Ruth to the plate I could have stood on my head and no one would have known the difference. The Babe is one fellow, and I'm another and I could never be exactly like him. I don't try, I just go on as I am in my own right."

Gehrig's own right was quite acceptable to the Yankees' management and fans. After being inserted into the Yankees' starting lineup on June 1, 1925, as a replacement for injured first baseman Wally Pipp, Gehrig played in a record 2,130 consecutive games. With his play and health mysteriously diminishing, "The Iron Horse" finally asked to be removed from the lineup on April 30, 1939. Two years later, Gehrig died from the debilitating neuromuscular disorder amyotrophic lateral sclerosis, still commonly known as "Lou Gehrig's Disease," which had ended his career. Gehrig was a paragon of stability throughout the 1930s, a depressing decade in dire need of solid heroes. In a 17-year career with the Yankees, which was foreshortened by his premature death, Gehrig collected 493 home runs, 1,888 runs scored, and 1,990 runs batted in, and posted a .340 career batting average, a .447 on-base average, and a .632 slugging average, becoming one of baseball's greatest all-time hitters. "The Iron Horse" drove in more than 100 runs for 13 consecutive seasons, averaging 147 runs batted in per season during that span, and still holds the American League single-season record of 184 runs batted in, the Major League single-season record of 301 runs produced (runs scored plus runs batted in minus home runs, which are counted in both totals), and the Major League career record for grand slam home runs with 23. "Larrupin' Lou" played for seven American League pennant winners and six World Series champions, and was a key player in two Yankees dynasties, first with Babe Ruth and later with Joe DiMaggio.

As America entered the Great Depression, baseball's best team was the Philadelphia Athletics.[234] Flush with revenues from the successful Roaring Twenties, Connie Mack had assembled a stunning array of talent in the City of Brotherly Love. This phalanx of stars, featuring Jimmie Foxx, Mickey Cochrane, and Al Simmons at bat and in the field and Lefty Grove, Rube Walberg, and George Earnshaw on the mound, won three consecutive American League pennants from 1929 through 1931 and World Series championships in 1929 and 1930. During his 20-year Major League career, Foxx led the American League in home runs four times, runs batted in three times, and in batting average twice, including 1933 when he won the "Triple Crown."[235] "The Beast" tallied career totals of 534 home runs (including 58 in 1932), 1,921 runs batted in, 1,751 runs scored, a .609 slugging average, and a .325 batting average, while being named the American League's Most Valuable Player three times. "Double X" had 13 consecutive seasons with more than 100 runs batted in and 12 consecutive seasons with at least 30 home runs, averaging 40 home runs per season during that span. "Black Mike" Cochrane, baseball's finest catcher, maintained a .320 batting average over 13 seasons and was twice accorded the honor of Most Valuable Player in the American League. Simmons maintained a batting average of .334 over a 20-season career in which he collected 2,927 hits, hit 307 home runs, drove in 1,827 runs, and scored 1,507 runs. Grove won 300 games over 17 seasons, including eight years with at least 20 wins and 31 wins in 1931 when he was named the American League's Most Valuable Player. He led the American League in earned run average nine times. Bill James rates Grove "[t]he greatest pitcher of all time, period."[236] Unfortunately for Philadelphia's fans, the Great Depression's austerity forced the Athletics to sell each of these great players to competing clubs.[237] The Athletics would never again challenge in Philadelphia.[238] Unequal financial resources created a sharp division between teams with financial muscle and those without. While wealthy teams could purchase the players necessary to win championships, poorer teams were forced to sell their stars to survive.

A number of other players were also helping the American public forget, at least temporarily, the realities of life during the Great Depression. The Senators' star outfielder Goose Goslin and the Athletics' outstanding catcher Mickey Cochrane were both sold to the Detroit Tigers to help their teams recoup financial losses. Cochrane and Goslin teamed with sluggers Hank Greenberg and Charley Gehringer to lead the Tigers to pennants in 1934 and 1935. Goslin averaged .316 over 18 seasons, while collecting 2,735 hits, 1,483 runs scored, and 1,609 runs batted in. Greenberg, the first player to break the $100,000 annual salary mark and the game's first Jewish star, hit 331 home runs over a 13-season career abbreviated by more than four years of military service, while winning four American League home run crowns (including 58 home runs in 1938), leading the league in runs batted in four times, and batting over .300 nine times. Gehringer maintained a batting average of .320 over 19 seasons with 1,774 runs scored (including twelve seasons with over 100 runs scored), and 1,427 runs batted in (including seven seasons in which he drove in more than 100 runs).

Although many of baseball's brightest hitting stars were playing in

Lefty Grove

the American League, the senior circuit's blend of hitting and superior pitching also ensured exciting action during the Great Depression. In 1930, in a year in which a livelier baseball was used,[239] the Chicago Cubs' Hack Wilson set the single season National League home run record of 56, which would stand until 1998 when Mark McGwire demolished it. The hard-drinking Wilson's total of 190 runs batted in during that year (191 according

Hank Greenberg

to recent reports) remains the Major League's single season record.[240] In that year, the National League batting average was .303 and the junior circuit batted .288. Six National League teams had team batting averages higher than .300. In the same year, New York Giants star Bill Terry posted a .401 batting average, becoming the last National Leaguer to hit .400. The following year, a less lively ball was introduced.[241] In a 14-year career with the Giants, Terry hit over .300 in ten consecutive years and retired with a lifetime batting average of .341, second highest in National League history to Rogers Hornsby. Chuck Klein of the Phillies also was proceeding with a Hall of Fame career in which he would win four home run titles and a "Triple Crown" in 1933. Other top National League hitters included Mel Ott, who hit 511 home runs, amassed 1,860 runs batted in, and scored 1,859 runs in 22 seasons with the New York Giants, and Johnny Mize who hit 359 home runs and drove in 1,337 runs, while maintaining a .312 batting average and a .562 slugging average in a 15-season career with the Cardinals, Giants, and Yankees which was shortened by three years of military service during World War II.

The New York Giants and Chicago Cubs fielded strong teams throughout the 1930s, with the Giants winning three pennants and the Cubs two. Probably the most memorable National League team of the 1930s, however, was the St. Louis Cardinals, who became a symbol of the Depression-era austerity gripping the nation when they drew only 325,000 home fans during their 1934 World Series championship season.[242] The "Gas House Gang," which led the National League in hits, runs scored, runs batted in, doubles, stolen bases, slugging average, and batting average in 1934, featured a rough-hewn and unkempt, but intimidating, lineup of hitters, including James Anthony "Rip" Collins (who batted .333 with 35 home runs and 128 runs batted in, while leading the league in total bases and slugging average and tying Mel Ott for the home run crown), John Leonard Roosevelt "Pepper" Martin, dubbed by scribes the "Wild Horse of the Osage" (who led the league in stolen bases), Frankie Frisch, and Joseph Michael "Ducky" Medwick (who batted .319, tallied 106 runs batted in, scored 110 runs, and led the league in triples with 18 in 1934 and won the "Triple Crown" in 1937, the last National League player to do so). The Redbirds also fielded a strong pitching staff anchored by the incomparable Jerome Hanna "Dizzy" Dean and his brother Paul "Daffy" Dean. Dizzy won 133 games in six years with the Cardinals, including 30 in 1934, while Brother Paul won 19 games in each of 1934 and 1935. Unfortunately, injuries truncated both Dean brothers' careers.[243] Dizzy also delighted baseball fans with his zany antics and malapropisms and exasperated the Cardinals' general manager, Branch Rickey. Rickey told his son, "I completed my college course in three years. I was in the top 10 percent of my class in law school. I am a Doctor of Jurisprudence. I am an honorary Doctor of Laws.... You have to admit boy that I am an educated man.... And I like to believe that I am an intelligent man.... Then will you please tell me, why in the name of common sense, I spent four mortal hours today conversing with a person named Dizzy Dean."[244]

In 1936, a 17-year-old farm boy from Iowa, Robert William Andrew "Rapid Robert" Feller, burst upon the scene as a pitcher for the Cleveland Indians. In his first Major League game, Feller struck out 15 batters. Later in the season, he struck out an American League record 17 batters in a game. He then returned home to finish high school before resuming a Major League career in which he would win 266 games, lead the American League in strikeouts seven times, and top the American League in wins six times, in spite of missing almost four seasons in his prime for military service during World War II. The hardest-throwing Major League pitcher of his day, Bob Feller pitched three no-hitters and twelve one-hitters, while tallying 2,581 career strikeouts.

Also in 1936, the New York Yankees purchased the contract of an injury-prone, 21-year-old outfielder from the San Francisco Seals in exchange for $25,000 and five players. The young Joseph Paul DiMaggio, a smooth, almost effortless, center fielder whose sweet swing combined power and beauty, had hit safely in 61 consecutive games for the Seals in 1934. One year after the departure of the great Babe Ruth, DiMaggio debuted with the Yankees in grand style. In 1936, the rookie DiMaggio hit .323 with 29 home runs, 132 runs scored, 125 runs batted in, and a league-leading 44 doubles and 15 triples. Lou Gehrig hit .354, blasted 49 home runs, drove in 152 runs, and scored 167 runs to lead the powerful Yankees to another World Series championship. The 1936 Yankees became the first, and only, team to have five players drive in more than 100 runs in a season: Gehrig (152), DiMaggio (125), Tony Lazzeri (109), Bill Dickey (107), and George Selkirk (107). Led by Gehrig, and then DiMaggio, the Yankees won four consecutive World Series from 1936 through 1939. In that four-year span, DiMaggio averaged 34 home runs, 130 runs scored, 140 runs batted in, and hit .341. With an ailing and retired Gehrig out of the lineup in 1939, DiMaggio hit a league-leading .381 and paced the Yankees to another World Series championship.[245]

The Great Depression forced Major League Baseball owners to find new ways to earn revenues. In 1935, the Cincinnati Reds became the first Major League team to feature night baseball, as President Franklin Roosevelt activated the light switch for the first Major League night game from the White House, 400 miles from Cincinnati's Crosley Field.[246] The Reds played seven night games in 1935, one against each National League opponent. Although night baseball had been popular in the minor leagues and Negro leagues for several years, the majority of the Major Leagues' conservative owners initially believed there was no future in night baseball, claiming that the great tradition of baseball being played in sunshine was

Bob Feller

being undermined. According to Washington Senators owner Clark Griffith, "high class baseball cannot be played at night under artificial light." Griffith also opined that night baseball was "just a step above dog racing."[247] Most owners resisted night baseball until they saw how the Reds profited by playing under artificial light. Night games brought a new group of working fans, who were unable to attend during the day. In their

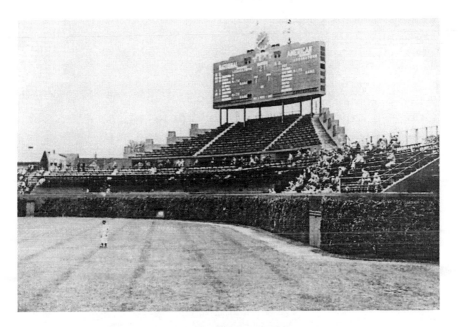

Wrigley Field, Chicago

seven night contests in 1935, the Reds' attendance averaged 18,620 per game.[248] In their 69 daylight games, the Reds drew only 4,699 per game.[249] A year earlier, their home attendance averaged only 2,685 per game.[250] As the Reds' attendance and revenues increased, other owners' concerns regarding the erosion of baseball's traditions faded. By the end of the 1930s, most teams had followed the Reds' example. The Chicago Cubs, playing in the cozy confines of Wrigley Field, however, did not host a night game until 1988.

While a gloomy economic cloud hung over the country throughout the 1930s, the financial fortunes of some teams began to improve near the end of the decade. In 1939, under the leadership of owner and radio mogul Powel Crosley and his visionary general manager, Leland Stanford "Larry" MacPhail,[251] the Cincinnati Reds purchased a number of players who helped them win the National League pennant. Pitchers Paul Derringer and Bucky Walters, purchased from the Cardinals and the Phillies, respectively, combined to win 52 games. Unlike free agency of the last quarter of the 20th century, however, star players who were sold to new teams were not the beneficiaries of large cash payments. Instead, the entire sales proceeds accrued to the teams disposing of their players. In 1941, the perennially hapless Brooklyn Dodgers, under new general manager Larry MacPhail, who had previously rebuilt the Cincinnati Reds, went on a

buying spree and cap-
tured the National
League pennant with
the aid of several pur-
chased stars, thus re-
inforcing a system of
haves and have-nots
which still exists in
Major League Base-
ball.

In another effort
to raise revenues, ra-
dio broadcasts of games
commenced and the
sale of local radio
broadcast rights began
in earnest.[252] Many
Major League owners
initially resisted radio
broadcasts of games in
their home markets
because they believed
radio would erode live
attendance. Although
radio broadcasting of
Major League teams
began in 1921, home

Larry MacPhail

games of New York's three Major League teams were not broadcast until
1939, after Larry MacPhail became general manager of the Dodgers.[253] By
1939, broadcasting income totaled 7.3 percent of total club revenues, up
from 0.3 percent in 1930. Although each team negotiated, and retained
the proceeds from, its own radio broadcasting rights, the lucrative rights
to the World Series were negotiated collectively and evenly divided among
all teams.[254]

Chapter 5

RESURRECTION

There is always some kid who may be seeing me for the first or last time. I owe him my best.
—Joe DiMaggio

Did they tell me how to pitch to Ted Williams? Sure they did. It was great advice, very encouraging. They said he has no weakness, won't swing at a bad ball, has the best eyes in the business, and can kill you with one swing; he won't swing at anything bad, but don't give him anything good.
—Bobby Shantz

I've had pretty good success facing Stan [Musial] by throwing him my best pitch and backing up third base.
—Carl Erskine

While Adolf Hitler's Luftwaffe, storm troopers, and panzers were conquering Europe in the late 1930s and early 1940s, the isolationist lobby in the United States blocked American involvement in the conflict. Americans were concerned about the actions of the Axis powers, but only as observers. The devastating bombing of Pearl Harbor on December 7, 1941, changed that status and precipitated the entry of the United States into World War II. In April 1941, however, America was still "neutral" except for the Lend-Lease of equipment and supplies to Great Britain. The Major Leagues' last peacetime baseball season until 1946 would be one of its most memorable. There was concern during the season that America would enter the European war. In May, President Franklin Roosevelt announced: "I have today issued a proclamation that an unlimited national emergency exists. We will not hesitate to use our armed forces to repel attack." The

Joe DiMaggio at bat.

anticipated declaration of war did not come, however, and America remained on the sidelines for another seven months. War may have been hell in Europe, but in America the Church of Baseball still occupied center stage.

The 1941 season spotlighted new leading men whose exploits and style symbolized the official passing of the torch from Ruth and Gehrig to a new generation of compelling and passionate players.[255] Like Ruth two decades earlier, Joe DiMaggio was a perfect fit for New York.[256] He possessed an elegance and sophistication that belied his humble roots as the son of an Italian immigrant fisherman living in San Francisco. Santiago, the principal character in Ernest Hemingway's novel, *The Old Man and the Sea*, observed, "I would like to take the great DiMaggio fishing. They say his father was a fisherman. Maybe he was as poor as we are and would understand."[257] Like thousands of other poor boys in Major League Baseball's history—former miners, farmers, factory hands, and immigrants— DiMaggio definitely understood. "A ball player's got to be kept hungry to become a big-leaguer," said Joe. "That's why no boy from a rich family ever made the big leagues." While there was nothing in DiMaggio's upbringing to prepare him for life in the cosmopolitan fishbowl of New York City, the slugger had an innate understanding for more than baseball. Like most star players of his day, every contract negotiation proved to be a harrowing and frustrating affair. After DiMaggio's stellar 1937 sophomore season, the Yankees' general manager informed DiMaggio that his contract demands for 1938 were only $3,000 less than the great Lou Gehrig, who had been a Yankees star for 13 years. DiMaggio responded that Gehrig was grossly underpaid.[258] Coming into the 1941 season, DiMaggio held out for a higher salary. The previous season had been DiMaggio's fifth in the Major Leagues and the first that failed to yield a World Series winner's check. It was hardly DiMaggio's fault. He had produced 31 home runs, 133 runs batted in, and a .353 batting average, to win his second consecutive American League batting crown.

If there were any doubts whether DiMaggio was worth his salary, those doubts were erased in 1941 when the "Yankee Clipper" put together a season for the ages.[259] On May 15, 1941, DiMaggio had two hits in four at bats. Over the next 55 games, he would embark on one of the most memorable journeys in baseball history. DiMaggio's hitting streak became *the* daily news. America was more obsessed with the Yankee Clipper's pursuit of batting immortality than with advances by Hitler and his Nazis in Europe. With the advent of radio broadcasts and increased newspaper coverage of baseball, fans were kept apprised of the Yankee Clipper's streak. From coffee shops in Manhattan to steak houses in Texas, the first question invariably was "How did DiMaggio do today?" DiMaggio handled the media horde in his usual manner, accommodating but detached. On June 29, DiMaggio's streak stood at 40, one game shy of George Sisler's American League record and four short of Wee Willie Keeler's Major League mark. In the first game of a doubleheader against the Washington Senators, DiMaggio got a hit off Dutch Leonard to tie Sisler. In the nightcap, he collected two more hits off Red Anderson to become the first American Leaguer to hit in 42 consecutive games. Three games later, Keeler's record was also eclipsed. The streak finally ended on July 17 in a game against the Cleveland Indians. The man now known as "Joltin' Joe" DiMaggio had energized the country by hitting in 56 consecutive games. In the game in which the streak ended, DiMaggio hit three hard grounders to the left side of the infield, but each time sparkling defensive plays resulted in outs. After the streak was broken, DiMaggio started another streak, hitting safely in 16 more consecutive games. The closest anyone has come to DiMaggio's 56-game mark in the last 61 seasons is Pete Rose who recorded a 44-game hitting streak in 1978. DiMaggio had proved he was worth the money. His hitting streak brought a whole new wave of fans into the game as had Ruth's prodigious power in the 1920s.

DiMaggio's teammates marveled at his exploits. "He had great wrists and hit balls like rockets," said Bobby Doerr. "It always seemed as if he hit the ball hard every at bat." Yet DiMaggio was also a private man who cultivated an imperious manner, rarely socialized with other players, and was parsimonious to a fault. "He led the league in room service," said one teammate. According to another teammate, Jerry Coleman, "DiMaggio seldom showed emotion. One day after striking out, he came into the dugout and kicked the ball bag. We all went 'ooooh.' It really hurt. He sat down and the sweat popped out on his forehead and he clenched his fists without ever saying a word. Everybody wanted to howl, but he was a god. You don't laugh at gods." Over a 13-year career with the New York Yankees, the only Major League team for which he played, Joe DiMaggio epitomized excellence on the field. The "Yankee Clipper" hit 361 career home runs, drove in 1,537 runs, had a lifetime batting average of .325 and a career .579 slugging average, and was baseball's finest center fielder in a career shortened by military service and injuries. He led the American League in home runs twice, runs batted in twice, won two batting titles, and was named the American League's Most Valuable Player three times. He played on ten American League pennant winners and nine World Series championship teams.

When DiMaggio's consecutive games hitting streak ended in July, the eyes of the baseball world shifted to focus squarely on young Boston Red Sox hitting sensation Theodore Samuel "Ted" Williams.[260] A West Coast boy like DiMaggio, Williams grew up in San Diego. Unlike DiMag-

Ted Williams at bat.

gio, Williams cared little about the defensive part of baseball. Ted was interested only in hitting. "A man has to have goals," said Williams, "for a day, for a lifetime, and that was mine, to have people say, 'There goes Ted Williams, the greatest hitter who ever lived.'" Williams broke in with his home town San Diego Padres of the Pacific Coast League in 1936. In 1938, he won the American Association's "Triple Crown" in Minneapolis, where his batting coach was Rogers Hornsby. The next season, as a rookie with the Boston Red Sox, Williams drove in 149 runs to lead the American League, while slugging 31 home runs and batting .327. The "Kid" had arrived! By mid–September of the 1941 season, Ted's batting average was above .400 as he attempted to become the first American League hitter to achieve that lofty level since Harry Heilmann hit .403 in 1923. Like DiMaggio earlier in the season, the country was now tuned in to the daily exploits of the "Splendid Splinter." Coming into the last day of the season, a doubleheader in Philadelphia, Ted's average was .3995, a number which when rounded off would have put him at .400. His manager suggested that the "Kid" sit out the final two games to preserve this vaunted mark, but Williams appeared at the ballpark ready for his date with history.[261] The Yankees had already clinched the American League pennant, so the only suspense was Ted's flirtation with .400. In two games, "Teddy Ballgame" collected six hits in eight at bats to finish the season with a .406 average, a level that no player has approached in the last 60 years.[262] Forgotten in the hullabaloo surrounding DiMaggio's hitting streak and Williams's batting average was the fact that Williams also led the American League in home runs (37), runs scored (135), bases-on-balls (145), and slugging average (.735), while posting one of the greatest hitting seasons ever. Ted's 120 runs batted in fell just short of DiMaggio's 125.

In 19 seasons with the Boston Red Sox, the only Major League team for which he played, Ted Williams posted a career .344 batting average and a career .634 slugging average, hit 521 home runs, and tallied 1,839 runs batted in, 1,798 runs scored, and 2,019 bases on balls, in spite of missing nearly five seasons to military service in World War II and the Korean conflict. The "Splendid Splinter" won six batting titles—the final one at age 40 after hitting .388 at age 39. He also led the American League in slugging average nine times, runs batted in four times, runs scored six times, and home runs four times, won two "Triple Crowns," and was twice named the American League's Most Valuable Player. He holds the highest Major League career on-base percentage and is second only to Babe Ruth in career slugging average. Williams and Ruth are the only two players in Major League Baseball history whose career slugging averages were at least twice that of the league average.

Williams and DiMaggio, both West Coast boys, greatly increased fan interest in Major League Baseball in disenfranchised western locales. The advent of national radio broadcasts of baseball games and the increase in space that newspapers were allocating to sports sections was expanding Major League Baseball from its northeastern roots. As the American population began a westward migration, fueled by the Great Depression and World War II, fans in larger cities such as Los Angeles and San Francisco began to clamor for Major League Baseball.

The 1941 season also witnessed the arrival of a National League rookie who would become the greatest player in the history of the senior circuit. Stanley Frank "Stan the Man" Musial, the son of a Polish immigrant mill worker, had commenced his professional career as a pitcher, but had injured his throwing arm in the minor leagues and was converted to an outfielder.[263] The 20-year-old Musial embarked on the first of his 22 Major League seasons in September 1941 and, in his twelve-game September debut, hit .426. He would never hit lower than .300 until he was 38 years old. During his career, Stan broke virtually every National League hitting record, while serving as a spokesman for, and model citizen of, the game. Musial won seven National League batting titles and led the National League in slugging average six times, hits six times, total bases six times, runs scored five times, runs batted in twice, doubles eight times, and triples five times. He hit over .300 for 17 consecutive seasons and was named the National League's Most Valuable Player three times. In 1948, in one of the most spectacular seasons in Major League history, Musial led the National League in batting average (.376), on-base percentage (.450), slugging average (.702), combined on-base percentage and slugging average (1.152), hits (230), doubles (46), triples (18), total bases (429), runs scored (135), runs batted in (131), extra-base hits (103), and runs created (227), and was second in home runs (39) to Ralph Kiner and Johnny Mize, each of whom hit 40. If a Musial home run had not been rained out early in the season, he would have won not only the National League's "Triple Crown," but would have led the league in all thirteen important batting categories. As a 41-year-old grandfather in 1962, Musial challenged for another National League batting crown, posting a .330 batting average and a .508 slugging average, the highest slugging average ever recorded by a player over 40 years old.

Although Musial remained a Cardinal for his entire career, he briefly contemplated jumping to the Mexican League in 1946 where he was offered a five-year contract for $175,000. With half of this amount to be paid as a signing bonus, this must have been a substantial temptation, considering Musial's $13,500 annual Cardinals salary.[264] In 1947, the Cardinals offered a $21,000 salary to Musial, who was by then a two-time National League Most Valuable Player. Musial rejected the offer, which was substantially lower than the salaries paid to Hank Greenberg ($85,000), Bob Feller ($72,000), Joe DiMaggio ($43,750), and Ted Williams ($75,000), and briefly held out for a higher salary.[265] Because of the reserve system, however, Musial was unable to sign with any Major League team other than the Cardinals, and he was forced to accept $31,000.[266] In spite of his consistent excellence, the reserve system continued to depress Musial's salary throughout his career. From 1951, when he received a $25,000 salary increase to achieve a then National League high of $75,000, until 1958, when he became the National League's first $100,000 player, Musial did not receive a salary increase.[267]

For a variety of reasons, including his reticence, avoidance of unnecessary contact with the press, and the fact that he played his entire Major League career in St. Louis, not a media center such as New York, Stan Musial's exploits are less widely known today than those of his contemporaries DiMaggio and Williams, whose reputations have increased since their playing days ended. Was Musial's career less exemplary than those of DiMaggio and Williams, or has his lack of self-promotion and existence away from the glare of America's media centers diminished his feats? Musial played in 24 All-Star Games (tied with Willie Mays for most appearances) and received more votes for Most Valuable Player than any man in history, being voted Most Valuable Player three times and second in voting four times. Sabermetrician and author Bill James has concluded that Musial was probably the most respected player, by press, fans, and other players, of the post–World War II era. According to James, "to the extent that a consensus has developed that lifts [Ted] Williams over Musial as the greatest left fielder of the forties, and thus the greatest left fielder of all time, I cannot agree with that consensus. Look, I am not saying anything at all negative about Ted Williams. The further we go in the analysis of batting statistics, the closer we come to being forced to accept the conclusion that Williams, not Babe Ruth, was the greatest hitter who ever lived. I think he was the second-greatest left fielder who ever lived. That's not criticism. But if I had to choose between the two of them, I'd take Musial in left field, Musial on the base paths, Musial in the clubhouse, and Williams only with the wood in his hand. And Stan Musial could hit a little, too."[268]

When Musial retired from the Cardinals (the only Major League team for which he played) in 1963 after posting a career batting average of .331 and a career slugging average of .559, he held over 50 Major League and

Stan Musial at bat.

National League records, including career Major League records for total bases (6,134) and extra-base hits (1,377) and career National League records for games played (3,026), at-bats (10,972), hits (3,630), doubles (725), runs scored (1,949), and runs batted in (1,951). His career totals in bases on balls (1,599) and home runs (475) were second in National League history only to Mel Ott's. Ott, a left-handed batter, who then held the

National League career home run record (511), played his entire career in the Polo Grounds with its inviting right field fence only 257 feet away[269] and hit only 188 home runs away from his home park. "Stan the Man" played his entire career in Sportsman's Park (later renamed Busch Stadium) where the wall was 320 feet from home plate down the right-field line and 370 feet in the power alleys, 11½ feet high, and fronted by a 33–37 foot high screen. In comparison, the left field dimensions of Boston's Fenway Park are 310 feet down the base line and 379 feet in the power alley, capped by the legendary 37 foot high "Green Monster."[270] In 1955, the Cardinals removed the screen for one year. In that year, Musial hit 22 home runs in Sportman's Park, more than in any other season. More total home runs were hit in Sportsman's Park during the 1955 season than in any other year. In 1956, the screen was re-installed.[271] How many Musial home runs became doubles into Sportsman's Park's non-green monster?

The inscription on the base of an eight-foot high bronze statue of Musial at bat located outside Busch Stadium in St. Louis contains Major League Baseball commissioner Ford Frick's famous tribute: "Here stands baseball's perfect warrior. Here stands baseball's perfect knight."

The Yankees defeated the Brooklyn Dodgers, under the leadership of Larry McPhail as general manager and Leo Durocher as field manager, in the 1941 World Series, but the hitting feats of DiMaggio and Williams made for one of the most captivating seasons in Major League Baseball's history. On December 7, 1941, "a date which will live in infamy," carrier-dispatched airplanes of the Japanese Imperial Navy bombed and strafed the American naval fleet and Army, Navy, and Air Corps facilities at Pearl Harbor, Hawaii. America officially went to war with Japan and her allies, Nazi Germany and Fascist Italy. Although Major League Baseball continued to be played throughout World War II, players were not exempt from military service and several top stars were pressed into duty. For the next four years, Major League rosters were depleted of top talent. Players such as 15-year-old Joe Nuxhall for the Cincinnati Reds, who two months prior to his Major League debut had been a junior high school pitcher, one-armed Pete Gray of the St. Louis Browns, and Bert Shepard whose lower leg had been amputated in a German prisoner-of-war camp substituted for the departed stars.[272] In 1942, the Yankees' Joe Gordon, in by far his best season ever, was named the American League's Most Valuable Player in spite of leading the league in only three statistical categories: strikeouts, grounding into double plays, and errors. In 1944, the perennially woeful St. Louis Browns surprised the rest of baseball's depleted squads and made their only World Series appearance in franchise history, eventually succumbing to the Cardinals, their co-tenant in Sportsman's Park. Led by the slugging exploits of Stan Musial and Enos "Country" Slaughter, a tight defense anchored by Marty "Slats" Marion, Walker Cooper, and Terry Moore, and solid pitching by Mort Cooper, Johnny Beazley, Max Lanier, Red Barrett, and Harry "The Cat" Brecheen, the Cardinals were the closest thing to a National League dynasty since John McGraw's Giants twenty years earlier. During the five seasons from 1942 to 1946, the Redbirds won four pennants and three World Series titles. Their only failure during this period was in 1945 when both Musial and Slaughter spent the entire season in military, not baseball, uniforms.

In August 1945, World War II ended and the world entered the nuclear age, when the United States Army Air Forces dropped atomic bombs on Hiroshima and Nagasaki, Japan. Many major leaguers who had missed playing time to serve their country made their way back to baseball, but most arrived too late to affect the 1945 pennant race. "I can't conceive of either team winning a single game," said Chicago writer Warren Brown, when asked for a prediction of the outcome of the 1945 World Series between the Chicago Cubs and the Detroit Tigers. Even with wartime stars such as the Cubs' Stan Hack and Phil Cavarretta, who won the 1945 National League batting title, and Tigers pitcher Hal Newhouser, who was named the American League's Most Valuable Player in both 1944 and 1945, and returning star Hank Greenberg, both clubs still had a wartime look. In a poorly played World Series, the Tigers held on to win in seven games. Nevertheless, America was joyous. The long war was over and the institutions that defined the way of life Americans fought to maintain, including the World Series, would take on an even greater significance.

America's boys were back to play baseball in 1946. DiMaggio and Williams, each of whom had missed three full seasons, came marching home. Bob Feller returned after nearly four years in the Navy. Other stars rejoined the game. Perhaps more significant and meaningful for baseball than the return of top-flight talent from overseas, however, were the death in November 1944 of commissioner Kenesaw Mountain Landis at the age of 78 and the social changes that had occurred in America as a result of the war. Landis, who had been in complete control of baseball since 1920, left a legacy of autocracy, arbitrariness, bigotry, and protection of the status quo. Never again would the Major Leagues' franchise owners permit an outsider to wield such power.

World War II had profoundly changed America. Women entered the workplace in large numbers for the first time. Blacks migrated from the rural South to Northern cities. Blacks and whites migrated West to occupy defense industry jobs. The power of the media, particularly radio, increased. Governmental control was further centralized. Although most Americans now wanted to return to their pre-war lives, America would never be the same. How would Americans adapt to the post-war world? What further changes were in store for Major League Baseball and post-war America?

APOCRYPHA

My skin is against me.
    —Bud Fowler

It matters not what branch of mankind the player sprung from with the fan, if he can deliver the goods. The Mick, the Sheeney, the Wop, the Dutch, and the Chink, the Cuban, the Indian, the Jap, or the so-called Anglo-Saxon—his "nationality" is never a matter of moment if he can pitch, or hit, or field. In organized baseball there has been no distinction raised—except tacit understanding that a player of Ethiopian descent is ineligible—the wisdom of which we will not discuss except to say by such rule some of the greatest players the game has ever known have been denied their opportunity.
    —The Sporting News, 1923

There is a catcher that any big league club would like to buy for $200,000. His name is Gibson. He can do everything. He hits the ball a mile. And he catches so easy he might as well be in a rocking chair. Throws like a rifle. Bill Dickey isn't as good a catcher. Too bad this Gibson is a colored fellow.
    —Walter Johnson

I am an invisible man. No, I am not a spook like those who haunted Edgar Allan Poe; nor am I one of your Hollywood-movie ectoplasms. I am a man of substance, of flesh and bone, fiber and liquids—and I might even be

said to possess a mind. I am invisible, understood, sim-
ply because people refuse to see me.
                              —Ralph Ellison, *Invisible Man*

During the Great Depression, players in the "Major Leagues" played in the shadow of Babe Ruth and the Roaring Twenties. But Gehrig, Greenberg, and Foxx were not the only baseball stars playing in a shadow. Another group of baseball players operated in a darker and more pervasive shadow, performing legendary feats that were shielded from the eyes of most Americans. Their exploits were not reported in mainstream newspapers and their statistics were not recorded for baseball's posterity. This shadowy existence was not the consequence of a temporary phenomenon such as the retirement of a great player or a depressed economy, but of a permanent condition of pigment.[273]

From baseball's inception until after World War II, the so-called "national pastime" was hardly national. Membership on baseball's first organized team, the New York Knickerbockers, was restricted to white Anglo-Saxon "gentlemen" of an appropriate economic and social background. In 1867, Philadelphia's Pythians baseball club, comprised entirely of black players, was denied membership in the National Association of Base Ball Players.[274] When the National League was formed in 1876, although there was no official rule banning blacks, there was a "gentlemen's agreement" among owners of the league's teams, hardly a group of gentlemen, to exclude blacks from the league.

In the 1870s and 1880s, a few black players found jobs in white professional baseball in the supposedly more liberated northeastern United States. In 1878, Bud Fowler (originally named John W. Jackson), who ironically was raised in Cooperstown, New York, became the first black player to join a white professional team.[275] In 1884, Moses Fleetwood "Fleet" Walker, who had attended Oberlin College and the University of Michigan Law School, became the first black Major League player when he competed in 42 games with the Toledo Blue Stockings of the American Association, which was then considered to be a "Major League."[276] After suffering an injury and receiving threats from rival teams, however, Walker was released. Fowler, Fleet Walker, Fleet Walker's brother Welday, Ulysses S. "Frank" Grant, George Washington Stovey, and other blacks later played in the International League.[277] Insults and abuse from fans, opposing players, and racist teammates made these black players' lives intolerable. In Toronto, a supposedly liberal Canadian city to which slaves had escaped through the so-called "underground railroad" during the American Civil War, fans chanted "Kill the Niggers." Chicago White

Stockings Hall of Fame player and manager Adrian "Cap" Anson threatened to remove his team from the field rather than compete against a team with black players. In 1887, International League owners voted to ban any future contracts with blacks.[278] Other leagues soon followed the International League's example and excluded blacks. For the next 60 years, blacks would be excluded from "organized" baseball.

During the late 19th century, a number of all-black traveling teams began to garner renown in "barnstorming" tours. Perhaps the most famous of these clubs, the Cuban Giants, began to tour in 1885, passing themselves off as His-

Moses Fleetwood Walker

panics to avoid offending white audiences.[279] Other teams such as the Page Fence (Michigan) Giants, the Lincoln (Nebraska) Giants, the Chicago Unions, and the Cuban X Giants emulated the success of the original Cuban Giants and competed with local teams and one another during the 1890s and in the early 20th century.[280] After the turn of the 20th century, few integrated teams existed at any level. A notable exception was the All-Nations Team which included Blacks, Native Americans, Hispanics, Asians, and Caucasians and was owned by white Kansas City businessman J.L. Wilkinson.[281] The first Negro baseball league, the League of Colored Baseball Clubs, was formed in 1887.[282] It folded two weeks later.[283] Undercapitalized attempts to create all-black leagues in the late 19th century and early 20th century failed.[284]

The founding father and guiding force of "organized" black professional baseball was Andrew "Rube" Foster.[285] Bright, articulate, forceful, and charismatic, Foster rose through Negro baseball's ranks from star pitcher to field manager to team owner to league organizer and executive.[286] As a field manager, Foster was a brilliant tactician whose teams employed the bunt, the steal, and the hit and run.[287] In 1920, Foster, now the dominant character in black baseball, convinced seven other owners

Andrew "Rube" Foster (second from right) and other (unidentified) Negro League franchise owners.

of top teams to form the National Association of Professional Baseball Clubs, which came to be known as the Negro National League.[288] This eight-team league consisted of Foster's Chicago American Giants, the Chicago Giants, the St. Louis Giants, the Cuban Stars, the Detroit Stars, the Dayton Marcos, the Indianapolis ABCs, and the Kansas City Monarchs.[289] All teams in the new league were controlled by black businessmen, with the exception of J.L. Wilkinson's Kansas City Monarchs, which featured the black stars from Wilkinson's former All-Nations Team.

Over the next decade, black baseball expanded and the Eastern Colored League and Southern Negro League were formed.[290] These rival leagues and unaffiliated barnstorming teams undermined the Negro National League's profitability, but increased national interest in black baseball. In the late 1920s, the financially strapped Eastern Colored League and Southern Negro League folded. Foster retired from baseball in 1926 and died in 1930.[291] The Negro National League could not survive the combination of the Great Depression and the loss of Foster's leadership. In 1930, the league disbanded and organized black baseball ceased to exist.[292]

Although the black baseball leagues were defunct, powerful touring black teams such as J.L. Wilkinson's Kansas City Monarchs, wealthy Pittsburgh businessman Cumberland Posey's Homestead Grays, and Pittsburgh numbers racketeer Gus Greenlee's Pittsburgh Crawfords remained popular on the barnstorming circuit.[293] Wilkinson's Monarchs pioneered night baseball, employing a portable lighting system which illuminated the field of play and permitted the Monarchs to play several games each day (and night).[294] On tour, black ballplayers confronted multiple hardships—substandard playing conditions, inadequate food and accommodations, racism, and little money. They did, however, have the opportunity to earn at least a meager living working in their chosen field. Posey's Homestead Grays, one of the strongest teams ever, boasted a roster that included, at various times, Smokey Joe Williams, Josh Gibson, Martin Dihigo, Oscar Charleston, Judy Johnson, Buck Leonard, and Cool Papa Bell. Greenlee's Crawfords spent liberally, raiding top players from other clubs, to assemble one of the most imposing collections of baseball talent in history, including future Hall of Famers Gibson, Charleston, Johnson, Bell, and Satchel Paige.[295]

In 1933, the Homestead Grays, Pittsburgh Crawfords, New York Cubans, Philadelphia Stars, Baltimore Elite Giants, and Newark Eagles, all controlled by black gangster businessmen, combined to form a new Negro National League.[296] In 1937, J.L. Wilkinson and his Kansas City Monarchs joined the all-black teams of other Midwestern and Southern owners to form the Negro American League. Together, the Negro National League and the Negro American League became known as the Negro Leagues.[297] The champions of the two leagues met annually in the Negro World Series, but the highlight of the Negro Leagues calendar was the annual East-West All-Star Game played in Chicago.[298] Top black entertainers of the day, including Louis Armstrong, Duke Ellington, Billie Holiday, and Cab Calloway, joined capacity crowds to enjoy the festivities. Armstrong, a leading supporter of black baseball, owned a team called the New Orleans Secret Nine.

In addition to official Negro League games, black teams still played a variety of white and black professional and semi-professional opponents on annual barnstorming tours throughout America and the Caribbean. The official Negro League seasons were always short in comparison to the number of games played on tour. White teams also barnstormed throughout the 1920s, 1930s, and 1940s, as white Major League ballplayers sought to supplement their regular-season incomes. Games between white and black teams were intensely contested affairs that provided action and entertainment to black and white spectators. Although the white Major Leagues were now dominated by the power game introduced by Babe Ruth, the black game featured speed, daring, flair, and high energy, in addition to superb pitching, hitting, and defense. In a marriage of entertainment and baseball, players on many black teams also entertained their crowds by performing pantomime routines and clowning. Teams such as the Zulu Cannibals and the Ethiopian Clowns perpetuated the basest black stereotypes and became known as much for their minstrel shows as for baseball.

The Negro Leagues and black barnstorming survived the Great Depression and prospered during World War II when increased employment and income and a scarcity of consumer goods resulted in a dramatic growth in attendance. Black baseball became a vital component of the fabric of black urban life, providing a source of pride to the black public and contributing significantly to the economies of the black communities in which teams played, by providing employment for blacks and revenues for black-owned hospitality, entertainment, and related businesses.

Although the black press in major cities regularly reported on official Negro League games, the far more numerous barnstorming games, which were played against varying levels of competition, received less consistent coverage.[299] White mainstream newspapers provided virtually no reporting of black baseball games, whether "official" or otherwise. Accordingly, much of black baseball's history was recorded long after the fact from second-hand sources, often vastly embellished.[300] Because of this paucity of reliable reporting on black baseball, statistics are suspect and inconsistent[301] and the history and legends of black baseball are shrouded in ambiguity and uncertainty. It is clear, however, that in the first half of the 20th century, black baseball teams featured some of the greatest players in baseball's history. In barnstorming contests between all-black teams and all-white teams with Major League players, black teams won the majority of such games against their paler rivals. Although it is impossible to discuss all of the great players of the Negro Leagues who never were permitted to play in the white Major Leagues, a few deserve special attention.

According to Negro League contemporaries and white Major League players against whom he played on the barnstorming circuits, Oscar Charleston was probably the greatest overall player in black baseball. John McGraw contended that Charleston was the best baseball player of any color that he ever saw. During a long career, Charleston, who was born in Indianapolis, played with a number of teams, including the Indianapolis ABCs, Chicago American Giants, St. Louis Giants, Pittsburgh Crawfords, Homestead Grays, and in Cuba. A fiery and dramatic center fielder who played shallow, a daring and fleet base runner, a powerful hitter, a fierce competitor, and an accomplished showman, Charleston combined all the qualities of a Major League superstar except skin tone. Charleston retired as a player three years before Jackie Robinson's first game for the Dodgers. Oscar hit .340 in "official" Negro League play and .330 against white Major Leaguers. He later coached, managed, and scouted for several teams.[302]

Oscar Charleston

Josh Gibson

Black baseball's greatest hitter was the muscular, barrel-chested Josh Gibson, star catcher for the Pittsburgh Crawfords and Homestead Grays. Born in Georgia, Gibson grew up in Pittsburgh and later starred for Pittsburgh's Negro League teams. Renowned for his prodigious clouts, Gibson's Hall of Fame plaque credits him with "almost 800 home runs." He may have hit more than 1,000. From accounts of his contemporaries, including many by white Major Leaguers, Gibson was unparalleled as a catcher, thrower, hitter, and slugger. Many consider him the greatest catcher of all time, white or black. In "official" Negro League play, Gibson hit .351 and blasted 224 home runs. Against white Major League pitching, Josh hit .376. He died of a stroke at the age of 35, three months before Jackie Robinson's Major League debut.[303]

Another great blackball slugger was Buck Leonard, first baseman of the Homestead Grays, who batted clean-up behind Josh Gibson for many years. A powerful left-handed hitter and agile fielder, Leonard played 23 years in the black leagues, batting .335, but was nearly 40 years old when Jackie Robinson broke the Major League color barrier and never played in the white Major Leagues.[304]

John Henry "Pop" Lloyd was a smooth fielding, hard hitting shortstop known as the "Black Wagner" in reference to Pittsburgh Pirate great Honus Wagner. "I felt honored that they would name such a great player after me," said Wagner after watching Lloyd play. A gentleman and fine representative for baseball off the field, Lloyd was one of baseball's greatest players on the field. His lifetime batting average for a succession of teams in the black leagues was .337, but much of his career preceded accurate statistics.[305] Other top blackball shortstops included Dick Lundy, Dobie Moore, and Willie "Devil" Wells.[306]

Other great Negro League stars included James "Cool Papa" Bell, Cristobal Torriente, Martin Dihigo, Norman "Turkey" Stearnes, Mule Suttles, Judy Johnson, Ray Dandridge, and Oliver Marcelle. Bell, generally credited as being the fastest runner in baseball history, played for more than two decades, but retired too early to make the white Major Leagues. He was known as a clever hitter, daring base runner, and sparkling defensive player. Torriente, a burly Cuban, was a fast runner, powerful hitter, strong and accurate thrower, and fine defensive player who was rated as one of the greatest outfielders in blackball. In a career that lasted over 20 years and ended in the mid–1930s, Torriente hit .336 in "official" Negro League play and .436 against white Major League players. Another superb Cuban player was Martin Dihigo. Believed by many of his contemporaries to be the greatest overall baseball player who ever lived, Dihigo played every position on the field except catcher. He had great range and ability as a fielder, hit for average and power, and was a star pitcher for more than two decades. Stearnes was a prodigious slugger who hit more "official" Negro League home runs than any other player, including Josh Gibson. Combining power and consistency, he had a lifetime batting average of .332 in the Negro Leagues and hit .378 against white Major League players. Another powerful Negro League player was

Mule Suttles, a huge and imposing slugger who hit gargantuan shots. John-son, Dandridge, and Marcelle were a trio of outstanding black ball third basemen who ruled the hot corner as slick fielders and fine hitters.[307]

Leading the Negro Leagues in showmanship, if not also in athletic prowess, was the great Leroy "Satchel" Paige.[308] Paige, one of many great black baseball players to hail from Mobile, Alabama, was long and lean, and possessed a rubber whip for an arm. The outlandish and shamelessly self-promoting Paige was the best known of all Negro League players and one of baseball's greatest pitchers, black or white, of all time. While slug-gers Josh Gibson and Buck Leonard became known as the black Ruth and Gehrig, it was Satchel Paige's blazing fastball, pinpoint control, and flair that drew blackball's crowds. Paige was even hired out to teams who expe-rienced difficulty selling tickets because it was known that, with Satchel's name on a program, a full house was guaranteed. "I ain't ever had a job," said the always-quotable Paige, "I just always played baseball." Report-edly born in 1906 (although an earlier date is likely), Paige pitched for a succession of Negro League and black barnstorming teams throughout the 1920s, 1930s, and 1940s. Although Paige's best years were clearly behind him by the time Jackie Robinson broke the white Major League color bar-rier in 1947, Satchel was signed by the Cleveland Indians in 1948 and pitched competitively in the Major Leagues until he was more than 50 years old, even making a cameo appearance for the Kansas City Athletics in 1965 when he was approximately 60 years old. Credited for winning 147 "official" games in the short-season Negro Leagues, Paige reportedly pitched in literally *thousands* of games over his long career. How much of Paige's story is true and how much is legend will never be known. Paige's performance against white Major League hitters convinced many in white baseball's management and the general public that black players were equal to their white counterparts. Paige experienced unforgettable battles against the great Cardinals pitcher Dizzy Dean during post-season barn-storming tours. "If Satch and I were pitching on the same team, we would clinch the pennant by July fourth and go fishing until World Series time," observed Dean. Unfortunately for Cardinals' fans, this was not to be.

Other great blackball pitchers included "Smokey" Joe Williams, "Cannonball" Dick Redding, and "Bullet" Joe Rogan. Williams, a hawk-nosed, half–Indian, half-black Texas fireballer reportedly threw harder than Walter Johnson or Satchel Paige. When a group of Negro League veterans and sportswriters were asked to name the best Negro League pitcher of all time in the early 1950s, Williams, not Paige, was their choice. Another black hurler with plenty of heat was "Cannonball" Redding. Red-ding reportedly once struck out Babe Ruth three times on nine pitches.

Leroy "Satchel" Paige

Perhaps the best "pitcher" of the Negro Leagues, however, was Rogan, whose repertoire combined a blazing fast ball and an array of other pitches, including an exceptional curve and a palm ball.[309]

    Many white Major League stars were duly impressed by the black players against whom they competed on the barnstorming circuit. John McGraw rated Oscar Charleston the greatest player ever, black or white.

Walter Johnson called Josh Gibson the best catcher in baseball. "The greatest player I ever saw was a black man," said St. Louis Cardinals, New York Giants, and New York Yankees first baseman Johnny Mize. "His name is Martin Dihigo. I played with him in Santo Domingo in winter ball in 1943. I thought I was having a pretty good year myself down there and yet they were walking him to get to me." Dizzy Dean called Satchel Paige the greatest pitcher he had ever seen. By the late 1930s and early 1940s, black players were proving themselves eminently worthy of Major League careers. How much longer would they have to wait?

During World War II, baseball's chronic manpower shortage resulted in white-only Major League rosters featuring individuals who were exempted from the draft because they were supporting families or were medically unfit to be conscripted for military service. During this period, Major League rosters even included a 15-year-old pitcher and a one-armed player. "How do you think I felt when I saw a one-armed outfielder?" lamented Negro League star Chet Brewer. Pitcher Nate Moreland summarized the plight of black players: "I can play in Mexico, but I have to fight for America where I can't play."

In 1942, Major League Commissioner Kenesaw Mountain Landis announced, "There is no rule, formal or informal, no understanding, subterranean or otherwise, against hiring Negro players."[310] Efforts by Major League owners and potential owners such as Bill Veeck and the Washington Senators' Clark Griffith to sign black players, however, were rebuffed by Landis. In 1943, before Bill Veeck purchased the Cleveland Indians, he sought to acquire the Philadelphia Phillies, which he intended to stock with a number of Negro League stars. Landis learned of Veeck's plans and immediately the team was sold to a safer purchaser.[311] When the Pittsburgh Pirates attempted to sign Josh Gibson in 1943, Landis blocked the Pirates' move stating, "Colored ballplayers have their own league. Let them stay in their own league. I have said everything that is going to be said on that subject, the answer is no."[312] When Leo Durocher was quoted in 1942 as stating that a number of players in the Negro Leagues were good enough to play in the Major Leagues and that he would be willing to sign and manage them, Landis rebuked Durocher and forced him to retract his statement and say that he had been misquoted.[313] While hypocritically denying in public that any impediment existed to signing black players, the bigoted Landis stood as an implacable opponent of baseball's integration until his death in 1944.

In early 1945, the deceased Landis was succeeded as commissioner by former United States Senator and Kentucky Governor Albert Benjamin "Happy" Chandler. Viewed by Major League Baseball's owners and those

Bill Veeck

favoring integration as a Southern caretaker who would maintain the status quo, Chandler surprised many by stating, "If a black boy can make it on Okinawa and Guadalcanal, hell, he can make it in baseball." A legion of black baseball fans agreed. Black activists galvanized their communities and organized groups of picketers at Major League ballparks. "If we are able to stop bullets, why not balls?" queried one sign outside Yankee Stadium.[314]

 Integration efforts, accelerated by changes in America's demographics; black participation in the armed services and defense industries during World War II; increased play between barnstorming black and white teams and on integrated military teams; and pressure by owners of various white Major League and minor league teams who wished to employ black talent, generated forces that ultimately would challenge the exclusionary practices of "organized" baseball.[315] The winter leagues of California had showcased a number of talented black players. The Los Angeles Angels of the Pacific Coast League had attempted to integrate their roster, but other owners in the league quickly quashed the plan.

Many aspects of American life were changing, but baseball was not one of them. For professional baseball's first eighty years, the winds of change blew about as fast as a lazy knuckleball. More than eighty years after Abraham Lincoln signed the Emancipation Proclamation, Major League Baseball still did not admit black men to its ranks. Baseball's owners, aided by politicians and jurists espousing sentimental encomiums in lieu of rational discourse, had refused to extend to baseball and black players even the most basic rights granted by the United States Constitution. Labor and civil rights may have been at the forefront of 20th century America, but baseball defined the country's culture. Major League Baseball's ownership and management bore a heavy moral burden. Their public mandate was simple: protect the good of the game. Their private agenda was simpler: maintain control of the game and its profits. Although the death of Landis had removed a major obstacle to integration of the Major Leagues, racism and fundamental economics were deeply ingrained in many Major League owners who feared that the presence of blacks on rosters could greatly diminish white attendance and reduce revenues and franchise values. In 1945, a Major League Committee on Baseball Integration was created. Predictably, the committee never issued a report or made any recommendations.

Chapter 7

DELIVERANCE

There is no rule, formal or informal, no understanding, subterranean or otherwise, against hiring Negro players.
—Commissioner Kenesaw
Mountain Landis, 1942

"[A] baseball box score is a democratic thing. It doesn't tell how big you are, what church you attend, what color you are, or how your father voted in the last election. It just tells what kind of baseball player you were on that particular day.
—Branch Rickey to Jackie Robinson

A life is not important, except in the impact it has on other lives.
—Jackie Robinson

Every time I look at my pocketbook, I see Jackie Robinson.
—Willie Mays

It took two men of uncommon valor to drag Major League Baseball's ownership and management kicking and screaming into the 20th century.[316] Brooklyn Dodgers president, general manager, and part owner Wesley Branch Rickey was a flamboyant, overbearing, sanctimonious, and verbose orator who had reshaped the business of baseball during the first half of the 20th century. A graduate of Ohio Wesleyan University and the University of Michigan Law School, Rickey had briefly been a catcher for the St. Louis Browns, but his greatest abilities were not displayed on the playing field. Rickey worked his way up through baseball's hierarchy, beginning as a scout and becoming, successively, a coach, field manager, chief executive, and part owner of a team. In the process, he completely restructured the St. Louis Cardinals, molding them into a National League powerhouse of the 1920s, 1930s, and 1940s. Nicknamed by sportswriters the "Mahatma" and "El Cheapo" for his demi-godlike and parsimonious characteristics, Rickey spent 25 years with the Cardinals in a number of roles, most prominently as the club's president and general manager. As the Cardinals' general manager, Rickey devised the modern farm system, using and abusing that system to permit the Redbirds to achieve success for years against better-financed teams from larger markets and to become the most profitable and consistently successful National League team.

After leaving St. Louis in 1942 to restructure and inspire the hapless Brooklyn Dodgers organization, Rickey saw an opportunity to realize his destiny. Rickey later recounted how his experiences as a collegiate coach in 1904 had shaped his ideology. Apparently, one of Rickey's black players, Charlie Thomas, upon being denied lodging in a hotel with the rest of his teammates, broke down sobbing and rubbing his hands. "'Black skin, black skin,'" Thomas lamented, "'If only I could make them white!'"[317] According to Rickey, this experience had a profound and lasting impact on him. "'I couldn't face my God much longer knowing that His black creatures are held separate and distinct from His white creatures in the game that has given me all I own,'" recalled Rickey.[318]

Beginning with his arrival in Brooklyn in 1942, Rickey quietly set into motion a series of events that would culminate in the integration of Major League Baseball. Disguised behind a public plan to establish a Brooklyn Brown Dodgers team in a new all-black United States League,[319] Rickey and his scouts scoured the United States, Mexico, and the Caribbean for black stars to stock the Brooklyn Dodgers and integrate Major League Baseball.[320] The inscrutable organizational genius knew that, as with his earlier establishment of the Cardinals farm system, if properly planned and executed, signing of large numbers of black stars would provide a huge advantage to his team and would pay dividends for years to come. The shrewd Rickey also realized that New York's large black population represented enormous potential revenue as spectators if they could be induced to attend games to view black players. By 1945, Rickey was close to bringing his master plan to fruition. The only decision remaining was which black player to choose to be the first to breach the color barrier. The "first" had to be the right man on and off the field. Rickey and his scouts carefully assessed both established black stars and younger players and narrowed the choice to three individuals: Roy Campanella, a 24-year-old, half-black, half–Italian eight-year veteran catcher for the Baltimore Elite Giants; 19-year-old Newark Eagles rookie pitching phenomenon Don

Branch Rickey

Newcombe; and 26-year-old Kansas City Monarchs shortstop Jack Roosevelt Robinson.[321]

After a protracted period of careful observation and subterfuge, Rickey finally identified Jackie Robinson as the man who would be the pioneer.[322] The Georgia-born and California-raised Robinson had a number of qualities that appealed to Rickey. Robinson had attended college at

UCLA, where he had starred in football, track, and basketball, in addition to baseball. He had been an officer in the United States Army, although he had been court-martialled and nearly dishonorably discharged for insubordination for his refusal to sit in the back of a bus. He was physically attractive, intelligent, and articulate. He was mature and had life experiences outside baseball. Although he was playing successfully in the Negro Leagues, his professional baseball career had been relatively short and he had little association with the gangsters who owned and operated the Negro Leagues.

On August 28, 1945, Jackie Robinson was asked to visit Branch Rickey in Brooklyn. Rickey outlined his plans to Robinson and asked if Jackie was up to the task of being the first black man to play Major League Baseball since the brief appearance of Moses Fleetwood Walker in 1884. Rickey did not trivialize the magnitude of the task he was asking Robinson to undertake, admonishing Jackie about the difficulties that would lie ahead and asking him to promise to "turn the other cheek" for at least three years to ensure that this "great experiment" would become a success. He also asked Robinson to promise that he would not disclose the signing to anyone outside his immediate family until Rickey was ready to make his plans public. "Jackie," Rickey began, "there's virtually nobody on our side. No owners, no umpires, very few newspapermen. And I'm afraid that many fans will be hostile. We'll be in a tough position. We can win only if we can convince the world that I'm doing this because you're a great ballplayer, a fine gentleman." Robinson agreed to Rickey's terms and was signed to a contract with the Montreal Royals in the International League, Brooklyn's top farm club, with a promise that if his performance was up to Major League standards, he would be promoted to the Dodgers.[323]

Although Rickey did not initially intend to announce the signing of Robinson until early 1946, by which time he expected to have signed a number of other black stars, political pressures required that this timetable be accelerated. In the New York City municipal elections in the fall of 1945, the integration of baseball became a *cause célèbre* for a number of black and white candidates, including incumbent Mayor Fiorello LaGuardia.[324] LaGuardia, who had earlier worked with Rickey to establish a committee to study the integration of baseball,[325] was eager to announce that baseball would commence signing black players as a result of the committee's work. Yielding to LaGuardia's pressure, Rickey announced on October 23, 1945 that the Montreal Royals had signed Jackie Robinson to a contract.[326] Rickey's concern about delaying the announcement until he had time to sign other stars would prove to be unwarranted. No other National League team included a black player on its roster until

1949. Rickey was able to secure contracts with Campanella, Newcombe, Jim "Junior" Gilliam, Dan Bankhead, and other black players who helped form the nucleus of the powerful Dodgers teams of the 1950s.

On April 18, 1946, Jack Roosevelt Robinson became the first black man in the 20th century to openly compete in white "organized" baseball when he played for the Montreal Royals in their game in Jersey City, New Jersey. Rickey had calculated, correctly as it turned out, that cosmopolitan and Canadian Montreal would be a far more hospitable environment than most United States cities for the first black player in an otherwise white league. What neither Robinson nor Rickey could control, however, was the treatment to which Jackie was subjected on the road, where he was forced to dine and room apart from his teammates. Everywhere Robinson and the Royals went, they attracted record crowds and hostile fans. Robinson was jeered, taunted, hit by pitches, and spiked as he fielded his position at second base.[327] The toll on Robinson was overwhelming, but so was his performance. In the 1946 season with Montreal, in spite of constant pressure, Robinson hit for a .349 average and scored 113 runs, as the Royals won both the International League pennant and the Little World Series, the championship of white minor league baseball.

In a secret meeting held in 1946, 15 of the 16 owners of Major League Baseball teams voted to continue to exclude blacks from the Major Leagues. The only dissenting vote came from the Brooklyn Dodgers.[328] Baseball's owners were still concerned that the presence of blacks on Major League rosters would discourage white attendance. They also were concerned that the presence of black players on Major League rosters might "lessen franchise value."[329] The Major Leagues issued a report claiming that integration of baseball would be harmful to the Negro Leagues and to black ballplayers. Following the owners' meeting, Rickey met with new Commissioner Chandler to enlist his support for integration. Chandler pledged his support for Rickey's plan in spite of the unanimous position of the other owners.

By early April 1947, Rickey still had not promoted Robinson to the Dodgers. Robinson was quoted as saying that he felt Branch Rickey was a fair man and that, when his play warranted it, he would be promoted to the Dodgers. "I do not resent being with Montreal," said Robinson. "I can understand that a lot of people might feel that my showing in my first year was that of a flash in a pan." In spite of a strong season in Montreal in 1946 and a sparkling spring training performance with the big club, however, a potentially explosive situation had to be defused by Rickey before Robinson could join the Dodgers. A group of older, mostly Southern, Dodgers players led by Dixie Walker, Eddie Stanky, and Bobby Bragan

Jackie Robinson attempting to steal home.

petitioned Rickey to block Robinson's promotion to the Dodgers.[330] Younger Dodger players, notably Pee Wee Reese and Pete Reiser, refused to support the petition[331] and Rickey threatened to trade any players who opposed Robinson's presence on the team. On April 10, Robinson was promoted. The protesters were quietly traded after the 1947 season.[332]

On April 15, 1947, Jackie Robinson played his first Major League game in Ebbets Field, Brooklyn. "The debut of Jackie Robinson was quite uneventful, even though he had the unenviable distinction of snuffing out a rally by hitting into a remarkable double play," wrote Arthur Daley of Robinson's debut.[333] "The muscular Negro minds his own business and shrewdly makes no effort to push himself. He speaks quietly and intelligently when spoken to and already has made a strong impression." In spite of published reports, Robinson's debut was highly eventful. "He knew he had to do well," said teammate Duke Snider. "He knew that the future of blacks in baseball depended on it. The pressure was enormous, overwhelming, and unbearable at times. I don't know how he held up. I know I never could have." Robinson was probably asking himself the same question. Once again, Robinson was forced to dine and room separately from his teammates on the road and, once again, he was the target of insults, taunts, brush-back pitches, high spikes, death threats, and threats of harm to his family.

Ebbets Field, Brooklyn.

Rumors circulated that the St. Louis Cardinals planned to strike rather than play against Robinson and the Dodgers. National League President Ford Frick admonished the potential strikers: "If you do this you will be suspended from the league. You will find that the friends you think you have in the press box will not support you, that you will be outcasts. I do not care if half the league strikes. Those who do it will encounter quick retribution. They will be suspended, and I don't care if it wrecks the National League for five years. This is the United States of America, and one citizen has as much right to play as another. The National League will go down the line with Robinson, whatever the consequence."[334] No strike materialized. Several St. Louis players deny that a strike ever was threatened.[335]

Overcoming a slow start, Robinson put together a fine freshman season, hitting .297 with 31 doubles, 5 triples, 12 home runs, 125 runs scored, and a league-leading 29 stolen bases. Wherever Robinson and the Dodgers went, record crowds appeared. Robinson's breakthrough performance earned him *The Sporting News'* inaugural Rookie of the Year award. In October 1947, Jackie Robinson became the first black player to appear in a World Series.

While Robinson was mounting a high profile campaign in Brooklyn, the Cleveland Indians, under the guidance of baseball's most progressive owner, Bill Veeck, quietly signed Negro Leagues star Larry Doby in July 1947, and Doby became the first black player to compete in the American League. Doby moved immediately from the Newark Eagles to the Indians and, used sparingly, batted a paltry .156. The St. Louis Browns, eager to increase attendance, signed Willard Brown and Hank Thompson from the Kansas City Monarchs. After the Dodgers called up pitcher Dan Bankhead in August, five black players were in the Major Leagues. But Brown and Thompson were quickly released when the Browns' attendance did not improve, and both Doby and Bankhead were marginal contributors, leaving the focus squarely on Robinson.

Baseball, the most American of games, played naturally by the most American of men, repeatedly tested Robinson's fortitude. During one game in particular, repeated jeering and taunting from the Phillies, led by Southern manager Ben Chapman, almost proved to be Robinson's undoing. "For one wild and rage-crazed minute, I thought, to hell with Mr. Rickey's noble experiment," recalled Robinson. "What a glorious, cleansing thing it would be to let go.... I could throw down my bat, stride over to the Phillies dugout, grab one of those white sons of bitches and smash his teeth in with my despised black fist. Then I could walk away from it and I'd never become a sports star. But my son could tell his son someday what his daddy could have been if he hadn't been too much of a man."[336]

As promised to Rickey, however, Robinson managed to leash his temper, enduring three years of dignified deferral. In 1949, free of the shackles of self-denial, Robinson was an aggressive and possessed force who neither gave nor took any quarter. "They better be prepared to be rough this year," said Robinson, "because I am going to be rough on them."[337] He was rough on other National League teams that year, winning the batting title with a .342 batting average, 38 doubles, 12 triples, 16 home runs, 122 runs scored, 124 runs batted in, and a league-leading 37 stolen bases. His performance earned him the National League's Most Valuable Player award during a season in which he refused to back down from any challenge on the field or off. Robinson now insisted on staying at the same hotels as his teammates on the road and refused to enter through rear service entrances. This new, more aggressive, attitude was observed and criticized by the media. "I learned that as long as I appeared to ignore insult and injury, I was a martyred hero to a lot of people who had sympathy for the underdog," recalled Robinson. "But the minute I began to sound-off—I became a swell-head, wise-guy, an 'uppity' nigger."[338]

In 1948, Larry Doby blossomed in Cleveland and his .301 average in the regular season and .318 average in the World Series led the Indians to their last Major League championship of the 20th century. Doby went on to have a fine 13-year career with the Indians, White Sox, and Tigers. Another player on the Indians' 1948 roster was 42-year-old (at least) pitcher Satchel Paige. After being called up in July, the venerable Paige won six games and recorded a 2.48 earned run average. Thereafter, Satch played in five different Major League seasons.

In spite of the obvious success of Robinson and Doby, baseball was moving slowly to bring other black players to the Major Leagues. In 1949, the New York Giants promoted former Negro Leaguers Monte Irvin and Hank Thompson. Two years later, Irvin and Thompson teamed with rookie Willie Mays to form an all black outfield that led the Giants to the National League pennant. In the next four years, Negro League graduates Mays, Sam Jethroe, Joe Black, and Jim Gilliam successfully won the National League Rookie of the Year award. The Dodgers' Roy Campanella became not only the best catcher in baseball, but one of the game's best players in the early 1950s, winning the National League's Most Valuable Player award in 1951, 1953, and 1955. Major League Baseball was now officially integrated, but integration was superficial at best. As late as 1953, only six of the Major Leagues' 16 teams had a black player on their rosters.[339] By the beginning of the 1957 season, only 26 black players were on Major League rosters, 18 in the National League and eight in the American League.[340] In a comment that was as much a sad indictment of America as it was praise for Major League Baseball, the Giants' Monte Irvin said, "baseball has done more to move America in the right direction than all of the professional patriots with all their cheap words."

In the 1950s, Major League teams, particularly the Dodgers and the Giants, also began to mine the rich and previously untapped baseball resources of the Dominican Republic, Puerto Rico, Cuba, and other Caribbean nations. Orestes "Minnie" Minoso, the "Cuban Comet," was signed by the Cleveland Indians in 1948 and traded to the Chicago White Sox in 1949. In 1954, Vic Power joined the Philadelphia Athletics. Originally signed by Rickey's Dodgers, but claimed by Pittsburgh after an unsuccessful effort by the Dodgers to hide him on their unreserved roster, Roberto Clemente, the greatest Latin star, debuted with the Pirates in 1955. In 1958, Felipe Alou became the first of three Alou brothers to play for the Giants. In 1960, future Hall of Famers Juan "The Dominican Dandy" Marichal and Orlando "The Baby Bull" Cepeda debuted with the Giants.[341]

By the time Jackie Robinson retired after the 1957 season, only the Philadelphia Phillies, Detroit Tigers, and Boston Red Sox had yet to include a black player on their rosters. The Red Sox, the Major Leagues' last all-white holdout, added Elijah "Pumpsie" Green to their roster in 1959.[342] Teams such as the Dodgers and Giants, which were in the vanguard of integration, would find great success on the field in the 1950s and 1960s. The previously hapless Dodgers won six National League pennants and one World Series during Robinson's ten Major League seasons. With the exception of the Yankees, whose wealth ensured that they were always stocked with top white players, those teams that were slow to integrate suffered the consequences. A striking example of this reality was the decline of the once-powerful St. Louis Cardinals.

During the final years of white-only Major League Baseball, the Cardinals, guided by Branch Rickey, were the National League's dominant team. From 1942 to 1946, the Cardinals won four National League pennants and three World Series. Located in a heavily segregated city that was the most southern and most western outpost of the Major Leagues until 1955, however, the Cardinals did not add a black player to their roster until 1954, nine years after Jackie Robinson signed his contract to play in Montreal, and did not employ black or Latin players in significant numbers until the 1960s. Not surprisingly, the Cardinals did not win a National League pennant between 1946 and 1964.[343]

During that same period, the Dodgers won seven National League pennants and the Giants won three. Many of the National League's greatest stars of that era, including Jackie Robinson, Roy Campanella, Willie Mays, Hank Aaron, Frank Robinson, Ernie Banks, and Roberto Clemente, were black and the teams on which they played dominated the National League. In eleven of the fifteen years from 1949 through 1963, black players were named the National League's Most Valuable Player.

Although the Cardinals still had the National League's last white superstar, Stan Musial, his all-white supporting cast was weak and his own abilities declined as the 1950s drew to a close. It would not be until 1964, a year after the great Musial's retirement, that a Cardinals team again would win a National League pennant and the World Series. Ironically, that team, and subsequent Cardinals pennant winners in 1967, 1968, 1982, 1985, and 1987 featured black and Latin stars such as Bob Gibson, Lou Brock, Curt Flood, Bill White, Julian Javier, Orlando Cepeda, Ozzie Smith, George Hendrick, Willie McGee, Lonnie Smith, Joaquin Andujar, Terry Pendleton, Vince Coleman, and Tony Pena.

Today, the roster of every Major League team is rich in black and Latin talent. While black and Latin players have gained acceptance on the field, however, they have hardly earned common rights. "On the field, blacks have been able to be super giants," said Hank Aaron. "But, once our playing days are over, this is the end of it and we go to the back of the bus again." Larry Doby similarly observed, "[w]e bring dollars into club treasuries when we play, but when we stop playing, our dollars stop." In spite of being one of the game's greatest players and foremost ambassadors in the Caribbean, Roberto Clemente was often ridiculed by the Pittsburgh press for being lackadaisical and a malingerer.

With Jackie Robinson's integration of Major League Baseball, a revolution in playing style also occurred. Robinson, employing an aggressive style of play and daring base running, hallmarks of the Negro Leagues, dictated a style that would come to define the National League for decades to come. The game, as played in the National League, became faster, more exciting, and less dependent on home runs for scoring. This is not to say that power was not, or is not, an important part of the game played by blacks, but the National League's leading home run hitters of the 1950s and 1960s, Mays, Aaron, Banks, and Frank Robinson, combined speed and power in a way that most white players, with the exception of a few players such as DiMaggio, Musial, and Enos Slaughter, of that era and the preceding one, did not. The power game introduced by Babe Ruth transformed baseball in the 1920s from a game of speed, controlled hitting, tight pitching, and low scores to a game dominated by power. The Negro Leagues' style of play, as later introduced by blacks in the Major Leagues, combined power, speed, and aggressiveness, and transformed baseball again. In the 54 seasons since Jackie Robinson was named the National League's Most Valuable Player in 1949, 32 of the individuals who have been named Most Valuable Player in the National League have been black or Latin and 21 of the individuals who have been named Most Valuable Player in the American League have been black or Latin. In the slower to integrate American League, the first black Most Valuable Player was Elston Howard in 1963.

Blinded and crippled by diabetes, Jackie Robinson died of a massive heart attack on October 24, 1972, at the age of 53. The pioneer integrator of previously all-white Major League Baseball had been heavily involved in business and various community and civil rights causes following his retirement from the game. Robinson's impact on Major League Baseball was monumental, but his impact on America was not limited to the baseball field. Jackie Robinson's legacy is manifested in the historic Supreme Court desegregation and civil rights cases of the 1960s and 1970s, the advancement of black Americans in all walks of life, and the hope and raising of consciousness that Robinson's breaking of the color barrier provided to generations of people of color. Equally important, according to Leonard Koppett, Robinson's integration of baseball had a historic and lasting impact on *white* Americans because it "compelled millions of decent white people to confront the fact of race prejudice—a fact they had

been able to ignore for generations before.... Millions of people, and especially children, found nothing wrong with the fact that there were no black
ball players [in the white Major Leagues]. These decent people weren't
against blacks.... They simply never questioned a system that excluded
them.... The consequences of the waves [Robinson's] appearance made
spread far beyond baseball, far beyond sports, far beyond politics, even
to the very structure of a culture."[344]

As a sad irony, although Jackie Robinson's integration of the white
Major Leagues created new opportunities for blacks in Major League Baseball and other fields, Robinson's historic feat signaled the end of participation by blacks in some arenas. The acceptance of Robinson and other
blackball stars in the white leagues drew the final curtain on the Negro
Leagues, black ownership of baseball teams, black management, and, tragically, black baseball spectators. With the demise of the Negro Leagues,
no black was to manage a top team until Frank Robinson was hired by
the Cleveland Indians in 1975. No black served as a Major League general
manager until the Atlanta Braves hired Bill Lucas as their general manager. Even today, almost none of Major League Baseball's top management and administrative positions are filled by blacks or Latins and few
blacks or Latins serve as managers, coaches, or scouts. Although black
spectators once thronged to see Negro Leagues and black barnstorming
games, black and Latin attendance at Major League contests today is minimal. Finally, the contributions made by the Negro Leagues to the economy, social fabric, and pride of black communities are but a distant
memory.

Was Jackie Robinson the correct choice to be the "first"? This question could be debated forever by baseball fans and sociologists. Was Jackie
Robinson the best black baseball player available in 1946? The answer to
this question is decidedly in the negative. Although Robinson was a talented and exciting player, men such as Oscar Charleston, Josh Gibson,
Satchel Paige, and Buck Leonard had greater baseball abilities and far
more productive careers in the Negro Leagues. But all of those men were
a decade or more older than Robinson, were more closely associated with
the Negro Leagues and their gangster owners, and lacked many of Robinson's other attributes. Future Major League superstars such as Hank
Aaron, Willie Mays, and Frank Robinson were teenagers or younger in
1945 when Robinson signed his Montreal contract. Among Robinson's
contemporaries such as Roy Campanella, Monte Irvin, and Larry Doby,
Robinson's education, personal qualities, and determination set him apart.
The wisdom and parameters of Rickey's selection process guided him to
the correct man for this historic task. The shrewd Rickey realized the type

of pressures that would be placed on the chosen man. He knew that something more than a great ballplayer would be required. In Jack Roosevelt Robinson, Branch Rickey and America got that something more. The right man both on the field and off the field. An intelligent, mature, educated, dignified, proud man who had enough wisdom and courage to "turn the other cheek" when that was required, even though his insides told him to do otherwise, and enough heart and integrity to be more aggressive and militant when that was warranted. A man who could be admired not only by the Negro race, but by all members of the human race.

Chapter 8

DIASPORA

It is arguable that baseball has been better—more multi-dimensional, nuanced, and surprising—since the fifties. But baseball has never before or since been more purely American, or more perfectly congruent with an era. With its relentless emphasis on the "big bang" style of offense, baseball was brimming over with energy. And nothing is more characteristic of this axe-swinging, forest-clearing, prairie-breaking, concrete-pouring, skyscraper-raising nation than the exuberant belief that energy, sheer straight-ahead power, is an unmixed blessing and the right approach to most things. Soon after the fifties ended, domestic turmoil and foreign entanglements made American life seem more solemn and complicated. But before the clouds lowered and America came of middle age, back in the fifties when there were still lots of day games and doubleheaders, the national pastime, like the nation, seemed uncomplicated.

—George Will

A baseball club is part of the chemistry of the city. A game isn't just an athletic contest. It's a picnic, a kind of town meeting.

—Michael Burke

World War II finally ended with the dropping of American atomic bombs on Hiroshima and Nagasaki in August 1945. The war in Europe had ended in May of that year as American and English forces advancing east in Germany met Russian armies moving west. In July and early

August, Soviet Premier Joseph Stalin, British Prime Minister Winston Churchill, and American President Harry S Truman met at Potsdam, outside Berlin, to chart the direction of the post-war world. Disagreements and antagonisms surfaced between Stalin, on one side, and Truman and Churchill, on the other. The expressed position of the United States was to infuse Europe and Asia with Anglo-American concepts of liberty, equality, and democracy and to strengthen the economies of the defeated countries to prevent future wars. The Soviet Union, which had borne much of the brunt of the war, was justifiably concerned with rebuilding its own country and economy, protecting its borders, and ensuring that its neighboring countries posed no future threats and were "sympathetic" to Russia's centralized, autocratic government. The "Cold War" that resulted from these conflicting objectives shaped America's foreign policy for much of the remainder of the 20th century and led to further conflicts that resulted in great losses of human life and profound changes in American society. In the immediate post–World War II period, however, Americans accepted the basic tenets of American doctrine. We were victorious in World War II, we were the only country that possessed atomic weaponry, we had the strongest economy in the world, and we were confident in our mission and standing in the world. The task that now faced American leaders was how to convert America from a nation geared to win a war to a peacetime economy in which the benefits of America's democratic structure and prosperity could be shared by its 140 million people.

Less than one week after the Japanese surrender on the United States battleship *Missouri* in Tokyo Bay, President Truman sent to Congress a 21-point domestic program that included increased unemployment compensation, an increase in the minimum wage, tax reform, crop insurance for farmers, extension of government controls over business for an additional year, federal aid to housing to make possible the construction and purchase of one million new houses each year, and protection against unfair labor practices.[345] Within months, a proposal for national health insurance was added.[346] In 1947, President Truman sent a 10-point civil rights program to Congress.[347] In July 1948, he banned racial discrimination in federal government hiring practices and ordered an end to segregation in the military.[348]

World War II had returned the United States to prosperity and, in the post-war period, the country consolidated its position as the world's richest economy. The United States' gross national product increased from approximately $200 billion in 1940 to $300 billion in 1950 to more than $500 billion in 1960. Many factors contributed to this growth, including an increase in the manufacture and sale of automobiles to an increasingly mobile society, a housing boom precipitated by the sale of houses to returning servicemen who were able to take advantage of inexpensive mortgages under the G.I. Bill, Cold War defense spending, and explosive growth in the manufacture and sale of televisions and other consumer products.

Post-war America also witnessed changes in the types of businesses and jobs that dominated the country's economy. Major corporations became larger. Fewer workers were involved in the production of goods and more became employed in service businesses. Farmers left the land and joined the urban workforce. Companies began to offer guaranteed annual wages, long-term employment contracts, and fringe benefits.

Post-war America was on the move. Boys and girls who departed from family farms for the war or defense industry jobs were not eager to return to their rural roots. A post-war baby boom markedly increased the country's population. Millions of blacks migrated from farms in the South to industrialized jobs in the North and West. Populations in the West and Southwest increased rapidly, a trend which would continue throughout the 20th century. City dwellers departed the inner cities and moved to new suburbs which offered affordable housing to accommodate the post-war baby boom. Businesses abandoned the cities to join individuals who had moved to the West and to the suburbs. New highways created better access to the West and to the suburbs. The urban landscape was redefined.

The pervasive optimism that gripped America in 1945 was similar to that at the end of World War I in 1918. Unlike the conclusion of the First World War, however, implementation of the Marshall Plan in Europe seemingly assured that the roots of a lasting and effective world peace were in place. It was now time for America to spend and enjoy. American manufacturing switched from military output to consumer products such as automobiles, refrigerators, washers, dryers, and televisions. By the mid–1950s, the United States, with only six percent of the world's population, produced two-thirds of the world's manufactured goods. America's rapidly expanding economy created growth in jobs, wages, and consumer spending, particularly for leisure activities. In the immediate post-war period, this resulted in increased attendance at Major League Baseball games. The combination of the attractions of other leisure pursuits (including hunting, fishing, bowling, and golf), the popularity of television, the exodus of whites from America's cities to its suburbs, and the extended dominance of New York City's three Major League teams for more than a decade, however, ultimately eroded Major League Baseball's attendance.

By the beginning of the 1946 season, virtually all Major League players who had served their country were back and ready to resume their baseball careers. The Boston Red Sox easily won the 1946 American League pennant and, after a hard-fought pennant race and a playoff game, the St. Louis Cardinals fended off the Brooklyn Dodgers for the National League pennant. In a World Series in which neither the Red Sox's great star, Ted Williams, nor the Cardinals' great star, Stan Musial, shone brightly, the Cardinals defeated the Red Sox in the first complete season after World War II and the final season of white-only Major League Baseball.

Until Jackie Robinson was promoted to the Brooklyn Dodgers in 1947, little had changed in Major League Baseball for the half century following the National Agreement in 1903. The Major Leagues still constituted sixteen teams, with eight in each league, which were concentrated in ten cities in the Northeastern quarter of the United States, with three teams in New York, two in each of Boston, Philadelphia, Chicago, and St. Louis, and one in each of Pittsburgh, Cleveland, Cincinnati, Detroit, and Washington, D.C. The Major Leagues' most Western and Southern outpost was St. Louis, 26 hours by train from Boston, the Major Leagues' most Northern and Eastern city. No Major League franchise had moved since the National Agreement. With the exception of the short-lived Fraternity of Professional Base Ball Players and the Federal League in 1912–15, no serious challenge had been mounted to the primacy of Major League Baseball's monopoly since the National Agreement. With World War II ended, the autocratic commissioner Kenesaw Mountain Landis dead and replaced by a more compliant Albert "Happy" Chandler, night baseball established, and an eager middle-class fan base, Major League Baseball's owners looked expectantly to huge post-war profits, a return to normality, and continued stability.

In 1945, the year in which World War II ended, Major League Baseball's attendance again finally exceeded 10 million, its level in 1930. In 1946, attendance increased 71 percent to 18.5 million, a new season record, as eleven of the Major Leagues' sixteen teams set new franchise attendance records and the Yankees became the first team to draw more than 2 million fans in a season.[349] By 1948, total Major League attendance exceeded 20 million. In 1948, the American League champion Cleveland Indians drew 2.620 million spectators, a record not exceeded until 32 years later when the New York Yankees drew 2.627 million fans.[350] During the four seasons immediately following World War II, fourteen of the sixteen Major League teams posted new attendance records.[351] Major League teams now also had their games broadcast by radio and their home games televised. Baseball's owners were profiting at a rate greater than ever before. The profits were not proportionate, however, and problems began to appear. In 1949, attendance declined for the first time since World War II, a trend that would continue throughout the 1950s.[352] The 1948 average Major League attendance of 1.3 million per team would not again be achieved until 1976.[353]

The first indication that the post-war period would bring change was in 1946, when the Pascual brothers provided a challenge to the Major Leagues' monopoly by luring a number of Major League players to play in the Mexican League.[354] According to reports, Stan Musial was offered a five-year $175,000 contract to play in Mexico (a substantial increase on his $13,500 salary with the St. Louis Cardinals) with 50 percent of this amount to be paid as a signing bonus, and Hal Newhouser was offered a total of $500,000 in salary and bonus for a three-year contract (his Detroit Tigers salary was $45,000 per season).[355] Although the Pascuals were unable to sign Ted Williams, Joe DiMaggio, Stan Musial, Hal Newhouser, or any of the other top stars they desired, their open pocketbooks did convince a number of Major League players to jump to Mexico. The conditions in Mexico proved not to be conducive to American players, however, and by the end of the following season all had returned to the United States where they hoped to return to the Major Leagues.[356]

Commissioner Chandler denied the renegades re-entry into the Major Leagues and blacklisted all players who had jumped to the Mexican League from playing in the Major Leagues for five years. Four of the blacklisted players filed lawsuits alleging violations of the federal antitrust laws. The blacklisted players ultimately were reinstated.[357] Around the same time that the Mexican League blacklist suits were commenced, other challenges to the century-old reserve system were mounted in antitrust lawsuits lodged by disgruntled players.[358] Although most of these cases were quietly settled by Major League Baseball's owners, one case wended its way through the federal court system and was decided by the United States Supreme Court. In that case, *Toolson v. New York Yankees*,[359] George Edward Toolson, a former Yankees farmhand who had been assigned to another team against his will and was blacklisted for failing to report to the new team, challenged Major League Baseball's reserve system under federal antitrust legislation. As discussed in Chapter 2 of this book, in his historic 1922 decision in *Federal Baseball Club of Baltimore, Inc. v. National League of Professional Clubs*,[360] Justice Oliver Wendell Holmes created an "exemption" for organized baseball from the application of the federal antitrust laws. Holmes's decision in *Federal Baseball* was based on the determination that baseball did not involve interstate commerce and, therefore, the federal courts had no power to regulate it. In the years between *Federal Baseball* and *Toolson,* the Supreme Court had greatly expanded the scope of what constituted interstate commerce and had distinguished the *Federal Baseball* decision in other cases involving sports and entertainment crossing state lines. It seemed likely that the *Toolson* court would reverse the *Federal Baseball* decision. Surprisingly, however, the Supreme Court, over dissents by two justices, refused to overturn *Federal Baseball,* noting that Major League Baseball's owners had made investment decisions in reliance on a belief that organized baseball was exempt from the antitrust laws.[361] The Supreme Court also invited the Congress to remedy this situation by enacting specific legislation to address the application of the antitrust laws to baseball.[362] This decision confirmed the reserve system, the owners' most powerful tool in controlling players and their salaries, and strengthened the owners' belief in the unassailableness of their control over baseball. Throughout the 1950s, 1960s, and 1970s, this control was repeatedly challenged.

The breaking of the Major Leagues' color barrier by Branch Rickey and Jackie Robinson also demonstrated that changes in American society in the post-war world would result in changes to baseball. In integrating "organized" baseball, Branch Rickey had challenged one of the Major Leagues' most enduring bonds, the "gentlemen's agreement" to exclude blacks, and new Commissioner Chandler had supported Rickey's action over the objection of the other 15 owners. Chandler's support of Rickey, approval of minimum salaries and a pension plan for players, 1947 suspension of Leo Durocher, investigation of recruiting abuses, veto of a proposed raise in ticket prices, and failure to keep baseball out of costly and dangerous antitrust litigation ultimately cost him his job. In 1950, Chandler's contract was not renewed and he resigned.[363] The commissioner's powers had been circumscribed sharply after the death of Landis. Now they would be curtailed further. The owners decided that their new commissioner should be National League President Ford Frick, a former sportswriter and ghostwriter for Babe Ruth, a man they considered to be a baseball insider and one whom they knew they could control.[364]

America's union membership had increased dramatically during World War II and, by the end of the war, 36 percent of America's non-agricultural work force was unionized. In 1946, Robert Murphy, a Boston lawyer, organized the American Baseball Guild as a players' union for Major League players.[365] The union's goal was a minimum annual salary of $6,500, 50 percent of the sale price being paid to a player if he was sold, and arbitration of certain disputes.[366] Although Murphy was unsuccessful in securing sufficient votes to call a strike and the union was dissolved,[367] the existence of the union and the challenge by the Mexican

League caused Major League Baseball to amend the standard player contract and the Major League regulations to increase the minimum player salary to $5,500, increase spring training expense payments (thereafter called "Murphy Money"), provide $500 in expenses to players traded or sold to another club, limit the maximum salary cut in a renewed contract to 25 percent, provide minimal medical coverage and expense payments, and provide for consideration of a pension plan.[368]

In 1950, war broke out in Korea and again a number of Major League players were called into action. Ted Williams, an experienced Marine fighter pilot who had already spent three years in the military during World War II, would spend another two years away from baseball. Several younger players, including Willie Mays and Whitey Ford, also were inducted. The Korean conflict would have a far less significant effect on baseball, however, than World War I or World War II.

In 1949, Charles Dillon "Casey" Stengel became manager of the New York Yankees,[369] the Brooklyn Dodgers' Jackie Robinson was named the National League's Most Valuable Player, and the New York Giants roster included Monte Irvin and Hank Thompson, both graduates of the Negro Leagues. During the 1950s and early 1960s, the Yankees produced a continuous stream of top-line white talent. The Dodgers and Giants, Major League leaders in integrating their teams, fielded top teams during the same period. For the decade from 1949 through 1958, a New York–based team played in the World Series every year and, in six of those ten seasons, New York teams faced each other. In 1951, all three New York teams were featured in post-season action.[370]

During the twelve seasons from 1946 through 1957, the Yankees drew an average of 1.85 million fans, the Dodgers' average attendance was 1.3 million, and the Giants averaged over one million in attendance. For each of these teams, however, attendance declined in the 1950s.[371] The combination of the location of the teams' stadiums in deteriorating slum neighborhoods, movement of middle-class white fans to new suburbs, insufficient automobile parking, and vast increases in television viewing contributed to the diminished attendance. The Yankees' attendance dropped from 2.2 million in 1948 to 1.5 million in 1957. During the same period, the Dodgers' attendance declined from 1.8 million to 1 million and the Giants' attendance fell from 1.6 million to only 650,000. Overall, attendance for New York's three Major League teams plummeted by 43 percent in the decade.[372]

Fan interest in most of the rest of the country also declined in this era dominated by New York teams. With the exception of Cleveland's

Municipal Stadium, all Major League ballparks in use in the early 1950s had been built between 1909 and 1923 and most were now located in deteriorating neighborhoods with insufficient parking for automobiles.[373] From the Major Leagues' record attendance of 20.9 million in 1948, total attendance fell to 14.4 million in 1953.[374]

In 1951, Bill Veeck, Jr., son of the former President of the Chicago Cubs, acquired the St. Louis Browns. Veeck had purchased the Cleveland Indians in 1946 and built that team into the 1948 World Series champion. Through then-pioneering promotions, Veeck increased the Indians' attendance from its total of 558,000 in 1945 to an all-time Major League high of 2.6 million in 1948, exploited the depreciation and capital gains provisions of the federal tax laws, and sold the Indians realizing a healthy profit.[375]

In acquiring the perpetually hapless Browns at a time when the St. Louis Cardinals were also in dismal condition, Veeck believed he could infuse the Browns with talent, ideas, and promotions and drive the Cardinals out of St. Louis. His promotional ideas in St. Louis included sending a midget, Eddie Gaedel, to the plate as a pinch hitter and hiring Satchel Paige as a relief pitcher.[376] In 1953, however, the Anheuser-Busch brewery acquired the Cardinals. Busch's money made it clear that the Browns would remain the less successful occupant of St. Louis's Sportsman's Park. At the same time, the Braves were suffering in Boston and the Athletics were struggling in Philadelphia as less successful teams in two-team cities that could only support one club.[377]

Veeck had repeatedly irritated his fellow baseball owners, and particularly the more conservative National League owners, with his flamboyant promotions, revenue sharing ideas, and suggestions for changing baseball's established order. After Busch's purchase of the Cardinals, Veeck again was prepared to annoy the other owners. In March 1953, one month before the season was scheduled to commence, Veeck proposed that the Browns be moved to Milwaukee, where a new ballpark of Major League standards was being constructed. But Milwaukee also was home to the American Association's Brewers, which were the top farm club of the Boston Braves. The Braves owners, realizing their own situation in Boston was hopeless, objected to Veeck's proposal and requested that they be permitted to move the Braves to Milwaukee instead of allowing the Browns to relocate there. Major League owners vetoed the unpopular Veeck's request and approved the transfer of the Braves.[378] In their first year, the Braves drew 1.8 million fans in Milwaukee, the highest attendance figure in National League history and more than six times the 281,278 fans they had drawn a year earlier in Boston. The Milwaukee Braves drew appoxi-

mately two million spectators per season throughout the 1950s[379] in the
new Milwaukee County Stadium, which was located adjacent to super-
highways, had extensive automobile parking facilities, and was located
away from Milwaukee's downtown area.[380]

In 1954, Veeck again petitioned to move the Browns—this time to
Baltimore.[381] Veeck was again rebuffed by other owners, who believed that
they could persuade him to get out of Major League ownership if they
forced him to keep the Browns in St. Louis. Ultimately, the Browns were
permitted to move, but on the condition that Veeck sell the team to a
local group in Baltimore where they were moved and renamed the Orioles.[382] In 1954, the Orioles drew more than one million fans in Baltimore,
three and one-half times as many as the Browns had drawn in St. Louis
in 1953.[383]

In 1955, the Athletics, whose 1954 attendance in Philadelphia was
only 300,000, moved to Kansas City, where they played in the refurbished
Municipal Stadium and drew 1.4 million fans.[384] Finally, after half a century of franchise stability, three Major League teams had changed cities
within three years, the benefits of moving had clearly been demonstrated
to baseball's owners, and the benefits of having a Major League Baseball
team had clearly been demonstrated to cities that desired Major League
status. But each of these three moves involved teams that were poorly supported second teams in two-team cities and each of those teams was facing financial collapse if it remained in its original home city.[385]

Concerned by their own declining attendance, the Brooklyn Dodgers'
owner, Walter O'Malley, who had wrested control of the team from
Branch Rickey in 1950, and the New York Giants' owner, Horace Stoneham, sought new publicly financed stadiums in Brooklyn and Manhattan, respectively, which they believed would improve their teams' financial
positions.[386] These proposals were rejected by municipal authorities.[387]
Although both the Dodgers and the Giants made profits in the 1950s in
Ebbets Field and the Polo Grounds, respectively, in part because they also
received substantial television revenues by 1950s standards, their profits
were declining and future financial improvement did not appear likely in
their existing ballparks. Both O'Malley and Stoneham, cognizant of the
improved situations in Milwaukee, Baltimore, and Kansas City, began to
investigate other locations for their teams. Stoneham prepared to move
the Giants to Minneapolis, where his top farm club was playing in a newly
constructed stadium and he anticipated the ability to develop regional
rivalries with the Milwaukee Braves, Chicago Cubs, and St. Louis Cardinals. O'Malley made plans to move the Dodgers to Los Angeles, which
promised to provide a new ballpark and cable television revenues in an

enthusiastic market that was now accessible by transcontinental air travel.[388]

By the mid–1950s, the Pacific Coast League had practically become a third major league. Two Los Angeles–based teams were drawing approximately two million spectators annually, more than the combined attendance for the Dodgers and the Giants.[389] The move of Major League Baseball to the West Coast was inevitable, and Walter O'Malley, baseball's shrewdest and most profit-driven owner, wanted to be the owner who would mine the California gold. O'Malley convinced Stoneham of the promise of the West Coast and, in 1958,

Walter O'Malley

the Dodgers moved to Los Angeles and the Giants moved to San Francisco.[390]

After announcing the Giants' departure from New York, Stoneham told a *New York Journal-American* reporter, "I feel bad for the kids. I've seen lots of them at the Polo Grounds. But I haven't seen many of their fathers lately."[391] Although the Dodgers and Giants did not face immediate financial disaster if they remained in New York, their attendance and profits had declined. Moving to what had become America's most populous and fastest-growing state brought immediate financial rewards. In 1958, their first year in California, the Dodgers and Giants drew 1,845,556 and 1,272,625 fans, respectively, substantial increases from their 1957 totals of 1,028,258 and 653,923, respectively.[392] They would soon be the beneficiaries of new, publicly subsidized ballparks that would result in further increases in attendance and profitability.[393] In their first three seasons in California, the Dodgers and Giants doubled their attendance in their last three years in New York.[394] In their inaugural year in the new Dodger Stadium in 1962, the Dodgers drew more than 2.5 million fans.[395]

Dodger Stadium, Los Angeles

Fans who had been left behind by the Braves in Boston, the Browns in St. Louis, the Athletics in Philadelphia, and especially the Giants in New York and the Dodgers in Brooklyn experienced abandonment, betrayal, and outrage. For the first time since the National Agreement in 1903, Major League Baseball teams, which provided cohesiveness, tradition, character, continuity, and economic value to communities, had been moved. At the time of the National Agreement, America's total population was 80 million, the population of New York was 3.5 million, the population of Philadelphia was 1.3 million, the populations of Boston and St. Louis were nearly 600,000 each, the population of Baltimore was 500,000, the population of San Francisco was 350,000, the population of Milwaukee was nearly 300,000, and the population of Los Angeles was only about

100,000.[396] By the time of the five Major League franchise moves of the 1950s, the country's population had doubled to approximately 160 million, the populations of metropolitan New York, Philadelphia, Milwaukee, and the San Francisco Bay Area had approximately doubled, and the populations of Boston and St. Louis had increased by approximately 50 percent, but the population of the greater Los Angeles area was approximately 30 times as large.[397] During the fifteen years following World War II, the inner-city populations of New York, Philadelphia, Boston, and St. Louis declined while America's suburban populations, particularly in Western and sun-belt cities, rose dramatically. After a half century of franchise stability and concentration in ten cities, five teams were moved and five new cities added in five years. Only Chicago remained a two-team city. The moves can be partially explained by demographics and economic forces, but the dominant reason was financial gain. Larger markets and reduced competition meant greater profits to team owners.

Four times during the 1950s, Congress held hearings on baseball.[398] In those hearings, a number of Major League owners and managers, current and former players, economists, labor leaders, and others presented

Casey Stengel testifying in Congress, flanked by Mickey Mantle and Ted Williams.

testimony. Major League Baseball's reserve system was scrutinized in light of the federal antitrust laws, interstate commerce, and the United States Supreme Court's decisions in *Federal Baseball* and *Toolson*. In each of those hearings, many subjects were discussed, disagreement and confusion prevailed, and ultimately no congressional action was taken. After the famous congressional hearings in 1958 in which both Casey Stengel (extensively) and Mickey Mantle (briefly) testified, the congressional committee reviewing the applicability of the federal antitrust rules to baseball concluded: "Legislation is not necessary until the reasonableness of the reserve rules has been tested by the courts. If those rules are unreasonable in some respects, it would be inappropriate to adopt legislation before baseball has had an opportunity to make such modifications as may be necessary."[399]

Movement of the Dodgers and Giants from New York became a major political issue in America's most populous city. Lawyer and Democratic Party heavyweight Bill Shea was appointed to head a commission to obtain a replacement National League franchise for New York.[400] After a petition for a National League expansion franchise was rebuffed, Shea attempted to convince the owners of each of the Philadelphia Phillies, Pittsburgh Pirates, and Cincinnati Reds to move their teams to a new stadium to be built on the site of the Worlds Fair in Queens. The owners of those franchises decided not to move their teams. Shea co-opted Branch Rickey, now an advisor to the Pittsburgh Pirates, to assist in bringing a new team to New York. Shea and Rickey, convinced that the National League was unlikely to grant New York an expansion franchise, proposed that the existing Major Leagues recognize a new third Major League, the Continental League, with teams in New York, Houston, Minneapolis, Toronto, Denver, Atlanta, Dallas, and Buffalo.[401] The Major League owners seriously considered the proposal which would have required the Continental League owners to compensate the existing owners and would have reduced legislative pressure in Washington.[402] Concluding that it was not in their interests to permit the creation of a new league, however, each of the existing Major Leagues voted to expand to ten teams. Expansion franchises were granted to the Continental League's ownership groups in New York and Houston, the Washington Senators moved to Minneapolis and became the Minnesota Twins, a replacement franchise was installed in Washington, D.C. (influence in the nation's capital was still desirable), an American League franchise for Los Angeles was granted to Gene Autry, and the Continental League was disbanded.[403] Each expansion team purchased its players from existing teams in its league.[404] Again, threats to the

Charles O. Finley

Major Leagues' monopoly had been repelled and the owners remained in control.

In 1960, Chicago insurance executive Charles O. Finley acquired the Kansas City Athletics.[405] Although the Athletics had drawn well in Kansas City immediately after their move in 1955, by the time Finley purchased the team, attendance had declined.[406] Finley was an irascible and flamboyant individual with plans to improve the quality of the Athletics team, increase attendance through promotions, and enhance the team's profitability.[407] Finley unsuccessfully negotiated with Kansas City civic officials to provide a new publicly financed ballpark, which he believed would increase attendance. Frustrated by his lack of success, Finley threatened to move the team to Atlanta, Dallas, Denver, Louisville, New Orleans, Oakland, or Phoenix.[408] At the same time, attendance in Milwaukee had declined to one-third of its peak years. Atlanta offered the Braves' new ownership, a Chicago-based syndicate headed by William Bartholomay and Jack Shaffer, a new stadium, media money, and the opportunity to be the Major Leagues' first team in the South. Major League owners approved the move of the Braves to Atlanta for 1966, but rejected the disliked Finley's request to move. After much maneuvering involving a number of teams, and several threatened antitrust actions, the owners finally approved Finley's move of the Athletics to Oakland and its new Oakland-Alameda County Coliseum for 1968, and new American League franchises were awarded to Kansas City and Seattle for 1969.[409] Not to be outdone, the National League awarded new franchises to San Diego and Montreal for 1969.[410] After the 1969 season, the Seattle Pilots franchise was relocated to Milwaukee and became the Brewers.[411] After the 1971 season, the Washington Senators moved to Dallas/Fort Worth where they became the Texas Rangers.[412] For 50 years, the Major Leagues had been fixed at 16 teams in 10 inner cities in the Northeastern quarter of the United States. In less than two decades, the Major Leagues' diaspora resulted in 24 teams in 20 metropolitan areas and two countries.

The combination of expansion and franchise relocation substantially increased Major League attendance. In 1952, the last season before franchise movement began, total Major League attendance was 14.6 million. By 1969, Major League attendance was 27.2 million. Total attendance in the 1960s was 63 percent greater than in the 1950s.[413]

As discussed in Chapter 7 of this book, the introduction of black players into Major League Baseball changed the nature of the game, particularly in the National League. With the exception of the Yankees, who continued to be able to attract and acquire the best young white players because of their relentless success and large revenue base, most of the best young players in the game were black or Latin. In the National League, several players who ultimately would challenge all-time Major League records debuted in the 1950s. In New York, the Giants introduced the incomparable Willie Mays, and later in San Francisco they added future Hall of Famers Juan Marichal, Orlando Cepeda, and Willie McCovey. While they still called Brooklyn's Ebbets Field home, the Dodgers featured Negro Leagues graduates Jackie Robinson, Roy Campanella, Jim Gilliam, Don Newcombe, and Joe Black and white stars Duke Snider, Pee Wee Reese, and Gil Hodges. Later, in Los Angeles, Sandy Koufax, Don Drysdale, Maury Wills, and Tommy Davis would continue the rivalry with the Giants that had begun in New York, with the Dodgers winning pennants in Los Angeles in 1959, 1963, 1965, and 1966 and the Giants winning their first pennant in San Francisco in 1962.

In Milwaukee, Hank Aaron joined Warren Spahn, Lou Burdette, and Eddie Matthews to form a team that would win National League pennants in 1957 and 1958. With the exception of Philadelphia's "Whiz Kids" in 1950, led by Richie Ashburn, Robin Roberts, and Jim Konstanty, and Chicago's great Ernie Banks, the Phillies and Cubs displayed their usual ineptitude. Until 1960 and 1961, when young stars such as Roberto Clemente and Frank Robinson, respectively, began to dominate, the Pirates and Reds were perennial second-division teams.

In spite of the continued excellence of Stan Musial, particularly in the first half of the 1950s, the Cardinals were in serious decline, badly hampered by their delay in recruiting black players. At the end of the 1963 season, after 22 seasons with the Cardinals, the great Musial finally retired at age 42. The following season, the Cardinals, energized by young stars from their farm system such as Bob Gibson, Julian Javier, and Tim McCarver, and anchored by veteran Cardinals such as Ken Boyer and players acquired in judicious trades such as Lou Brock, Curt Flood, Bill White, and Dick Groat, the Cardinals won the first of their three National League pennants in the 1960s. In 1967 and 1968, aided by newcomers Orlando Cepeda and Roger Maris, and with a pitching staff that included Gibson, Steve Carlton, Ray Washburn, and Nelson Briles, the Cardinals again won pennants.

In 1969, the "Miracle Mets," led by Tom Seaver, Jerry Koosman, Gary Gentry, and Tommy Agee, erased seven years of complete frustration and returned a World Series championship to New York City. Las Vegas odds-makers had quoted 100 to 1 odds against the chances of the Mets winning the National League pennant, but a combination of strong, young pitching and timely hitting led the team to the regular-season National League East title, a sweep of the Atlanta Braves in the National League Championship Series, and a five-game victory over the heavily favored Baltimore Orioles in the World Series.

The Yankees, combining the solid pitching of Whitey Ford, Vic Raschi, Allie Reynolds, Eddie Lopat, Bob Turley, Ralph Terry, and Jim Bouton with the hitting of Mickey Mantle, Yogi Berra, Bill Skowron, Elston Howard, and Roger Maris, dominated the American League from 1949 through 1964. During this sixteen-year period, the Yankees won fourteen American League pennants and nine World Series championships, failing to appear in the World Series only in 1954 and 1959. For other American League teams, there was little cheer. The Indians won the pennant in 1954 and the White Sox won in 1959, but both failed in the World Series. In the 1961 season, Mickey Mantle battled teammate Roger Maris for the American League home run title all season. When the season finished, Mantle had hit 54. But Maris, the American League's Most Valuable Player in both 1960 and 1961, had tallied 61, exceeding Babe Ruth's 1927 total of 60, one of baseball's most cherished records.

After the demise of the Yankees following the 1964 season, Boston, Detroit, Minnesota, and Baltimore emerged as the top teams in the American League. In 1966, the Baltimore Orioles' Frank Robinson won the American League's "Triple Crown" and in 1967 the Boston Red Sox' Carl Yastrzemski became the last Major League "Triple Crown" winner, in each case leading their teams to American League pennants. Robinson also became the only man ever to be named Most Valuable Player in both Major Leagues, having been accorded that honor while playing for the Cincinnati Reds in 1961 and while playing for the Baltimore Orioles in 1967. In 1968, Denny McLain became the Major Leagues' last pitcher to win 30 games in a season, in a year in which his Detroit Tigers won the American League pennant and defeated the St. Louis Cardinals in the World Series.

Two trends were established on the field in the 1950s and 1960s which have had lasting effects: relief pitching and base stealing. In the 1950s, relief pitchers began to be used with frequency. Philadelphia Phillies' relief pitcher Jim Konstanty, with 74 relief appearances, 16 wins, and 22 saves, was named the National League's Most Valuable Player in 1950. By the 1960s, relief pitchers were no longer only washed-up or ineffective starters and by the 1970s pitchers were trained in the minor leagues to be relief pitchers, particularly for short relief "closer" roles, as teams found that dominant closers were increasingly important to success. In 1962, Dodgers shortstop Maury Wills stole 104 bases, breaking Ty Cobb's record which had been established nearly half a century earlier. This led to a renewed emphasis on the stolen base which came to be employed as a devastating offensive weapon by Wills, Lou Brock, Vince Coleman, Rickey Henderson, and other players.

The Major Leagues' greatest players in the quarter century following World War II were Ted Williams, Stan Musial, Joe DiMaggio, Willie Mays, Hank Aaron, Yogi Berra, Roy Campanella, Frank Robinson, Roberto Clemente, Mickey Mantle, Warren Spahn, Sandy Koufax, Don Drysdale, Juan Marichal, Whitey Ford, and Bob Gibson.

The careers of Williams, Musial, and DiMaggio are discussed in detail in Chapter 5 of this book. "Joltin' Joe" DiMaggio retired after the 1951 season when injuries no longer permitted him to play like Joe DiMaggio. Ted "The Splendid Splinter" Williams played through the 1960 season, missing a total of five seasons to military service, and hit a home run in his final at-bat. Characteristically, Williams refused to acknowledge the crowd's cheers for his final clout. As John Updike reported in *The New Yorker*, "He didn't tip his cap. Though we thumped, wept and chanted 'We want Ted' for minutes after he hid in the dugout, he did not come back. Our noise for some seconds passed beyond excitement into a kind of immense, open anguish, a wailing, a cry to be saved. But immortality is nontransferable. The papers said that the other players, and even the umpires on the field, begged him to come out and acknowledge us in some way, but he never had and he did not now. Gods do not answer letters." Stan "The Man" Musial finally retired after the 1963 season, a 42-year-old grandfather who had challenged for the National League batting title by hitting .330 a year earlier, and who had played for the Cardinals for 22 remarkable seasons from before America's entry into World War II in 1941 until less than two months preceding President John F. Kennedy's assassination in 1963.

Willie Mays, a true five-tool Major Leaguer, began his professional career with the Birmingham Black Barons of the Negro Leagues, joined the New York Giants in 1951, and became one of the greatest and most exciting players in the history of the game. A dramatic center fielder, daring base runner, and accomplished power hitter, Mays won a National League batting title and led the National League in slugging average five times, triples three times, home runs four times, runs scored twice, and stolen bases four times. He was the first Major Leaguer to hit 300 home runs and steal 300 bases. During his 22-year Major League career, the "Say Hey Kid" collected 3,283 hits, 660 home runs, 2,062 runs scored, 1,903 runs batted in, and posted a lifetime batting average of .302 and a lifetime slugging average of .557. Willie won eleven Gold Gloves and was twice named the Most Valuable Player in the National League.[414]

Henry Aaron began his professional career with the Indianapolis Clowns of the Negro Leagues and joined the Milwaukee Braves in 1954.

Willie Mays playing stickball in Harlem.

Hank Aaron at bat.

Less flamboyant than Mays, "Hammerin' Hank" quietly but relentlessly established numerous Major League records, including career marks for home runs (755), total bases (6,856), extra-base hits (1,477), and runs batted in (2,297). He is second in Major League career at-bats (12,364) and third in games played (3,298), hits (3,771), and runs scored (2,174).

Aaron won two National League batting titles, captured four home run crowns, four times led in runs batted in, three times won Gold Gloves, and was named the National League's Most Valuable Player in 1957. In his 23-year Major League career, Hank maintained a career .305 batting average and a lifetime .555 slugging average.[415]

Lawrence "Yogi" Berra was a standout catcher and timely hitter for the Yankees in the 1950s. The winner of three American League Most Valuable Player awards, Berra anchored the great Yankees teams of the 1950s and played in 14 World Series, ten times on winning teams.

Roy Campanella played eight seasons with the Baltimore Elite Giants of the Negro Leagues before moving on to the Brooklyn Dodgers in 1948. He was the Major Leagues' finest catcher in the 1950s, a dangerous hitter, and was named the National League's Most Valuable Player three times.[416]

Frank Robinson is the only player to have been named Most Valuable Player in both Major Leagues, in 1961 with the Cincinnati Reds and in 1966 with the Baltimore Orioles. In his 21-year career, the intense Robinson led his league in home runs once, runs scored three times, runs batted in once, batting average once, and slugging average four times. He

Roy Campanella (right) blocking the plate from Bobby Thompson.

won the American League "Triple Crown" in 1966. After retiring from the game in 1976 with career totals of 586 home runs, 2,943 hits, 1,829 runs scored, 1,812 runs batted in, a .294 batting average, and a .537 slugging average, Frank Robinson became the first black man to manage a Major League team.

Roberto Clemente, the greatest Latin player in Major League history, won four National League batting titles in an 18-year career with the Pittsburgh Pirates in which he collected 3,000 hits. A spectacular outfielder and base runner, Clemente was the National League's Most Valuable Player in 1966. He died in an airplane crash in 1972, while delivering food and medical supplies to Nicaragua, which had been ravaged by a massive earthquake.

Mickey Mantle was Major League Baseball's most feared switch hitter, belting 536 home runs in his 18-year career with the New York Yankees. A fine fielder and runner, in spite of career-long illness and injuries to both of his knees, Mantle was probably the Major Leagues' fastest runner before injuries and hard living slowed him. Mantle won the American League "Triple Crown" in 1956 and was named the American League's Most Valuable Player three times. He posted a career batting average of .298, a career slugging average of .557, and collected 1,677 runs scored and 1,509 runs batted in. Mantle participated in twelve World Series, playing on the winning team seven times.[417]

Warren Spahn won more games than any left-handed pitcher in Major League history. In his 21-year career, Spahn won 363 games, leading the National League in wins eight times, earned run average three times, complete games nine times, innings pitched four times, and strikeouts four times. Spahn won 20 or more games in 13 different seasons and posted a lifetime earned run average of 3.09. He won the Cy Young Award in 1957 and pitched no-hitters when he was 39 and 40 years old.

After six disappointing seasons, Sandy Koufax became baseball's most dominating pitcher, posting a 111–34 record with 100 complete games and 33 shutouts from 1962 through 1966. He led the National League in earned run average in all five of those years and in wins and strikeouts in 1963, 1965, and 1966, winning the Cy Young Award in all three of those years. He won 165 games and recorded a lifetime 2.76 earned run average during his 12-year career with the Brooklyn and Los Angeles Dodgers. Koufax threw four no-hitters, including a perfect game. He was forced to retire prematurely after the 1966 season at age 30 because of arthritis in his pitching arm. He became the youngest player ever admitted into the Hall of Fame.[418]

Don Drysdale was Sandy Koufax's right-handed counterpart in the

Top: Roberto Clemente at bat. *Bottom:* Mickey Mantle at bat.

Warren Spahn

great Dodgers pitching rotation of the 1960s. Drysdale led the National League in wins in 1962 and strikeouts in 1959, 1960, and 1962. He posted a lifetime 2.95 earned run average and collected 209 wins in a 14-year career. He was known for intimidating right-handed batters with his inside pitching.

Juan Marichal won 243 games over a 16-year career, twice leading the

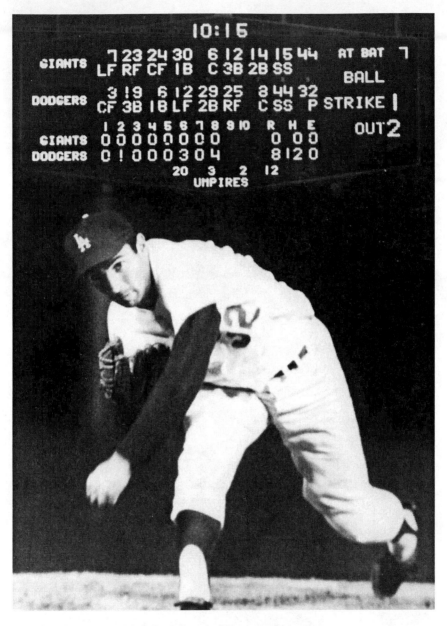

Sandy Koufax pitching a perfect game.

National League in wins and twice in innings pitched. The "Dominican Dandy" won more than 20 games in six seasons and posted a lifetime earned run average of 2.89.

Edward "Whitey" Ford anchored the pitching staff of the perennial champion New York Yankees of the 1950s and early 1960s. Ford led the

American League in wins three times, winning percentage three times, earned run average twice, and innings pitched twice. He won 236 games in a 16-year career, posted a lifetime 2.75 earned run average, recorded a .690 lifetime winning percentage (the highest for any 200-game winner), and set all-time World Series records for wins and scoreless innings.

Bob Gibson won 251 games in a 17-year career with the Cardinals, recorded a 2.91 lifetime earned run average, collected ten Gold Gloves and, like Drysdale, intimidated National League hitters. In 1968, Gibson posted a 1.12 earned run average, the lowest in modern baseball history. A former college and Harlem Globetrotters basketball player, Gibson won two Cy Young Awards, a National League Most Valuable Player award, pitched seven straight wins in the World Series, and was the first pitcher since Walter Johnson to record 3,000 career strikeouts. Gibson's renowned intensity is demonstrated by Roger Angell's account of Gibson's encounter with a former teammate: "His roommate, Bill White, was traded away and White told me that the first time he came up to bat against his old roommate, he knew he would be hit. And he said Gibson hit him right up under the neck. And [that] was a message saying, 'We're not roommates anymore.'"[419]

Other notable players of the period included Richie Ashburn, Al Kaline, and Lou Brock; sluggers Duke Snider, Willie McCovey, Ernie

Bob Gibson

Banks, Eddie Matthews, Rocky Colavito, Harmon Killebrew, and Ralph Kiner; and pitchers Ferguson Jenkins, Robin Roberts, Early Wynn, and Jim Palmer. Ashburn, a fleet and sure center fielder from Tilden, Nebraska, was the Phillies' leadoff hitter and best baserunner during the 1950s. Always a hustler, Ashburn collected 2,574 hits and maintained a .308 batting average over 15 seasons. At the age 20, Kaline became the youngest player to win a batting title when he hit .340 in 1955. In 22 seasons with the Detroit Tigers, Kaline amassed 3,007 hits and won ten Gold Gloves. Lou Brock combined batting ability (3,023 hits and a lifetime batting average of .293), speed (118 stolen bases in a season and a career total of 938, both Major League records at the time of his retirement), and occasional power in 19 superb seasons with the Cubs and Cardinals. Edwin "Duke" Snider of the Brooklyn Dodgers was the third of the great New York center fielders of the 1950s, with Mickey Mantle of the Yankees and Willie Mays of the Giants. He hit 407 career home runs and holds the National League career records for World Series home runs (11) and runs batted in (26). Willie McCovey was a devastating slugger who hit 521 home runs over a 22-season Major League career. Playing in four decades, McCovey intimidated pitchers, leading the National League in home runs three times and slugging average three times, and was named the National League Most Valuable Player in 1969. Ernie Banks, one of the most feared power hitters of his era, won successive National League Most Valuable Player awards in 1958 and 1959 in spite of playing on losing teams. Banks, who began his career with the Kansas City Monarchs of the Negro Leagues, hit more home runs while playing shortstop than any player in history (293) until Cal Ripken broke that record, and hit a total of 512 home runs in his career. "Mr. Cub" led the National League in home runs twice, runs batted in twice, and slugging average once. Eddie Matthews, a sweet-swinging, smooth-fielding third baseman, led the National League in home runs twice and hit a total of 512 home runs in his 17-year career. Colavito, Killebrew, and Kiner were classic power hitters who amassed career home run totals of 374, 573, and 369, respectively.

Jenkins won a career total of 284 games over 19 seasons, winning 20 or more games in seven seasons. Roberts (who was later to play a pivotal role in convincing Marvin Miller to serve as the executive director of the Major League Baseball Players Association) won 286 games over 19 seasons, including six consecutive seasons with at least 20 wins. Wynn won 300 games over 23 seasons, winning at least 20 games in five seasons. Palmer won 268 games in an 18-year career with the Baltimore Orioles. Palmer, who won at least 20 games in eight seasons, received three Cy Young Awards and posted a .286 career earned run average.

Several rule changes occurred in the 1950s and 1960s that influenced the game.[420] In 1950, to encourage offensive production, the strike zone was narrowed. In 1959, a new rule was enacted which required ballparks constructed after that date to have right field and left field fences at least 325 feet from home plate. To reduce home runs and scoring, in 1963, the strike zone was expanded and pitcher's mounds were raised.[421] By 1968, as a result of the combination of higher pitching mounds, larger stadiums, and the increased strike zone, Major League home runs had declined by 60 percent.[422] The consequent decline in scoring, when combined with the general stagnation in Major League Baseball in the late 1950s and early 1960s, resulted in decreased attendance.[423] In 1968, the "Season of the Pitcher," Denny McLain won 31 games, Bob Gibson posted a 1.12 earned run average and 13 shutouts, the National League had a collective batting average of .243, the American League had a collective .230 batting average, only six Major League hitters batted at least .300, Carl Yastrzemski won the American League batting championship with a .301 average and was the only American League player to hit .300, the lowest number of runs were scored since the Dead Ball Era, 21 percent of all games were shutouts, more than five percent of all games finished with a score of 1–0, and attendance declined further.[424] To increase scoring and attendance, pitchers mounds were lowered and the strike zone narrowed for the 1969 season. Batting averages, home runs, and attendance rose.[425] Major League Baseball's owners were reminded of a lesson their predecessors had learned from Babe Ruth's exploits and their effects on attendance in the 1920s and 1930s—fans want to see runs and especially home runs.

Baseball's attendance in most cities decreased throughout the late 1950s and most of the 1960s,[426] resulting from a combination of relentless Yankees dominance, reduced scoring, increased television viewing, and diversion of attention to other events, including civil rights activities, the war in Vietnam, and other sports, particularly professional football. Franchise movements and expansion franchises, however, resulted in increases in total attendance. Several new Major League owners operated media enterprises, including the Columbia Broadcasting System which acquired the Yankees in 1964.[427] This combination of team ownership and the ability to transmit the team's entertainment product by television created vast new opportunities for owners and created new challenges for Major League Baseball. Television proved to be a mixed blessing for the Major Leagues. It eroded attendance at games, but by the 1960s broadcast revenues were an increasingly important component of overall income, particularly to franchises in media centers. Major League owners and their commissioner had not yet realized the full potential of telecasting or the enormous potential of marketing logoed products. In 1946, the Major League owners barred television broadcasts of games beyond a 50-mile radius of the ballpark.[428] In 1949, this rule was eliminated, except that later "Game of the Week" telecasts were blacked out in Major League cities.[429] The combination of Major League expansion and radio and television coverage of Major League games conspired to inflict grave injury on the minor leagues in the 1950s and early 1960s. Minor league attendance declined by 75 percent and, ultimately, two-thirds of the minor leagues disbanded.

Although franchise shifts and expansion were now occurring, the rights granted to players were virtually unchanged since the reforms that had been made in 1946 in the wake of the threats posed by the Mexican League and Robert Murphy's American Baseball Guild. The players had little representation with ownership. Their only formal contact was through the pension committee, where the players' proposals were consistently ignored. In 1953, the players' requests for modest changes to the pension plan were flatly rejected by the owners.[430] The players' efforts to be represented by legal counsel and for a 20 percent increase in the $6,000 Major League minimum salary also were rebuffed.[431] Finally, in 1954, the owners agreed to fund the players' pension plan with revenues from the All-Star Game and the World Series, but would not agree to increase the amount of the pensions.[432] That year, the Major League Baseball Players Association was formed to represent the players in pension matters.[433] In 1958, the Players Association requested that 20 percent of Major League Baseball's gross receipts be allocated to player compensation.[434] Again, the owners refused. Player salaries averaged between $10,000 and $25,000 during the 1950s and 1960s, with Joe DiMaggio, Hank Greenberg, Ted Williams, and Stan Musial receiving baseball's first $100,000 salaries.[435] Minimum salaries increased from $6,000 in 1946 to $7,000 by 1960 to $10,000 in 1969.[436] In 1962, a new and improved players' pension scheme was adopted.[437]

In one of Major League Baseball's first attempts at collective wage bargaining, Sandy Koufax and Don Drysdale negotiated jointly with Dodgers' owner Walter O'Malley for increased salaries for the 1966 season.[438] Koufax and Drysdale, who had combined to lead the Dodgers to World Series championships in 1963 and 1965, held out from spring training in 1966 to demonstrate their resolve. "The goal," recalled Sandy Koufax, "was to convince them that they would have to approach us not as indentured servants but as coequal partners to a contract, with as much dignity and bargaining power as themselves."[439] O'Malley was outraged at Koufax and Drysdale. "'Baseball is an old-fashioned game with old-fashioned traditions. If we allowed this [concerted] entry business to take hold, it would lead to practices not possible to tolerate.'"[440] Ultimately, the Dodgers provided raises of nearly 50 percent to Koufax and Drysdale.[441] Although the raises were less than Koufax and Drysdale had sought, they demonstrated the enhanced bargaining power that could be achieved through collective action.

Players' experiences with Major League owners throughout the post–World War II period generally reflected the desires of owners to return to the pre-war model of complete domination. In the post-war world, however, numerous changes had occurred that made it unlikely that this historic model could continue to prevail. Post-war labor advances, civil rights developments, social changes, and alterations in the game, including franchise movement, expansion and the consequent creation of more jobs, and television money, coupled with the owners' arrogant refusal to negotiate to address those conditions, created situations that would contribute to future conflicts between the owners and the players and among owners.

As the 1950s and 1960s progressed, great changes were evident in American society. The civil rights movement, sparked by Jackie Robinson's historic integration of Major League Baseball, gathered momentum. In 1954, the United States Supreme Court decided the case of *Brown v. Board of Education*,[442] in which it overturned the judicial doctrine of "separate but equal" treatment of minorities which had been established in the 1896 Supreme Court case of *Plessy v. Ferguson*.[443] In the 1950s and 1960s, Congress enacted comprehensive civil rights legislation and legislation establishing Medicare, Medicaid, aid for schools, and housing reform.[444] In 1956, however, the Eisenhower administration, eager to maintain French support for Soviet containment in Europe, began to provide economic and military aid to France's former colony in Indochina. Successive administrations, convinced that the fall of Vietnam to Communist nationalist Ho Chi Minh would result in the loss of other Asian countries to Communism, escalated economic and military aid to Vietnam. By 1968, 540,000 American troops were stationed in Vietnam.[445] Americans viewed their first televised war, witnessing bloody battles and ineffective military campaigns in which the United States spent $150 billion, more than 58,000 American lives were lost, and more than 300,000 Americans were wounded.[446] Americans, particularly the young, protested American involvement in Vietnam and in 1973 a cease fire agreement was signed.[447] The United States had lost its first war, many Americans now questioned the values that their country sought to uphold, and the consensus supporting United States foreign policy eroded. Young Americans also began to reject the stable living patterns of their middle-class parents and to seek alternatives. Hair and clothing styles changed dramatically, the use of illegal drugs increased, and a new sexual permissiveness prevailed.

As a result of Jackie Robinson's integration of "organized" baseball in 1946, the movement of five teams including the Dodgers and Giants in the 1950s, the expansion of the Major Leagues to 24 teams in 20 metropolitan areas in two countries in the 1960s, and judicial, legislative, and labor challenges to Major League Baseball in the 1950s and 1960s, baseball experienced more changes in the 25 years following World War II than it had in the previous 50 years. Those changes would all seem trivial, however, in comparison to the changes that were on deck.

Chapter 9

GOD PROFANED!
APPLE PIE BLASPHEMED!

Every contract, combination in the form of trust or oth-erwise, or conspiracy, in restraint of trade or commerce among the several States, or with foreign nations, is declared to be illegal.
> —The Sherman Antitrust Act
> (1890)

Like a fugitive slave law, the reserve rule denies [the base-ball player] a harbor or a livelihood, and carries him back, bound and shackled, to the club from which he attempted to escape.... He goes where he is sent, takes what is given him, and thanks the Lords for life.
> —John Montgomery Ward
> (1889)

I once loved this game. But after being traded four times, I realized that it's nothing but a business. I treat my horses better than the owners treat us. It's a shame they've destroyed my love for the game.
> —Dick Allen

By the mid–1960s, America had finally awakened from its post–World War II slumber. The country's innocence had been shattered on November 22, 1963, by the assassination of its young and dynamic President, John F. Kennedy. Civil rights workers had been beaten and murdered in Mississippi and Alabama. Martin Luther King marched for equality, cities burned, American boys fought in Southeast Asia, and the Beatles appeared on *The Ed Sullivan Show.*

America was awake but the national pastime was still sleeping. Ted Williams, Stan Musial, and Warren Spahn, the last remaining stars who had played in the Major Leagues' all-white era, had finally retired. The New York Yankees dynasty, which had won 14 of the 16 American League pennants from 1949 through 1964 and, in the process, transformed an entire generation of disillusioned baseball enthusiasts into professional football fans, had finally collapsed. A number of Major League franchises had moved to new cities and both Major Leagues had expanded the numbers of their teams. But the ownership of Major League Baseball was essentially unchanged. The O'Malleys, Stonehams, Griffiths, and other owners were smug with their baseball cartel and its monopoly practices, protected by a judicially enforced antitrust exemption which protected its "contractual" reserve system.

Over the next decade, the country would explode in rage and righteousness. When Martin Luther King was assassinated the day before the scheduled opening of the Major Leagues' 1968 season and riots ensued throughout America, commissioner William "Spike" Eckert declared that it was up to individual teams to determine whether they would cancel games. Black and white Pittsburgh Pirates players voiced outrage and refused to play. Grudgingly, Eckert cancelled opening day games. Some players, such as Willie Mays in San Francisco, were recruited for public service announcements, urging residents of black neighborhoods to show restraint. The war in Vietnam continued to sharply divide the country. In spite of outrage in American cities and on university campuses, however, little anti-war sentiment was expressed in Major League Baseball, America's most conservative sport.

A surprising voice of dissent was heard from venerable former Red Sox slugger Ted Williams, a veteran of both World War II and the Korean conflict. "The war in Vietnam was another undeclared war which was a huge mistake," said Williams. "If I had a kid in Vietnam, I'd be screaming." Nevertheless, baseball was a content anachronism in a period of massive upheaval. America needed a bedrock and the owners of Major League Baseball were happy to provide it.

In spite of changes in civil and labor rights occurring throughout American society, Major League Baseball's labor relations had scarcely evolved over a century. Baseball's owners clung to a plantation mentality in which players were the property of the franchises that paid them. Pain killers, uppers, and downers were accepted, and even encouraged, by management if it helped keep players performing and alert during the rigors of a lengthy season. After winning 27 games and losing only nine in 1966, Los Angeles Dodgers' pitcher Sandy Koufax was regarded as one of the greatest pitchers in baseball's history. Koufax had averaged 24 victories and 307 strikeouts over the previous four seasons. At only 30 years of age, Koufax seemed destined to dominate like few pitchers had before him. One month after leading the Dodgers to the 1966 World Series championship, however, Koufax announced his retirement. "I don't know if cortisone is good for you or not," Koufax said. "But to take a shot every other ball game is more than I wanted to do, and to walk around with a constant upset stomach because of the pills and to be high half the time during a ballgame because you're taking painkillers, I don't want to have to do that."[448] In taking this stand, Koufax laid bare the risks many athletes would take to keep performing. But few baseball players made principled stands in the mid–1960s. The control by Major League Baseball's owners was still too powerful.

In the boxing ring, the loquacious and irrepressible young heavyweight champion of the world, Cassius Marcellus Clay, now known as Muhammad Ali, was more outspoken. In demanding his rights and refusing to be inducted into the United States Army to participate in a different form of fighting in Vietnam, Ali took an honorable and courageous stand that was made somewhat easier by plying his trade in an individual sport. But American team sports, and Major League Baseball in particular, were not ready for the flamboyant or intelligent black athlete. Not in the mid–1960s.

Baseball players, and black players in particular, needed first to liberate themselves before they could effect group change. Although Jackie Robinson had broken organized baseball's color barrier in 1946, the struggle continued for most black players. Black stars of the 1960s, including Willie Mays, Hank Aaron, and Frank Robinson, still seethed over the treatment they had received over the years. Like Jackie Robinson, their anger would manifest itself in aggressive play on the field. Although black players had finally been accorded some basic rights, such as the ability to stay in the same hotels as their white teammates during the regular season, in spring training in the South their accommodations remained separate because most teams' Florida hotels had white-only policies. Although a disproportionate number of Major League Baseball's star players were black, a majority of the remaining roster spots were filled by whites. But for a black player, even a heralded star, to survive in baseball, he would have to steer clear of the slightest whiff of controversy. Baseball players in general had few rights and black players had even fewer.

Two players, one perhaps unwittingly and the other because of unshakable principles and courage, would come to embody the struggle of not only the black man in America, but also the baseball player in the Major Leagues. Dick Allen was a prodigious and flamboyant physical talent and an individual who played by his own rules. Allen's clashes with Major League Baseball's antiquated management typified the problems of the times: an unyielding force meets an immovable object. Curt Flood was a superb baseball player with courage and convictions. Flood's clash with Major League Baseball's owners changed the business of baseball forever. After the paths of Allen and Flood crossed, Major League Baseball was never the same.

If Dick Allen had played in the era of Nike and ESPN's SportsCenter, he would have been celebrated for more than his spectacular athletic talents. But Allen, unlike many modern sporting mercenaries, was not drunk with self-promotion. Allen was his own man. Hall of Fame slugger Willie Stargell recounted to Allen's autobiographer, Tim Whitaker: "Dick Allen played the game in the most conservative era in baseball history. It was a time of change and protest in the country, and baseball reacted against all that. They saw it as a threat to the game. The sportswriters were reactionary too. They didn't like seeing a man of such extraordinary skills doing it his way. It made them nervous. Dick Allen was ahead of his time. His views and ways of doing things would go unnoticed today."[449] Unfortunately for Dick Allen, talent has no opportunity to select the generation in which it shines.

Allen was the "discovery" of John Ogden, a wizened baseball hand and Philadelphia Phillies scout who had been around the game long enough to have pitched to Babe Ruth in 1929. After reading a newspaper story about a 16-year-old, power-hitting shortstop who played on a men's semi-pro team, Ogden headed for Wampum, Pennsylvania, about an hour outside of Pittsburgh, for a personal look at Dick Allen. What he saw when he arrived simply overwhelmed him. "I go back 53 years in baseball and nobody, nobody, was ever as powerful as Allen," said Ogden. "Not even Babe Ruth had the power to the opposite field that Allen does. I knew I had been looking 30 years for this boy. I wasn't going to lose him." In those days, Major League scouts had to wait until prospects graduated from high school or turned 18 years old before signing them to contracts. Minutes after his high school graduation ceremony, Dick Allen asked John Ogden, "Where's that paper to sign? I want to go play ball." Ogden quickly provided a contract and a pen.

Perhaps Allen was doomed from the moment he signed that contract with its $60,000 bonus which was, as newspaper columnists of the day often reminded readers, the highest bonus ever paid to a black athlete.[450]

Allen was a quiet and imposingly built young man with an easy smile who had never traveled more than an hour beyond Wampum. His mother was well-respected in this small steel and cement manufacturing town of approximately 1,000 residents, where blacks and whites mingled with minimal conflict. A war for civil rights may have been raging in America, but the battlefield seemed not to encompass Wampum, Pennsylvania.

The 18-year-old Dick Allen's perspective on race relations was forever changed, however, as he disembarked from his first-ever airplane flight in Clearwater, Florida, on his way to the Phillies' camp. Allen was initially confused by the two separate airport doors, one for whites and the other for blacks. Dick was eventually whisked away, past the Phillies' downtown hotel, to the house of a black woman where he was provided a room. "After a while," Allen recounted to sportswriter Melvin Durslag, "the Phillies felt I might be lonesome so they sent me company. It was Marcelino Lopez, the Cuban pitcher now with Baltimore. We were great company for each other. He didn't speak English and I didn't speak Spanish."

In 1963, after playing in the minor leagues in Magic Valley, Utah, and Williamsport, Pennsylvania, the Phillies assigned Allen to their new Triple A team in Little Rock, Arkansas. Allen became that state's first black professional baseball player and encountered marchers with signs that read "DON'T NEGRO-IZE BASEBALL" and "NIGGER GO HOME."[451] Allen called his oldest brother, Coy, to tell him he wanted to do just that. Phillies' General Manager John Quinn, scout John Ogden, and Coy Allen flew to Little Rock to persuade Dick to remain in Arkansas.[452] Allen stuck it out, slugging 33 home runs and driving in 97 runs with the Little Rock club before a late-season call-up to the Phillies. The parent club could no longer ignore its powerful prodigy.

In 1964, the Phillies were a woeful franchise with baseball's most poisonous "fans," who would boo first and ask questions later. In fairness to Phillies' supporters, they had a right to jeer. The Phillies had captured National League pennants only twice in their history, in 1915 and 1950, and the franchise had yet to produce a World Series champion. Old Connie Mack Stadium, originally known as Shibe Park, had become a den of hostility and scarcely qualified as the ideal stage for an ultra-sensitive young black man from tiny Wampum, Pennsylvania, with a hefty signing bonus, to make his Major League debut.

In 1964, Dick became the first black player in Philadelphia baseball history to win a starting job in his rookie year. Young Dick, now referred to as "Richie" by Philadelphia's scribes, immediately displayed the awe-inspiring power that would become the hallmark of his career and thrilled the perpetually sour Philly fans. Halfway through 1964, the impossible was occurring: the Phillies were in first place and their rookie slugger appeared to be leading them to a National League pennant.

The media, fans, and local politicians jumped aboard the Allen bandwagon. Most seasoned baseball hacks had never seen anyone like Allen. While there was no denying the athleticism necessary to perform at the highest levels of baseball, a number of its great practitioners had been men of notable girth and less than optimal conditioning. But not Dick Allen. He was a physical specimen who inspired an almost homoerotic awe from some writers. "He is accused of having arms like Popeye and that isn't true," wrote Leonard Shecter. "Only his forearms are like Popeye's. The rest of the arm is much bigger. Thick through the shoulders, massive of chest, thin in the waist, the 5-11, 185 pound Allen could be described as having the perfect build. But he is so muscular there is distortion. The muscles in his buttock are so bunchy that he looks in tight pants as though he has a baseball glove in each back pocket. This gives him a sort of gander walk that is short of being perfect." According to another Philadelphia sportswriter, "Stripped to the waist, Rich Allen looks as if he could have stolen his upper torso from the Rodin Museum."[453]

Allen was a prodigiously talented athlete. Although he was only 5 feet 11 inches tall, he could not only dunk a basketball with either hand, he could touch a spot 16 inches above the rim.[454] He was the most natural of athletes performing the most difficult of maneuvers in such a simple and sublime way that he confounded and infuriated the legions of mortals around him. He was graceful, powerful, unfailingly independent, and black.

It seemed like such an unfair advantage to be Dick Allen. Almost all stories about Allen began by recounting that he had been paid the highest signing bonus ever for a black athlete. By the second or third paragraph, it would be noted that his last home run had traveled 500 feet or more into uncharted territory at Connie Mack Stadium. Bespectacled and introspective, powerful and sinewy, Allen was a beguiling contradiction. Irascible and typically understated Phillies manager Gene Mauch marveled at Allen's incredible maturity. "I've never known an athlete with a better mental attitude," said Mauch. "He never gets too high when things are going good and he never gets downhearted when they are going bad." This was Philadelphia, right? The town where they boo the national anthem! The City of Brotherly Love was awash in love for Dick Allen, at least as long as he had a bat in his hands.

As the 1964 season reached its climax, two things seemed clear: Dick Allen would be the National League's Rookie of the Year and the Phillies would win the National League pennant. Philadelphia's baseball fans had not expressed this sort of optimism since the success of their beloved "Whiz Kids" in 1950. Allen finished his freshman season with a .318 batting average, 219 hits, 38 doubles, a Major League–leading 13 triples, 29 home runs, 91 runs batted in, a Major League–leading 125 runs scored, a Major League–leading 41 errors, and a new National League record 138 strikeouts, easily capturing Rookie of the Year honors. Unfortunately, the Phillies suffered a less happy fate. With ten games remaining to play, the Phillies held a seemingly comfortable six-game lead.

Dick Allen

After losing all ten of those games, Philadelphia finished the season one game behind the fast-closing St. Louis Cardinals.

Something died in Dick Allen after that first year in Philadelphia. The shy young slugger from Wampum was gone forever, replaced by a talented, yet elusive, enigma. In spite of debuting in an era renowned for dominant pitching, Allen's rookie season had been one of the most productive in Major League history. But all the statistics were for naught, he admitted, because his team did not win. So Dick scratched his head and shrugged his mighty shoulders. Somewhere between the boos and the cheers, the incessant cat-calls, the "nigger-baiting" in Florida, Little Rock, and Philadelphia, somewhere between hitting 29 home runs and making 41 errors, somewhere between being the franchise's most exciting talent in 20 years and its most reviled in 80 years, and somewhere between Richie and Dick, Allen decided to take a stand.

When the Phillies made their pilgrimage south for spring training in 1965, they did so without their best player. Allen was not happy with his contract and decided to hold out. The media were highly critical of the brooding young star. "Can you imagine wanting more money to play baseball?" The seeds of hostility were irreversibly sown and Allen battled the Philadelphia media and fans. The same writers who referred to him as "humble" during his rookie season now found him to be an "enigma" and an "ingrate." "Allen Not Earning Big Salary," headlines declared. Naturally, Phillies fans concurred. The Phillies were still a second division club. In spite of posting big numbers at the plate, Allen had to be the problem. By now, Allen had begun wearing a batting helmet on the field to protect himself from projectiles launched by local "fans," causing his teammates to bestow upon him the nickname "Crash."[455] "They would throw change, chicken bones, half pints, anything they could find," Allen later told *Sports Illustrated*. But Allen had no batting helmet to protect his home, where "fans" threw rocks through his windows, dumped garbage and drove over his lawn, threatened his wife on the telephone, and taunted his young children.

In 1965, Phillies first baseman Frank Thomas pushed Allen too far. Thomas was frustrated by his lack of playing time and found a target for his displeasure in Allen. "Shine my shoes, boy?" Thomas would often ask the Phillies' black players. On July 3, 1965, during the Phillies' batting practice, Thomas responded to gibes from Johnny Callison and Allen by screaming to Allen, "What are you trying to be, another Muhammad Clay, always running your mouth off?" Allen snapped and hit Thomas with a left to the jaw. Thomas swung back with a bat and hit Allen on the shoulder. The Phillies immediately released Thomas and forbade anyone in the organization to discuss the fight.[456] Thomas resorted to radio and television for sympathy. "All they had to do was call a press conference and clear things up," Allen said later. "They wouldn't. They had a losing team, they had to get people out to the park, so they said, 'Boo that black sumbuck. Go ahead, he won't say anything.'" And Allen wouldn't, his vow of silence mandated by management. So what else could he do? Hold out for more and more money, that's what.

After posting a .317 batting average, slugging 40 home runs, scoring 112 runs, driving in 110 runs, and recording a National League–leading slugging average of .632 in 1966, Allen held out again. He avoided spring training in 1967 and was eventually rewarded with a $85,000 contract, which according to numerous media reports was the most ever paid to a fourth-year player. "So what?" said Allen, knowing he was worth it. "They [the Phillies] say I'll make the money later," Allen repeated to *Sport* magazine. "But I say why pay for something you're not going to get? Say you're buying a 1955 Cadillac. You won't pay the price just because it's been around. In '55 when it was qualified to do the job, you paid full price for it. Now it's not worth it. A ballplayer should be paid for his production, not seniority. Seniority don't drive in any runs. If it did Ty Cobb would still be playing." Irrefutable logic to Allen, but not to the Philadelphia media and fans. The more money Allen made, the more he was resented and the more bizarre his behavior became. Dick missed curfews and batting practice. He would show up 15 minutes before game time and pronounce himself ready to play. Even more infuriating to management was the fact that he could do so and still be their best hitter.

In August 1967, Allen severed two tendons and the ulnar nerve in his right hand when his hand broke through the headlight of a car he was pushing.[457] Later, he was arrested in a fight in a bar (charges were later dropped) and missed team airplane flights. After appearing late for a game in New York, he was suspended for 20 days.[458] The Philadelphia media blamed Allen for causing two managers, Gene Mauch and Bob Skinner, to be fired. On the field, however, Dick continued to post enviable numbers.

In spite of his fine on-the-field performance, Allen was hardly blameless and he knew it. His love for horses not only helped him to forget his problems on the field, it kept him away from the ballpark. He purchased a number of racehorses and spent much of his time at the racetrack, although rarely betting large amounts.

Allen's aloofness toward baseball, and in particular Philadelphia, further infuriated local scribes. They became much less tactful in their reporting about him and his off-the-field behavior. "Richie Allen, who has been known to over-swing both on and off the field...." began one story. "Allen's diet is equally divided between imported and domestic," another scribe reported. It was true, Allen was resorting to the bottle for refuge from the Philadelphia fans' constant jeering. Yet, his performance on the field never faltered. Baseball and boozing were a combination associated with some of the game's biggest stars from Ty Cobb and Babe Ruth to Mickey Mantle and Whitey Ford. An important difference for those players, of course, was that they were white and the media seldom reported it. But Dick Allen was different: he was black, outspoken, belligerent, and fair game.

Larry Merchant had a front row seat for the Dick Allen phenomenon, as an editor and writer for the *Philadelphia Daily News* and the *New York Post*. Merchant told writer Tim Whitaker that Allen was too hot to ignore. "In terms of hot copy, Richie Allen was right up there with the epic personalities of the sixties," said Merchant. "Everything was so titanic about Allen—from his home runs into the light towers to his fights with management. He was a walking headline. He was the guy everybody wanted to write about. Problem was, he didn't understand the relationship between the press and a superstar. He didn't take any responsibility for his image." When pressed by Whitaker whether the media also had a responsibility to their readers and themselves to at least try to understand and interpret Allen's complexities irrespective of his superstar status, Merchant was hardly compassionate. "Maybe," he replied. "But understand, Allen was a good story—and that's what journalism is all about. Getting the story. Look, when a guy gets in a fight with a teammate, then doesn't show up at the ballpark a few times and blames it on traffic, then pushes his hand through a headlight, things escalate to the point where everybody just thinks he's a fuck-up, and that's what we wrote."[459]

Dick Allen came of age in the mid–1960s and early 1970s, a time when it was hip to be rebellious. But Allen was far more hip than rebellious. He was just being his own man. "Richie Allen arrived at the ballpark looking as if he got his clothes out of Currier & Ives," Jim Murray once wrote. "The lace shirt, the bell-bottomed trousers, the Edwardian coat, the jodhpurs, the purple gold-rimmed glasses made him look like a guy on his way to a duel."[460] "My sign, Pisces, is two fish—one going along with the flow, cool; the other fighting the current," Allen told *Sports Illustrated*. "I can't do anything that isn't me. But I've found that if you go along with these guys it saves a whole lot of trouble. But it isn't me. But the trouble isn't either." But, hey man, it was the '60s and Richie was hangin' with Joe Willie Namath at his swinging Bachelors III club and diggin' the Temptations, James Brown, Marvin Gaye, Al Green, and Aretha Franklin. And in this era of free love, Allen felt compelled to indulge, in spite of being married at the tender age of 22. Allen did it all.

Try as he might, Allen just couldn't lie low. It was bad enough that the local hacks made a meal of him, but even the national scribes couldn't resist his charisma. When NASA's astronauts came back from walking on the moon in 1969, they were feted with a two-page spread in *Life* magazine. In the same issue, Allen warranted four pages. Of course, all the astronauts did was walk on the moon for a few minutes. According to conventional logic, Dick Allen had been living on the moon for years.

Not surprisingly, Allen yearned for an escape from Philadelphia. In 1969, after six seasons with the Phillies, in which he averaged 30 home runs, 90 runs batted in, 98 runs scored, and a batting average exceeding .300, Allen got his wish. In a trade of troubled and troublesome star players, Philadelphia sent Dick Allen, Octavio "Cookie" Rojas, and Jerry Johnson to the St. Louis Cardinals in exchange for Tim McCarver, Joe Hoerner, Byron Browne, and All-Star center fielder Curt Flood.[461] Finally, Allen was liberated. But one man's freedom would become another man's prison.

Curt Flood grew up in predominantly black Oakland, California, and spent most of his minor league career playing in the Deep South. Playing in the South required more than a cultural adjustment, it was a complete affront to Flood's senses. In his autobiography, *The Way It Is,* Flood recounted how the constant racial abuse he encountered almost shattered his will: "I used to break into tears as soon as I reached the safety of my room. I felt too young for this ordeal."[462] Introspective but resilient, Flood endured and became a key member of the powerful St. Louis Cardinals teams of the 1960s. Together with Bob Gibson, Bill White,

Curt Flood

Lou Brock, Julian Javier, Julio Gotay, Orestes "Minnie" Minoso, and Orlando Cepeda, Flood helped integrate Major League Baseball in one of America's most racially divided cities. Flood captured seven straight Gold Glove awards, set a record by playing 226 consecutive games without making an error, and posted a .987 lifetime fielding percentage, while maintaining a career batting average of .293. *Sports Illustrated* deemed Flood to be "The Best Centerfielder in Baseball," declaring that his defensive acumen exceeded that of even the great Willie Mays. In the clubhouse and on the field, Flood was a natural leader who served as co-captain of the Cardinals from 1965 through 1969. He became my favorite Cardinal after Stan Musial's retirement in 1963.

There was another side to Curt Flood that frightened and intimidated the secular world of Major League Baseball. Flood was from Oakland, home of the Black Panthers, and agreed with many of the basic principles of black power. He was a man of intellect, which automatically made him suspect to baseball's owners, and he was a black man making noise in a game controlled by white men. Flood was an accomplished portrait painter, owned his own photography business, and was as comfortable in the company of the era's political activists as he was in the clubhouse.

In 1968, the Cardinals were baseball's best-paid team, becoming the first club to have a $1 million payroll.[463] During that season, Curt Flood batted over .300 and the Cardinals won the National League pennant. In negotiations for his 1969 player contract, Flood asked Cardinals owner August "Gussie" Busch for a raise to $100,000 from his $72,500 1968 salary. The imperious Busch, a firm practitioner of baseball's patriarchal approach, was incensed by Flood's audacious request and the activities of the Major League Baseball Players Association during the 1968-1969 offseason. After further discussions and a brief holdout, Flood ultimately received a salary increase to $90,000.[464] During spring training in 1969, Busch openly admonished his players in a clubhouse sermon, drawing into question their work ethic, attitudes, and continued support by the fans.[465] According to Busch, the players had become complacent and the fans had become critical of their effort and performance. Didn't the players realize how privileged they were to be making a living at this, the greatest of American games? Busch's pompous attempt to enhance team morale and define the team's mission backfired. After capturing three National League pennants and two World Series championships in a four-year period, the 1969 Cardinals skidded to fourth place, Flood's batting average slipped to .285, and an increasingly disenchanted Flood became more vocal in his protest against baseball's archaic practices.

In early October 1969, in Richard Nixon's first year as President, shortly after the New York Mets won their first World Series championship, and less than three months after Neil Armstrong became the first earthling to walk on the moon, Curt Flood received a telephone call from Jim Tooney, a mid-level Cardinals official, advising him that he had been traded to the Philadelphia Phillies.[466] At 31 years of age, Flood did not want to leave St. Louis. He had previously been traded from the Cincinnati Reds to St. Louis where he had established friendships and business interests. Flood had grown accustomed to St. Louis, where black players were more readily accepted than in Philadelphia.

Flood decided not to accept his transfer to the Phillies and wrote to Major League commissioner Bowie Kuhn:

> Dear Mr. Kuhn:
>   After twelve years in the major leagues, I do not feel that I am a piece of property to be bought and sold irrespective of my wishes. I believe that any system which produces that result violates my basic rights as a citizen and is inconsistent with the laws of the United States and of the several States.

It is my desire to play baseball in 1970, and I am capable of playing. I have received a contract offer from the Philadelphia club, but I believe I have the right to consider offers from other clubs before making any decisions. I, therefore, request that you make known to all Major League clubs my feelings in this matter, and advise them of my availability for the 1970 season.

Sincerely,

Curt Flood[467]

In reply, Kuhn informed Flood that his choices were limited to playing for the Phillies or not playing professional baseball.

Emboldened by a few of his more activist friends, Flood decided to bring a legal action against Major League Baseball in hopes of eradicating the game's reserve system. Flood sought support from the Major League Baseball Players Association.[468] Although executive director Marvin Miller had begun to gain some momentum in elevating the consciousness of the union's members to assert their rights, many were still worried about the implications of Flood's suit. During a meeting between Flood and the union's executive board, Giants player representative Tom Haller addressed some of the concerns secretly being voiced. Noting that the 1960s was a period of black militance, Haller asked Flood whether he wanted to bring the legal action because he was black and Major League Baseball was discriminatory.[469] Flood deftly responded to this pointed question by noting that, although he believed he had been the object of discrimination, organized baseball's policies and practices affected all players equally and his color was beside the point. Miller warned Flood of the dangers of bringing a legal action, the unlikelihood of success, the fact that the owners had far greater resources and influence than Flood, the probable vindictiveness of Major League Baseballs' owners, and the reality that Flood's Major League Baseball career was probably finished if he went forward with a lawsuit. Flood acknowledged Miller's advice, but reiterated his determination to proceed.[470] After being convinced of Flood's sincerity, integrity, and convictions, the union overcame its initial reluctance and threw its full support behind Flood.[471] Arthur J. Goldberg, former United States Supreme Court Justice, United States Ambassador to the United Nations, United States Secretary of Labor, legal counsel for the United Steelworkers of America, and long-time critic of Major League Baseball's reserve system, was enlisted to head Flood's legal team.[472]

Curt Flood was now prepared to attack Major League Baseball, that most sanctified, and sanctimonious, American institution. Although his actions would constitute nothing short of blasphemy, Flood later explained that he had no other recourse. "I'm a child of the sixties, I'm a man of the 60's. During that period of time this country was coming apart

at the seams. We were in Southeast Asia.... Good men were dying for
America and for the Constitution. In the southern part of the United
States we were marching for civil rights and Dr. King had been assassinated, and we lost the Kennedys. And to think that merely because I was
a professional baseball player, I could ignore what was going on outside
the walls of Busch Stadium [was] truly hypocrisy and now I found that
all of those rights that these great Americans were dying for, I didn't have
in my own profession."[473]

On January 16, 1970, Curt Flood filed suit against commissioner
Bowie Kuhn and the owners of Major League Baseball's 24 teams in the
United States District Court for the Southern District of New York. Flood
asserted that Major League Baseball's reserve system violated United States
Federal antitrust laws. Flood had been grilled by his colleagues in the
Major League Baseball Players Association and briefed by Goldberg and
his legal team. He understood that, irrespective of the outcome, his baseball career was finished. Prior to the trade, Flood had been earning an
annual salary of $90,000, a significant amount in 1970. Only 31 years old,
he would still have had at least four or five prime earning years ahead of
him. Flood knew all this, but he was undeterred. He was a black man bat-
tling the white power structure during a time of heightened hostility and
black militancy. Major League Baseball would demonize him, painting
Flood as a man who was attempting to destroy the most cherished and
traditional of American institutions at a time when the country desperately needed a semblance of order and a link to simpler times. "If the
newspaper was typical," Flood recalled, "it lied that a victory for Flood
would mean the collapse of our national pastime. God profaned! Flag des-
ecrated! Motherhood defiled! Apple pie blasphemed! The animal was furious. Them niggers is never satisfied."[474]

In his autobiography, former Major League Commissioner Bowie
Kuhn recounts the conservative nature of Major League Baseball's owners.[475] Not surprisingly, Cardinals owner Gussie Busch, a man who had
battled against union intrusions into his breweries for decades, was aghast
at Flood's behavior. "With considerable emotion, [Busch] advised
reporters that he could not fathom what was happening in our country,"
Flood wrote. "He declared that my recalcitrance was somehow related to
the unrest on American campuses. He was absolutely right. And when he
said that he could not understand it, he was absolutely right for the second time in a day."[476]

Major League Baseball's reserve system, established by William A.
Hulbert and the National League in the 1870s, had bound players and
depressed salaries for nearly a century. Prior to adoption of the reserve

system, player compensation had absorbed approximately 60 percent of total baseball revenues. When the Major Leagues' reserve system achieved its full fruition, less than 15 percent of Major League revenues was paid in salaries. After the demise of the reserve system in the 1970s, player salaries increased again to constitute nearly approximately 53 percent of Major League Baseball's total reported revenues in 1999.[477] By combining the reserve system and a perpetual team option on a player's services, once a player signed the standard form players contract, he was the property of the team with which he signed until he was traded or sold to another club, released, or retired. The player had no ability to negotiate to supply his services to other teams and the owner retained total control.

If Flood were hoping to tap into the social and civil unrest of the times, he would find it difficult making a case for a highly paid baseball player as a champion of reform. He would clearly have to tackle baseball on a larger stage by demythologizing the sport and exposing it for the callous and oppressive business that it was. This would prove to be no mean feat. Not only was Flood forced to battle baseball's owners and management, he received little support from his fellow players.[478] Only Jackie Robinson, Hank Greenberg, and Jim Brosnan, all of whom were now retired, and maverick former owner Bill Veeck testified on behalf of Flood.[479] At one time or another, Robinson, Greenberg, and Veeck had all been pariahs in Major League Baseball.

In spite of having retired more than a decade earlier, the graying and dignified Robinson was still an outspoken and unyielding firebrand. Robinson refused to participate in old-timers games and other official baseball functions until he saw progress in the hiring of blacks in management. Like many pioneers before him, his position as a seminal figure would not be fully accorded him until after his death. But Jackie Robinson still terrified Major League Baseball. As baseball's first Jewish star in the 1930s, Greenberg, like Robinson after him, had been subjected to vicious racial abuse. "There was added pressure being Jewish," Greenberg later recalled. "How the hell could you get up to home every day and have some son of a bitch call you a Jew bastard and a kike and a sheeny and get on your ass without feeling the pressure?"[480]

Nevertheless, baseball's ownership was smug. Flood and the Major League Baseball Players Association could only produce four men who had the nerve to testify against the game and they were willing to testify only because they no longer needed the game. The owners still controlled baseball and it was obvious that, if an individual wished to make his livelihood in the game, he would steer clear of helping Curt Flood. Not a single contemporary player came forward to assist Flood, who put his career on

the line to improve the players' cause. Indeed, management recruited players to testify against Flood. Flood later recalled, "My guys, my colleagues
didn't stand up with me. And I can't make any excuse for them. Had we
shown any amount of solidarity, if the superstars had stood up and said,
'We're with Curt Flood,' if the superstars had walked into the courtroom
in New York and made their presence known, I think that the owners
would have gotten the message very clearly and given me a chance to win
that case."[481] "If I had six hundred players behind me, there would be no
reserve clause," Flood concluded.[482]

But the cavalry never arrived, which made Flood's next task much
easier. It was time to take a sledgehammer to some of baseball's sanctimonious myths and Flood chose to do so by writing *The Way It Is,* both
an autobiography and an exposé of baseball. "I was offended by the disparity between American reality and American pretension," Flood wrote.
"I wanted reality upgraded, pretension abolished. Above all, I saw life as
all of a piece. The hypocrisies of the baseball industry could not possibly
have been sustained unless they were symptoms of a wider affliction.
Wherever I turned, I found fresh evidence that this was so. Baseball was
socially relevant, and so was my rebellion against it. The knowledge fueled
and fortified me."[483] It was one thing to go after Major League Baseball's
ownership and management; even the general public was becoming aware
of their parochial and dictatorial manner. But going after heroes was
another matter. Echoing the lurid revelations of pitcher Jim Bouton's *Ball
Four,*[484] Flood recounted the debauchery of Major League Baseball—the
matter-of-fact sexual arrangements made with legions of baseball groupies
and the daily ingestion of lethal drugs to help players survive the grind of
lengthy seasons. Bouton had recently outraged baseball's players and
establishment with his detailed chronicle of baseball's sexual excesses,
drugs, racial friction, profanity, and parsimonious proprietors. So sensa-
tional was Bouton's book that it sold more copies faster than any previous sports-related book. Naturally, Bouton and Flood were reviled by
players and management alike for revealing baseball's dirty secrets.

Flood went on to vilify baseball's management for its treatment of
ballplayers, who had become no more than a "a consignment of goods"
and "chattel." Flood wrote, "baseball's terminology betrays its essential
attitudes, which are those of animal husbandry. Baseball regards us as
sheep, livestock with which higher forms of life may tamper at will."[485]

The Sherman Antitrust Act of 1890[486] prohibits contracts, combinations, and conspiracies in restraint of interstate commerce. The Clayton
Antitrust Act of 1914[487] gives private individuals the right to sue for recov-

ery of treble damages for violations of the antitrust laws. Because it seemed clear that Major League Baseball was engaged in interstate commerce and that Major League owners had contracted, combined, and conspired to restrain the movement of players, the legal foundation for Flood's suit seemed solid. As discussed in Chapters 2 and 8 of this book, however, the United States Supreme Court had previously ruled otherwise. In 1922, in *Federal Baseball Club of Baltimore, Inc. v. National League of Professional Clubs*,[488] in an opinion written by Justice Oliver Wendell Holmes which displayed highly questionable logic, the Supreme Court held that Major League Baseball did not constitute a business engaged in interstate commerce and, thus, was not an appropriate subject for the federal courts to regulate. This watershed opinion created the so-called "antitrust exemption" for Major League Baseball. In spite of the specious reasoning of this opinion, and broad extensions by the judiciary of the scope of the federal interstate commerce power in the decades after that opinion was rendered, in 1953 the United States Supreme Court affirmed the *Federal Baseball* decision in *Toolson v. New York Yankees*.[489] These apparently controlling decisions were cited as authority by the United States District Court for the Southern District of New York and the United States Court of Appeals for the Second Circuit, both of which courts decided against Flood. United States District Court Judge Irving Ben Cooper stated categorically, "Baseball has been the national pastime for over one hundred years and enjoys a unique place in our American heritage. The game is on a higher ground, it behooves us to keep it there."[490] Surprisingly, however, the United States Supreme Court granted Flood's petition for *certiorari* to review the lower courts' decisions "in order to look again at this troublesome and unusual situation."

When United States Supreme Court Justice and ardent baseball enthusiast Harry Blackmun delivered the Supreme Court's affirmation of the decisions of the United States District Court and the United States Court of Appeals for the Second Circuit, he began by listing 88 legendary baseball players and cited "Casey at the Bat" and "Tinker to Evers to Chance."[491] The Supreme Court recognized that Major League Baseball was engaged in interstate commerce, but noted, "If there is an inconsistency and illogic in all this, it is an inconsistency and illogic of long standing that is to be remedied by the Congress and not by this Court."[492] In a stinging dissent that dismissed the specious reasoning of the majority decision, Justice Thurgood Marshall, who had served as counsel to the NAACP and argued *Brown v. Board of Education*[493] in the Supreme Court, urged that the "virtual slavery" of Major League Baseball's reserve system should be eliminated.[494]

Although the Supreme Court denied Flood's claim, his historic challenge to baseball's omnipotence signaled the beginning of the end of the owners' unilateral control over players and their salaries. Flood's willingness to battle Major League Baseball later emboldened others to question the iron control of baseball's owners. Moreover, as indicated above, the specious holdings of *Federal Baseball* and *Toolson,* cited as controlling in the two lower Federal court decisions in *Flood v. Kuhn,* were based on Justice Holmes's contorted 1922 logic, reasoning that was much harder to justify a half century later. Because Major League Baseball's legal counsel were concerned that these cases would be reversed by the Supreme Court in *Flood,* they argued in the Supreme Court that, because the players were now represented by the Major League Baseball Players Association, the reserve system was an issue for collective bargaining, not a matter for federal antitrust litigation. Under the National Labor Relations Act, labor agreements are generally not required to comply with antitrust legislation if unions agree to their exemption from such laws. Although this argument may have helped the owners to win the *Flood* case, it provided the lever that ultimately enabled the players to pry open the reserve system's chains in the Messersmith-McNally arbitration which is discussed in Chapter 10 of this book. Because of Curt Flood, future generations of baseball players will not be bound for their careers to their initial employers or find that the federal antitrust rules which protect other workers do not apply to them.

Twenty-six years after the United States Supreme Court delivered its decision in *Flood v. Kuhn,* the United States Congress enacted the Curt Flood Act of 1998,[495] which repealed the judicially created antitrust exemption for baseball, but only with respect to labor relations for Major League baseball players. The Curt Flood Act amends the Clayton Act[496] to provide that practices "directly relating to or affecting major league baseball players" are subject to the federal antitrust laws. The Curt Flood Act specifically excludes from its coverage minor league baseball, the amateur draft, relations between the major and minor leagues, franchise relocations, intellectual property, broadcasting rights, and major league umpires, all of which continue to be exempted from the application of the federal antitrust laws.

After testifying on behalf of Curt Flood, Jackie Robinson made a rare Major League appearance to throw out the first ball of the 1972 World Series. Robinson, only 53 years old but ravaged by diabetes and heart disease, toured the clubhouses of the Cincinnati Reds and the Oakland A's. Although Robinson had only been retired from the game for 15 years, a number of younger players, both black and white, had never heard of this pioneer of the Major Leagues' integration. They would not have an opportunity to get to know him much better. Ten days later, Jackie Robinson died.

Now out of baseball and officially out of work, Curt Flood had experienced enough of apple pie and the greatest country in the world. He moved to Europe and continued his painting career in anonymity.[497] Although he made an ill-fated attempt to resume playing with the Washington Senators in 1971,[498] Flood's baseball career effectively ended with his 1969 letter to commissioner Bowie Kuhn. On January 20, 1997, Curt Flood succumbed to throat cancer and died at the age of 57. "It's sad," former teammate Lou Brock told the *St. Louis Post Dispatch*, "most of the pioneers end up with an arrow in their backs. And he certainly was one of those who had an arrow in his back. As a pioneer, he never got his just due. God will amend that." Andy Messersmith told the *San Francisco Examiner* that Flood "was the guy who started it all. The idea of mobility, or restricted mobility, in baseball, all of that started with his incident in St. Louis. But he was also a big mover in the equality aspects, not just baseball. He had a lot of things to say about a lot of issues. Fortunately, a lot of people listened to what he had to say."

In one of his last interviews, a reflective Flood lamented the end of his innocence to a reporter from the *San Francisco Chronicle*. "I believed in the great American dream. I believed if you were right that nine smart men on the Supreme Court would say that. I believed if you were right, people would understand and be compassionate." But Flood expressed few regrets about the position he had taken. "I lost money, coaching jobs, a shot at the Hall of Fame. But when you weigh that against all the things that are really and truly important, things that are deep inside you, then I think I have succeeded. People try to make a Greek tragedy of my life, and they can't do it. I'm too happy. Sometimes the simplest concepts, like morality, are the most difficult for people to understand." Flood never admitted any bitterness or animosity toward the players of today and their multi-million dollar contracts. He simply stated that they were getting the rights the players of his generation had been so unjustly denied.

After playing the 1970 season in St. Louis, Dick Allen spent the next seven seasons shuffling among four other teams. In 1972, while playing for the Chicago White Sox, Allen was named the American League's Most Valuable Player. Allen even had another stint with the Phillies, helping that team win the 1976 National League East title. In 14 Major League seasons, Allen hit 351 home runs with a career batting average of .292. "'Richie played with fire in his eyes, always,'" said former Cardinals and Giants star Orlando Cepeda. "'Never read that in no newspaper.'"[499]

Yet, it is difficult to escape the view that Dick Allen was a wasted talent. Bill James has concluded that Allen was "[t]he second-most controversial player in baseball history, behind Rogers Hornsby. Allen had baseball talent equal to that of Willie Mays, Hank Aaron, or Joe DiMaggio, and did have three or four seasons when he was as good as a player as anyone in baseball, but lost half of his career or more to immaturity and emotional instability."[500]

Allen's contribution to transforming Major League Baseball from a plantation system to the modern free agency system pales in comparison to that of Curt Flood. But as Major League Baseball's first flamboyant, outspoken, and unapologetic black star, Allen was an important figure in baseball's transformation. But Allen also was a serious man who was active in players' union matters. According to Marvin Miller, executive director of the Major League Baseball Players Association, "I recall the positive contributions of many players at [the meeting in 1969 to approve holdouts from signing 1970 player contracts until players benefits and pension plan issues were settled], but for some reason I recall most vividly Dick Allen. Always an impressive figure, he came to the meeting dressed in a dashiki. He did not speak in the early part of the meeting but later spoke with quiet dignity in a fashion that indicated he had been listening carefully. He was eloquent and forceful, and the other players listened intently. He didn't speak as a superstar, but as a player who understood both the issues and the importance of the players' moving forward as a group. I wish some of the writers who were so quick to jump on him in later years had seen him in this light."[501]

Allen's behavior played a significant role in changing the manner in which journalists approach baseball stories. For many years, baseball writers such as Dick Young of the *New York Daily News* were mouthpieces for management, ready to publicly humiliate players who stepped out of line. Allen forced a number of writers to consider their actions more carefully. Three writers in particular, Jim Murray of the *Los Angeles Times,* Art Spander of the *San Francisco Examiner* and *The Sporting News,* and Melvin Durslag of the *Los Angeles Herald-Examiner,* found Allen to be a unique treasure in a world of sporting robots. According to Murray, "On the Phillies, he stands out like Man O' War in a mule barn. Richie Allen so clearly belongs in a World Series that the fans of Philadelphia are furious at him for not getting into one."[502] Murray also attempted to answer a number of charges leveled against Allen in Philadelphia. "He drinks. Does he now? Well, that makes him unique in baseball. Think what it might have done to Babe Ruth's career."[503]

Spander has long considered himself to be the bard of the baseball field, often prefacing his columns with quotes from the likes of Shakespeare, Yeats, and Joyce. Writing in 1974, after Allen "retired" from the White Sox with two weeks remaining in the season, Spander invoked Henry David Thoreau: "If a man does not keep pace with his companions, perhaps it is because he hears a different drummer. Let him step to the music he hears, however measured or far away." Spander went on to observe that Allen had provoked a chorus of ridicule from sportswriters who were jealous of him. "Because Allen, a marvelous talent on the baseball field, didn't conform to their standards, he was strange, indeed frightening. After all, anyone who could walk out of a $225,000 occupation couldn't be completely normal, could he?"[504]

In Allen, Durslag saw baseball's last poet. Durslag described how Allen tried to be a model citizen when he was traded to the Los Angeles Dodgers in 1970. "He came to camp on opening day and he never left. He granted interviews to every segment of the media. When the season began he got to the park at 5 p.m. each day and took infield and batting practice and did more interviews on radio and television. Do you know what happened to this poor man? After two months he was hitting .230. Healthily disillusioned, he found the remedy. He went back to reporting at 7:30, forgot about infield and batting practice and shut off the interviews. And soon he was hitting .295 and leading the club in homers and RBI's. So no one knows better than Richie the perils of conformity, and he rejects a system that could shorten a man's time in the game." When Allen's Major League career had seemingly come to an end in 1977, after Oakland A's owner Charlie Finley suspended him for taking a shower during the sixth inning of a game, Durslag realized baseball would miss Dick more than he would miss it.

"It is very hard to know Allen and dislike him," Durslag wrote. "Fellow players like him. Few managers he has left put the knock on him. Ownerships usually give him a good reference, too. Dick engages in few arguments, rarely is belligerent, has been known to get into only one fight in 17 years in baseball—and he didn't provoke that one. When he leaves a club, it isn't often in a storm of protest. He just sort of eases out the door, vanishes and isn't seen again, not bothering to explain the reasons for his departure." When Allen suggested that he might play in Japan, Durslag further speculated that playing baseball and living in Japan would seem a likely environment for Dick Allen, a poet in search of utopia. "And the masses join in bidding him sayonara."[505]

Curt Flood and Dick Allen, two seemingly dissimilar characters, had a front row seat for the most turbulent of times in America and in baseball. Both Dick Allen and Curt Flood were their own men who joined Jackie Robinson in helping to liberate future generations of Major League baseball players.

Chapter 10

EMANCIPATION

All persons held as slaves ... shall be then, thenceforth, and forever free....
        —President Abraham Lincoln (1862)

Players have been bought, sold and exchanged as though they were sheep, instead of American citizens. "Reservation" ... became for them another name for property rights in the player.... By a combination among themselves, stronger than the strongest trust, the owners were able to enforce the most arbitrary measures, and the player had either to submit or get out of the profession in which he had spent years attaining proficiency.
        —National Brotherhood of Professional
        Base Ball Players' Manifesto attacking
        the National League of Professional
        Baseball Clubs (1889)

I think $200,000 for one year is the limit any star can hope to make. I also think that the player who seeks and gets that much may be pricing himself right out of the game.
        —Wes Parker

Let me get this straight. The owners are about to shut down baseball when it's more prosperous than it's ever been, and the players are the ones who have to get their urine tested?
        —Ron Darling on the eve of the 1990
        Major League Baseball owners' lock-out

In the quarter century that followed Curt Flood's courageous decision to challenge Major League Baseball's reserve system in the federal courts, many memorable events occurred in Major League Baseball. Longstanding records were broken. Expansion and franchise movements continued to alter baseball's map. Veteran greats retired. Exciting new stars emerged. Thrilling pennant races and post-season action were witnessed by ever larger audiences. A new breed of owner appeared. Scandals stained the game's integrity. But the most dramatic and compelling events of those 25 years occurred off the field, where ownership and players squared off in a series of epic conflagrations for control of Major League Baseball and its finances. These battles were fought and won not with pitching, defense, speed, and home runs, but by lawyers, economists, accountants, and arbitrators.

As discussed in Chapter 2 of this book, Columbia Law School graduate and New York Gothams shortstop and field captain John Montgomery Ward established baseball's first labor union, the Brotherhood of Professional Base Ball Players, in 1885.[506] In 1889, after disputes with the National League and the American Association over a number of issues including the National League's implementation of a fixed salary classification system, the Brotherhood formed a new Players League which did not employ a reserve system[507] and provided greater rights to players.[508] But the poorly capitalized Players League folded after only one season of play. With the demise of the Players League, the Brotherhood also disappeared. Three other efforts at player unionization, the League Protective Association (1900–02), the Baseball Players' Fraternity (1912), and the American Baseball Guild (1946), met similar fates.[509] Finally, in 1953, when the average Major League player's salary was approximately $13,000, the Major League Baseball Players Association was formed to attempt to improve the amounts of, and method of funding, player pensions.[510] For the first several years of its existence, the Major League Baseball Players Association's sole accomplishment was to obtain the owners' agreement to fund the players pension with 60 percent of the revenues from the All-Star Game and the World Series and to raise the annual minimum player's salary to $6,000.[511] During those years, the Major League Baseball Players Association was financed by Major League Baseball's owners.[512]

With the pension plan scheduled to expire in 1967, the Players Association became concerned that the players' pension would be eliminated or downgraded.[513] At that time, the pension was of crucial importance to the players. Few players were college-educated or had skills other than baseball. The Major League annual minimum salary was only $6,000 and the average player salary was approximately $19,000.[514] Few players were able to fund their retirement from savings and even fewer could expect

John Montgomery Ward

lucrative careers after their playing days ended. Total salary and pension costs to Major League owners accounted for only 18.5 percent of reported Major League revenues.[515] Several leaders of the Major League Baseball Players Association decided that a new full-time spokesman for the union was needed to address the pension issue.

One of the Major League Players Association's leaders, pitcher Robin Roberts, asked Dean George Taylor of the University of Pennsylvania's Wharton School of Finance, one of America's foremost labor authorities, for a recommendation. Professor Taylor recommended Marvin Julian Miller, the chief economist for, and assistant to the president of, the United Steelworkers of America.[516] Miller, the 48-year-old son of working-class immigrant parents, had grown up in Brooklyn as a Dodgers fan, worked his way through New York University, and, for the next quarter century, worked in a number of labor-related jobs, both in the public and private sectors.[517] In 1966, after several interviews with leaders of the Players Association, and in spite of stiff opposition from many players who were conservative, suspicious of collective labor action, and exceedingly wary of hiring a spokesman with a union background, Miller was named executive director of the 500-member Major League Baseball Players Association.[518] Fortunately for Miller, the players had exceedingly low expectations from the Players Association. According to Jim Bouton, "If they [the Major League owners] had just said, 'We'll raise the minimum salary to $10,000, then raise it $1,000 a year for the next twenty years. Then we'll throw in an annual cost-of-living increase on the meal money.' If they'd have just done something like that, nobody would have looked to Marvin Miller. But with everything they did, they helped Marvin."[519]

When Miller became executive director of the Major League Baseball Players Association, the union had only $5,400 in its bank account.[520] The owners immediately withdrew their financial support of the union and Miller had to find other ways to fund its activities.[521] Miller immediately negotiated a contract with Coca-Cola to feature players' likenesses under bottle caps.[522] He also convinced the players to contribute $344 each in annual dues, to be deducted from the players' salaries.[523] Miller established the first permanent offices for the Players Association on Park Avenue in New York City[524] and hired Richard M. "Dick" Moss, a former associate legal counsel of the United Steelworkers of America, as legal counsel to the Players Association.[525] From these humble beginnings, Marvin Miller effected the most radical changes in the history of baseball.

Shortly after accepting his position with the Players Association, Miller began the time-consuming and strenuous process of educating players, assembling information regarding current employment conditions,

Marvin Miller (center) with player representatives.

and listening to player grievances on a variety of issues.[526] Prior to Miller's efforts, the Players Association did not even have comprehensive information on its members' salaries. The Players Association had not previously gathered such information and the owners were eager to keep the information confidential. Miller assembled the information and disseminated it to all players. Many players were surprised and angered to learn that management had deceived them in salary negotiations by alleging that comparable players' salaries were lower than their true compensation.[527] In 1967, the average annual Major League salary was $19,000 and the median annual salary was $17,000. Seven percent of Major League players received the minimum salary of $6,000 and 40 percent were paid $12,000 or less.[528]

The experience of Miller and Moss in labor matters, and particularly their work in the Steelworkers Union, one of America's most sophisticated and aggressive unions, brought new levels of competence and understanding to the Players Association. Miller's careful education of the players slowly raised their consciousness. Cardinals player representative Tim McCarver recalls Miller's efforts to educate the players. "The most remarkable thing to me, looking back, is what a patient man Marvin Miller was. He realized how disparate his knowledge of negotiating and contracts was from ours. So he educated the player reps and they educated the rest. It was a very slow, methodical process. He never let the cart get before the horse. Everything was building from a base."[529] Phillies player representative Bob Boone also reflected on Miller's style. "He was a master at never telling anybody how to do anything. He would just ask questions until you could see the answer for yourself. Marvin was a master at leading you down the right road."[530]

Miller and Moss began to negotiate with the owners on a variety of player issues, including the pension. In 1967, the owners appointed John Gaherin, former president of the Publishers Association of New York and a labor negotiator with more than two decades of experience in a variety of industries, as their principal labor negotiator.[531] The negotiations between the owners' representatives and the Players Association exposed fundamental differences in the objectives of players and owners. Players sought improved pensions and other benefits, modest advances in compensation, fair treatment, and basic due process. The owners' principal concerns were money and complete control over all aspects of baseball, especially player compensation. In themes that were to recur in future negotiations between players and management, players discovered that ownership was ossified, rigid, unyielding, and deceptive. These discoveries and the players' increasing awareness of labor and civil rights issues resulted in the players becoming more militant and ultimately achieving greater gains than if ownership had made reasonable concessions and negotiated honestly.

The owners strenuously resisted dealing with Miller and the Players Association. They refused to accept the premise that anyone could interfere with the manner in which they operated their businesses. American League President Joe Cronin advised Marvin Miller shortly after he was elected as executive director of the Major League Baseball Players Association: "Young man, I've got some advice for you that I want you to remember.... The players come and go, but the owners stay on forever."[532] Dodgers owner Walter O'Malley gave Gaherin a message to take to Miller. "Tell that Jewish boy to go on back to Brooklyn," said O'Malley.[533] The Jewish boy stood firm. So did the players. In 1968, Miller persuaded Major League Baseball's owners to engage in collective bargaining with the Players Association, the first time the owners had so consented. Under the National Labor Relations Act, management and labor are required to meet and negotiate over terms and conditions of employment and both sides must bargain in good faith on such issues. If either side fails to bargain in good faith, the other can file an unfair labor practice charge with the National Labor Relations Board. By early 1969, after a threatened players' strike over the owners' failure to upgrade the players' pension plan or negotiate fairly,[534] Miller had convinced the owners to accept the terms of the Basic Agreement, the first collective bargaining agreement between baseball's owners and players, a critical initial step in improving players' rights. In this initial collective bargaining agreement, the minimum annual Major League player salary was increased from $7,000 to $10,000, spring training and meal money were increased, a formal grievance procedure with appeal to the commissioner was established, the maximum salary cut for renewed contracts was reduced from 25 percent to 20 percent, the annual contribution to the pension plan was nearly tripled from $1.5 million to $4.1 million, various player benefits were improved, and a joint owner-player study of "possible alternatives to the reserve clause as now constituted" was authorized.[535]

Additional gains were made by the Players Association in subsequent negotiations. In 1970, the minimum salary was increased from $10,000 to $12,000 for 1970, $13,500 for 1971, and $15,000 for 1972, the players' share of playoff revenues was increased from 50 percent to 60 percent, the owners recognized the Players Association as the "sole and exclusive collective bargaining agent for all Major League Players," the players were permitted to use agents in negotiating contracts for the first time, and the owners agreed to arbitrate all player grievances not involving "the integrity of the game" before a neutral arbitrator.[536] Of these gains, impartial arbitration would prove to be the most important. The arbitration procedure proposed by Marvin Miller had long been used to resolve economic disputes in the steel industry. Each arbitration would be held before a three-member arbitration tribunal. Major League Baseball's owners would appoint one arbitrator, the Major League Baseball Players Association would appoint one arbitrator, and the owners and the Players Association would agree on a third "neutral" arbitrator. The owners' appointee, John Gaherin, would always vote in favor of the owner; the Players Association's appointee, Marvin Miller, would always vote in favor of the player; and consequently, the neutral arbitrator would decide the case. The neutral arbitrator was appointed to serve in all baseball arbitrations. Either the owners or the Players Association could dismiss the neutral arbitrator, but dismissal would not be effective for an arbitration that was already in progress. In 1970, the average Major League annual salary increased to $29,000, an increase of $5,000 over 1969 and $10,000 higher than the 1965 average.[537]

In 1972, the Major League Baseball Players Association sought further improvements in the pension plan and medical benefits. The owners flatly refused. To establish the credibility of their bargaining position, the members of the Players Association voted 663–10 to effect a work stoppage before the beginning of the 1972 season if their demands were not satisfied.[538] The owners were incensed by the threatened strike. "We voted unanimously to take a stand," said Cardinals owner August "Gussie" Busch. "We're not going to give them another goddamn cent! If they want to strike, let them strike."[539] The rigidity of the owners' position began to galvanize the highly competitive players. The players went on strike and, ten days after the scheduled opening of the regular season, the owners yielded and accepted the same deal that Miller had proposed before the strike.[540] The strike ended and Major League Baseball resumed play.[541] The players' collective action and solidarity had been successful and they experienced the first of what would become a string of significant victories over the owners during the next two decades. Their success also eroded the owners' sense of invincibility and emboldened the players to take further, more aggressive, action. But the vindictive owners punished those players who dared to serve as player representatives, trading or releasing two-thirds of them.[542]

During the 1972 strike negotiations and those that followed, resulting in a new three-year collective bargaining agreement in early 1973, Miller urged the end of the reserve system.[543] The owners refused the Players Association's request, realizing that a free market in players would dramatically increase player salaries. But instead of flatly rejecting the players' position, the owners agreed to resolve by arbitration future disputes over player compensation for players with at least two years of Major League service.[544] The owners had represented to the United States Supreme Court in *Flood v. Kuhn* that the reserve rules were a matter for collective bargaining. Moreover, as discussed above, the owners had agreed in 1970 that all arbitrations not involving the integrity of the game would be conducted by an impartial arbitrator jointly selected by the owners and the players. Marvin Miller suggested a refinement of the owners' arbitration proposal. The owner and the player would each submit a proposed salary figure and the arbitrator would select which of those figures he believed was more reasonable. He would have no power to determine any other compensation level. This system of "final offer arbitration" provided incentives for the owners to make reasonable offers and for the players to make reasonable demands.[545] It also meant that the players' compensation automatically increased in every arbitration because the owners offered salaries higher than those which would have been paid in the absence of the arbitration.[546] At the time, however, most Major League owners believed arbitration was a reasonable compromise for avoiding free agency and would not be costly to them.[547]

The astute Oakland Athletics owner Charles O. Finley, however, foresaw the effect of salary arbitration. "We'll be the nation's biggest assholes if we do this," observed Finley. "You can't win. You'll have guys with no baseball background setting salaries. You'll have a system that drives up the average salary every year. Give them anything they want, but don't give them arbitration."[548] Dick Meyer, president of the St. Louis Cardinals and an experienced labor negotiator at the Anheuser-Busch brewery, also anticipated the adverse impact of arbitration on the owners, predicting, "This will be baseball's ruin."[549] Finley was the only owner who favored complete free agency for all players, realizing that the resulting glut of players on the market would actually reduce salaries. "Let them be free agents every year," Finley presciently counseled. "It'll flood the market with players; it'll keep salaries down."[550] But the owners' ossified stance on player movement, their own egos, and their dislike of Finley would not permit them to accept his advice.

In another significant concession in the 1973 agreement, the owners agreed that players who had played in the Major Leagues for at least ten years and with the same team for at least five years could reject being traded.[551] Under these new rules, Curt Flood could have vetoed his trade from the Cardinals to the Phillies and probably would have received the salary increase the request of which caused him to be traded. Unfortunately for Flood, by the time the owners had accepted these changes to preserve the reserve system, he had lost his case in three federal courts and was out of baseball.

Even without free agency, salary arbitration began to increase salaries. Most arbitration cases were won by the players and, even in those cases that the players lost, they received higher compensation than they would have under the old system.[552] Moreover, many disputes were settled by negotiation before arbitration decisions were issued. Now it was time for other issues to be addressed.

Major League Baseball's reserve system is based on a complicated set of documents, including the Major League Rules, the Basic Agreement, and the Uniform Players Contract, particularly the "reserve clause" and the "option clause" of the Uniform Players Contract. The reserve clause binds a player to his team by prohibiting him from playing with another team during the period of his contract and for the following year. The option clause permits an owner that is unable to reach agreement with a player to unilaterally renew the player's contract for one year. The Players Association interpreted the option clause to mean that owners could renew a player's contract, but only for one year. Owners interpreted the clause to mean that a player's contract could be renewed for one year, but that the option clause which was part of the contract was also renewed, resulting in a perpetually renewable contract.[553]

Since the beginning of the National League's existence, teams had required players to sign contracts containing these clauses and refused to let them begin playing in a season until the contract was signed. In 1969, New York Yankees pitcher Al Downing became the first player to play in spring training without signing a new contract.[554] During the 1970s, several players were allowed to begin playing without signing, so long as they signed contracts before the season ended. In 1972, Cardinals catcher Ted Simmons decided to play out his option year, but in August he signed a new contract with a substantial raise.[555] In 1973, several players decided to play out their options, but during the year all of them were either signed to new contracts or released.[556] In 1974, Yankees relief pitcher Sparky Lyle and San Diego outfielder Bobby Tolan decided to play out their options. Lyle signed a new contract shortly before the end of the season.[557] Tolan had not signed a new contract by the end of the season and the Players Association filed a grievance alleging that Tolan was now a free agent. The case was never heard, however, because Tolan signed a new contract in December.[558]

At the end of the 1974 season, another opportunity to challenge the reserve system arose. Oakland Athletics pitcher Jim "Catfish" Hunter had signed a two-year contract at the beginning of the 1974 season which provided for one-half of his $100,000 annual salary to be paid to him directly and the remainder to be paid to an investment company which would provide Hunter an annuity after he retired from baseball. This deferred income would not be currently taxable to Hunter. Oakland owner Charles O. Finley paid Hunter the portion of his salary that the contract required to be paid directly. After learning that the portion to be paid to the investment company would not be deductible for tax purposes in the year of payment, however, Finley refused to pay the deferred amount.[559] Hunter and the Major League Baseball Players Association protested this failure in writing. Finally, in early October, after Hunter had won 25 games, posted a 2.49 earned run average, and led Oakland to its third consecutive World Series championship, Finley tendered a check for the deferred amount directly to Hunter. Hunter refused the check, filed a grievance under the collective bargaining agreement, and submitted the dispute to arbitration.[560] Hunter's standard form player contract provided Hunter with two remedies for Finley's failure to pay.[561] One choice was to have the payment made in full to the designated investment company. The contract's alternative remedy was that "[T]he Player may terminate this contract.... if the Club shall default in the payments to the Player." Hunter elected to terminate the contract. On December 13, 1974, Major League Baseball's neutral arbitrator, Peter Seitz, declared that Jim Hunter was a free agent.[562]

Hunter was now able to negotiate with all 24 Major League teams. Two weeks later, after fielding offers from virtually every team,[563] he signed a five-year, $3.5 million contract with the New York Yankees, at an average annual salary seven times his $100,000 salary with Oakland.[564] The benefits of arbitration and free agency were immediately apparent to all players and the detriments were equally obvious to all owners. American League President Lee MacPhail observed, "This has shown everybody exactly what free agency could amount to."[565]

The Hunter arbitration involved a pure breach of contract claim and did not challenge the reserve system directly, but it did open the players' eyes to the compensation that would be available if they were free agents. In 1975, a direct challenge to the reserve system was made. Andy Messersmith was the Los Angeles Dodgers' most successful pitcher in the mid–1970s. In negotiations with the club for his 1975 contract, Messersmith, who wanted to remain with the Dodgers, requested that the contract contain a no-trade clause. No team had ever granted a no-trade clause to a player, and Dodgers owner Peter O'Malley was not prepared to be the first.[566] But Messersmith was adamant in his demand. "The money was incredible, but they wouldn't bring the no-trade to the table. I'd gotten stimulated by Marvin [Miller] and Dick [Moss]. Now I understood the significance of what this was all about. I was tired of players having no power and no rights."[567] The Dodgers refused Messersmith's request for a no-trade clause and exercised the option clause in the Major Leagues' standard player's contract to renew his contract for 1975, providing him a $25,000 raise in the process.[568]

Messersmith played out the 1975 season without signing a contract, winning 19 games and posting a 2.29 earned run average. After the end of the 1975 season, Messersmith and the Players Association filed a grievance under Major League Baseball's collective bargaining agreement, asserting that the arbitrator should declare that Messersmith was a free agent and permitted to negotiate with all 24 Major League teams.[569] A grievance was also filed on behalf of former Montreal Expos pitcher Dave McNally who had played during the 1975 season without signing a contract. McNally had been traded to the Expos from the Baltimore Orioles after the 1974 season and retired in June after experiencing recurring arm problems. Although he was retired, McNally was technically still reserved by the Expos.[570]

The owners responded that free agency was not within the province of the arbitrator and filed a lawsuit in the United States District Court seeking to prevent the arbitration of the grievances.[571] The Players Association pointed out to the court that, in the previous five years, Major League Baseball's arbitrators had decided 16 cases involving reserve issues and the owners had not sought to prevent such arbitrations. The court convinced the parties to take the case to the arbitrator, but told the owners they could return to court to contest the arbitrator's jurisdiction over the grievance if they lost the arbitration. Thus, the future of the reserve system would

Andy Messersmith

turn on the arbitrator's interpretation of the option clause, Paragraph 10A of the Uniform Players Contract, which provided: "If prior to March 1, player and club have not agreed ... the club shall have the right ... to renew this contract for the period of one year on the same terms." Messersmith and the Players Association argued that this meant the Dodgers could renew his contract for only one year; *i.e.,* 1975. In 1967, a California court had accepted this interpretation of an identical provision in the National Basketball Association's standard player contract in the San Francisco Warriors' case against Rick Barry.[572] Conversely, the owners argued that the option clause should be interpreted as permitting the contract to be renewed for successive one-year periods "on the same terms," which included the one-year option.

Major League Baseball's neutral arbitrator, Peter Seitz, cognizant of the potential impact of dismantling Major League Baseball's reserve system, wanted to avoid making a ruling. Seitz warned the owners' representatives of his likely decision in the arbitration and attempted to achieve a compromise between the parties or a delay in rendering his decision to permit the parties to fashion a substitute for the reserve system.[573] "Take this case out of my hands. Negotiate with the players and settle your differences," Seitz pleaded with the owners' representatives.[574] Inexplicably, the owners insisted on an immediate ruling. On December 23, 1975, they got one. Seitz ruled that McNally and Messersmith were free agents.[575] The owners immediately fired Seitz (which they were permitted to do now that the arbitration was completed) and returned to the United States District Court to challenge the arbitrator's jurisdiction.[576] Seitz later recounted his attempts to encourage the owners to negotiate and their rejection of those efforts. "I begged them to negotiate, but the owners were too stubborn and stupid. They were like the French barons in the twelfth century. They had accumulated so much power they wouldn't share it with anybody."[577] That court confirmed the arbitrator's jurisdiction, noting that the owners had agreed to the collective bargaining agreement which provided for the arbitration of disputes not involving the integrity of the game. The court also approved the reasoning of the arbitrator's decision.[578] The owners appealed the District Court's decision to the United States Court of Appeals which affirmed the decision of the lower court.[579] Thus, all Major League players would become free agents one year after the expiration of their current contracts. McNally remained retired but Messersmith signed a three-year contract with the Atlanta Braves for an average of $600,000 per season.[580]

Both the owners and the Players Association realized that unlimited free agency would not be favorable to their respective interests.[581] Except for Charlie Finley, the owners would have preferred to return to the old reserve system, even with salary arbitration.[582] The players, of course, would not agree to do so, but Marvin Miller realized that complete free agency would provide too much competition in the market and depress the salaries that players could achieve.[583] Thus, a limited form of free agency, which provided benefits to both the owners and the players, was the subject of the next collective bargaining agreement. The owners, desperate to recover some control over player movement, staged a brief lockout of spring training facilities prior to the 1976 season.[584] After the spring training camps were opened, the owners commenced their negotiations for the new collective bargaining agreement with presentations and public statements predicting impending doom for Major League Baseball because of salary increases resulting from free agency. They provided extensive financial information to the Players Association to support their claims of poverty, but much of this information later was proved to be false. Miller, who realized that time was on the players' side after the Messersmith ruling, patiently negotiated with the owners' representatives and kept the players' representatives informed of the proceedings.[585] Finally, a compromise was negotiated in a new collective bargaining agreement which was effective for 1976 through 1979. Any player who had completed at least six years' service in the Major Leagues could become a free agent and negotiate for a new contract with up to 12 of the 24 Major League teams. A player who had completed at least five years' service in the Major Leagues could demand to be traded and, if his demand were not satisfied, he could immediately become a free agent. If a player became a free agent, he could not again become a free agent until he completed five further Major League seasons. Players not yet eligible for free agency would still be eligible for salary arbitration after three years of Major League service, as in the period before free agency. Players with fewer than three years service were subject to the same treatment as under the old reserve system. The contribution to the pension fund was also increased and the minimum annual Major League salary was increased from $13,500 to $19,000 for 1976 and 1977, and to $21,000 for 1978 and 1979.[586] The owners, however, demanded something more. Recalling the joint negotiation and holdout by Los Angeles Dodgers pitchers Sandy Koufax and Don Drysdale before the 1966 season, the owners wanted a contractual prohibition against players acting collectively in free agency negotiations.[587] The Players Association was willing to agree to this proposal, as long as the prohibition was reciprocal.[588] Thus, the new collective bargaining agreement provided that neither players nor teams would act in concert in free agency matters.[589] The owners would later regret their insistence on this provision.

Following the 1976 season, the first free agency market resulted in a number of significant new contracts and substantial player movement. Players, who were successful in their chosen profession because of their competitive nature, competed in a new arena to become more highly compensated than their peers and confirm their superiority. The majority of these players were now represented by agents, who were successful in pitting competitive and egotistical owners against one another in bidding for their clients' services. Equally competitive owners improvidently offered large long-term contracts to free agents.[590] In a single year, the average Major League salary increased from $51,501 to $76,066.[591] Moreover, most new contracts were signed for multiple years, replacing the prior practice of one-year pacts. Several of these new long-term contracts proved to be imprudent for owners, as players became injured, disaffected, or simply proved to have ordinary skills. During the four-year period under the new collective bargaining agreement, 164 players became free agents, the average annual Major League player salary increased to $113,558 (nearly six times the average salary when Miller became executive director of the Major League Baseball Players Association in 1966 and more than double the average salary before free agency), and Nolan Ryan became the first player to receive a $1 million annual salary.[592]

In 1979, the owners' representatives and the Major League Baseball Players Association met again to discuss the terms for a new collective bargaining agreement for the period beginning in 1980. Experienced labor negotiator Ray Grebey had replaced John Gaherin as the owners' chief negotiator.[593] The owners, as always, were focused on player compensation. The owners' experiences with free agency had convinced them that the players were too well remunerated and that some restriction on their ability to move was necessary if salaries were to be brought under control. The Players Association was generally satisfied with the manner in which limited free agency was working and were suspicious, justifiably it would turn out, of the owners' claims of financial ruin. In the five-year period following free agency, the average annual Major League salary more than tripled from $44,676 in 1975 to $143,756 in 1980.[594] Baseball revenues, both from ticket sales and broadcasting rights, and net income after player salaries, however, increased sharply during the same period in spite of free agency, as attendance increased by nearly 40 percent and overall revenues increased by 66 percent.[595] Even where players did not become free agents, the new system resulted in long-term contracts replacing one-year pacts. In 1975, only Catfish Hunter had a multiple-year contract. By 1980, over 40 percent of Major League players had long-term contracts.[596] Nevertheless, in 1980 player salaries totaled only 28 percent of total Major League revenues.[597]

The owners presented two alternative proposals for dealing with their concerns about increased player compensation: scaled salaries and compensation for free agents. In the first of these alternatives, each player would be paid a flat salary based on number of years of service.[598] Under the second alternative, any team that signed a free agent would compensate the free agent's former team with one of its other players who had a comparable value.[599] The Players Association completely rejected the scaled salary alternative. Although the Players Association also refused to accept the owners' compensation proposal because a team would have too great a disincentive to sign a free agent, Miller offered a counterproposal to the owners' compensation plan. Each team that lost a free agent would be entitled to an amateur draft choice from the signing team and all teams would contribute money to a fund from which each team that lost a free agent could receive cash compensation. The owners rejected this compromise, but dropped their scaled salary proposal.[600]

The parties agreed that compensation was the only issue separating them. The owners asked for federal mediation, and experienced mediator Ken Moffett was appointed to conduct the mediation.[601] The players voted to strike until a new collective bargaining agreement was signed. Marvin Miller suggested that a new collective bargaining agreement be signed immediately, but that the free agency compensation issue be referred to a committee to study for one year.[602] The owners refused Miller's suggestion and demanded that the compensation issue be settled as part of the collective bargaining agreement. More negotiations followed until the parties announced that a compromise had been reached at 5:00

a.m. on the day the players were scheduled to strike.[603] The compromise was a new four-year collective bargaining agreement in which the annual Major League minimum salary was increased from $30,000 to $35,000, a new pension plan was instituted, pension fund contributions were sharply increased, salary arbitration was available to any player who had served at least two years in the Major Leagues, and the free agent compensation issue was deferred for one year as Miller had suggested.[604]

Although the players again had made significant advances at the owners' expense, the agreed logistics for deciding the compensation issue sowed the seeds of future conflict: If no agreement on the issue was achieved before February 15, 1981, the owners could put their free agent compensation proposal into effect during the following five days. If the owners' compensation proposal were put into effect, the players could announce before March 1, 1981, that they were prepared to strike and the strike would have to begin no later than June 1, 1981.[605] Both sides realized that a strike was likely. The owners purchased a $50 million strike insurance policy from Lloyds of London and created a $15 million strike fund.[606] The players also set aside funds to survive a strike.[607] On February 20, 1981, Ray Grebey announced that the owners were implementing a free agent compensation plan which would award a Major League player as compensation to any team that lost a "ranking player"; i.e., one who ranked in the upper 50 percent of plate appearances or innings pitched in his league. The player who would be provided as compensation would come from the team that signed the free agent, with the signing team retaining the ability to "protect" a number of its players.[608] On February 25, 1981, the Players Association announced the players' intention to strike and that the strike would commence on May 29, 1981.[609]

Meetings continued between the owners' representatives, the Players Association, and federal mediator Ken Moffett, but no progress was made.[610] The owners had taken a position and, still smarting from prior defeats at the hands of the Players Association, became hardened in their decision to stick with that position, even if the players carried out the strike. Cincinnati general manager Bob Howsam highlighted the importance of resolve in his challenge to the owners: "This is your only chance to achieve something. If you capitulate this time, you'll never achieve anything again. It's now or never."[611] The owners were certain that the players would not strike for long and, in any event, the owners had strike insurance.

On May 7, the Players Association filed a charge with the National Labor Relations Board, asserting that the owners were not bargaining in good faith.[612] On May 27, the National Labor Relations Board sought a temporary restraining order from the United States District Court to postpone the strike.[613] The owners and the Players Association agreed to delay any action until the court rendered its decision. During the court proceeding, Miller offered a compromise to the owners. All Major League clubs could "protect" a certain number of players and all remaining players in the Major Leagues would be put into a pool for selection by any team that lost a free agent.[614] Under this proposal, the team that lost a free agent would receive compensation for its loss, but the disincentive to signing a free agent would not exist. The owners rejected Miller's compromise and the court refused to issue the restraining order.[615]

The Players Association announced that the strike would commence on June 12 and would continue until a settlement on the compensation issue was achieved. On June 12, the players went on strike.[616] The owners remained convinced that the strike would not be lengthy, believing that once the players missed salary payments, now much larger than before and a more meaningful loss, they would crawl back and accept the owners' compensation system.[617] Player movement would be curtailed, salaries would be brought into line, and order would be restored. Exhibiting both lack of prescience and extraordinarily bad taste, Atlanta Braves owner Ted Turner outlined the owners' plan to defeat the Players Association and its executive director, Marvin Miller, who had been born with a deformed shoulder that caused him to carry his arm in an ungainly manner: "That gimpy-armed bastard. We'll run him out of town once and for all."[618] As usual, the owners failed to correctly assess the players' motives and their resolve.

The strike continued until August 11 and ultimately was settled only when the owners agreed that the free agent compensation system would be based on Miller's player pool compensation system which the owners had been offered before the strike, only nine free agents each year would be subject to Major League player compensation with all other free agents subject only to amateur draft pick compensation, and players who had at least 12 years of Major League service would not be subject to compensation.[619] The new collective bargaining agreement also provided for an increase of the annual minimum salary to $40,000 and counted strike days as credited service time.[620] The real reason the strike was settled was that the owners' insurance compensation ran out on August 8 and thereafter they had begun to suffer real financial losses.[621]

The 1981 strike was a disaster for owners, players, and fans. Both owners and players suffered financial losses. Marvin Miller estimates the direct losses to the owners after reimbursement by insurance was in excess of $70 million and that salary losses by players was approximately half that

Ted Turner

amount.[622] The owners' losses were permanent, however, while the players' losses were only temporary. The owners accomplished none of their important goals in forcing the strike. Free agency remained in effect, largely unrestrained by Major League player compensation. Average annual Major League player salaries continued to increase from $186,000 before the strike to $242,000 the following year, $289,000 in 1983, $329,000 in 1984, $371,000 in 1985, $597,000 in 1990, $890,000 in 1991, $1,172,000 in 1996, and more than $2 million in 2001.[623]

The 1981 strike produced other undesirable effects. Notable performances by Pete Rose, Fernando Valenzuela, Tim Raines, and other players were diminished when 712 Major League games were cancelled. Neither the Cincinnati Reds, which had the Major Leagues' best overall record, nor the St. Louis Cardinals, which had the best overall record in the National League East, made the playoffs as the season was separated into pre-strike and post-strike components with the winner of each segment entering post-season action. The New York Yankees, which had the third best overall record in the American League East, played in the World Series. Perhaps most importantly, however, the game and its players were diminished in the eyes of the fans. The majority of fans did not sympathize with striking players who collected average annual salaries of $186,000 and who were willing to withhold baseball from spectators to increase that compensation. In spite of predictions that the 1981 strike would permanently alienate fans, however, the 44.6 million in Major League attendance in 1982 exceeded the previous record of 43 million spectators posted in 1980.[624]

Further acrimonious negotiations were in store. The owners' representatives and the Major League Baseball Players Association began to meet in 1984 to set the terms for a new collective bargaining agreement to cover 1985–89. By now the principal negotiators on each side had changed. The owners' chief negotiator was now former American League president Lee MacPhail.[625] Marvin Miller had retired as the Players Association's executive director and, after being replaced briefly and unhappily by Ken Moffett,[626] had been succeeded by Donald Fehr, who had formerly served as the Major League Baseball Players Association's chief legal counsel.[627] Fehr continued to be assisted by Miller, who returned as a consultant after Moffet was fired.[628] The players were reasonably satisfied with the status they had achieved following the 1981 strike and in the existing collective bargaining agreement. The owners, of course, were not at all happy with the status quo and wanted to improve their position. Again, the owners' principal concern was player compensation.

The owners reiterated their claims that they were suffering enormous financial losses. Their proposal for curtailing those losses was threefold: each team would have an overall salary limit based on the average of the 1985 salaries paid by all teams, no team could sign a free agent or make a trade that would cause it to exceed the cap, and no player could receive compensation through arbitration that would exceed 200 percent of his previous year's salary.[629] The Players Association rejected this proposal and, on July 15, the players announced that they would go on strike beginning August 6.[630] The owners again announced their resolve and determination to improve their position. On August 6, the strike began. On August 7, a settlement was reached and, on August 8, play resumed.[631] The terms of the settlement once again provided significant gains to the players. No salary cap would apply, the contribution to the players' pension was doubled, the minimum annual Major League salary was increased by 50 percent from $40,000 to $60,000 and indexed for cost of living increases, the prior free agent compensation system was completely eliminated, and the period for a player's initial eligibility for salary arbitration was extended from two years to three years.[632] As discussed earlier in this chapter, the new collective bargaining agreement also provided that neither players nor teams would act in concert in free agency matters.[633]

In the 1970s, the difference between the players' salary proposals and those of the owners in arbitration were relatively insignificant, with the average difference being less than $20,000.[634] By the 1980s, however, the dramatic increases in salaries achieved through free agency began to be felt in arbitrations and all salaries began to rise dramatically. From 1980 to 1984, the average annual Major League salary more than doubled, reaching $329,408.[635] Players such as Fernando Valenzuela and Wade Boggs received arbitration awards in excess of $1 million.[636] Although the owners had some limited success in arbitrations, particularly in those in which they were represented by former Houston Astros general manager Tal Smith, now an arbitration consultant armed with a computerized database and a staff of analysts and lawyers,[637] most arbitrations were won by players. Baseball revenues, both from ticket sales and broadcasting rights, had continued to increase, but the owners claimed that they were experiencing devastating losses.

If the owners were losing money, it was because of their own excessive eagerness to sign free agents. During this period, legions of average players became wealthy as competitive and egotistical owners frenetically signed them to high salaried long-term contracts. As White Sox owner Jerry Reinsdorf observed, "Baseball is the only industry where I have to pay someone what my dumbest competitor pays."[638] Kansas City Royals owner Ewing Kauffman summarized the industry and illuminated the reasons for the high salaries paid in free agency. "You have twenty-six owners who are partners, and yet each owner tries to beat the other as much as he can in winning baseball games. So you're really not true partners, and you don't act like partners, and you don't run it like a partnership. You run it for the benefit of your own franchise."[639]

Money also came to assume increasing importance to egotistical and competitive players, as victories in free agency and salary arbitration became more meaningful than victories on the baseball field. Fred Lynn once observed, "Royalties are life and death matters, not baseball games." By the mid–1980s, contracts of even longer duration and higher average annual compensation were signed by Bruce Sutter, Dan Quisenberry, George Brett, Ozzie Smith, Eddie Murray, and other players.[640]

Although American League President Lee MacPhail and new Commissioner Peter Ueberroth counseled the owners to exercise self discipline and common sense, owners could not resist the chance to sign that one player who might put their teams over the top. MacPhail observed, "Most important is that all clubs practice common-sense economic self-restraint. We must rely on the unilateral, self-imposed restraints of each individual club to do what experience and reasonable expectations indicate is in its own best interest. We must stop daydreaming that one free agent signing will bring a pennant."[641] Ueberroth vigorously discouraged long-term contracts, admonishing the owners to exercise discipline. "Look in the mirror and go out and spend big if you want, but don't go out there whining that someone made you do it."[642]

After the 1985 season ended, an unusual phenomenon occurred. Several players declared themselves to be free agents. But, with the exception of a few fringe players who were no longer desired by their existing teams,

teams other than existing employers were not offering contracts to the free agents.[643] Had the owners all suddenly decided independently to exercise discipline and achieve control over their finances by refusing to pay higher salaries? New Major League Commissioner Peter Ueberroth had exhorted the owners to exercise fiscal prudence and "stop asking for the players to solve their financial problems." Had the owners followed Ueberroth's advice and individually practiced self-restraint? The Players Association didn't believe so. The players believed the owners were in collusion to depress Major League salaries.[644]

As discussed above, the owners had agreed in the collective bargaining agreements beginning in 1976 that they would not act in concert in free agency matters.[645] The Players Association filed a grievance with Major League Baseball's arbitrator, alleging that the owners had violated the collective bargaining agreement.[646] After reviewing considerable evidence which convincingly incriminated the owners, the arbitrator ruled that the owners had engaged in collusion.[647] The owners had provided information to one another regarding their desires to retain their own free agents and their negotiations with other free agents. It was clear that a tacit understanding existed that, if a free agent's prior team wished to retain the player, no other team would offer a contract to him. The owners engaged in similar concerted conduct after the 1986 and 1987 seasons.[648] Additional arbitrations were held and again the owners were found to have engaged in collusion.[649] The arbitrators determined that a number of players had been disadvantaged by the owners' collective activity and ruled that 20 players who had remained with their old teams were free agents again.[650] In addition, the arbitrators assessed a total of $280 million in monetary damages against the owners.[651]

The owners' collusion in violation of the 1985–89 collective bargaining agreement was fresh in the minds of the players when negotiations for the 1990–93 collective bargaining agreement began in 1989. The owners, ever hopeful they could control the escalation of player salaries, offered a comprehensive new proposal which they termed "an innovative Baseball Partnership."[652] Under this proposal, the players' overall salaries would be set at 48 percent of total baseball revenues (the 1989 level), scaled salaries would be paid to all players with fewer than six years of service in the Major Leagues, players with at least six years' Major League service would be free agents, each team would have a salary cap, and no free agent could be signed if the team's salary cap would be exceeded.[653] The Players Association, having no difficulty in recognizing another crude attempt by owners to limit free agency, refused the owners' proposal. The owners decided they could achieve leverage in negotiations by locking the players out from spring training camps until the players accepted the owners' proposal.[654] But again the owners backed down and provided gains to the players. The new collective bargaining agreement, which was not reached until two weeks before the 1990 season was scheduled to begin, increased the minimum annual Major League salary from $60,000 to $100,000 with cost of living increases, increased the contribution to the players' pension plan by nearly 60 percent, provided for no changes in free agency or arbitration, except that a small number of players would be eligible for salary arbitration after two, rather than three, years of Major League service, and did not include team or overall limits on player compensation.[655] The agreement also provided that, if the owners were again found to have colluded on free agency, they would pay the players treble damages, a committee would be formed to study baseball financial matters and revenue sharing, and either the owners or the players could reopen the agreement for further negotiation of major issues after three years.[656]

As the collusion cases faded into the background and the combined effects of free agency and salary arbitration again began to take effect, salaries increased dramatically. Until 1988, the highest annual salaries in Major League Baseball were approximately $2 million.[657] In 1990, the first $3 million salaries were paid.[658] In 1991, Jose Canseco signed a five-year contract at an average salary of $4.7 million per year.[659] In 1992, Roger Clemens signed a four-year contract at a $5.4 million average annual salary, Bobby Bonilla signed a four-year contract with a $5.8 million average annual salary, Ryne Sandberg signed a four-year contract at an average annual salary of $7.1 million, and Doug Drabek, a pitcher with four years of Major League experience, was awarded a $3.35 million salary in arbitration.[660] In 1993, Barry Bonds signed a six-year contract with an average annual salary of $7.24 million and Ruben Sierra received a $5 million salary in arbitration.[661] Between 1989 and 1992, the average Major League salary more than doubled.[662] Although revenues had steadily increased and, on an overall basis, matched salary gains, the owners again pleaded poverty and predicted the demise of Major League Baseball. They decided that they had to do something to halt the relentless escalation in salaries. In more than 20 years of negotiating with the Major League Baseball Players Association, however, the owners had lost virtually every significant battle and the players had realized remarkable gains. The owners now had a collective bargaining agreement that ran through the 1993 season. So what did they decide to do? On December 7, 1992 (the fifty-first anniversary of the Japanese attack on Pearl Harbor), the owners voted to reopen the collective bargaining agreement and force the players to strike until the owners achieved their financial objectives.[663] They fired commissioner Fay Vincent, appointed Milwaukee Brewers' owner Bud Selig as their acting commissioner, hired Richard Ravitch as their chief labor negotiator, and prepared for a fight.[664]

In spite of threats of a lock-out by the owners and a strike by the players, discussions drifted on throughout the 1993 season and the collective bargaining agreement expired on December 31, 1993. In early 1994, the owners met to attempt to reach a formula for sharing revenues among the franchises, provided the players agreed to salary caps.[665] The owners were unable to do so, but agreed they would not lock the players out of spring training or unilaterally institute changes.[666] The 1994 season began without an effective collective bargaining agreement. The owners presented a proposal for a new seven-year agreement which provided for the elimination of salary arbitration, setting of player salaries at 50 percent of Major League revenues, and team salary caps of 110 percent of the average team payroll.[667] The Players Association rejected the owners' proposal and made a counter-proposal which essentially would have retained the 1990–93 collective bargaining agreement with minor improvements.[668] The owners rejected the players' counter-proposal in late July.[669]

On July 28, the players announced that they would strike beginning August 12,[670] believing this would provide enough time to settle their difference with the owners before the playoffs and World Series were scheduled to begin. By that date, the players also would have received a majority of their 1994 salary payments. Because of the importance of pennant race, playoff, and World Series revenues, a season-ending strike would cause greater financial damage to the owners than the players.[671] In light of their prior experience in negotiating with the owners, the players did not believe the owners would forgo the playoff and World Series revenues. In spite of evidence to the contrary from prior strikes, the owners did not believe that the players would permit the strike to continue for the remainder of the season. On August 2, the players learned that a $7.8 million payment that should have been made to the players' pension fund had not been made.[672] On August 12, the players went on strike. Negotiations continued for the next month. The Players Association offered a compromise on the salary cap issue which would have imposed a tax on teams that exceeded a certain salary amount. For once, however, the owners did not yield. They rejected this proposal and, on September 14, acting commissioner Selig cancelled the remainder of the 1994 regular season, the playoffs, and the World Series.[673]

Over the following three months, sporadic negotiations occurred among the owners' and players' representatives and former Secretary of Labor William Usery, who had been appointed by President Bill Clinton to mediate the dispute. The Major League Baseball Players Association presented the owners with a comprehensive proposal that would have eliminated salary arbitration, permitted free agency after four years of Major League service, established a fixed salary structure for players with less that four years' service, imposed a payroll tax on teams that exceeded a specified salary amount, and given the players input into the selection of the commissioner, television contracts, and league expansion.[674] The owners made a proposal which contained a punitive payroll tax, but rejected the players' other proposals.[675]

Under the National Labor Relations Act, participants in a labor dispute are required to negotiate in good faith until the point of impasse, at which time management is allowed to unilaterally implement its last offer to the union. On December 23, 1994, the owners declared an impasse had been reached, abolished salary arbitration, and imposed the salary cap.[676] On December 27, the Players Association filed an action with the National Labor Relations Board, asserting that the implementation of impasse, the elimination of salary arbitration, the imposition of a salary cap, and the owners' refusal to bargain over wages were unfair labor practices.[677]

On March 2, 1995, Major League training camps opened.[678] How could that happen? Didn't the teams need players and weren't the players still on strike? Yes, and no. All clubs except the Baltimore Orioles (whose owner Peter Angelos is a labor lawyer who represents unions) and the Toronto Blue Jays (who were prevented from doing so under Ontario law) used replacement players; *i.e.,* retired Major League players, minor league players, and others, to staff their teams. On March 15, the National Labor Relations Board ruled that the owners had not bargained in good faith and sought an injunction from the United States District Court to prevent the owners from utilizing any of the new rules and to reinstate the expired collective bargaining agreement until the owners and players could adopt a new one.[679] On March 31, the court granted the injunction, and the grant was affirmed by the United States Court of Appeals.[680] The players' strike was cancelled, the ersatz players were themselves replaced by real major leaguers, the season opened on April 26, an abbreviated 144-game schedule was played, and the terms of the 1990–93 collective bargaining agreement continued to apply during 1995 and 1996.[681]

Negotiations for a new collective bargaining agreement continued throughout 1995 and 1996. Finally, on December 26, 1996, a new collective bargaining agreement was signed.[682] The minimum annual Major League player salary was increased from $109,000 to $150,000 for 1997, $170,000 for 1998, and $200,000 for 1999, the free agency and arbitration rules were unchanged, and any team whose payroll exceeded a specified amount ($51 million in 1997 increasing to $59 million in 1999) was required to pay a tax of 34–35 percent which would be deposited into a pool and used for revenue sharing by the smaller market franchises. In addition, the players contributed 2.5 percent of their 1996 and 1997 salaries to this revenue sharing pool, limited inter-league play was authorized, and a new Industry Growth Fund was established to promote the growth of baseball.[683] This fund was to have a board of directors comprised of equal numbers of representatives of the owners and the players and one additional member to be jointly appointed. Finally, the agreement contained a provision that required the owners and players to jointly request and cooperate in lobbying the United States Congress to enact legislation to repeal the judicially created antitrust exemption as it relates to Major League baseball players.[684] The new collective bargaining agreement covered 1996–2000 and the players had an option to extend the agreement to cover the 2001 season. In August 2000, the Players Association exercised that option, thereby deferring confrontation with the owners until after the 2001 World Series.

The balance of power between players and owners had fundamentally changed between the time Curt Flood filed his federal court action against Major League Baseball in 1970 and the signing of the new collective bargaining agreement in 1996. Major League salaries had increased exponentially. The minimum annual Major League salary was increased to $200,000 in 1999 under the new collective bargaining agreement, 33 times the $6,000 minimum salary in 1967 when Marvin Miller became executive director of the Major League Baseball Players Association. During the same period, the *average* annual Major League salary skyrocketed to more than 100 times the 1967 average of $19,000. A player was no longer required to remain with a team throughout his career. Veteran players could veto trades. Players and their agents had greater freedom and bargaining power in their relations with owners. Owners now bargained collectively with the Players Association.

But what effects would all these changes have on the field? How would the fans react? Would they continue to support a system in which an extremely well-compensated group of players engages in constant warfare with an extremely wealthy group of owners with complete disregard for the emotions and interests of the fans who finance both groups? Would fan loyalty survive the constant movement of players under free agency? Could Major League Baseball survive? If so, at what cost?

Chapter 11

ROLLING STONES

I am the most loyal player money can buy.
—Don Sutton

They [the players] all changed. Most of them got agents, and I ceased to talk to 'em. "Like to use this toilet paper?" "Dunno, I gotta talk to my agent."
—Bill "Spaceman" Lee

The difference between the old ballplayer and the new ballplayer is the jersey. The old ballplayer cared about the name on the front. The new ballplayer cares about the name on the back.
—Steve Garvey

I feel we're all overpaid. Every professional athlete is overpaid. I got a phenomenal contract—much more money than I ever thought I'd make. I wouldn't say I'm embarrassed by it, but deep down I know I'm not worth it. To my shame, though, I have to admit I asked for it.
—Fred Patek

During the last three decades of the 20th century, significant changes occurred within the United States and in its international relations. After nearly two decades of United States involvement in Indochina, National Security Advisor Henry Kissinger negotiated a cease-fire agreement with the North Vietnamese government in 1973. The war in Vietnam finally ended in 1975 when the government of North Vietnam consolidated its control over the entire country. After three decades of hostile relations between the United States and the Soviet Union, the two countries pursued a policy of *détente* in the 1970s and, in 1972, they entered into an arms control agreement limiting the growth of nuclear arsenals and restricting missile systems. The United States granted diplomatic relations to, and normalized relations with, the People's Republic of China. America's rate of population growth declined and its population grew older. Immigration policies changed to become less focused on Western Europe and the numbers of new immigrants from Asia and Latin America increased. Although the fringes of America's major political parties became more vocal and extreme and new political groups emerged, the platforms of the Republican and Democratic parties' national candidates moved closer to each other and on many issues began to blur. As the Soviet Union and its Eastern European satellites collapsed in the early 1990s, the United States emerged as the world's only economic and military superpower. America asserted itself in international relations, engaging in economic and limited military warfare in a variety of world trouble spots, including the Persian Gulf, South Africa, Latin America, and Eastern Europe. The United States' economy evolved from "smokestack industries" such as steel, textile, and automobile manufacturing toward service and technology industries. America and the world entered into a new information age. After two decades of economic recession and deficit financing, in the 1990s America enjoyed a decade of economic expansion and deficit reduction.

During that 30-year period, significant changes also occurred in Major League Baseball. As the 1970s began, Major League Baseball was dominated by the last four teams that would build dynasties in the era before free agency. Each of these four teams won five division championships and regularly competed against one another in post-season action in the seven-year period from 1969 to 1976. These powerful teams, built the old-fashioned way by scouting, minor league development, and judicious trades, were four of the greatest teams in Major League history.

In the five years from 1971 through 1975, Charlie Finley's Oakland A's won five consecutive American League West crowns, three consecutive American League pennants, and three consecutive World Series. The A's combined a splendid balance of starting pitching, relief pitching, hitting, power, speed, and defense. The A's starting pitching consisted of Jim "Catfish" Hunter, who won 106 games for the A's from 1970 through 1974, Vida Blue, who won 121 games for the A's from 1971 through 1977, Ken Holtzman, who won 77 games for the A's from 1972 through 1975, and John "Blue Moon" Odom, who won 70 games for the A's from 1969 through 1973. The A's relief pitching was anchored by Roland "Rollie" Fingers, who won 54 games and saved 112 games for the A's from 1971 through 1976. The A's offense was led by Reginald Martinez "Reggie" Jackson, Joe

Rudi, and Sal Bando. Jackson hit 253 home runs for the A's from 1968 through 1975, providing the team's leading power threat. Joe Rudi provided solid hitting and splendid defense during the same period. Sal Bando added powerful hitting and strong defense at third base and served as the A's field captain. Shortstop Campy Campaneris contributed speed and defense. First baseman and catcher Gene Tenace added strong hitting. The A's defeated the Cincinnati Reds in the 1972 World Series in seven games, beat the New York Mets in the 1973 World Series in seven games, and defeated the Los Angeles Dodgers in five games in the 1974 World Series. The "Swingin' A's" were a swashbuckling, belligerent, and boisterous bunch, clad in Charlie Finley's outrageous green and gold uniforms and white shoes, and sporting mustaches that Finley paid them to grow. They fought with Finley and one another. But they were also Major League Baseball's most successful team of the period immediately preceding free agency. Three members of the team, Reggie Jackson, Catfish Hunter, and Rollie Fingers, would ultimately be inducted into the Hall of Fame.

From 1970 through 1976, the Cincinnati Reds won five National League West championships, three National League pennants, and two World Series. The Reds were more conservative than the A's, both in manner and attire, but were the equal of the A's on the playing field, if not in pitching. From 1970 through 1977, four different members of the Reds were named the National League's Most Valuable Player, two of them twice. Offensively, third baseman Pete Rose and second baseman Joe Morgan set the table, with hits, walks, stolen bases, and aggressive base running. Johnny Bench was baseball's finest catcher and the team's leading power hitter. First baseman Tony Perez drove in runs. The remainder of the line-up featured power-hitting outfielder George Foster, smooth hitting and fielding outfielder Ken Griffey, Sr., star defensive center fielder Cesar Geronimo, and slick-fielding shortstop Dave Concepcion. The Reds' offensive attack and defensive prowess featured running, with Geronimo, Griffey, Morgan, Concepcion, and Rose all possessing superior speed. The Reds' speed and defense was well-suited to their new artificial surface ballpark, Riverfront Stadium, which debuted in 1970. The Reds' starting pitching featured Don Gullett, Gary Nolan, and Jack Billingham, and their relief pitching, which Manager Sparky "Captain Hook" Anderson used frequently, starred Rawly Eastwick, Will McEnaney, Clay Carroll, and Pedro Borbon. The "Big Red Machine" lost the 1970 World Series to the Baltimore Orioles in five games, lost the 1972 World Series to the Oakland A's in seven games, defeated the Boston Red Sox in the 1975 World Series in seven games, and swept the New York Yankees in the 1976 World Series. The Reds featured three future Hall of Fame players, Johnny Bench,

Joe Morgan, and Tony Perez; a Hall of Fame manager, Sparky Anderson; and another player who would be in the Hall of Fame if he had not disgraced himself and baseball by gambling on the sport, Pete Rose.

The Baltimore Orioles won five American League East championships, three straight American League pennants, and one World Series from 1969 through 1974. Earl Weaver's Baltimore Orioles team featured strong starting pitching, powerful hitting, and defense. The starting pitching staff included Jim Palmer, Mike Cuellar, Dave McNally, and Pat Dobson. In 1971, each of these four starters won at least 20 games. During his 19-year Orioles career, Palmer won 268 games, including at least 20 wins in eight seasons, and three Cy Young Awards. Cuellar won 139 games for the Orioles from 1969 through 1975. McNally won 133 games for the Birds from 1968 through 1974. The Orioles' power came from huge first baseman John Wesley "Boog" Powell, perennial Gold Glove third baseman Brooks Robinson, and star outfielder Frank Robinson, who during his lengthy career was named the Most Valuable Player in both Major Leagues, won the American League's "Triple Crown" in 1966, and hit a total of 586 home runs, still fifth on the all-time list. Defensive strength was provided by center fielder Paul Blair, second baseman Dave Johnson, shortstop Mark Belanger, and third baseman Brooks Robinson. The Orioles lost the 1969 World Series to the New York Mets in five games, defeated the Cincinnati Reds to win the 1970 World Series in five games, and lost the 1971 World Series to the Pittsburgh Pirates in seven games. Three members of those Oriole teams, Frank Robinson, Brooks Robinson, and Jim Palmer, and the team's manager Earl Weaver, have been inducted into the Hall of Fame.

The Pittsburgh Pirates won five National League East crowns, one National League pennant, and one World Series from 1970 through 1975. Unfortunately for these powerful Pirates teams, they played during the same era as the Big Red Machine and the Swingin' A's. The Pirates featured the incomparable Roberto Clemente and the powerful Willie Stargell, fine hitting from Dave Cash, Richie Hebner, Manny Sanguillen, and Al Oliver, solid starting pitching from Dock Ellis, Steve Blass, Nelson Briles, and Bob Moose, and relief pitching from Dave Giusti. The Pirates' attack took advantage of their new artificial turf ballpark, Three Rivers Stadium, which opened in 1970. But, too often, the Pirates faced the Reds in post-season competition. The Reds defeated the Pirates in the National League Championship Series in 1970, 1972, and 1975. In 1971, the Pirates dispatched the San Francisco Giants and the Baltimore Orioles and won the World Series. Two players on those Pirates teams, Roberto Clemente and Willie Stargell, are members of the Hall of Fame.

Pete Rose at bat.

After the landmark Andy Messersmith arbitration in 1975 and the dawn of the free agency era after the 1976 season, the method of building and retaining a winning Major League Baseball team changed dramatically. Player compensation skyrocketed and players moved freely from team to team and from league to league. No longer could a team patiently assemble the pieces of a winning team, confident that those pieces would remain in place because of the Major Leagues' reserve system. Team development in the free agency era focused on short-term goals, attracting top free agents and retaining a team's own free agents.

Catfish Hunter became the "Swingin' A's" first free agent after the 1974 season when he signed with the New York Yankees. At the beginning of the 1976 season, the A's traded impending free agents Reggie Jackson and Ken Holtzman to the Baltimore Orioles in exchange for Don Baylor and Mike Torrez. After the 1976 season, Sal Bando moved to the Milwaukee Brewers, Joe Rudi joined the California Angels, Rollie Fingers and Gene Tenace moved to the San Diego Padres, and Bert Campaneris joined the Texas Rangers. By the 1977 season, only Vida Blue remained of the A's stars of the early 1970s, as the no-longer-swingin' A's finished in last place in the American League West. By 1978, Blue also had departed.

The Reds fared somewhat better than the A's, with the nucleus of their "Big Red Machine" remaining intact throughout much of the 1970s. But

Tony Perez left for the Montreal Expos after the 1976 season, Pete Rose joined the Philadelphia Phillies after the 1978 season, and Joe Morgan returned to his original team, the Houston Astros, after the 1979 season.

The Orioles aged, but new players such as Lee May, Bobby Grich, Ken Singleton, Don Baylor, Mike Torrez, Wayne Garland, Mike Flanagan, Dennis Martinez, Scott McGregor, Doug DeCinces, and Eddie Murray were added throughout the 1970s. The aging Frank Robinson and Boog Powell were traded, as were Don Baylor and Mike Torrez.

The Pirates lost the great Roberto Clemente in an airplane crash on New Year's Eve 1972 when he was delivering relief supplies to earthquake victims in Managua, Nicaragua. Willie Stargell remained a prodigious slugger throughout the 1970s. He was joined by hitters Al Oliver, Richie Zisk, Dave Parker, and Bill Madlock, pitchers Bert Blyleven, John Candelaria, Bruce Kison, and Jim Bibby, and submariner reliever Kent Tekulve, as the Pirates won another National League pennant and World Series championship in 1979.

But for Major League Baseball's four greatest teams of the early 1970s, the years immediately following free agency have been difficult. Each of the teams was torn apart and rebuilt more than once, but, with the exception of the Orioles after the construction of their fabulous new ballpark at Camden Yards, which debuted in 1992, these four teams have been small-market or at best mid–market teams, which have been unable to match large-market franchises in the pursuit and retention of free agent players. The Oakland A's won the American League West crown in 1981 under Billy Martin. With new stars Mark McGwire, Jose Canseco, Rickey Henderson, Harold Baines, and Willie McGee, and strong pitching by Dave Stewart, Bob Welch, Mike Moore, and Dennis Eckersley, and led by Manager Tony Larussa, the A's won three successive American League pennants in 1988–90, losing the 1988 and 1990 World Series to the Los Angeles Dodgers and Cincinnati Reds, respectively, and defeating the cross–Bay San Francisco Giants in the earthquake-interrupted 1989 World Series. With a corps of promising youthful stars, the A's returned to post-season action in 2000 and 2001, but lost hard-fought playoff series to the New York Yankees in each of those years. The Reds won the National League West crown in 1979, but did not return to post-season action until 1990, when they won the National League pennant and swept the Oakland A's in the World Series. The Reds have not appeared in post-season play since that season. The Orioles won the American League pennant in 1979, but lost to the Pittsburgh Pirates in the World Series. They were

Opposite: Camden Yards, Baltimore.

American League and World Series champions in 1983, led by Eddie Murray and Cal Ripken, Jr., as they defeated the Philadelphia Phillies. The Orioles also appeared in post-season action in 1996 and 1997, but have not won an American League pennant since 1983. Except for 1979, when they won a National League pennant and the World Series, the Pirates have not again appeared in a World Series, although they were National League East champions in 1990, 1991, and 1992, with teams featuring Barry Bonds, Bobby Bonilla, and Andy Van Slyke, and pitchers Doug Drabek and John Smiley. Each of those players ultimately departed as free agents.

Following the 1976 season, the first free agency market resulted in a number of significant new contracts and substantial player movement. The New York Yankees were particularly aggressive in signing big-name free agent talent, including Reggie Jackson, Catfish Hunter, and Rich "Goose" Gossage. Those free agent stars, combined with an existing Yankees nucleus that included Thurman Munson, Mickey Rivers, Lou Piniella, Graig Nettles, Chris Chambliss, and Willie Randolph, and pitchers Ron Guidry, Mike Torrez, and Sparky Lyle, led the Yankees to defeat the Los Angeles Dodgers' fine teams in the 1977 and 1978 World Series. Those Dodgers teams featured Steve Garvey, Dave Lopes, Bill Russell, Ron Cey, Reggie Smith, Rick Monday, and Dusty Baker and pitchers Don Sutton, Burt Hooten, Tommy John, Rick Rhoden, and Charlie Hough. On their way to winning American League pennants in 1976, 1977, and 1978, the Yankees dispatched the Kansas City Royals which won American League West crowns in each of those years. Those Royals teams starred George Brett, Frank White, Hal McRae, Amos Otis, Al Cowens, and Darrell Porter, and pitchers Dennis Leonard, Larry Gura, and Paul Splittorff.

The Major Leagues in the late 1970s were characterized by player movement, both as a result of free agency and trades engineered to offset the expected impact of impending free agency. Because of free agency, it became harder for franchises to build and maintain consistently good teams in the 1980s. The most consistent teams of the 1980s were the Kansas City Royals and Oakland A's in the American League and the Los Angeles Dodgers and St. Louis Cardinals in the National League.

The Royals, featuring George Brett, Willie Wilson, Hal McRae, and Frank White, starting pitchers Larry Gura, Dennis Leonard, Bud Black, and Brett Saberhagen, and relief pitcher Dan Quisenberry, were American League West champions in 1980, 1984, and 1985, won American League pennants in 1980 and 1985, and defeated the St. Louis Cardinals in the 1985 World Series. The Dodgers, featuring Steve Garvey, Dave Lopes, Ron Cey, Bill Russell, Pedro Guerrero, Dusty Baker, and Kirk Gibson and pitchers Fernando Valenzuela, Bob Welch, Jerry Reuss, and Orel Hershiser, won

National League West crowns in 1981, 1983, 1985, and 1988, and National League pennants and World Series championships in 1981 and 1988 for Manager Tommy Lasorda. The swift Cardinals, with George Hendrick, Lonnie Smith, Tommy Herr, Keith Hernandez, Ozzie Smith, Willie McGee, Terry Pendleton, and Vince Coleman, starting pitchers Joaquin Andujar, Bob Forsch, John Tudor, and Danny Cox, and relief pitchers Bruce Sutter and Ken Dayley, won National League East crowns in 1981, 1982, 1985, and 1987, won National League pennants in 1982, 1985, and 1987, and defeated the Milwaukee Brewers in the 1982 World Series for Manager Whitey Herzog. As the 1980s closed, the revived Oakland A's, featuring "Bash Brothers" Mark McGwire and Jose Canseco and superb pitching by Bob Welch, Dave Stewart, and Dennis Eckersley, won three consecutive American League pennants for Manager Tony Larussa. The National League demonstrated the parity of free agency with six different pennant winners in the six years from 1986 through 1991.

In 1991, the Atlanta Braves reached the World Series for the first time and began a decade of excellence marked by the superb starting pitching of Tom Glavine, Greg Maddux, and John Smoltz, and offensive support by a capable, if constantly changing, crew of hitting stars including Terry Pendleton, Ron Gant, David Justice, Otis Nixon, Fred McGriff, Chipper Jones, Andres Gallaraga, Brian Jordan, and Andruw Jones. During that eleven-year period, the Braves won ten National League East crowns (the Braves were trailing the Montreal Expos in the strike-shortened 1994 season, the only year in that eleven-year span in which the Braves did not top the National League East), National League pennants in 1991, 1992, 1995, 1996, and 1999, and the World Series championship in 1995 for Manager Bobby Cox.

In the early 1990s, the American League's dominant team was the Toronto Blue Jays, which combined the hitting of Joe Carter, Roberto Alomar, Dave Winfield, John Olerud, Paul Molitor, and Devon White with the pitching of Jack Morris, Juan Guzman, Jimmy Key, and Dave Stewart to win American League East crowns in 1991, 1992, and 1993, and American League pennants and World Series championships in 1992 and 1993. The Cleveland Indians, with Jim Thome, Matt Williams, Kenny Lofton, David Justice, Roberto Alomar, Sandy Alomar, and Manny Ramirez won five consecutive American League Central crowns from 1995 through 1999, the American League Central title in 2001, and American League pennants in 1995 and 1997, but have not won a World Series since 1948.

The New York Yankees won American League East championships and American League pennants in 1996 and 1998–2001, and World Series championships in 1996, 1998, 1999, and 2000 for Manager Joe Torre.

George Steinbrenner's latest Yankees "dynasty" combined superstars Derek Jeter and Bernie Williams with solid professionals Tino Martinez, Paul O'Neill, Chuck Knoblauch, and Scott Brosius, interchangeable designated hitter and outfield combinations of veteran stars such as Darryl Strawberry, David Justice, Glenallen Hill, Tim Raines, and Chili Davis, strong starting pitching from David Wells, Andy Pettite, David Cone, Roger Clemens, and Orlando Hernandez, and remarkable relief pitching by John Wetteland and Mariano Rivera to win four World Series championships in five years. The first World Series of the new millennium pitted these latter day Bronx Bombers against the National League champion New York Mets, who play their home games in Queens. This "subway series," the first in New York since 1956, elicited great joy and fan enthusiasm in America's most populous city, but provided considerably milder entertainment to Major League Baseball fans in America's heartland, West, and South, who have tired of witnessing Yankees victory parades. In the 2001 World Series, the Yankees lost in seven hard fought and dramatic games to the Arizona Diamondbacks.

During the 1970s and 1980s, a number of Major League Baseball's most hallowed and longstanding records were broken. In his first at-bat in Major League Baseball's opening day on April 4, 1974, Hank Aaron hit his 714th career home run to tie Babe Ruth's 39-year-old career Major League record. Four days later, Aaron hit number 715 to become Major League Baseball's all-time home run king. Aaron ended his 23-year Major League career in 1976 and is Major League Baseball's career leader in home runs (755), runs batted in (2,297), total bases (6,856), and extra-base hits (1,477), second in career at-bats (12,364), third in career games played (3,298), hits (3,771), and runs scored (2,174), and eighth in career doubles (624). Also in 1974, Lou Brock stole 114 bases to break Maury Wills's single-season Major League record of 104 and Bob Gibson became the first pitcher since Walter Johnson to reach 3,000 career strikeouts. Brock had career totals of 3,023 hits, 1,730 runs scored, and 938 stolen bases, leading the National League eight times and holding the Major League career stolen base record at the time of his retirement. Gibson, the greatest right-handed pitcher of his era, ended his career with 251 wins, 3,117 strikeouts, and a 2.91 career earned run average. Willie Mays ended his brilliant career in 1973 with lifetime totals of 660 home runs, 3,283 hits, 337 stolen bases, 1,903 runs batted in, 2,062 runs scored, and eleven consecutive Gold Gloves. Also in 1973, Nolan Ryan collected 383 strikeouts to break Sandy Koufax's single-season record of 382. Before he finally ended his 27-year career in 1993, Ryan won 324 games, struck out an incredible 5,714 batters, had 26 games with at least 15 strikeouts, and pitched seven no-hit games, including no-hitters at 43 and 44 years old. In 1981, Pete Rose broke Stan Musial's 18-year-old National League career hits record (3,630) and, in 1985, he broke Ty Cobb's 57-year-old Major League career hits record (4,191). When Rose ended his 24-year career in 1986, he was Major League Baseball's career leader in games (3,562), at-bats (14,053), and hits (4,256), was second in career doubles (746), and was fourth in career runs scored (2,165).

Other players who had outstanding careers and who played pre-dominantly after the 1960s include Steve Carlton, Tom Seaver, Gaylord Perry, Jim "Catfish" Hunter, Phil Niekro, Rollie Fingers, Jim Palmer, Dennis Eckersley, Lee Smith, Jeff Reardon, Willie Stargell, George Brett, Mike Schmidt, Dave Winfield, Reggie Jackson, Ozzie Smith, Brooks Robinson, Carlton Fisk, Robin Yount, Dick Allen, Joe Morgan, Johnny Bench, Paul Molitor, Eddie Murray, Andre Dawson, Rod Carew, Gary Carter, Wade Boggs, Kirby Puckett, Cal Ripken, Jr., Tony Gwynn, and Mark McGwire.

Steve "Lefty" Carlton pitched 24 seasons in the Major Leagues, winning 329 games with an earned run average of 3.22 and 4,136 strikeouts. He won four National League Cy Young Awards and struck out more batters than any left-handed pitcher in Major League history. Tom Seaver won 311 games in 20 Major League seasons with a 2.86 earned run average and 3,272 career strikeouts. Seaver won three National League Cy Young Awards. Gaylord Perry, whose pitch assortment included the Major Leagues' last great spitball, won 314 games over 22 seasons. Jim Hunter won 224 games in his career, posting five consecutive 20-win seasons in the 1970s. He had a lifetime earned run average of 3.26, won the American League Cy Young Award in 1974, and pitched a perfect game. Phil Niekro relied primarily on an outstanding knuckleball to accumulate 318 victories. Rollie Fingers posted 341 saves, winning both the American League's Cy Young Award and Most Valuable Player award. Jim Palmer won 268 games and three Cy Young Awards in his 19-year career with the Baltimore Orioles. Originally a starting pitcher, but later converted into a closer, Dennis Eckersley is the only Major League pitcher who has won at least 100 games (197) and saved at least 300 games (390). Big Lee Smith won 71 games and established a career Major League record of 478 saves while maintaining a career 3.03 earned run average. Jeff Reardon won 73 games, saved 367 games, and maintained a career 3.16 earned run average.

Willie Stargell hit 475 home runs and drove in 1,540 runs in his 19-year Major League career with the Pittsburgh Pirates. He twice led the National League in home runs, led his team to World Series championships twice, and was named co-winner of the National League's Most

Valuable Player award in 1979. George Brett, who played 21 seasons with the Kansas City Royals, is the only player in Major League history to combine for at least 3,000 hits (3,154), 300 home runs (317), 600 doubles (665), 100 triples (137), and 200 stolen bases (201). Mike Schmidt was the National League's leading power hitter in the late 1970s and 1980s. In an 18-year career with the Philadelphia Phillies, Schmidt hit 548 home runs, leading the National League in home runs eight times, and posting 13 years with at least 30 home runs and three years with at least 40. The finest fielding third baseman of his day, winning eight consecutive Gold Gloves, Schmidt amassed career totals of 1,596 runs batted in and 1,506 runs scored and was named the National League's Most Valuable Player three times. Dave Winfield was a power-hitting, smooth fielding star for 22 Major League seasons. He hit a total of 465 home runs and collected 3,110 career hits. During his 20-year career, Reggie Jackson was one of Major League Baseball's leading power hitters. "Mr. October" hit 563 home runs, drove in 1,702 runs, struck out a Major League–record 2,597 times, and won the American League's Most Valuable Player award in 1973. Ozzie Smith was probably the finest fielding shortstop, and possibly greatest defensive player, of all time. The "Wizard of Oz" (or "Wizard of Aahs") led the St. Louis Cardinals to World Series appearances in 1982, 1985, and 1987. Brooks Robinson was the American League's leading defensive third baseman for two decades. He also amassed 2,848 hits, including 268 home runs, in a 23-year career with the Baltimore Orioles. Robin Yount had 3,142 hits and 251 home runs in a 20-year career with the Milwaukee Brewers and was named the American League's Most Valuable Player twice, once as a shortstop and once as a center fielder. Dick Allen was one of Major League Baseball's leading power hitters, blasting 351 home runs over 15 seasons and winning the American League Most Valuable Player award in 1972. Joe Morgan was the 5 feet 7 inch tall catalyst for Cincinnati's "Big Red Machine" of the 1970s. A fine fielder, hitter, and base runner, Morgan won consecutive National League Most Valuable Player awards in 1975 and 1976, as the Reds won World Series championships in both years. Johnny Bench was baseball's leading catcher in the 1970s and early 1980s. Bench hit 389 career home runs, won ten Gold Gloves, and was twice named the National League's Most Valuable Player in a 17-year career with the Cincinnati Reds. Carlton Fisk played in 24 seasons for the Red Sox and White Sox, catching a record 2,226 Major League games. He retired with a career .269 batting average, 2,356 hits, 376 home runs, 1,330 runs batted in, and 1,276 runs scored. Paul Molitor, who primarily served as a designated hitter during his 21-year American League career, retired with career totals of 3,319 hits, 605 doubles, 114 triples, 234 home runs,

1,780 runs scored, 1,307 runs batted in, and 504 stolen bases. Eddie Murray, who with Cal Ripken, Jr. provided the power for the Baltimore Orioles in the 1980s, collected 3,255 career hits, 504 home runs, 1,627 runs scored, and 1,917 runs batted in, becoming one of only three players to combine at least 500 home runs and 3,000 hits, the other two being Hank Aaron and Willie Mays. Andre Dawson was a superb fielder, base runner, and hitter whose career was sadly shortened by injuries to his knees. He posted career totals of 2,774 hits, 438 home runs, 1,591 runs batted in, 1,373 runs scored, and 314 stolen bases and was named the National League's Most Valuable Player in 1987. Rod Carew won seven American League batting titles, collecting 3,053 hits, 1,424 runs scored, and 1,015 runs batted in in his 19-year career. He was named the American League's Most Valuable Player in 1977. Gary Carter won three Gold Gloves and collected 2,092 hits, including 324 home runs, in a 19-year National League career, primarily with the Montreal Expos and New York Mets. Wade Boggs collected 3,010 hits and posted a .328 lifetime batting average in 18 Major League seasons. Kirby Puckett maintained a .318 lifetime batting average, hit 207 home runs, and collected 1,085 runs batted in and 1,071 runs scored in a 12-year career which was tragically truncated by glaucoma. Cal Ripken, Jr., retired from Major League Baseball following the 2001 season, after 21 seasons with the Baltimore Orioles. Major League Baseball's "Iron Man," Ripken surpassed Lou Gehrig's longstanding Major League record for most consecutive games played, finally stopping his streak at 2,632. Ripken collected 3,184 hits and 431 home runs in his career and won two American League Most Valuable Player awards. In his 20-year Major League career, the recently retired Tony Gwynn amassed 3,141 hits and eight National League batting titles, and posted a .338 lifetime batting average. Mark McGwire, who announced his retirement on November 11, 2001, was the most consistent home run hitter in the history of Major League Baseball. In his 16-year Major League career, which was interrupted and finally abbreviated by a succession of injuries, "Big Mac" hit 583 home runs (sixth on the all-time list) in only 6,187 at-bats, for a Major League career-best one home run in each 10.6 times at bat. His 70 home runs in 1998 was the single-season Major League record until it was broken by Barry Bonds in 2001. McGwire is the only Major League player ever to have accounted for more than two-thirds of his total bases by home runs. More than one-half of all Major League players hit twice as many doubles in their careers as home runs. McGwire is the only player in Major League history to have hit twice as many home runs as doubles. He is also the only player in Major League history to have more extra-base hits than singles.

A number of current Major League players are proceeding with careers that are likely to lead to eventual induction into the Hall of Fame. For some of these players, it is still too early to tell whether their careers will have the duration and continued excellence that justifies that honor. For a few players, however, barring injury, the Hall of Fame seems only to be waiting for the conclusion of great careers and the required five-year retirement period. Such players include Roger Clemens, Greg Maddux, Randy Johnson, Barry Bonds, Sammy Sosa, Ken Griffey, Jr., and Rickey Henderson.

Roger Clemens, Major League Baseball's leading right-handed power pitcher since the retirement of Nolan Ryan, has won 293 games in his career and has received the American League Cy Young Award a record six times. In his 19-year career to date, the 39-year-old "Rocket" has a lifetime earned run average of 3.15 and has amassed 3,909 strikeouts, including 20 in a single game on two different occasions. In 2001, Clemens became the first Major League pitcher to post a 20–1 record. Greg Maddux has been Major League Baseball's leading control pitcher for the last decade. Thus far in his 17-year career, Maddux has won 273 games with a 2.83 earned run average and 2,641 strikeouts and has won the National League's Cy Young Award four times. Randy Johnson has been the Major Leagues' leading left-handed power pitcher over the last decade. The 6 feet 10 inch tall "Big Unit" intimidates batters and has won 224 games over the last 15 years, with a 3.06 career earned run average and 3,746 strikeouts. Johnson won the American League Cy Young Award in 1995 and has won four consecutive National League Cy Young Awards (1999–2002). Barry Bonds has been Major League Baseball's greatest all-around player for the last decade. An excellent fielder, runner, and hitter, Bonds is the only Major League player to have hit over 400 home runs and stolen over 400 bases in his career. In his 17-year career to date, Bonds has hit 613 home runs, driven in 1,652 runs, scored 1,830 runs, stolen 484 bases, recorded a .585 slugging average, and won an unprecedented five National League Most Valuable Player awards. In 2001, he set a new single season Major League home run record (73). He also is a Gold Glove outfielder. In his 14-year career to date, Sammy Sosa has accumulated 499 home runs, 1,347 runs batted in, 1,215 runs scored, and 233 stolen bases. He has hit at least 50 home runs in four separate seasons, joining Babe Ruth and Mark McGwire as the only players to have done so. Sosa exceeded 60 home runs in 1998, 1999, and 2001, becoming the only player to have three 60-home run seasons and joining only Mark McGwire with more than one season with at least 60 home runs. The American League's best all-around player during the 1990s, Ken Griffey, Jr., moved to the National League for the new millennium, where his success has been hampered by injuries. In his 14-year career to date, "Junior" has tallied 468 home runs, 1,358 runs batted in, 1,237 runs scored, 176 stolen bases, and a .562 slugging average. He also has been a Gold Glove center fielder ten times. Rickey Henderson was Major League Baseball's greatest leadoff hitter for two decades. He holds Major League records for both single season (130) and career (1,403) stolen bases, and for career bases on balls (2,179) and runs scored (2,288). He also has collected 3,040 hits, including 295 home runs.

Other players who have not yet achieved these levels of sustained excellence, but who appear to have the necessary talent and may need only additional healthy years in their careers to attain comparable success, are Jeff Bagwell, Manny Ramirez, Alex Rodriguez, Juan Gonzales, Ivan Rodriguez, Mike Piazza, Nomar Garciaparra, Derek Jeter, Jeff Kent, Roberto Alomar, Rafael Palmiero, Todd Helton, Jason Giambi, Gary Sheffield, Vladimir Guerrero, Larry Walker, Chipper Jones, Pedro Martinez, Curt Schilling, Tom Glavine, John Smoltz, and Mariano Rivera.

Major League Baseball has expanded three times since the 1960s and two franchises have changed cities during that period. In 1970, after only one season in Seattle, the Seattle Pilots moved to Milwaukee and became the Milwaukee Brewers. In 1972, the second Washington Senators team moved to Arlington, Texas, and became the Texas Rangers. The American League added two new franchises for the 1977 season. A new Seattle Mariners franchise was awarded to replace the franchise that moved to Milwaukee in 1970. A second Canadian franchise was also established, in Toronto. The National League added two new franchises for the 1993 season, the Florida Marlins and the Colorado Rockies. Each of those teams paid $95 million for the right to become a member of the Major Leagues. Two new Major League franchises were also added for the 1998 season, with the Arizona Diamondbacks joining the National League and the Tampa Bay Devil Rays becoming members of the American League. Each of these teams paid $130 million for its Major League franchise. At the same time, the Milwaukee Brewers moved from the American League to the National League. The American League now has 14 teams and the National League has 16 teams.

With the exception of seasons suffering from the effects of Major League Baseball's several labor disputes, baseball attendance has grown steadily over the past thirty years. In 1970, the Major Leagues drew a total of 28.7 million fans, with the National League accounting for 16.7 million and the American League drawing 12 million.[685] By 1980, National League attendance had increased to 21.1 million and the American League drew

Barry Bonds at bat.

21.9 million fans, for a total attendance of 43 million.[686] By 1990, total Major League attendance was 54.8 million, as American League attendance increased to 30.3 million and the National League drew 24.5 million spectators (the American League had two more teams than the National League).[687] In 1991, Toronto became the first team to draw four

Alex Rodriguez

million fans, repeating that feat in 1992 and 1993.[688] In 1993, in its first season in the National League, the Colorado Rockies set the all time single-season Major League attendance record at 4,483,350.[689] In 2000, Major League Baseball set a new total annual single-season attendance record of 72.7 million, as nine teams drew over three million spectators. Major League attendance remained steady at 72.6 million in 2001, as eight teams reported paid attendance in excess of three million, 20 teams drew over two million fans, and only the Montreal Expos failed to draw at least one million spectators (642,745). In 2002, Major League attendance declined to 67.9 million, as six teams reported attendance in excess of three million, 18 teams drew over two million fans, and only the Florida Marlins (813,118) and Montreal Expos (812,045) failed to attract at least one million spectators.

Salaries began to accelerate more rapidly in the early 1980s as the combination of free agency and arbitration began to take effect. From 1980 to 1984, the average annual Major League salary more than doubled, reaching nearly $330,000, and baseball's most highly compensated players were paid in excess of $1.5 million per season.[690] By the early 1990s, Major League Baseball's average annual salary increased to $1 million and the highest-salaried players were paid in excess of $7 million per season.[691] In 1997, Albert Belle signed a 5-year contract with the Chicago White Sox for an average of $11 million per season. In 1998 and 1999, Mike Piazza and Kevin Brown signed 7-year contracts for average annual salaries of $13 million and $15 million, respectively. By 2000, the average annual Major League salary was approximately $2 million. After the 2000 season, new salary heights were achieved. The Toronto Blue Jays extended the contract of Carlos Delgado for four years at a salary of $17 million per season. The Texas Rangers signed former Seattle Mariners superstar shortstop and free agent Alex Rodriguez to a 10-year contract for total compensation of $252 million, an average of $25.2 million per season, higher than the entire payroll for the 2001 Minnesota Twins and nearly *three times* as much as the aggregate salaries paid to *all* Major League Baseball players in 1966, the year in which Marvin Miller became executive director of the Major League Baseball Players Association![692] The Boston Red Sox signed former Cleveland Indians slugger and free agent Manny Ramirez to an 8-year contract for total compensation of $160 million, an average of $20 million per season. The New York Yankees extended the contract of their young superstar shortstop Derek Jeter for 10 years for total compensation of $189 million, an average of $18.9 million per season. The Colorado Rockies inked left-handed pitcher Mike Hampton to an 8-year contract for total compensation of $121 million, an average of $15.125 million per season. Right-handed pitcher Mike Mussina signed a 6-year contract with the New York Yankees for total compensation of $88.5 million, an average of $14.75 million per season. The *average* Major League player's salary in the 2001 season increased to approximately $2.15 million. Fewer free agents achieved huge salaries after the 2001 season. The most significant free agent signings were the New York Yankees' luring of former Oakland A's star Jason Giambi with a 7-year, $120 million contract ($17.1 million average annual salary) and the San Francisco Giants' retention of Barry Bonds with a 5-year, $90 million contract ($18 million average annual salary).

Chapter 12

YOU CAN'T SMOKE ASTROTURF

I don't know. I never smoked Astroturf.
> —Frank Edwin "Tug" McGraw,
> when asked if he preferred grass
> or artificial turf

Every ball park used to be unique. Now it's like women's
breasts—if you've seen one, you've seen both.
> —Jim Kaat

Mr. Speaker, I rise to condemn the desecration of a great
American symbol. No, I am not referring to flag burn-
ing; I am referring to the baseball bat. Several experts
tell us that the wooden baseball bat is doomed to extinc-
tion, that major league baseball players will soon be
standing at home plate with aluminum bats in their
hands. Baseball fans have been forced to endure count-
less indignities by those who just cannot leave well enough
alone. Designated hitters, plastic grass, uniforms that
look like pajamas, chicken clowns dancing on the base-
lines, and of course the most heinous sacrilege, lights in
Wrigley field. Are we willing to hear the crack of a bat
replaced by the dinky ping? Are we ready to see the
Louisville slugger replaced by the aluminum ping dinger?
Is nothing sacred? Please, do not tell me that wooden bats
are too expensive, when players who cannot hit their
weight are being paid more money than the President of
the United States. Please, do not try to sell me on the
notion that these metal clubs will make better hitters.

What is next? Teflon baseballs? Radar-enhanced gloves? I ask you. I do not want to hear about saving trees. Any tree in America would gladly give its life for the glory of a day at home plate. I do not know if it will take a con- stitutional amendment to keep the baseball traditions alive, but if we forsake the great Americana of broken- bat singles and pine tar, we will have certainly lost our way as a nation.

—United States Congressman Richard H. Durbin in a speech in the United States House of Repre- sentatives

Major League Baseball's owners and players have committed a mul- titude of crimes over the game's long and varied history, some felonies and some mere misdemeanors. Some were premeditated and others were committed without forethought. Many of the owners' greatest crimes, particularly in race and labor relations, are recounted in other chapters of this book. Some of the players' crimes, particularly in labor matters and greed, are also discussed elsewhere in this book. But a number of other crimes, involving the game itself and artificial elements that have influenced the game, have also been committed. In many cases, these crimes have been committed with ostensibly legitimate goals in mind. But, by introducing artificial and foreign elements to the greatest of games, the game itself and its special place in America has been diminished.

Professional baseball's earliest ballparks, which held approximately 1,000–2000 spectators each, were rather simple affairs, wooden grand- stands with no shade or amenities for spectators.[693] Near the end of the 19th century, newer, more permanent, ballparks, which provided seating for approximately 10,000–20,000 spectators each, such as the Polo Grounds in New York, Lakefront Park in Chicago, and the Baker Bowl in Philadelphia, began to appear, typically located in the centers of cities and on or near subway or trolley lines or other public transportation.[694] Between 1909 and 1923, Major League Baseball's first great building boom replaced primitive wooden grandstands with modern steel and concrete stadiums offering new levels of comfort for baseball's fans. These parks continued to be sited in central locations convenient to public trans- portation.[695] After World War II, another building boom replaced some of the earlier stadiums and accommodated Major League Baseball's fran- chise movements and expansion. Increasingly, the newer parks were located in suburban areas and provided extensive parking facilities for spectators' automobiles.[696] Still, these new stadiums were essentially improved versions of baseball's older parks. All this changed, however, in 1962 with the opening of the Harris County Domed Stadium in Houston, Texas, also known as the "Astrodome."

Dubbed by its creator, real estate developer and former Houston mayor Judge Roy Hofheinz, as the "Eighth Wonder of the World," the Astrodome was a revolutionary structure which cost more than twice as much as Dodger Stadium in Los Angeles which was completed in the same year. Domed to insulate spectators from Houston's oppressively hot and humid summers, the temperature and humidity-controlled Astrodome contained three stadium clubs, the world's largest bar, extended dugouts to give more spectators the ability to sit behind the players, corporate VIP suites and skyboxes, wild color schemes, and the world's first animated and "exploding" electronic scoreboard.[697]

Although the Astrodome was a financial success and popular with many fans, as a baseball park it was a disaster. It proved impossible for fielders to follow fly balls under the stadium's massive Lucite dome. Experiments with colored baseballs failed and the dome was painted. Fielders could now track the ball, but the grass on the field died. With no immediate solution to the problem, the Astros painted the stadium's soil green. Finally, Monsanto Chemicals developed a synthetic grass surface which was first used in the Astrodome. The age of Astroturf was born.[698] Eventually, ten Major League teams used Astroturf in their stadiums. Owners loved it. It was cheaper to install and maintain than grass. Fewer field staff were required. Fields drained more easily and could be cleared of rain, snow, or other debris more quickly. Baseball and other field sports became faster and could be played indoors in locations with unreliable weather. Unfortunately, the incidence of serious knee, foot, toe, and other injuries on Astroturf fields far exceeded those on natural grass. Moreover, a major component of baseball's timeless and rustic appeal disappeared when it was played indoors on a synthetic surface.

> The expensive Houston experiment does not truly affect the players or much alter the sport played down on the field, but I think it does violence to baseball—and, incidentally, threatens its own success—through a total misunderstanding of the games's old mystery. I do not agree ... that a ballpark is a notable center for socializing or propriety, or that many spectators will continue to find refreshment in returning to a giant living-room—complete with manmade weather, wall-to-wall carpeting,

clean floors and unrelenting TV shows—that so totally,
so drearily resembles the one he has just left.
—Roger Angell

The Astrodome influenced stadium design and construction for a quarter of a century. Beginning in the late 1960s, numerous new cold, artificial, and soulless multi-purpose stadiums were erected.[699] Examples of such stadiums are Busch Stadium in St. Louis, Riverfront Stadium in Cincinnati, Three Rivers Stadium in Pittsburgh, and Veterans Stadium in Philadelphia. Other domed stadiums appeared in Seattle, Minneapolis, and Toronto. Typically these stadiums held approximately 50,000–60,000 spectators, were symmetrical, featured playing fields covered with Astroturf, were publicly financed, featured large exploding electronic scoreboards and outrageous sound systems, and could accommodate baseball, football, soccer, rock concerts, tractor pulls, monster truck competitions, and other events. Unlike the ballparks constructed in the Major Leagues' first major concrete and steel building boom in 1909–1923, the ballparks built in the 1960s and 1970s were typically not built in inner cities near subway or trolley lines, but were located in suburban locations near super-highways and featured vast automobile parking facilities. Unfortunately for players and fans, the new stadiums were not favorable to the game of baseball. In addition to the injuries discussed above, the artificial surfaces and the hard padding that served as a foundation for such surfaces changed the manner in which the game was played. Ground ball singles, including chops of pitches into the Astroturf in front of home plate, became more common. Infielders played deeper and balls hit into the outfield gaps quickly gathered momentum and became extra base hits. Because of the need to accommodate multiple types of events, these stadiums generally featured extensive foul territory, which had the combined effects of discouraging offense because of additional foul outs and moving spectators farther from the field of play. Fortunately, many of these stadiums have already been replaced or substantially remodeled or will be within the next couple of years. In 2000, the Seattle Kingdome was demolished and the Mariners began to play in new Safeco Field, an outdoor, natural grass facility which is more conducive to good pitching than scoring runs. Also in 2000, the Houston Astros abandoned the Astrodome for new Enron Field (since renamed Minute Maid Park), an outdoor, natural grass ballpark that encourages offense. In 1999, their last year in the Astrodome, the Astros hit 168 home runs and scored 823 runs and their opponents

Opposite: Astrodome (interior), Houston.

hit 128 home runs and scored 675 runs. In 2000, their first year in Enron Field, the Astros hit 249 home runs and scored 938 runs and their opponents hit 234 home runs and scored 944 runs. In 2000, the San Francisco Giants finally left Candlestick Park to move into new Pacific Bell Park in San Francisco's China Basin. In 2001, the Pittsburgh Pirates moved from Three Rivers Stadium to the new PNC Park and the Cincinnati Reds moved from Riverfront Stadium/Cinergy Field to the new Great American Ball Park. Many of these new ballparks feature retro themes and offer greater viewing enjoyment and amenities for spectators, continuing a trend that commenced when the Baltimore Orioles moved into Camden Yards in 1992, and that has been followed in recent years by the Ballpark in Arlington, Texas, Jacobs Field in Cleveland, Comiskey Park in Chicago, Turner Field in Atlanta, Coors Field in Denver, and Bank One Ballpark in Phoenix.

With the exception of a handful of owners and front-office executives in Major League Baseball and the Negro Leagues, notably Bill Veeck, Larry MacPhail, and Rube Foster, baseball had long eschewed extensive marketing and promotion to attract and increase the enjoyment of spectators. Teams led by Foster, MacPhail, and Veeck had featured creative marketing and on-the-field promotions in the 1920s, 1930s, and 1940s, but these activities were generally frowned upon by Major League Baseball's owners, particularly those in the more conservative National League. Judge Hofheinz's Astrodome set new standards in artificial and often tasteless promotions. The Astrodome's scoreboard featured an electronic cannon, an electronic trumpet, and electronic hands which relentlessly encouraged fans to clap and scream "Charge!" in unison. The Astros' promotions were relatively tasteful and subdued, however, in comparison to the panoply of gimmicks employed by Kansas City and later Oakland A's owner Charlie Finley. Finley tried nearly everything to bring fans to his team's games. Every day seemed to be a theme day of one type or another, contests of all varieties were held on the playing field before games, and various efforts were made to improve the game's offense. Finley attempted to have the American League use yellow or orange balls, which he argued were easier to see.[700] Finley paid his players to wear mustaches and long hair to attract younger fans. Eschewing the white home and gray road uniforms of other Major League teams, Finley's A's were clad in flashy green and gold uniforms and shod in white spikes. Finley encouraged his "Swingin' A's" to play with dash, flash, and panache.[701] Other teams followed Finley's example in the 1970s, including the Houston Astros whose

Opposite: Astrodome (exterior), Houston.

outrageously multicolored uniforms Charlie Hough said looked as if they belonged to a Hawaiian softball team, the Chicago White Sox who sported hideous short pants and V-necked pullover jerseys, and the San Diego Padres whose brown and yellow uniforms Steve Garvey said made the Padres players look like tacos.[702] Finley also argued that all World Series games should be played at night when both children and working people would be at home and able to watch the games on television.[703] In spite of initial resistance, this idea, like many other Finley suggestions, ultimately was accepted by Major League Baseball's owners. Promotions also have become a regular part of each Major League franchise's efforts to increase and maintain attendance.

Another of Finley's proposals was adopted in 1973, when the American League, in an effort to increase offense and generate spectator interest, introduced the controversial designated hitter rule.[704] The rule, which had been used in the minor leagues for a number of years, was intended to increase hitting by removing hapless pitchers from teams' batting orders. For many years preceding the introduction of the designated hitter rule, the American League had been weaker offensively than the National League. In 1972, the last season before the American League's adoption of the rule, the National League batters scored 824 more runs, hit 186 more home runs, and posted a collective batting average nine percentage points higher than their American League counterparts.[705] In 1973, the collective American League batting average increased by 20 percentage points and American League home runs and runs scored increased by nearly one-third.[706] The implementation of the rule increased American League attendance, as spectators came out in greater numbers to witness aging hitting stars such as Hank Aaron, Frank Robinson, Orlando Cepeda, Billy Williams, and Tony Oliva who could no longer play regularly in the field. In 2001, the average salary for American League designated hitters was $5.65 million, more than $1 million higher than any other position.[707]

The designated hitter rule has not always produced the desired effect, however, and has completely changed the strategy of managing games in the American League. Although the pitcher does not bat and a manager can use a better hitter to replace him in the line-up, the other team is not forced to remove a still-effective pitcher at a crucial point in a game during which a pinch hitter otherwise might be used. A more effective way to have generated offense would have been to eliminate the pitcher's position in the line-up and allow only eight hitters to bat. Under such a system, each team's best hitters would have more opportunities to hit and offensive production would increase.

Of course, many rule changes could be made that would increase or decrease offense. The use of fielders' gloves could be outlawed or improved. Titanium or nuclear-powered bats could be introduced at the Major League level. Baseballs could be made still livelier. All ballparks could be designed to yield runs as easily as Coors Field. The game could be changed to feature offensive and defensive squads. If pitchers do not have to bat, why should middle infielders, except possibly Robbie Alomar, Jeff Kent, Alex Rodriguez, Nomar Garciaperra, Derek Jeter, Bret Boone, and Rich Aurelia? Free substitution of players could be permitted. Major League Baseball could continue to adjust the strike zone and the pitcher's mound on a regular basis. By continually making changes that improve or harm baseball's offense and defense, however, the integrity of the game is imperiled. Baseball, more than any other game, depends upon tradition. Baseball is revered in part because it is the game closest to its past. Serious baseball fans know about players of past generations and enjoy comparing the feats of modern stars to those of yesteryear's heroes. Although such efforts are at best an inexact science, even for Bill James and other sabermetricians, they become impossible and meaningless when artificial, external factors eliminate all basis for logical comparison. In any event, the American League adopted the designated hitter rule in 1973 and continues to employ it. The National League continues to reject using it. At the time the American League introduced the rule, National League President Chub Feeney proclaimed, "We'll continue to play by baseball rules." I am delighted the National League does so.

Perhaps the most persuasive argument for discontinuing the use of the designated hitter in the American League is that it simply has outlived its purpose. When the designated hitter rule was introduced, Major League Baseball was still attempting to recover from the doldrums of the 1960s. In 1968, Carl Yastrzemski won the American League batting title with a .301 average, the cumulative batting average in the American League was .230, Denny McLain won 31 games, Don Drysdale pitched 58⅔ consecutive scoreless innings and six straight shutouts, Bob Gibson won 22 games including 13 shutouts and posted a 1.12 earned run average, and 21 percent of all Major League games were shutouts. Immediately before the adoption of the designated hitter rule in the American League in 1973, both the National League and the American League averaged approximately four runs per game per team. By 2000, Major League scoring had increased to more than five runs per game per team in the National League and approximately five and one-half runs per game per team in the American League. Overall, the difference in scoring between the American League, which employs the designated hitter, and the National League, which does not, is of little significance. In 2001, primarily as a result of an expanded strike zone, runs per game fell in the Major Leagues to 9.55 per game and most other offensive statistics declined. In 2002, scoring declined further to 9.24 runs per game.

Since the introduction of the designated hitter rule in the American League, scoring has increased in both Major Leagues for a variety of reasons. Today's players are bigger, stronger, and generally in better physical condition than their counterparts of past years. Babe Ruth was considered to be a huge and superhuman figure in the 1920s. He was six feet two inches tall and, before adding substantial weight later in his career, a little over 200 pounds. Hardly a behemoth by today's standards. Players today also are more physically developed than earlier players because of better training and nutrition and use of weights and exercise equipment. But strength is only marginally important in hitting a baseball; bat speed is the most relevant factor. In spite of the 1998 furor over Mark McGwire's use of creatine and androstenedione to hasten his recovery between workouts, the six feet five inch, 250 pound Big Mac's ability to drive balls out of Major League ballparks had less to do with the diameter of his biceps than the tremendous leverage and bat speed he generated. McGwire was simply the greatest pure home run hitter in Major League history. Can anyone really believe that creatine and androstenedione are responsible for McGwire regularly hitting balls more than 500 feet or that, even if those supplements had some marginal effect, he wouldn't just as regularly have hit balls 450 feet without them? These days, 160 pound second basemen are regularly hitting home runs! What is the reason for all that power?

There are a number of reasons. First, in spite of vigorous denials by the commissioner's office, most seasoned observers believe that the Major Leagues introduced a livelier ball in 1993. Second, for a number of years the strike zone has been shrinking, although the Major Leagues made some effort to remedy this condition in 2001. Third, the quality of Major League pitching, and particularly middle relief pitching, has been diluted by expansion, a decline in the number of top athletes who elect to become pitchers, and the increased numbers of pitchers on each team's pitching staff. Fourth, the design and composition of today's bats, which have larger barrels, denser wood, and thinner handles than bats in previous decades, contribute to increased bat speed. Fifth, today's players are bigger and stronger than ever before, the result of a combination of factors including better diets, weight training, better overall physical fitness, and in some cases steroid use. Former players such as Ken Caminetti and Jose Canseco have reported that an overwhelming majority of Major League players have used steroids. Sixth, because of what Mark McGwire, Sammy Sosa, Junior Griffey, Barry Bonds, and others have accomplished in recent years, there is an increased emphasis on hitting home runs, not only for "power hitters" but for all hitters. When McGwire led the Major Leagues in home runs with 70 in 1998, Rickey Henderson led the Major Leagues in stolen bases with 66. That was the first season since Maury Wills broke Ty Cobb's single-season base stealing record in 1963 that the Major League home run champion hit more home runs than the stolen base leader had stolen bases. Major League Baseball is in another transitional period, perhaps as significant as that which occurred when Babe Ruth began hitting home runs in the early 1920s. At least for the time being, power has replaced speed and finesse as baseball's prime commodity. In even recent times, the offensive contributions of middle infielders were typically limited to getting on base, bunting to advance runners, employing hit-and-run tactics, and running the bases with proficiency. With increasing focus on, and financial rewards for, hitting home runs, however, middle infielders, like other players, are increasingly swinging for the fences. Seventh, and perhaps most significantly, those fences are closer and, because of ballpark configurations and geography, easier to reach.

There is no doubt that it is easier to hit a home run in Minute Maid Park than it was in the Astrodome or that it is easier to hit home runs and score runs in Coors Field than any other Major League ballpark. For several years, the Colorado Rockies teams had a number of players such as Andres Gallaraga, Dante Bichette, Vinny Castilla, and Larry Walker who were constant home run threats. The new-look Rockies were only 13th in the National League in home runs during the 2000 season, but still scored more runs (968) than any team in Major League Baseball in the last century except the 1930 St. Louis Cardinals (1,004). In spite of more pitcher-friendly enforcement of the strike zone in 2001, the Rockies still managed to score 923 runs. In all Major League ballparks other than Coors Field, the *losing* team scores ten or more runs in only about one out of every 229 games, or about once every three seasons; in the 2000 season in Coors Field this occurred in one out of every 18 games, or about four and one-half times each season, almost *thirteen* times as frequently. Not quite as bad as Lakefront Park—into which the Chicago White Stockings moved in 1883, which featured dimensions of 198 feet down the left field line, 190 feet down the right field line, and 300 feet to dead center, and where Major League home runs records were set in 1884 and which stood until Babe Ruth burst upon the scene—but not really Major League standard either.

Fans love to see runs scored and home runs hit. Increasingly, the Major Leagues' shrinking strike zone and lively baseball encourage offensive play, and Major League ballparks are being built and reconfigured to provide more runs and especially more home runs. During 2000, Major League Baseball's 30 teams hit 5,693 home runs (2.34 per game), more than the 5,528 home runs (2.28 per game) hit in 1999, previously baseball's most prolific home run season, and 87 percent more than the 3,038 home runs (1.44 per game) hit in 1992, the last season before the two expansions of the Major Leagues which added the Colorado Rockies, Florida Marlins, Arizona Diamondbacks, and Tampa Bay Devil Rays. In 2001, the number of home runs per game decreased to 2.25, as most Major League offensive statistics declined in the wake of an increased strike zone. In 1992, 37 Major League players hit at least 20 home runs. In 2000, 37 players had hit at least 20 home runs before the All-Star Game! Over the entire 2000 season, 96 players hit at least 20 home runs and 47 players hit at least 30 home runs. In 2001, 80 players hit at least 20 home runs and 50 players hit at least 30 home runs. In 2002, 81 players hit at least 20 home runs and 28 players hit at least 30 home runs. In the 1990s, more players hit 50 home runs in a season than in the 1940s, 1950s, 1960s, 1970s, and 1980s *combined*. To baseball's traditionalists, artificial enhancements of the game that pander to the desires of unknowledgeable fans for ever-increasing home run totals is an unforgivable devaluation of the game.

Another bastardization of the game was proposed by commissioner Bud Selig in 1997. Fortunately, after substantial public outcry, that proposal was rejected by Major League Baseball's owners. The proposal would have resulted in about one-half of all Major League teams changing leagues in an effort to arrange closer geographical groupings and heighten "local" rivalries. If this "radical realignment" actually had been effected, a century's baseball history would have been erased, the significance of the World Series destroyed, and Major League Baseball irredeemably cheapened. One of Major League Baseball's greatest attributes is its tradition. Tradition sets baseball apart from other sports whose alignments change regularly. To *radically* realign anything within the game of baseball risks the destruction of what makes baseball special. Baseball is a conservative game with a liberal agenda and should remain so. Apparently, however, few of Major League Baseball's owners realize or respect this fact and even fewer appreciate that they are guardians of a great public trust.

But baseball's owners are not solely to blame for the Major Leagues' ills. Players have been guilty of many of baseball's crimes. Perhaps the greatest of the players' current crimes is their greed and their willingness to withhold the game from the fans to accomplish their goals of even greater compensation. It is undeniable that many of baseball's owners historically treated players dreadfully. With the exception of an increasingly smaller group of aging players who can recall the owners' collusion in the late 1980s, however, few of today's players have experienced harsh treatment by owners. To the contrary, today's players are highly, often obscenely, compensated. Their bickering with owners over perceived unfairness no longer rings true to baseball's fans. With the exception of players such as Mark McGwire, who accepted significantly less than his market value to play in St. Louis, who decided not to hold the Cardinals' franchise to a $30 million, two-year contract extension when he felt that injuries would no longer permit him to contribute to the team at an appropriate level, and who regularly contributed a significant portion of his salary to charities, and Ken Griffey, Jr., who made financial concessions to play in Cincinnati, players are now typically viewed as overpaid, spoiled, arrogant brats who are unworthy of fans' affection.

As Jim Bouton's *Ball Four*[708] and Curt Flood's *The Way It Is*[709] recount, the Major League Baseball player's lifestyle has long included easy and frequent sexual fulfillment. Particularly public examples of such behavior included Babe Ruth's off-the-field escapades, Wade Boggs's affair with Margo Adams, and Steve Garvey's paternity of several children by different women.[710]

Players also have indulged in other behaviors that have adversely affected the game. Alcohol abuse has clearly had an impact on baseball games and on many Major League players from baseball's earliest days until the present. Notable players whose careers and lives were undoubtedly affected, and even abbreviated, by alcohol include Mike Kelly, Cap Anson, Ed Delahanty, Ty Cobb, Tris Speaker, Grover Cleveland Alexander, Babe Ruth, Hack Wilson, Jimmie Foxx, Don Newcombe, Mickey Mantle, Whitey Ford, Billy Martin, Sam McDowell, Dennis Martinez, Bob Welch, Darrell Porter, Lenny Dykstra, and Albert Belle, to name only a few.

Although you can't smoke Astroturf, this has not meant that Major League Baseball's players have not indulged in other substances. As aging radicals such as Timothy Leary encouraged the youth of America to "tune in, turn on, and drop out" in the 1960s, recreational drug use and free love became the rage. Those who abstained were "square." Initially, baseball was decidedly square. Major League Baseball players' early forays into the drug counter-culture seem almost laughable in hindsight. For example, New York Yankees upstart Joe Pepitone became the first recorded player to bring a hair dryer or marijuana into a Major League clubhouse. During spring training in Florida one year, Pepitone was cleaning the stems and seeds from a bag of weed when his roommate, Mickey Mantle, walked in.

"What's this?" asked Mantle.
"It's marijuana," replied Pepitone.
"What's it do?" Mantle asked again.
"It makes you relaxed and it makes you laugh," Pepitone said.
"Well, let's try some," said Mantle.

Pepitone proceeded to roll a joint and shared it with Mantle before their afternoon game. During the game Mantle struck out four times. Normally, Mantle would be extremely upset when he struck out, often cursing and throwing his helmet. After each strikeout on this afternoon, however, Mantle gingerly returned to the dugout and placidly sat in a corner, giggling uncontrollably. After the game, Mantle approached Pepitone and said, "I don't know what that shit is, but keep it away from me."

Reflecting the times, many Major League Baseball players experimented with drugs during the 1960s and 1970s. The combination of increasingly high disposable incomes, easy access to drugs, and abundant free time contributed to drug usage. Amphetamines and barbiturates were widely used, and even dispensed by team physicians and trainers. The Pittsburgh Pirates' free-spirited pitcher Dock Ellis reportedly threw a no-hitter in 1970 while stoned on LSD.

Over the last two decades, a number of Major League players have been arrested and convicted for possessing drugs, primarily cocaine. Among the convicted offenders are Ferguson Jenkins, Orlando Cepeda, John "Blue Moon" Odom, Steve Howe, Alan Wiggins, Pascual Perez, Willie Wilson, Vida Blue, Willie Mays Aikens, Jerry Martin, Darryl Strawberry, LaMarr Hoyt, Denny McLain, Maury Wills, and Otis Nixon. Others who have admitted to using cocaine or who have been implicated in cocaine trials but who were not tried include Keith Hernandez, Lonnie Smith, Dave Parker, Dale Berra, Darrell Porter, Enos Cabell, Jeffrey Leonard, Dock Ellis, Dwight Gooden, John Milner, Paul Molitor, Claudell Washington, Dick Davis, Tim Raines, Lee Lacy, Rod Scurry, Dusty Baker, J.R. Richard, Derrell Thomas, Joe Pepitone, and Joaquin Andujar. But these players were only the tip of the iceberg. During celebrated drug trials in Pittsburgh in 1986, Keith Hernandez testified that, in the early 1980s, 40 percent of all Major League Baseball players used cocaine.[711] Clearly, this degree of drug use affected the quality of play in that period. Tim Raines has confessed that he slid head first into bases to avoid breaking the vial of cocaine he kept in the back pocket of his uniform pants.[712] The Pittsburgh Pirates brought a legal action against Dave Parker alleging that the quality of his play had declined as a result of drug use.[713] Although Major League Baseball suspended and fined a number of such individuals, (e.g., Steve Howe was suspended seven times for drug and alcohol-related offenses), Darryl Strawberry's recent legal and personal problems, the recent death of Darrell Porter, and the recent exposures of widespread steroid use by Major League players confirm that illegal drugs continue to cast a cloud over Major League Baseball.

Another cloud that has intermittently hung over Major League Baseball's history is gambling. Gambling has existed in baseball since at least the 1860s, during baseball's "amateur" days, when fixing games, or "hippodroming," was common.[714] The National League, which was formed in 1876 under a banner of freedom from the foul influences of gamblers, experienced its first gambling scandal in 1877, when four members of the Louisville Grays threw the pennant. The National League banned the "Louisville Four" for life.[715] Attempts reportedly were made to fix the 1903, 1905, and 1914 World Series.[716]

Major League Baseball's most infamous gambling experience was the "Black Sox" scandal in which eight members of the American League champion Chicago White Sox conspired with gamblers to throw the 1919 World Series.[717] Although they were acquitted in a court of law, Commissioner Kenesaw Mountain Landis banned all eight players from the Major Leagues for life.[718] Legends Ty Cobb and Tris Speaker were permitted by the American League to resign as players/managers in 1926 when it became known that they had gambled on fixed games in 1919, but Commissioner Landis surprisingly reinstated both men.[719]

Manager Leo "The Lip" Durocher was suspended by commissioner Albert "Happy" Chandler in 1947 for a variety of unsavory acts, including consorting with gamblers. Denny McLain was suspended in 1970 for participating in a bookmaking operation. Mickey Mantle and Willie Mays were suspended from involvement in baseball activities long after their retirements and inductions into the Hall of Fame because they served as greeters in Atlantic City casinos. Oakland Athletics owner Charlie Finley and Atlanta Braves owner Bill Bartholomay were forced to sell their stock in a corporation that owned casinos and reportedly had organized crime connections. George Steinbrenner was suspended in 1990, in part because of his involvement with a gambler. In 1991, Lenny Dykstra was suspended for gambling offenses. But none of these suspensions involved betting on baseball games.

Baseball's most recent, and continuing, gambling scandal involves commissioner Bart Giamatti's 1989 lifetime banishment of Major League Baseball's all-time Major League hits leader and compulsive gambler, Pete Rose. commissioner Giamatti hired an investigator who assembled a plethora of evidence regarding Rose's betting on baseball games. Rose still contends he is innocent and is openly campaigning for reinstatement and election to the Hall of Fame. Major League Baseball has thus far refused to yield to Rose's pleas.[720]

The high crimes and misdemeanors discussed in this chapter are despicable, but are made all the more so because they undermine the only part of baseball that has endured more than a century of owner and player greed and stupidity: the game itself. The owners and players must no longer permit such artificial invasions into the sport which imperil the game we love. The Church of Baseball must not be subjected to such sacrilege.

Chapter 13

This Bud's for You

It seems I'll have to show somebody who's running this game.
> —Commissioner Kenesaw
> Mountain Landis on suspending
> Babe Ruth in 1922

Walter O'Malley is the true commissioner of baseball, not Bowie Kuhn. Kuhn does what he is told.
> —Bill Veeck

I apologize for calling the baseball commissioner the village idiot. In fact, I apologize to all the village idiots out there for doing them a disservice.
> —Charles O. Finley on Bowie
> Kuhn

Who would accept a job with Marge Schott's dog, Ted Turner, and George Steinbrenner as your boss?
> Commissioner Peter Ueberroth

In early 1993, the owners of Major League Baseball's franchises conducted a search to locate the ideal candidate to serve as the ninth commissioner of the game and to replace the eighth commissioner, Fay Vincent, who had been forced to resign the previous September. They put together a laundry list of requirements that few people could meet. They concluded that the following qualities should be possessed by the new commissioner:

- strategic thinking and problem solving abilities,
- intelligence and analytical ability,
- strong marketing, planning, and implementation skills,
- consensus-building ability,
- accessibility to the owners,
- charisma,
- sensitivity,
- warmth,
- pleasant personality,
- good sense of humor,
- dynamism,
- self confidence,
- poised and commanding personal style,
- innovation,
- motivation,
- positiveness,
- aggressiveness,
- strength of character,
- experience in dealing with the media,
- ability to act decisively, when necessary, in the best interests of baseball,
- unflinching loyalty and obedience to the owners, and
- ability to leap tall buildings in a single bound.[721]

When Milwaukee Brewers owner Allan Huber "Bud" Selig was named chairman of the Executive Council of Major League Baseball (effectively interim commissioner) on September 9, 1992, a search committee was appointed to unearth a worthy candidate. Not surprisingly, it would take more than five years to find a suitable candidate. Perhaps even less surprisingly, given the stated qualifications, the successful candidate would be the same Bud Selig. On July 9, 1998, Selig was officially named the ninth commissioner of Major League Baseball. The charade was finally over. After 71 years of purportedly being run by outsiders, and more than five years without an "official" commissioner, Major League Baseball's owners eliminated the artifice and lodged public control of the game in the hands of one of their own.

As discussed in Chapter 2 of this book, in 1901, a former Cincinnati sportswriter, Byron Bancroft ("Ban") Johnson, frustrated by repeated attempts to acquire a franchise in the National League, changed the name of the Western League, in which he was a franchise owner, to the "American League" and declared that the league was a "Major League," the equal of the senior National League. The American League aggressively pursued players and soon featured a number of former National League stars. The American League also was aggressive in awarding franchises and attracting spectators.[722] In 1903, a portentous National Agreement was signed between the National League and the American League, calling for two separate but equal Major Leagues. Thereafter, a three-member National Commission, comprised of the presidents of both leagues plus a chairman, controlled baseball[723] until baseball's most disgraceful on-the-field episode, the fixed 1919 World Series, provoked an outcry for a new leader to provide honesty and order to the game. Actually, the National Commission was experiencing difficulties before the 1919 World Series. Chicago Cubs shareholder Albert D. Lasker had formulated a plan for restructuring the administration of Major League Baseball. Lasker's plan would have created a new tripartite commission to rule baseball, but the members of that body would be eminent persons without financial connections to the game.[724] Initially, the proposal was met with lukewarm interest by the owners, but after the Black Sox scandal became public, Lasker's plan gained greater support and a search commenced to identify an honest and impartial eminence to serve as Major League Baseball's figurehead. According to the manifesto drafted by the owners, this man would have to be "of unquestionable reputation and standing in fields other than baseball whose mere presence would assure that public interests would first be served, and that therefore, as a natural consequence, all existing evils would disappear."

After considering the appointment of former President of the United States and future Chief Justice of the United States Supreme Court William Howard Taft, United States Army General John J. Pershing, and former Secretary of the Treasury William G. McAdoo, Major League Baseball's owners found their man in a Chicago courtroom. Kenesaw Mountain Landis, a cantankerous, bigoted, egotistical, jingoistic, erratic, headline-grabbing federal judge in the United States District Court in Chicago, had garnered fame as a trustbuster by ruling against John D. Rockefeller's Standard Oil.[725] Landis also had issued a summons for the arrest of German Kaiser Wilhelm II on charges of murdering a Chicago resident who was a passenger on the sunken ocean liner *Lusitania* and demanded that the Kaiser be extradited to his Chicago courtroom.[726] As discussed in

Chapter 2 of this book, during the Major Leagues' battle with the Federal League, Landis also had performed a valuable service for the baseball establishment. Landis's refusal to grant an injunction to the Federal League to prevent the Major Leagues' employment of the reserve system and blacklisting had resulted in a favorable settlement of the case for the established Major Leagues.[727] Five years later, Judge Landis's prior service made him the obvious choice to be appointed as Major League Baseball's first commissioner. The owners offered Landis chairmanship of a new three-member "Board of Control" over Major League Baseball. Judge Landis refused, demanding complete control. Yielding to Landis, the owners granted him the absolute power, for seven years, to investigate and punish wrongdoing and arbitrate all Major League disputes.[728] The owners also relinquished all rights to publicly complain about Landis's decisions or to seek legal redress therefrom. Only one owner, Phil Ball of the St. Louis Browns, refused to agree.[729] For the next 71 years, an "outsider" ostensibly would run Major League Baseball. Ironically, the appointment of a commissioner marked the demise of the commission.

Landis was filled with the oratory and piety that baseball's owners so desperately needed. "The opportunities for real service are limitless," said Landis upon being appointed in late 1920. "I have been devoted for nearly 40 years. On the question of policy, all I have to say is this: 'The only thing in anybody's mind now is to make and keep baseball what the millions of fans throughout the United States want it to be.'" Landis was passionately devoted to baseball and to preserving its integrity. "Baseball is something more than a game to an American boy," he declared. "It is his training field for life work. Destroy his faith in its squareness and honesty and you have destroyed something more; you have planted suspicion of all things in his heart." At the dedication ceremony for the new National Baseball Hall of Fame and Museum in Cooperstown, New York, in 1939, Landis stated, "I should like to dedicate this museum to all America, to lovers of good sportsmanship, healthy bodies, clean minds. For those are the principles of baseball."

Landis believed that, in order to perform the job of commissioner properly, it was necessary to rule with impunity, because Major League Baseball's owners were incapable of policing themselves and one another. Thus, he admonished the owners, "The impression was that there had grown up in baseball certain evils not limited to bad baseball players; that men who controlled ball clubs in the past had been guilty of various offenses and the time had come where somebody would be given authority, if I may put it brutally, to save you from yourselves."

The diminutive Landis made men twice his size cower. He did not

Kenesaw Mountain Landis

tolerate owner dissent, appeals of his rulings, or public criticism of him. Two months after assuming office, Landis demanded that the Major League owners sign a "Pledge of Loyalty" which stated: "We the under-signed, earnestly desirous of insuring to the public wholesome and high class baseball, and believing that we ourselves should set for the players an example of sportsmanship which accepts the umpires' decisions without complaint, hereby pledge loyally to support the commissioner in his important and difficult task; and we assure him that each of us will acquiesce in his decisions even when we believe them mistaken, and that we will not discredit the sport by public criticisms of him or one another."[730]

In the summer of 1921, eight members of the Chicago "Black Sox," who were accused of throwing the 1919 World Series to gamblers, were tried and acquitted in a Chicago court under highly questionable circumstances.[731] Accustomed to having his own judicial decisions overturned by higher courts, Landis, now commissioner of Major League Baseball, returned the favor and reversed the trial court's decision. "Regardless of the verdict of juries," Landis said, "no player that throws a ball game; no player that undertakes or promises to throw a ball game; no player that sits in a conference with a bunch of crooked players and gamblers where the ways and means of throwing games are planned and discussed and does not promptly tell his club about it, will ever play professional baseball."[732] With that sweeping edict, Landis banned all eight accused White Sox players from baseball for life.[733] He also forced New York Giants owner Horace Stoneham and manager John McGraw to divest their interests in a race track and casino operation in Havana, Cuba.[734] During his first five years in office, Landis banned twelve other players for life for various reasons. Some of these decisions were justified; others were questionable.[735] Many of the banned players were high-profile contributors to their clubs, a fact that hardly endeared Landis to many owners. Over the next 80 years, only one player, Pete Rose, would receive a life sentence.

Of course, gambling was not new to baseball. The 1877 National League pennant had been thrown by the Louisville Four.[736] Attempts reportedly had been made to fix the 1903, 1905, and 1914 World Series.[737] Both Ty Cobb and Tris Speaker were permitted by the American League to "resign" from their positions as players and managers in 1926 when it became known they had gambled on fixed games in 1919.[738] After reviewing the evidence against Cobb and Speaker, however, Landis surprisingly reinstated both men. Speaker played another year and Cobb played two more seasons.[739]

Landis even had the temerity to suspend Babe Ruth for the first thirty-nine days of the 1922 season for insubordination when Ruth ignored Landis's order to cease his participation in post-season barnstorming.[740] In spite of pleas by New York Yankees owner Colonel Jacob Ruppert that he was losing his box office king, and in spite of fan petitions bearing thousands of signatures, the commissioner held firm. Kenesaw Mountain Landis was in charge of Major League Baseball!

Not only offending players were visited with the wrath of Landis. The judge abhorred the minor league farm system initially developed by the St. Louis Cardinals' general manager Branch Rickey and successfully employed by a few other clubs. Landis viewed the farm system as a form of bondage. In 1938, the commissioner freed 73 prospects controlled by the St. Louis Cardinals. A year later, he liberated 90 players from the Detroit Tigers organization.[741]

For all the benefits Landis may have brought to Major League Baseball, perhaps his most enduring legacy was as an avowed opponent of racial integration. In spite of his public assurances that there was no rule preventing blacks from playing in the Major Leagues, Landis managed to keep baseball the exclusive domain of whites during his 24-year reign. Privately, the judge firmly maintained that spectators would never pay to watch black players. As discussed in Chapter 6 of this book, Landis used his power and influence to prevent several Major League teams from employing black players. In his autobiography, *Veeck—as in Wreck,* maverick baseball owner Bill Veeck related how he had been too forthright with Landis on the issue of integration. In 1944, Veeck was interested in buying the Philadelphia Phillies and stocking that team's roster with stars from the Negro Leagues. "I felt he [Landis] was entitled to prior notification of what I intended to do," Veeck wrote. "I was aware of the risk I was taking although, to be honest, I could not see how he could stop me. The color line was a 'gentleman's agreement' only. The only way the commissioner could bar me from using Negroes would be to rule, officially and publicly, that they were 'detrimental to baseball.' With Negroes fighting in the war, such a ruling was unthinkable. Judge Landis wasn't exactly shocked but he wasn't overjoyed either. His first reaction, in fact, was that I was kidding him. The next thing I knew I was informed that Nugent (the Phillies owner), being in bankruptcy, had turned the team back to the league and that I would therefore have to deal with the National League President, Ford Frick. Frick promptly informed me that the club had already been sold ... for about half what I had been willing to pay. Word reached me soon enough that Frick was bragging all over the baseball world—strictly off the record, of course—about how he had stopped me from contaminating the league."[742]

In 1944, Major League Baseball's owners, still fearful of the aging Landis, granted him a new seven-year contract extension that would expire when he was 85 years old.[743] Landis died five months later.[744] His steely grip on the commissioner's office and on baseball loosened only by his death, Landis was the game's unchallenged dictator for 24 years. With Landis's passing, the liberated owners moved quickly to redefine the powers of the office of commissioner and assure themselves a greater voice in their business. Both election and renewal of the commissioner's contract would now require the approval of at least 75 percent of Major League Baseball's owners, compared to the previous requirement of a simple majority.[745] Cincinnati Reds president Warren Giles explained, "The commissioner is vested with such sweeping powers that we decided it would be better to have one who is acceptable to at least three-fourths of the clubs than a mere majority. There was no thought of making it difficult for any commissioner to gain reelection. We had no idea at the time this measure was adopted who the next commissioner would be."[746]

The next commissioner would be a United States senator and former Kentucky governor, Albert Benjamin "Happy" Chandler.[747] With baseball's immunity from federal antitrust laws coming under scrutiny in Congress, Chandler was particularly attractive to the owners because of his perceived influence in Washington, D.C.[748] Many viewed Chandler as simply a caretaker of baseball's exclusive domain. But Chandler would prove to be a pleasant surprise and a "happy" departure from the stern Landis.

Chandler was installed as Major League Baseball's second commissioner on July 12, 1945, but only after insisting that the owners restore Landis's "loyalty pledge," making all of Chandler's decisions final.[749] Chandler was forced, however, to accept the three-fourths majority necessary for renewal of his term of office after his seven-year contract expired. The ebullient Chandler later recounted in his autobiography the rude awakening he received in dealing with his constituency. "Many of the owners were greedy," Chandler recalled. "They were cruel to the players and umpires. They abused the fans. They tried to dominate me. But I fought them. I took charge."[750]

Among the events that marked Chandler's tenure as commissioner was his dealing with the treatment of renegade players who had jumped to the Mexican League and then attempted to return to the Major Leagues, the suspension of Leo "The Lip" Durocher, and the integration of "organized" baseball by Jackie Robinson. It was not until later in his life that he was accorded proper credit for his role in Major League Baseball's integration.

The Mexican League was the brainchild of Mexican millionaire Jorge Pasquel, who offered large sums of money in an attempt to lure baseball's biggest stars south of the border.[751] Among the players wooed were Ted Williams, Stan Musial, and Hal Newhouser, who turned down lucrative offers. Eighteen Major League players did jump, however, and Chandler ruled quickly that any player signing with a Mexican League club would be suspended from Major League Baseball for five years. A few years later when Danny Gardella, one of the suspended players, took baseball to court over the illegality of Major League Baseball's anti-trust exemption, Chandler arranged an out-of-court settlement and reinstated all of the suspended players.[752] Chandler wisely realized that baseball's reserve system and antitrust exemption were built on the flimsiest of legal structures, and that deficiencies in that structure could be exposed by a serious legal challenge.

The Durocher affair was far more explosive, at least to the press. As a player and manager, the abrasive Durocher had been both reviled and adored. Durocher was also a darling of the media. Judge Landis had first summoned Durocher to his office in 1941 and warned him of the perils of consorting with gamblers, including tough-guy movie star George Raft.[753] Chandler later met with Durocher and gave him a list of people to avoid.[754] Durocher, twice married previously, married again, this time to Laraine

Day, a glamorous film star fifteen years his junior who was married to another man at the time her relationship with Durocher began. The marriage resulted in a spate of negative publicity for Durocher and baseball. A little later, some inflammatory comments made by Durocher and directed at the Yankees, particularly his former Dodgers boss and now Yankees co-owner Larry MacPhail, landed Leo "The Lip" in more hot water. Although most felt Durocher was guilty of nothing more than bad judgment, Chandler believed it had become necessary for him to address the accumulation of negative events. Chandler

Albert B. "Happy" Chandler

suspended Durocher from baseball for one year.[755] According to *Time* magazine, "Commissioner Chandler has done the seemingly impossible. He has made Durocher a sympathetic figure."[756] In his statement announcing Durocher's suspension, Chandler made it clear that baseball would be held to a higher standard than society. "Leo Durocher has not measured up to the standards expected or required of managers of our baseball teams. As a result of the accumulation of unpleasant incidents in which he has been involved which the commissioner construes as detrimental to baseball, he is hereby suspended from participating in professional baseball for the 1947 season."[757]

With Judge Landis dead, forces began to mobilize to integrate Major League Baseball. Major League owners were not yet ready for integration, however, and were fearful of the effect that black players would have on white attendance, revenues, and franchise values. According to unofficial reports, Major League owners voted 15–1 in 1946 against integrating the Major Leagues, with the Dodgers' Branch Rickey's being the sole vote in favor of integration.[758] According to other reports, Indians owner Bill

Veeck, Cubs owner Phil Wrigley, and Giants owner Horace Stoneham supported integration.[759]

According to Chandler, Rickey requested an audience with the commissioner to seek his support for the Robinson move. Chandler recounted his telling Rickey that, as a former member of the Senate Military Affairs Committee, he was well aware of the sacrifices many blacks had made during the war. "Branch, I'm going to have to meet my Maker some day," Chandler wrote, "and if He asks me why I didn't let this boy play and I say it's because he's black that might not be a satisfactory answer. If the Lord made some people black and some white, and some red or yellow, He must have had a pretty good reason. It's my job to see the game is fairly played and that everybody has an equal chance. Bring him [Robinson] up. I'll sign the transfer. And Rickey brought him up and from then on everyone made Rickey sound like God almighty."[760]

In his autobiography, Chandler listed a number of matters during his tenure of which he was proud. "I handled the Mexican League raids, the threat of a player strike and other tough disputes. I banished Leo 'The Lip' Durocher for a full year for besmirching the game. I just didn't sit around. For the first time players got pensions and a fair shake on rights, pay and contracts. I helped integrate baseball. The avaricious owners began to boil. They finally greased the skids and railroaded me out."[761] A true politician, the gabby Chandler also spent much of his time as commissioner campaigning for reelection, a fact that grated upon some owners. A number of owners wanted Chandler out. They felt that he was too focused upon players' rights and did not adequately represent the owners.[762] When Chandler sought the extension of his term of office, the owners voted nine in favor of renewal and seven against.[763] In spite of carrying the majority, Chandler fell short of the three-fourths requirement. Chandler observed to his wife, "Mama, if Jesus Christ were commissioner, I'm not sure he could carry twelve votes."[764] Chandler's term ended on July 15, 1951.

Among the nearly 100 candidates Major League Baseball's owners considered to replace Chandler were former United States Postmaster James A. Farley, Chief Justice of the United States Supreme Court Fred Vinson, Federal Bureau of Investigation Director J. Edgar Hoover, and United States Army generals Douglas MacArthur and Dwight Eisenhower.[765] In the end, however, the job went to Ford Frick, a former New York sportswriter and the National League president for the previous 17 years.[766] Former commissioner Chandler greeted the choice of Frick with derision. "There was a vacancy when I left, and the owners decided to continue it." Chandler added, "Frick's sleep was not as long as Rip van

Winkle's, but it was equally deep."[767] Frick had apprenticed during the golden days of sports writing and, although he was hardly a peer to luminaries such as Damon Runyon, Grantland Rice, and Ring Lardner, Frick was a confidant of Babe Ruth and served as the ghostwriter of *Babe Ruth's Own Book of Baseball*.[768] Frick served as commissioner for 14 inauspicious years. According to Gabe Paul, who was involved in the management of four Major League teams, "He [Frick] never did anything. All he did was show up for work."[769] Frick was low-key by nature, saw no need to change his personality to fit the office, and tried to avoid as many petty problems as possible, concentrating on the larger picture.

Frick's tenure was defined by the reshaping of Major League Baseball's geography. From 1903 to 1953, the locations of Major League Baseball's sixteen franchises remained unchanged. In a ten-year period, beginning with the Boston Braves' move to Milwaukee in 1953, however, six franchises moved and four expansion franchises were awarded. Milwaukee, Baltimore, Kansas City, Los Angeles, San Francisco, and Minneapolis welcomed established clubs while the New York Mets, Houston Astros, Los Angeles Angels, and a new Washington Senators club, to replace the team that was relocated in Minnesota, came aboard as expansion teams. In spite of the controversial nature of some of these moves, particularly the Dodgers' departure from Brooklyn, the compliant Frick approved all of the transfers.

Although Frick ostensibly was running Major League Baseball, he seemed to act as the loyal servant of Dodgers owner Walter O'Malley.[770] When maverick owner Bill Veeck, now owner of the Chicago White Sox, attempted to seize control of the American League by positioning loyalists in several other franchises, he found out who ruled baseball. Veeck's longtime friend and Hall of Fame player Hank Greenberg was slated to be granted the new American League franchise in southern California. Frick had repeatedly stated that Los Angeles was "open" territory, but suddenly reversed himself and ruled that O'Malley had to be paid $350,000 as compensation for his territorial rights.[771] Greenberg was irate, refused to pay O'Malley the fee, and forfeited his claim to the franchise. In his autobiography, *Veeck—as in Wreck,* Veeck recalled the episode. "As we met to vote for the Los Angeles franchise, we discovered that Walter O'Malley was loaded down with objections about anybody coming into his private grazing grounds in Los Angeles. We discovered it when Ford Frick, that erstwhile apostle of the Open City, sent word from his office that some kind of fair and equitable settlement had to be made with O'Malley. Los Angeles wasn't an Open City any more; it was an Open City only to the degree Walter O'Malley wanted it to be. New York was still an

Open City but Los Angeles was not."[772] "Hank [Greenberg] and I launched a noisy campaign to force Frick into the open," continued Veeck. "The slogan of our campaign was 'Make Him Vote!'"[773] By convincing the American League owners to refuse O'Malley's demands, Veeck would have forced the reluctant Frick to vote to break a deadlock between the leagues. "The last thing in the world Frick wanted to do was to vote," wrote Veeck. "Frick was so anxious not to vote that he looked ill. Frick has a slogan of his own, a slogan that has served him throughout the years. It goes: 'You boys settle it among yourselves.' For that he gets paid $65,000 a year, not bad as things go these days."[774] In spite of the efforts of Veeck and Greenberg, the American League owners fell in line and O'Malley received both his $350,000 fee and the satisfaction of seeing Veeck and his allies thwarted.

Ford Frick will also always be remembered for his "asterisk." In 1961, both Roger Maris and Mickey Mantle of the New York Yankees were approaching the most sacred of Major League Baseball's records, Babe Ruth's single season record of 60 home runs. Because of changes in schedules resulting from expansion of the Major Leagues, the season had been extended from 154 to 162 games. By the middle of the summer, both Maris and Mantle were ahead of Ruth's pace. Frick, in spite of his mantra of non-intervention, decided to intervene in order to protect the legacy of his departed friend and hero, Babe Ruth. Frick issued a terse statement: "A player who may hit more than 60 home runs during his team's first 154 games will be recognized as having established a new record. However, if the player does not hit more than 60 after his club has played 154 games, there would have to be some distinctive mark in the record book to show that Babe Ruth's record was set under the 154-game schedule, and that the other total was compiled while the 162-game schedule was in effect."[775]

No mention was made of other records, such as pitching victories, total hits, runs scored, or runs batted in, which also could be affected by playing eight extra games in a season. Maris went on to hit 61 home runs and break Ruth's record on the final day of the season. Accordingly, both Babe Ruth's total of 60 home runs and Roger Maris's total of 61 home runs appeared in Major League Baseball's official record books. It was not until 1992, when commissioner Fay Vincent had the double entry removed from the record books for "Most Home Runs, Season," that Roger Maris was officially recognized as Major League Baseball's single-season home run record holder.[776]

To this day, no one has taken credit for the appointment of the obscure Air Force General William Dole "Spike" Eckert as the fourth commissioner of Major League Baseball. Upon Eckert's appointment, New York sportswriter Larry Fox observed, "My god, they've elected the Unknown Soldier."[777] According to maverick Oakland Athletics owner Charlie Finley, John Fetzer, chairman of the Detroit Tigers, first recommended Eckert. "Fetzer called me several weeks before the election," recounted Finley. "I had never heard of Eckert. Fetzer put the heat on me. He gave me a lot of bullshit on how good he would be."[778] Finley preferred former college and professional football star and United States Supreme Court Justice Byron "Whizzer" White. Finley recalled his visit with Justice White in Washington. "We had a nice meeting but he wasn't interested," said Finley. "He would have been a great commissioner. Instead, we wound up with a guy nobody knew, who knew nothing about sports. That's when I began to realize I was sitting with a bunch of dummies."[779]

Surprisingly, Eckert proved capable of handling a few of the Major Leagues' more contentious issues. University of Southern California star pitcher Tom Seaver had been signed to a $40,000 bonus by the Atlanta Braves while still in college, violating a Major League prohibition. Eckert voided the deal, fined the Braves, and arranged a special draft that resulted in the New York Mets signing the future Hall of Famer.[780] In spite of his minor successes, however, Eckert proved to be inept at his job. He was also often an embarrassment—once he referred to the "Cincinnati Cardinals." After less than four years on the job, Eckert was unceremoniously dumped by the owners. Although there was little doubt they had fired the general, the owners' statement at a press conference to announce Eckert's departure clouded the issue. "General Eckert has just delivered his resignation effective with the appointment of a successor. We have decided to accede to the general's wishes. We hold him in the highest esteem, especially for the integrity and honor with which he has conducted our affairs."[781] Dick Young wrote in the *New York Daily News,* "Some reporters dashed out of the room to phones, others took crouching steps toward club owners standing nearby to ask hushed questions, and as Eckert rambled on, telling pitiably of what he had tried to do, the Lords of baseball began chattering among themselves, ignoring him for the most part and one of them said, 'Get him off there.' It was rude, terribly rude. More than that, it was cruel. The newsmen agreed that William D. Eckert, in his darkest moment, had been the biggest man in the room."[782]

The simple truth was that the office of commissioner of Major League Baseball was little more than a charade. The owners would have preferred to run things themselves. But cognizant of the negative publicity that could ensue from such an action, they decided to appoint, albeit cautiously, another commissioner. When Walter O'Malley convinced Major League Baseball's owners to elect one of the National League's lawyers, Bowie Kent Kuhn, as baseball's fifth commissioner,[783] the owners prudently gave Kuhn only a one-year contract.[784] At six feet six inches in height, Kuhn had an imposing presence. He also had an aristocratic and imperious manner and a flair for public speaking. But with only a one-year contract, Kuhn was on probation. Kuhn's first year, 1969, coincided with the 100th anniversary of professional baseball. During his first year in office, Kuhn satisfied his constituency and the owners rewarded him with a seven-year contract.[785] He now had the security he craved and felt empowered to pursue a broader agenda.

While Kuhn lacked the pious tone of Judge Landis, his tenure was marked by a propensity to act in "the best interests of baseball." Kuhn used these powers to suspend New York Yankees owner George Steinbrenner for two years because of his conviction for illegal contributions to Richard Nixon's presidential campaign; suspend Detroit Tigers pitcher Denny McClain for gambling and other offenses; suspend already-retired Willie Mays and Mickey Mantle from baseball-related activities because of their promotional activities for casinos; restructure trades in which players decided to "retire" to obtain better terms; force Oakland A's owner Charlie Finley and Atlanta Braves owner Bill Bartholomay to sell their stock in a company that owned casinos and which allegedly had organized crime connections; block the sale of the Chicago White Sox to Edward J. De Bartolo, Sr., who also owned racetracks; and suspend Atlanta Braves owner Ted Turner for tampering with players under contract to other teams.[786]

Perhaps the most important and difficult issue with which Kuhn was faced was outfielder Curt Flood's refusal to accept a trade from the St. Louis Cardinals to the Philadelphia Phillies and his subsequent legal challenge to Major League Baseball's reserve system and anti-trust exemption. Like commissioners who preceded him, Kuhn was obliged to defend the indefensible. "Baseball could not operate on a league basis without the reserve clause," Kuhn testified during the Flood case, asserting that the reserve system was necessary to "maintain the integrity of the game and honesty among clubs and players."[787]

Unfortunately for Kuhn, his tenure coincided with the reign of Marvin Miller, the shrewd executive director of the Major League Baseball Players Association. Miller had long recognized that the commissioner was paid by the owners and, therefore, responsible to them. Historically, the league presidents and the commissioner had been responsible for handling all player grievances. This was hardly fair, argued Miller. "They could make any ruling they wanted. They could say up is down and down is up."[788] Miller successfully pleaded for the establishment of a three-member arbitration panel comprised of an owners' representative, a players' representative, and an impartial arbitrator to hear all player grievances except those involving the integrity of the game, which would continue to be decided by the commissioner.[789] Under this new system, Miller would automatically vote for the players, management's appointee would automatically vote in favor of the owners, and the impartial arbitrator, whose ruling was binding, would cast the deciding vote.[790] The office of the commissioner was effectively emasculated.

In late 1975, when arbitrator Peter Seitz made his landmark ruling against the reserve system and option clause in the Andy Messersmith–Dave McNally arbitration, and in effect created free agency, the owners and Kuhn were stunned. Kuhn had testified on behalf of baseball's feudal laws. "When we came down to this grievance," said Kuhn, "I was troubled by it because in seeking, as it does, to eliminate the reserve system, it raises a very grave question as to whether it touches the integrity and public confidence in the game that the commissioner should use his powers to withdraw this grievance from the process. The reserve system is necessary to protect not only the integrity but the economic viability of the game.... If our players were free to play out their options, you may be sure the worst results will ensue even to the point of seeming unreasonable in terms of unbalancing competition. The strongest clubs would surely buy the best players. There is not the slightest question about it."[791]

Kuhn was indeed prophetic, but he was also helpless. His dated version of "using his powers" to intercede in labor disputes was folly. The days of imperious decrees from Judge Landis had passed. Players had freedom and the commissioner's office had become an anachronism. Internally, the commissioner still ruled. But the players were no longer management's pawns. That stark reality eventually would be Kuhn's undoing.

Some of Kuhn's most memorable skirmishes were with "Superpest," Oakland Athletics' owner Charles O. Finley. In 1976, cognizant that his star players would soon become free agents and that he would be unable to retain those players because he could not compete financially with larger market clubs, Finley decided to sell his talent before they departed and he received nothing in return.[792] Conjuring up memories of similar mass sales of players by former Philadelphia Athletics owner Connie Mack in 1913 and 1932, on June 18, the last day before the trading deadline, Finley sold Vida Blue to the Yankees for $1.5 million and Joe Rudi and Rollie Fingers to the Red Sox for $1 million each.[793] For a total of $3.5 million, the powerful A's team that had won five consecutive American League

Bowie Kuhn

West crowns and three consecutive World Series in the early 1970s had been gutted.[794] Citing the "best interests of baseball," Kuhn nullified the sales.[795]

After a chorus of howling from both Finley and a number of baseball insiders, the flamboyant A's owner sued Kuhn, Major League Baseball, the American League, and the National League.[796] In cross-examination during the trial, Dodgers owner Walter O'Malley supported Kuhn's intervention. "My opinion is that we need a strong commissioner and that we would not be a self-disciplined, self-governed sport if we did not have one. We probably would be under a state or a federal athletic commission and that would be horrible."[797] O'Malley's real concern was that, if million dollar sales were sanctioned, million dollar salaries would inevitably follow. As Marvin Miller predicted, "[o]ne thing that Finley's foiled deal did ... was to jolt everyone who followed baseball into realizing what the services of All-Star players were worth.... Once figures like that were bandied about for the sale of players, then with free agency beginning at the end of that season, the money representing the value of the player would be going from owner to player, instead of owner to owner."[798] The court ruled in favor of Kuhn, O'Malley, and Major League Baseball. While questioning the wisdom of Kuhn's decision, the court agreed that the Major League Agreement bound the teams to the commissioner's decisions.[799] Kuhn's action and the court's ruling sounded an alarm to a number of other owners. "I like the commissioner," stated Yankees boss George Steinbrenner in a *New York Times* interview, "but no one man should have the power the baseball constitution gives the commissioner's office. It's too much power."[800] The owners would make certain that the next commissioner's powers would be greatly reduced.

George Steinbrenner

The luster would fade for Kuhn during a seven-week players' strike in 1981[801] that crippled baseball and demoralized its fans. The owners were upset that the commissioner felt he was above the labor fray and refused to intercede. Walter O'Malley had died a few years earlier; now it was his son Peter's turn to attempt to save their emissary Kuhn. But after years of openly playing favorites among owners, Kuhn was attacked by the disenfranchised as a group of primarily American League and newer National League owners moved to oust him.[802] Longtime Major League Baseball legal counsel Lou Hoynes lamented the erosion of influence by the primarily National League old guard. "We used to take new owners aside and take them to the woodshed, if necessary, to make sure they stayed with the program. We'd lost our authority. The center wouldn't hold."[803] The vote to extend Kuhn's contract for a third seven-year term was eleven in favor of extending and three against in the American League and seven in favor and five against in the National League, two votes short of the necessary three-fourths majority in both leagues.[804] "In anywhere but baseball that's a landslide," said a bitter Kuhn.[805]

Kuhn's departure promised to ensure a dilution of powers for the next commissioner. But, when the successful candidate turned out to be

Time magazine Man of the Year Peter Victor Ueberroth, momentum changed quickly. "He knew how badly we wanted him," recalled White Sox owner Jerry Reinsdorf. "He would have been dumb if he hadn't demanded the right to dictate the terms. He is a man of affluence and didn't need the job."[806] Ueberroth insisted that reelection no longer require a three-fourths majority; a simple majority with at least five affirmative votes in each league would be sufficient.[807] Ueberroth also convinced the owners to agree to increase the maximum amount the commissioner could fine a team from $5,000 to $250,000.[808]

As president of the Organizing Committee for the 1984 Summer Olympic Games in Los Angeles, Ueberroth turned the typically debt-ridden event into a $225 million surplus and redefined the business of sport.[809] Ueberroth instituted a policy of exclusivity for corporate partners. It was either Coke or Pepsi, but not both. Whoever bid the highest amount would have the right to call itself an official supplier to the Olympics and use the Olympic rings logo on its products. The owners of Major League Baseball hoped he could do the same for them. He could and did, concluding lucrative marketing arrangements with Gillette, *USA Today*, Equitable Life Insurance, Coca-Cola, Arby's, Rawlings, and others.[810] During his four and one-half years as commissioner, Ueberroth increased the owners' annual licensing and merchandising income from zero to $36 million.[811]

While Ueberroth was a financial boon for the owners, he could not disguise his contempt and disrespect for them. He often referred to them as "stupid" and "incompetent." Dodgers owner Peter O'Malley, whose family had exercised vast influence over previous commissioners, was a frequent target of Ueberroth's ire.[812] "My job would be to make the sport better," said Ueberroth before taking over, "not only for the owners but for the players, managers, coaches, minor leaguers, and most important for the fans."[813]

Ueberroth took no time for a honeymoon. Within days after assuming office, he quickly moved to avert an umpires' strike by supporting the position of the umpires.[814] Later, one day after the players walked out during the 1985 season, Ueberroth interceded in the strike and ordered the owners' negotiating representatives to settle immediately. Within a few hours, the terms of a new five-year collective bargaining agreement were finalized, much to the chagrin of a number of hard-line owners.[815] It was another example of Ueberroth's tough love. "The owners operate like sheep," said Ueberroth. "They always go in one direction or the other."[816]

But Ueberroth's authoritarian management and imperious manner would eventually imperil the owners. He admonished the owners to avoid providing long-term contracts to players "Look in the mirror and go out and spend big if you want, but don't go out there whining that someone made you do it."[817] For once, the owners acted in unison. The owners pledged to abstain from signing free agents to long-term, lucrative contracts and a three-year period of fiscal restraint and failure to sign free agents began in 1985.[818] Baseball's collective bargaining agreement provided, however, that in matters of free agency "Players shall not act in concert with other Players and Clubs shall not act in concert with other Clubs."[819] When the Major League Baseball Players Association charged

Peter Ueberroth

that the owners had acted in concert in violation of the collective bargaining agreement, Ueberroth denied there had been any collusion. "They aren't capable of colluding," he insisted. "They couldn't agree on what to have for breakfast."[820]

After reviewing overwhelming evidence to the contrary, Major League Baseball's arbitrator disagreed, finding the owners guilty of concerted action, declaring some players that had remained with their teams to be free agents, and ultimately fining the owners a total of $280 million plus interest, to be distributed among players adversely affected by the owners' collusion.[821] Ueberroth insisted that, by urging the owners to act responsibly, he had done nothing wrong.[822] Nevertheless, 18 months before his contract was scheduled to expire, Ueberroth announced that he would not accept a second term.[823] Before he departed, however, Ueberroth negotiated the richest national television package in the history of Major League Baseball.[824]

In stark contrast to the authoritarian Ueberroth, Major League Baseball anointed a baseball romantic as the game's seventh commissioner. Angelo Bartlett Giamatti, a former professor of classical literature and president of Yale University and of the National League, fancied himself to be a Renaissance man.[825] Among Giammati's more daring literary efforts was a comparison of the Mets' trade of Tom Seaver to Masaccio's fresco *The Expulsion of Adam and Eve* in Florence's Brancacci Chapel.[826] But he was also an unabashed Boston Red Sox fan and thereby privy to an inherent cult of suffering.

Bart Giamatti stated on several occasions that his goal was to some day be president of the American League,[827] of which his beloved Boston Red Sox were a charter member. Although he never achieved his goal, Giamatti did become president of the National League and, by 1989, commissioner of Major League Baseball. "Academics love baseball," observed Giamatti. "Because of its history. Because it's susceptible to having a philosophy. Because it's been around awhile. Because the game allows you to get inside it. It's susceptible to endless quantification. That accounts for the bifurcation I encountered in the academic community between people who thought becoming the National League President was absurd and those who thought it was splendid."[828] Giamatti appointed as his deputy his friend Francis Thomas "Fay" Vincent, Jr., who, as a former Securities and Exchange Commission lawyer and corporate executive for Columbia Pictures and Coca-Cola, had far greater experience in business and finance matters.[829]

Giamatti's tenure will forever be defined by his lifetime suspension of Major League career hits leader Pete Rose. In his 24-year Major League career, "Charlie Hustle" had set a number of Major League career records, including all-time marks for games played, times at bat, and hits. Rose was also a compulsive gambler who consorted with gamblers, bookmakers, drug dealers, and petty criminals. A former Justice Department investigator appointed

A. Bartlett Giamatti

by Giamatti collected substantial evidence, much of it from two convicted felons, that Rose had violated a baseball golden rule by betting on baseball games while serving as manager of the Cincinnati Reds. Giamatti even asked a judge for leniency in the sentencing of one of those witnesses, Ron Peters, who had been convicted of cocaine trafficking, because Peters had presented evidence against Rose.[830]

Rose refused to admit guilt, but a settlement was reached in which Rose dropped a civil action that had been commenced against Giamatti and Major League Baseball. Rose was placed on the "Permanently Ineligible" list with a chance for reinstatement after one year, the commissioner agreed not to make any final findings or determination that Rose had bet on baseball games, and Rose signed a document acknowledging that "the commissioner has a factual basis to impose the penalty."[831] Shortly after the announcement of the settlement, Giamatti violated the terms of the settlement by publicly stating that Rose had bet on baseball.[832] Rose later was convicted of two counts of federal income tax evasion and was fined and imprisoned for five months.[833] To this day, Rose maintains his innocence and continues to campaign for readmission to baseball and induction into the National Baseball Hall of Fame.

Eight days after the announcement of his decision in the Pete Rose matter, and after only five months in office, Giamatti suffered a fatal heart attack at his summer home on Martha's Vineyard.[834] The media and Major League Baseball's ownership mourned the passing of this Renaissance man who had upheld the purity and integrity of the game.[835] A less flattering account of Giamatti was presented on his death by Marvin Miller, who believed Giamatti was a hypocritical stooge of the owners who had railroaded Rose without due process and then violated the terms of his settlement with Rose.[836] Miller's wife Terry wrote at the time:

> so, 2 weeks in a row bart captures the headlines. the week before it was his decision to ban pete rose from b.b. for life. whose life? m[marvin miller] is unforgiving, death notwithstanding. he abhors all the hypocrisy that has surrounded the commissioner, the unified voice of the media to label him a god and rose a villain. well, god heard, and he, you may remember, is a jealous god. thou shalt have no other gods before me. giamatti was like a biblical character as he announced his punishment of rose. he was angry, cold, severe, flag-waving, pennant-waving. he was the savior of the national pastime, of the nation itself. he had saved the nation from pete rose, the gambler, while handing it over to ron peters, the drug dealer, whose sentence he sought to have reduced. he died a hero. driving the money changers from the temple, employed by bigger money changers, he was looked upon as the great hope for the future of the game. not, mind you, to restore its integrity, but rather to rebuild its **appearance** of integrity. appearance is all. who better than a renaissance scholar to

*shield the lords of baseball from exposure to the light of honesty and fair play.
with bart to charm the public, the owners would be able to get away with anything. his death is a big blow to twenty-six owners and ten times that many
reporters and commentators who will no longer have their biased propaganda
sugar coated for them.*

*here lies a smooth talking casuist, a union-busting conservative, a simple fan
who was in over his head.*

*he did look a bit satanic, didn't he? had he perhaps signed a pact with the
devil to gain the post of commissioner of all the baseballs? and failed to pay up?
gambled and lost you might say, or is it truman capote's "more tears are shed
over prayers that are answered?"*[837]

Two weeks after Bart Giamatti's death, his deputy and friend Fay
Vincent was elected as Major League Baseball's eighth commissioner. In
spite of changes in the office and the authority vested in the commissioner,
Vincent was determined to control everything related to baseball. His
desire for control, and an unwillingness to submit to the authority of his
employers, Major League Baseball's franchise owners, would eventually
be Vincent's undoing. Within one month after assuming office, Vincent
faced his first crisis when an earthquake, registering 7.1 on the Richter
scale, ravaged the San Francisco Bay Area only 30 minutes before the third
game of the World Series between the San Francisco Giants and the Oakland A's. Vincent quickly postponed the World Series and said that baseball would return when the community was ready. During his three-year
reign, Vincent interceded in labor affairs, suspended Yankees owner
George Steinbrenner for two years without concern for due process, and
bullied and intimidated those who had the temerity to oppose the commissioner. Not surprisingly, the owners tired of Vincent's manner and a
vote of no confidence forced him to resign after only three years in office.[838]

To replace Vincent, the owners appointed one of their own, Bud
Selig, as interim commissioner. The interim label would stick for five and
one-half years, longer than the reign of any of the three preceding commissioners. In that capacity, Selig supervised the owners' negotiation of
a lengthy labor conflict with the Major League Baseball Players Association. In 1994, this conflict culminated in a mid–season players' strike. The
strike continued into September, and ultimately Selig announced the can-
cellation of the remainder of the 1994 season and the World Series, an
event that had come to define America.[839] The following spring, the owners locked out the striking players and conducted spring training with
replacement players.[840] Finally, after a 232-day work stoppage, the impasse
was settled and the regular Major League players returned.[841] Baseball was
back, but the damage to its image seemed irreparable. Not until 1998,

when Mark McGwire and Sammy Sosa chased and surpassed Roger Maris's single-season home run record, would baseball recover some of its prestige. In 2001, Major League Baseball's attendance exceeded 70 million for the fifth consecutive season, but total attendance dropped to 67.9 million in 2002. During his reign, Selig also has been successful in dividing each league into three divisions, introducing playoff wild cards, and instituting inter-league play, but he failed in his attempts to radically realign the leagues.[842]

Allan "Bud" Selig

While he may lack a "public mandate," perhaps no commissioner has been as active as Selig in attempting to address Major League Baseball's problems. Being an owner, of course, Selig has not faced the hostility and resistance encountered by many of his predecessors.

In January 2000, the owners voted to give commissioner Selig sweeping new powers, allowing him to block trades and, to a limited extent, redistribute Major League Baseball's wealth in order to restore competitive balance. The owners also agreed to equally divide Major League Baseball's future internet income. As an owner of a small market team, the Milwaukee Brewers, Selig has long been a proponent of revenue sharing. The text of the owners' resolution read as follows:

> *RESOLVED:*
>
> *WHEREAS, the Clubs have noted the trend toward an absence of competitive balance over the past several years in the conduct of the Championship Season; and*
>
> *WHEREAS, the Clubs believe that it is important that all Clubs have the opportunity to compete at a level that provides their fans a belief that their Club may in fact qualify for post season play; and*

> *WHEREAS, the Clubs have concluded that there is currently not an appropriate level of long-term competitive balance in Major League Baseball;*
>
> *NOW, THEREFORE, pursuant to the powers granted the commissioner under the Major League Constitution, the Clubs request that the commissioner take such action as he deems appropriate to ensure an appropriate level of long-term competitive balance in Major League Baseball.*

San Diego Padres owner Larry Lucchino proposed the move toward greater equity among owners. "Today baseball woke up and recognized there was an 800-pound gorilla sitting in our living room—the lack of competitive balance in the game," Lucchino said at the time. "Let's cure some of the problems. Enough is enough. Baseball has been for too long a big, old oil transport ship that takes forever to turn. Bud should take the rudder and turn ASAP." Selig was more circumspect: "I'm not going to get into the specific things I can and cannot do." Considering the history of divisiveness among Major League Baseball's owners, this is probably wise.

In testimony before the United States Senate Judiciary Committee Subcommittee on Antitrust, Business Rights, and Competition in November 2000, Commissioner Selig announced that "it is time for sweeping changes" in the economics of Major League Baseball. "I can assure that this system will be changed," Selig told the subcommittee.

After forcing Fay Vincent to resign, Major League Baseball's owners gutted the "best interests of baseball" power, weakening the commissioner's influence by limiting the use of that power to matters not subject to a vote by owners. Their owners' message was clear: "We rule baseball, not the commissioner." Now that the commissioner's office is occupied by one of their own, they seem more willing to delegate a portion of their power. Perhaps this willingness is limited, however, to the individual who currently occupies the office. On November 27, 2001, Major League Baseball's owners unanimously voted to extend Selig's term of office until 2006. By all reports, Selig is respected and well-liked by his peers, is a consensus builder, loves baseball, and appreciates baseball's historic significance. There is no evidence, however, of his ability to leap tall buildings in a single bound.

The commissioner is, and always has been, a creature of the owners. Major League Baseball Players Association executive director Marvin Miller once observed, "The concept of a mutual commissioner indicates no understanding of the labor-management relationship. It's a conflict of interests when you say 'We should have someone represent both sides.'

The owners have every right to hire somebody, pay him, tell him his duties and responsibilities, and fire him when they believe he has been unsatisfactory. What is fraudulent is when people are told the commissioner represents both sides."[843]

Chapter 14

Money Changers
in the Temple

---

*Baseball is such a wonderful sport it can survive even the
fat heads who run it.*
— Red Smith

*Baseball, like some other sports, poses as a sacred insti-
tution dedicated to the public good, but it is actually a
big, selfish business with a ruthlessness that many big
businesses would never think of displaying.*
—Jackie Robinson

*Gentlemen, we have the only legal monopoly in the coun-
try and we're fucking it up.*
—Ted Turner

*The dinner menu is lobster thermidor for the big-mar-
ket operators. And the small-market guys are saying
"Give us some of your lobster and we'll give you half of
our ham sandwich."*
—Tom Hardicourt

No baseball fan has ever paid to see an owner. The players and the
fans have always been baseball's most valuable resources, yet management
has claimed to own the game. In programs and advertisements promoting games in the 19th century, owners and boards of directors were billed
above players. From the birth of the reserve system in 1879 to its effective
demise in 1975, owners exerted their absolute control over the players and
the game. They conspired to exclude black players from the Major Leagues

257

for over 60 years. Protected by their "contractual" reserve system and an "exemption" from federal antitrust legislation created and confirmed by a fawning judiciary that employed circumlocution and effusive panegyrics instead of rational legal analysis, Major League Baseball's ownership deprived players of the basic labor rights enjoyed by the country's other workers. Major League Baseball players were bound in perpetual slavery to the teams that owned them, in a system that limited their compensation to levels that owners were willing to pay.

After 100 years of management abuse, emancipation and financial power eventually came to Major League Baseball players, not through the charity of the owners, but through concerted labor activity and the power of arbitrators and the courts. For a century, the owners stubbornly refused to negotiate with the players for a system of player compensation that was equitable to both players and owners and, at the same time, ensured the owners some ability to retain the services of or compensation for players in whom they had invested. Baseball was a game of tradition and the sportsmen-cum-proprietors who controlled the game continued to adhere rigidly to the reserve system until it was too late. In 1975, labor arbitrator Peter Seitz ruled that owners could only control a player for one year after the expiration of the player's contract. "The owners were stubborn and stupid," Seitz said later. "They had accumulated so much power they wouldn't share it with anybody." But their power base was about to erode.

As has been recounted in Chapter 10 of this book, from the time of Curt Flood's historic challenge to the reserve system through the end of the 20th century, a number of ugly labor impasses occurred. The negotiation of every labor agreement between the players and Major League Baseball's ownership proved to be a painful and public process. Invariably, the owners, blinded by their own self-importance and competitiveness and crippled by disunity in their ranks, lost. Meanwhile, the Major League Baseball Players Association, under the deft and consistent leadership of Marvin Miller and later Donald Fehr, became one of the strongest unions in America. While their brethren in basketball and football unions agreed to limit team payrolls and individual salaries, baseball players steadfastly resisted. In spite of relentless efforts by baseball's ownership to overhaul the game's compensation system, the players refused to budge. Although Marvin Miller has long been retired from active involvement in the Major League Baseball Players Association, his legacy of opposition to player "give backs" continues to guide the Players Association's negotiations. Ownership's absolute contempt of players for over a century has not been forgotten. The previous abuses and greed of Major League Baseball's "sportsmen of yore" remain a burden for today's Major League owners.

The momentous changes that have been wrought in Major League Baseball over the last 30 years have finally forced owners to share their profits with the men most responsible for creating them, the players. Players have become so lavishly compensated, however, culminating in Alex Rodriguez's 2001 signing of a ten-year, $252 million contract with the Texas Rangers, that they have alienated the general public. Yet, for many it is impossible to feel pity for the owners.

To understand the depth of the Major League Baseball Players Association's militancy and obstinacy, one must examine Major League Baseball's ownership over the last 130 years. In Major League Baseball's earliest days, powerful magnates such as William Hulbert and Albert Spalding systematically schemed to control all aspects of the game, crush competition, and minimize players' compensation. A number of rival leagues that challenged the Major Leagues' monopoly failed. By 1903, upon the signing of the National Agreement between the National League and the American League, the basic structure of the modern Major Leagues was established. Major League Baseball's franchises and ownership remained nearly static for the next half century. Major League Baseball's 16 owners were a self-regulating body who owned and administered the national pastime. Baseball's owners reasoned that the players should be grateful for their opportunity to play in the Major Leagues. It was a privilege, not a job. They also understood that few men of higher learning were present in Major League clubhouses and even fewer were present who understood the economics of supply and demand and the abusive power of cartels.

Although Major League Baseball's owners give the appearance of performing a great public service by providing the national pastime to millions of spectators, membership has its privileges. A rich man can own massive tracts of real estate and control numerous corporations, but if he purchases a Major League Baseball team, his public profile soars. Owners become the consorts of politicians and the rich and famous. Some can even forge national political careers. The attention is intoxicating to many Major League owners and those who aspire to become owners. Jacob Ruppert was a successful brewer. The Oakland Athletics' Haas family made a fortune from their family company, Levi Strauss. Del Webb was one of America's leading real estate developers. Philip Wrigley became fabulously rich selling chewing gum. Ray Kroc built the McDonald's hamburger empire. August "Gussie" Busch brewed Budweiser, the world's best selling beer. Charles Bronfman's family owned spirits giant Seagram. George Steinbrenner controlled a shipbuilding group. Ted Turner became a media magnate. Yet each of these owners achieved fame through the ownership of a Major League Baseball team. But involvement in baseball by these gentlemen was pure. They were merely providing the community with a service. They were sportsmen, hale and hearty, fraternal and jocular, who chose to spend their leisure time with their baseball teams instead of on their yachts.

One owner who was neither a sportsman nor a fan was the Brooklyn Dodgers' Walter O'Malley. It is entirely apropos that the most influential and astute baseball owner of the 20th century made his name, and a large part of his fortune, as a lawyer foreclosing mortgages during the Great Depression.[844] O'Malley was a financial opportunist who was more interested in the bottom line than the game. It was often said that, if O'Malley had his choice between his Dodgers winning the World Series in four games or losing it in seven, he would have opted for losing in seven because of the additional revenue.

The Brooklyn Dodgers were a civic treasure. Unlike their rivals from Manhattan and the Bronx, the Giants and the Yankees, respectively, who merely played in their boroughs, the Dodgers *were* Brooklyn. The Dodgers were an underachieving crew with some of the most passionate, partisan, and unconventional fans in baseball. A day at Ebbets Field was more than a baseball game, it was a community fair. The Dodgers Sym-Phoney, a rag-tag assemblage, serenaded the faithful with tuneless reverie. Ebbets Field featured cowbells and foghorns, but little quality baseball. In 1942, Branch Rickey arrived as part owner and president to rescue the moribund franchise. Rickey's financial acumen and baseball savvy helped to propel the Dodgers into a National League power. Eventually the hapless Dodgers, still known as "Dem Bums" but now more endearingly so, won National League pennants in 1949, 1952, 1953, 1955, and 1956 and defeated the hated cross-town Yankees in the 1955 World Series. It was a Brooklyn love affair in which everyone was smitten, everyone except Walter O'Malley.

Although Rickey redefined parsimony in his dealings with players, he was in many respects the polar opposite of his co-owner O'Malley. Both men loved to talk, eat, smoke cigars, and make money. Both had powerful personalities. But Rickey saw baseball not only as a source of money; he also loved the game and building baseball organizations. O'Malley saw only the bottom line. According to Rickey's biographer, Murray Polner, "To Rickey, baseball remained a civil religion which acted out public functions organized religion was unable to perform. O'Malley's faith rested on balance sheets and dividends."[845] In spite of successfully integrating baseball with Jackie Robinson in 1947, building the Dodgers organization into the best in baseball, developing the Dodgers team into a Major League power, and turning the Dodgers into the National League's most profitable franchise, Rickey was outflanked by the shrewd O'Malley and by 1950 found himself excluded from the Dodgers ownership picture. Soon O'Malley owned 100 percent of the Dodgers.[846] The farm system Rickey built would continue to bear fruit, however, and the previously hapless Dodgers became frequent participants in baseball's post season action. Over the second half of the 20th century, the Dodgers became, arguably, Major League Baseball's model franchise.

O'Malley's dispassionate rule of the Dodgers was a harbinger of doom. In 1953, he fired the Dodgers' much-loved broadcaster Red Barber, a man whose voice and passion defined the team. Barber was succeeded by another redhead, then-unknown Vin Scully.[847] According to the gloating O'Malley, Scully's replacement of Barber, whose salary was seven times as large as Scully's, was an example of shrewd business. O'Malley later bragged to his underlings, "Imagine a length of pipe that was full of peas. If you squeeze another pea in at one end, a pea is forced out the other. You put in Vin Scully at $7,500 here, and out there, at the other end, drops Barber at $50,000. That, gentlemen, is how you make money."[848]

But the next pea to drop out of O'Malley's pipe was the borough of Brooklyn and its passionate baseball fans. In spite of the success of the Dodgers as the most profitable franchise in the National League, O'Malley constantly cried poverty. Ebbets Field was quaint and charming, but the neighborhood around it had greatly deteriorated and O'Malley was stymied in his efforts to extract further profits from this woeful bandbox. The white middle-class fans O'Malley desired were now deserting the borough for pristine suburbs and were being replaced by an impoverished ethnic underclass. In what would become the standard refrain for new generations of sports team owners, O'Malley told Brooklyn's civic powers to either build him a new stadium or he would move the Dodgers to another city. O'Malley had witnessed the financial success of the Braves, which had moved from Boston to Milwaukee in 1953 and set new National League attendance records. O'Malley realized what that success could mean to the Dodgers and other teams, "If they take in twice as many dollars, they'll eventually be able to buy better talent. Then they'll be the winners, not us."[849] Rebuffed by Brooklyn's political leaders in his demand for a new stadium, O'Malley looked west toward the fertile climes of Los Angeles with its sprawling, post–World War II population base and promises of cable television riches.[850]

More than any event in Major League Baseball during the 20th century, Walter O'Malley's movement of the Dodgers from Brooklyn to Los Angeles exposed the true nature of baseball's greedy ownership. It was baseball's defining moment, the end of innocence when the motives of the

so-called "sportsmen" were laid bare. There was little uproar, and some
relief, when the Braves, Browns, and Athletics relocated from Boston, St.
Louis, and Philadelphia to Milwaukee, Baltimore, and Kansas City, respectively. Even the New York Giants, steeped in history and playing in the
country's number one market, could rationalize their move to San Francisco. After all, the Giants' attendance had dramatically declined in spite
of competitive teams. The Dodgers, on the other hand, had an unswerv-
ingly loyal fan base, were hardly in a state of financial distress, and were
Brooklyn's defining cultural icon.

From a business standpoint, however, the only standpoint that mat-
tered to O'Malley, the move to Los Angeles was brilliant. O'Malley built
his own shining baseball palace on a parcel of land, conveniently donated
by the City of Los Angeles, at the confluence of Los Angeles' new freeway
system.[851] O'Malley had been smitten by a visit to Disneyland and the ser-
vice-oriented atmosphere of the theme park.[852] The Dodgers adopted similar policies, serving the best hot dogs and the coldest beer to white
middle-class spectators who would enjoy comfortable seats offering prime
views of the pristine field in a clean and well-equipped stadium with ample
parking for their automobiles. O'Malley was hailed in Los Angeles as a
visionary, the man who had made baseball truly national. "Walter O'Malley moved the game to a new level," wrote legendary scribe Jim Murray
in the Los Angeles Times. Los Angeles County Supervisor Mike Antonovich
later reminded people how Walter O'Malley had the vision to create, "a
quality family oriented operation. It was the Dodgers who first broke the
color line in professional baseball. Peter O'Malley has expanded his father's
philosophy and today's team reflects the diversity of Los Angeles County's
10 million citizens." The betrayal, broken hearts, and devastation of loyal
fans in Brooklyn was a small price to pay to reshape Major League Baseball's geography.

Walter O'Malley's understanding of the business of baseball was far
ahead of its time. In the 1950s, he already comprehended what other owners would not appreciate for another decade or two, that the keys to extraordinary profits from *operating* a baseball team were a favorable stadium
situation and television revenues. He achieved both in Los Angeles. He
financed the new Dodger Stadium with a combination of public funding,
corporate sponsorship, and his sale of Ebbets Field.[853] In Los Angeles, he
found a vast new audience that was hungry for baseball and he had no
other Major League team as competition until the Angels arrived in the
early 1960s. By then, O'Malley and the Dodgers owned baseball in Los
Angeles, both at Dodger Stadium and on television.

Through his influence over other owners and commissioners, from

Ford Frick through Bowie Kuhn, O'Malley virtually controlled Major League Baseball. If O'Malley had wanted to own an expansion team in Los Angeles, he would have met little resistance. He could have sold the Dodgers to Brooklyn interests and started afresh in southern California. But O'Malley appreciated the value of the cachet attached to the Dodgers' name and felt no compulsion to relinquish their fertile farm system and organization. In lamenting the advent of concerted player bargaining in the mid–1960s, O'Malley observed, "Baseball is an old-fashioned game with old-fashioned traditions."[854] Obviously, those old-fashioned traditions did not apply to O'Malley's treatment of the aggrieved fans in Brooklyn.

In the mid–1960s, rumors abounded of Major League Baseball emulating the annual players drafts of the National Basketball Association and National Football League. The Dodgers' baseball scouts and farm system had routinely been the most astute in evaluating, selecting, and developing talent. A player draft, in which every team would have equal access to prospects, would clearly be of detriment to the Dodgers. But the shrewd and financially astute O'Malley realized that a draft would be good for the game. What he actually realized was that a draft would be good for Walter O'Malley. Players' signing bonuses had reached heady levels by 1964 when the Angels signed Rick Reichardt out of college for the then-record bonus of $205,000.[855] With a draft in effect, there would be no monetary competition for the owners in signing young players. The teams with the best scouting systems, particularly the Dodgers, would still dominate. But now it would cost a lot less money to sign a prized prospect. Not until the New York Mets' 1980 signing of Darryl Strawberry would an amateur player receive a signing bonus as high as that paid to Reichardt in 1964.[856]

In 1997, Walter's son, Peter, announced that his family was getting out of the baseball business. The game had become corporate and, with family puppets Kuhn and Frick long gone, the O'Malley influence had greatly diminished. The Dodgers had become the last franchise operated by a family with no outside businesses. "Family ownership is a dying breed," said Peter O'Malley. "It's a high-risk business, as high risk as the oil business. You need a broader base than an individual family to carry you through the storms. Groups or corporations are the wave of the future." Acting commissioner Bud Selig moved quickly to assure the good fans in southern California that this extremely profitable franchise, a perennial leader in attendance, would remain in place. "I want to assure the Dodger fans, Peter and the team, that we will work with them to keep the team in Los Angeles." Phew, what a relief!

In 1942, O'Malley paid $82,000 to acquire a 25 percent interest in the

Dodgers.[857] He acquired the remaining 75 percent of the team with dividends he received from his ownership of shares in the Dodgers. The O'Malley family reaped huge profits from the Dodgers for more than half a century. In 1997, Peter O'Malley found a better way to yield a return from his father's investment. He sold the Dodgers to Australian media baron Rupert Murdoch and his News Corporation for $350 million. It had been, to say the least, a fortuitous investment. Dad would have been proud.

In the early 1950s, television began to take America, if not Major League Baseball, by storm. In 1950, only nine percent of American households had televisions.[858] By 1954, televisions were present in 54 percent of American households.[859] By the early 1960s, approximately 90 percent of American families owned at least one television and many households boasted multiple sets.[860] For baseball's ownership, however, television was initially seen as an evil that would erode attendance at ballparks. A few more progressive owners may have seen this new medium as a promising method of enhancing and showcasing their product, with hopes of increasing ballpark attendance, but in the early 1950s the terms "progressive" and "baseball owner" were rarely used in the same sentence. In 1946, Major League owners banned televised broadcasting of Major League games beyond a 50-mile radius of the stadium in which a game was played.[861] In 1949, this ban was lifted, but, as discussed below, *Game of the Week* broadcasts were still blacked out in Major League cities.[862]

An early proponent of the use of broadcasting was Walter O'Malley.[863] O'Malley had favored the radio broadcasting of Dodgers games since the early 1940s, when the Yankees and Giants refrained from radio broadcasts of home games to preserve live attendance. The Dodgers played in the first televised World Series in 1947. O'Malley negotiated, and received substantial revenues from, baseball's first national television broadcast, the 1951 playoff game between the Giants and the Dodgers in which Bobby Thomson hit the "Shot Heard 'Round the World."[864] In 1949, commissioner Albert B. "Happy" Chandler sold the exclusive rights to broadcast the World Series for six years to the Gillette razor blade company for a fee of $1 million per year.[865] Not bad money for 1949. But Gillette immediately resold those broadcasting rights to the National Broadcasting Company for $4 million per year.[866]

In 1953, the American Broadcasting Corporation expressed interest in broadcasting a weekly Major League Baseball game. When ABC approached baseball's owners, it was agreed that they that could broadcast a weekly game, so long as the games were not televised in any of Major League Baseball's markets.[867] Thus, ABC's *Game of the Week* broadcast no games in New York, Chicago, Boston, Philadelphia, or any other Major League city, but the good folks in Mobile, Portland, Des Moines, Little Rock, East Podunk, and Albuquerque enjoyed the best that baseball had to offer. In 1955, the Columbia Broadcasting System replaced ABC in televising the *Game of the Week*.[868] I vividly recall watching those Saturday afternoon games, announced by Dizzy Dean and Pee Wee Reese, on my aunt and uncle's television set with its large box, small screen, and fuzzy black and white picture. Unfortunately, my house was still in the radio age. The owners' shortsighted greed guaranteed them exclusivity in their own markets while the game was popularized in the hinterlands. But it also guaranteed that their broadcasting revenues would be minimal and that the growth of the game would be stunted at a time when other sports such as professional football were gaining momentum. Exactly what the owners were promoting was also questionable. Because of the lack of proximity to Major League ballparks, the games being broadcast in distant locales could hardly be expected to attract fans to attend games. Nor did such broadcasts expand markets for Red Sox caps or Cardinals pennants because the owners refused to sell team merchandise, believing they were protecting the sanctity and dignity of their franchises.

What meager revenues baseball received from national television broadcasts ($895,000 in 1964) were not divided equally, but according to the number of television appearances made by each team. The networks, which were headquartered in New York, of course preferred to show the perennial champion New York Yankees and other popular teams such as the Dodgers, Giants, and Cardinals. In 1964, the New York Yankees received two-thirds of the total national broadcast money because they were easily the most televised team in baseball.[869] Those revenues swelled Yankees coffers, permitting the Bronx Bombers to out-spend and, consequently, out-play all other teams. Perhaps not coincidentally, CBS purchased the Yankees in 1964 and, effectively, paid those two-thirds of broadcasting fees to itself.[870] Thus, CBS recognized early the benefits of combining ownership of a premier Major League Baseball franchise and the ability to broadcast games.

Finally in 1965, Major League Baseball's owners assessed their national television package, addressed the inequities of the split of television revenues, and agreed to divide national broadcast revenues equally. In that year, the *Game of the Week* was first broadcast into Major League cities and national broadcast revenues increased to $5.7 million, six and one-half times the 1964 total.[871] Every team except the Yankees received at least three times as much in national broadcast revenues in 1965 as it had received in 1964. In 1966, a new contract was signed with NBC which permitted that network to televise the World Series, the All-Star Game, and the *Game of the Week* in 1966–68 for $11.8 million per year.[872] Still, professional football was receiving nearly three times as much in national broadcasting revenues as Major League Baseball.

National broadcasting revenues for Major League Baseball continued to rise throughout the remainder of the 20th century, as egotistical and competitive television networks and national sponsors including breweries, automobile manufacturers, and soft drinks giants paid ever greater amounts to televise baseball. NBC paid Major League Baseball an average of $16.5 million per year for exclusive national broadcasting rights in 1969–71.[873] NBC increased those fees to an average of $18 million per year for 1972–75.[874] NBC and ABC combined to pay Major League Baseball an average of $23.3 million per year for shared broadcasting rights in 1976–79.[875] In 1980, the first year in which national network revenues exceeded local broadcasting revenues, NBC more than doubled the average annual national broadcasting revenues to Major League Baseball for 1980–83 to $47.5 million.[876] After that contract expired, average annual national broadcasting revenues more than tripled as ABC and NBC combined to provide $187.5 million per year in 1984 through 1989.[877] Broadcast revenues continued to increase, as CBS paid an average of $265 million per year to broadcast Major League Baseball from 1990 through 1993.[878] During 1994 and 1995, Major League Baseball formed a partnership with the American Broadcasting Corporation and the National Broadcasting Corporation to create the ill-conceived and short-lived "The Baseball Network" which offered limited regional telecasts of games.[879] During 1996–1999, Major League Baseball received an average of approximately $425 million per season from its contracts with Fox, ESPN, and NBC.[880] Under contracts signed with ESPN and Fox in 2000, Major League Baseball will receive an average of $570 million annually for 2001–2005, $19 million per year for each of Major League Baseball's 30 teams.[881] And this is only part of the television broadcasting revenue story, a small part to some owners.[882]

The inescapable fact is that many of Major League Baseball's most serious and insidious problems today are the result of local revenues, particularly media revenues. Baseball is in serious trouble because of extraordinarily high media revenues, an inequitable and inefficient method of allocating those revenues, and player and franchise dislocations caused by the manner in which those revenues are allocated. How can that be? Aren't Major League Baseball's media revenues divided equally? Yes, and no. Major League Baseball equally divides among all 30 of its teams all *national* broadcasting revenues. But it does not equally divide *local* broadcasting revenues, and this unequal allocation of revenues provides the difference between financial profitability and loss and between success and failure on the field.

The difference between the revenues of Major League Baseball's highest revenue teams and its lowest revenue teams has never been higher and the gap is ever widening. The reason for this difference is the tremendous disparity in what is termed "local revenue." For this purpose, "local revenue" includes gate receipts, ballpark concessions, parking, advertising and publications, suite rentals, spring training and post-season revenues, and television, radio, and cable fees except for national network broadcasting revenues. Until the 1970s, "local" broadcasting revenues were relatively insignificant. As late as 1985, cable television revenues were only responsible for $1 of each $8 of television revenues received by Major League Baseball,[883] and that revenue was almost entirely earned by a few large-market teams.[884] In 1995, the year following the last players' strike, the difference between total revenues for baseball's highest revenue team (the New York Yankees at $97.7 million) and its lowest revenue team (the Pittsburgh Pirates at $24 million) was $73.7 million. In 1999, the difference between total revenues for baseball's highest revenue team (the New York Yankees at $177.9 million) and its lowest revenue team (the Montreal Expos at $48.8 million) was $129.1 million. Moreover, the difference between "local" revenues in 1999 for the Yankees ($175.9 million) and the Expos ($12 million) was an astonishing $164 million. In 1999, the Yankees' total revenue exceeded the *combined* total revenues of the *three* teams with baseball's lowest total revenues, and the Yankees' "local" revenues exceeded the *combined* local revenues of the *six* teams with baseball's lowest local revenues. In 2001, broadcasting revenues paid by "local" television and radio broadcasters to Major League Baseball teams totaled approximately $469 million,[885] most of which was received by teams in media centers or with ownership by media groups. New York Yankees managing owner George Steinbrenner has announced the formation of a new broadcasting company, the Yankees Entertainment and Sports ("YES") Network, that will feature his Yankees as well as the New Jersey Nets National Basketball Association team and the New Jersey Devils National Hockey League team which he acquired in 2000.

It comes as no surprise, then, that the Yankees' total payroll in 1999 ($92.4 million) was nearly six times as high as the lowest total team payroll (the Minnesota Twins at $15.8 million) and that the Yankees' total payroll exceeded the total *combined* payrolls of the *five* teams with baseball's lowest payrolls. It also comes as no surprise that the Yankees again had baseball's highest total payrolls in 2000, 2001, and 2002 ($114 million,

$125 million, and $135 million, respectively) and that the Yankees have won five of the last seven American League pennants and four of the last seven World Series championships. In 2001, the Yankees payroll was approximately five times as high as that of the Minnesota Twins, baseball's lowest payroll team, and more than the *combined* payrolls of the Minnesota Twins, Oakland A's, Montreal Expos, and Florida Marlins. In 2002, the Yankees' payroll was approximately four times as large as the payroll of the Tampa Bay Devil Rays, Major League Baseball's lowest paid team, and nearly as high as the *combined* payrolls of the Minnesota Twins, Oakland A's, Montreal Expos, and Tampa Bay Devil Rays. The World Series winner in each of the six years from 1996 through 2001 had one of the top six payrolls in baseball, the World Series loser in each of those six years had one of the top eight payrolls in baseball, and, except for the 2002 Minnesota Twins, all teams that have appeared in the National League and American League Championship Series in the last seven years have had payrolls in the top half of all Major League Baseball payrolls. Moreover, 249 of the 258 post-season games since the strike and lockout of 1994-95 (96 percent) have been won by teams with payrolls among the top half of all payrolls.

In the early 1970s, a new type of owner and a new type of problem entered Major League Baseball in the form of Robert Edward Turner III, the owner of a UHF television station in Atlanta who had acquired the National League's Atlanta Braves. The kooky, but shrewd Ted Turner televised Braves games sandwiched between classic movies and syndicated reruns of television programs such as *The Beverly Hillbillies, The Andy Griffith Show,* and *Leave It to Beaver.* Turner, dubbed "The Mouth of the South," was an imaginative and daring programmer who used his baseball broadcasts to promote and lead into other programming and other programming to promote and lead into his baseball broadcasts. His initial success permitted him to expand the reach of his broadcasting empire, by microwave relays and cable in the Southeast United States, and later by satellite transmission throughout the world. In many cases, Turner provided his broadcasting package free to cable companies, realizing that his advertising revenues would increase with the number of viewers of his programs. He parlayed this empire into the WTBS Superstation, Cable News Network, Time Warner Broadcasting, America Online/Time Warner, and a fortune.[886] Along the way, he irritated other owners with his brash, outspoken manner and his invasion of their territorial rights, but he also spawned a number of imitators, including superstations in New York, Chicago, and New England, many of which now own, or have significant interests in, Major League Baseball teams.

Rupert Murdoch's purchase of the Los Angeles Dodgers in 1997 angered several existing owners, particularly Atlanta Braves arch-rival Ted Turner. Several smaller market teams, already astonished by the free spending ways of Turner, the Yankees' George Steinbrenner, the Orioles' Peter Angelos, and others, were aghast at the prospect of Murdoch completely destroying their already shaky salary structure. Murdoch's purchase of the Dodgers was easily confirmed, however, and, within a few months, the team's annual payroll was increased to $80 million, the highest total ever.

Rupert Murdoch

But what does an $80–$100+ million team payroll buy these days? Although, as described above, a high payroll seems to be required to achieve post-season success, large salaries do not necessarily translate into wins. In spite of having Major League Baseball's fifth-highest payroll in 1999, Los Angeles finished with a disappointing 77 wins and 85 losses, 23 games behind the National League West champion Arizona Diamondbacks. Undeterred, the Dodgers waded back into the fray during the off-season, signing Toronto Blue Jays outfielder Shawn Green to a six-year deal averaging $15 million per season. In the 2000 season, the Dodgers paid two players, Kevin Brown and Shawn Green, $30 million, more than the total payroll of four other teams. With Major League Baseball's second-highest payroll in 2000, the Dodgers improved to 86 wins and 76 losses, but still finished 11 games behind the National League West champion San Francisco Giants. In 2001, the Dodgers increased their payroll to $109 million, third-highest in the Major Leagues, and still failed to reach the post-season playoffs, again winning 86 games and losing 76. In 2002, the Dodgers reduced their payroll to $95 million, still the fifth highest in the Major Leagues, but again failed to reach the playoffs, winning 92 games and losing 70. The Dodgers' 341 victories in 1999 through 2002 cost approximately $1.2 million in player salary per win.

In 2000, only three of the teams with the Major Leagues' ten highest payrolls, the Yankees, Braves, and Mets, even made the playoffs. In 2001, this improved as five of the teams with the Major Leagues' ten highest payrolls, the Yankees, Indians, Braves, Diamondbacks, and Cardinals, made the playoffs. In 2002, only four of the teams with Major League Baseball's ten largest payrolls, the Yankees, Diamondbacks, Braves, and Giants, reached the playoffs.

Maverick Major League Baseball owner Bill Veeck once said, "It isn't really the stars that are expensive. It's the high cost of mediocrity." Veeck must be turning in his grave at the contracts that currently exist in Major League Baseball. Consider, for example, the $6,536,612 annual salary paid by the Baltimore Orioles in 2001 to their outfielder Brady Anderson. Although Anderson once was an All-Star center fielder who hit 50 home runs in a season, his performance in 2001 resulted in 50 runs scored, 45 runs batted in, 8 home runs, and a batting average of .202. But Anderson is not the Orioles' only high-salaried, mediocre player. His teammate David Segui, who received a $6,658,731 salary in 2001, scored 48 runs, hit 10 home runs, and had 46 runs batted in. Mike Bordick earned $4,311,622 in 2001 for 32 runs scored, 30 runs batted in, 7 home runs, and a .249 batting average. In his final Major League season, Cal Ripken, Jr. was paid $6,300,000 to score 43 runs, drive in 60 runs, hit 14 home runs, and post a .239 batting average. These four players, who *combined* did not score or drive in 200 runs, received total income in 2001 of $23,806,965. If you are not troubled by the relative values of the Baltimore quartet, consider the combined 2001 salaries and production of the Boston Red Sox foursome of Dante Bichette, Jose Offerman, Mike Lansing, and Carl Everett who received salaries totaling $27,333,333 and combined to produce 227 runs scored, 190 runs batted in, and 43 home runs (Bichette—$7,000,000 salary, 45 runs scored, 49 runs batted in, 12 home runs, .286 batting average; Offerman—$6,750,000 salary, 76 runs scored, 49 runs batted in, 9 home runs, .267 batting average; Lansing—$6,250,000 salary, 45 runs scored, 34 runs batted in, 8 home runs, .250 batting average; and Everett—$7,333,333 salary, 61 runs scored, 58 runs batted in, 14 home runs, .257 batting average). The salaries paid to the Orioles quartet and the Red Sox foursome, respectively, exceeded the aggregate 2001 salaries ($23,744,083) paid to the entire Oakland A's starting infield (Jason Giambi, Frank Menechino, Miguel Tejada, and Eric Chavez), starting outfield (Johnny Damon, Jermaine Dye, and Terence Long), starting designated hitter (Jeremy

Giambi), starting catcher (Ramon Hernandez), three best starting pitchers (Tim Hudson, Mark Mulder, and Barry Zito), best middle reliever (Mike Magnante), and closing relief pitcher (Jason Isringhausen). These 13 Oakland A's contributed a total of 748 runs scored, 657 runs batted in, 174 home runs, 60 pitching wins, and 34 games saved. Incidentally, the A's won 102 games in 2001 while the Orioles managed only 63 wins and the Red Sox won 82 games.

If that is not enough to sicken you, consider the 2001 salaries and production of Matt Williams ($9 million salary, 58 runs scored, 65 runs batted in, 16 home runs, .275 batting average); Ray Lankford ($8.1 million salary, 58 runs scored, 58 runs batted in, 19 home runs, .252 batting average); David Justice ($7 million salary, 58 runs scored, 51 runs batted in, 18 home runs, .241 batting average); Chuck Finley ($8.9 million salary, 8–7 won-lost record and 5.54 earned run average); Joey Hamilton ($7.25 million salary, 5–6 won-lost record and 5.89 earned run average); and Kenny Rogers ($7.5 million salary, 5–7 won-lost record and 6.19 earned run average). For each of these hitters, each home run cost approximately half a million dollars in salary and for each of these pitchers, each game won cost in excess of a million dollars. In addition, a number of high-salaried players such as Mo Vaughn ($13,166,667), Albert Belle ($12,049,040), Frank Thomas ($9,927,000), David Wells ($9,250,000), Wilson Alvarez ($9,000,000), Alex Fernandez ($9,000,000), and Scott Erickson ($9,630,921) were injured for most or all of 2001 and contributed little or nothing to their teams.

The era of the mom and pop baseball store and the "gentleman sportsman" has ended. The Galbreaths no longer own the Pirates. The Carpenters are gone in Philadelphia. Philip Wrigley no longer sits in the owner's box in the Chicago ballpark that bears his name. Ray Kroc no longer owns the Padres. The Haas family has given up in Oakland. The Boston Red Sox franchise, owned by the Yawkey family since 1933, has finally been sold by the Yawkey Trust. Substantial "local" broadcasting revenues from New England Sports Network have permitted the Red Sox to finance payrolls of approximately $110 million in each of 2001 and 2002, the Major Leagues' second-highest payrolls in each of those years.

The ownership ranks of Major League Baseball today feature media icons such as America Online/Time Warner, News Corporation, The Walt Disney Company, Tribune Company, and Thomas Hicks's organization, all of which have realized the benefits of combining the ownership of a premier Major League Baseball team and the media apparatus to disseminate its product. No one understands the vast power of this combination better than Rupert Murdoch whose News Corporation holds the rights to televise not only Dodgers games, but also those of numerous other Major League teams. In theory, each Major League team has the exclusive (or shared in the case of metropolitan areas with more than one team) right to broadcast Major League Baseball within a defined territory. Moreover, in theory, Major League Baseball's cable television revenues are required to be shared, with the broadcasting team to receive 75 percent of the revenues and the other team to receive 25 percent of the revenues. In reality, however, "local" broadcasting revenues are understated, filtered through intermediate companies, and in the case of broadcasters and teams under common ownership manipulated to serve the owners' purposes. With satellite signals beaming games throughout the country and the world, the concept of "local" broadcasting is obsolete. Finally, the total value to AOL/Time Warner of broadcasting the Braves on the WTBS superstation, to the Tribune Company of telecasting the Cubs on the WGN superstation, or to Murdoch's News Corporation of televising the Dodgers on the Fox network and its affiliates is impossible to discern.

The "sportsmen" of this era are men such as George Steinbrenner, Peter Angelos, Jerry Reinsdorf, Eddie Einhorn, Tom Hicks, and Jerry Colangelo who appreciate the enormous value of media revenues, municipal and corporate funding, corporate sponsorship and promotion, and ultimately capital gains. At the other end of the spectrum are Major League Baseball's impoverished step-children, franchises such as the Montreal Expos, Minnesota Twins, Kansas City Royals, Pittsburgh Pirates, and Oakland A's. Although the low budget A's had remarkably successful seasons from their young and comparatively low-paid players from 1999 through 2002, and the low payroll Minnesota Twins reached the America League Championship Series in 2002, for the A's, the Twins, and the other Major League poor relations, there is little long-term hope. With no sharing of "local" media revenues, modest ballpark attendance, and no prospects of ever generating enough money to compete with the large market teams, they have become fodder for, and feeders to, the rich clubs. Consider that the Montreal Expos and Minnesota Twins receive $5–6 million in local media revenues annually while the New York Yankees may yield twenty times as much. "Yeah, but I didn't buy the Montreal Expos," points out Steinbrenner, "I bought the New York Yankees." Yankee "local" media revenues have increased even further under a new arrangement pursuant to which the Yankees games, which are now jointly owned with the New Jersey Nets National Basketball Association team and the New Jersey Devils National Hockey League team, are broadcast on the new Yankees Entertainment and Sports ("YES") Network.

As George Steinbrenner's high salaried Yankees collect more American League pennants (five in the last seven years) and World Series crowns (four in the last seven years), the Boss's self-centered view of Major League Baseball imperils the game. Back in the mid–1960s, even Walter O'Malley understood a certain degree of parity is necessary to sell baseball. The Christians at least have to put up a decent fight or fans will tire of seeing the Lions maul their victims. Like the hapless Washington Generals, who were mere foils to the star-studded Harlem Globetrotters basketball team, today's small-market Major League franchises offer a convenient and receptive stage for visiting large-market teams to showcase their skills and from which to beam their "local" television signals. They also provide a cost-effective method of developing talent for large-market teams when such players are eligible for salary arbitration and free agency. With increasing frequency, shrewd small and middle-market owners realize that it is more profitable to lose with a small payroll than a large one and are resigned to selling costly players to larger market teams. Teams that have no post-season illusions are willing to "dump" salaries to large-market teams that are willing to pay them. A particularly egregious recent example of this inequitable condition was the New York Yankees' acquisitions of Denny Neagle, David Justice, Jose Canseco, Glenallen Hill, Jose Vizcaino, and other players immediately preceding the July 31, 2000, trading deadline to buttress the Yankees' playoff drive and post-season roster. In 2001, the Yankees again acquired late season depth in purchasing Sterling Hitchcock and Randy Velarde for the late season pennant race and post-season playoff games. After their loss to the Arizona Diamondbacks in the 2001 World Series, the Yankees completely restructured their roster, acquiring free agents Jason Giambi, David Wells, Rondell White, and Steve Karsay and trading for Robin Ventura and John Vanderwal. Before the 2002 trading deadline, the Yankees assumed the salaries of Raul Mondesi and Jeff Weaver to provide greater depth for the playoffs.

Another area in which the finances of Major League teams vary widely is the ballparks in which teams play. Some teams continue to play in old-fashioned World War 1–era baseball parks, others in 1970s-era multi-purpose facilities, and still others in modern baseball-only facilities offering multiple sources of revenue to team owners. Major League Baseball experienced successive waves of building booms in the 20th century. From the first wave, the Major Leagues retain Yankee Stadium in the Bronx, Fenway Park in Boston, and Wrigley Field in Chicago. The owners of the teams that play in these classic ballparks have been grumbling increasingly in recent years about the need for new publicly financed stadiums. A number of "modern" ballparks such as Dodger Stadium in Los Angeles, Shea Stadium in Queens, and the Oakland–Alameda County Coliseum debuted in the 1960s. With the exception of Dodger Stadium, these parks are generally now outdated and will probably be substantially renovated or replaced in the next few years. In the 1960s and 1970s, new waves of multipurpose stadiums, some of which were covered with domes, and nearly all of which featured artificial turf, appeared. These included the Houston Astrodome (the "Eighth Wonder of the World"), Riverfront Stadium in Cincinnati, Busch Stadium in St. Louis, Three Rivers Stadium in Pittsburgh, Veterans Stadium in Philadelphia, and the Hubert H. Humphrey Metrodome in Minneapolis. Like many of the fashions of those decades, most of these stadiums have aged badly and many have already been substantially renovated or replaced. During the 1990s, a new group of retrodesign, baseball-only ballparks featuring restaurants, saloons, retail outlets, concessions, and other fan amenities began to dominate the Major Leagues. These parks include Camden Yards in Baltimore, Jacobs Field in Cleveland, Coors Field in Denver, the Ballpark at Arlington, Texas, and Bank One Ballpark in Phoenix.

Originally baseball parks were financed and owned by the teams that played in them. These parks were typically named after the owners of those teams; e.g., Wrigley Field, Ebbets Field, Comiskey Park, and Crosley Field. Partial or total municipal finance of ballparks became more common as Major League Baseball became national beginning in the 1950s, with the movement of the Braves from Boston to Milwaukee and later Atlanta, the Athletics from Philadelphia to Kansas City and later Oakland, the Browns from St. Louis to Baltimore, the Giants from New York to San Francisco, the Dodgers from Brooklyn to Los Angeles, the Senators from Washington, D.C. to Minnesota, and with expansion teams. Western and Southern cities vied with one another to attract such teams and become "Major League cities." Today, only four Major League teams (the Boston Red Sox, the Chicago Cubs, the Los Angeles Dodgers, and the St. Louis Cardinals) own their own ballparks.[887] The Red Sox and the Cardinals are seeking new, subsidized ballparks. A forerunner of modern stadium financing was Walter O'Malley's clever combination of public contribution of land and infrastructure and corporate promotion by Union Oil which financed the construction of Dodger Stadium.[888] Today, stadium finance is far more complicated and sophisticated with public finance, revenue bonds, tax incentives, ballpark naming rights, signage, corporate promotions, luxury clubs, corporate VIP box leasing and purchasing, theme activities, elaborate concessions, retail outlets, hospitality features, and the myriad of other schemes that increase the yield of some teams.[889] Baseball fields now have names such as Pacific Bell Park, Minute Maid Park, Coors Field, and Bank One Ballpark, which promote corporate sponsors that have paid vast sums to secure naming rights.[890] Negotiating a favorable package of stadium contracts and incentives can mean crucial economic differences to the finances of the teams that play in those stadiums. Coalitions of governments and businesses in cities that wish to attract Major League teams, and those that wish to retain them, bid vigorously to provide such packages, in the belief that being a Major League city will attract or retain businesses and jobs, increase municipal revenues, and produce positive psychological and social effects. Whether public finance of ballparks is an economically efficient allocation of public resources is the subject of much debate.[891] It is estimated that the average annual public subsidy to a Major League team is $10 million.[892]

The theory was long held in the parochial world of Major League Baseball that winning was the only way to sell tickets and that selling tickets was the only way to make a profit. Many of baseball's chief executives have historically been lifetime baseball men with, at best, a vague conception of public relations, marketing, or merchandising. With the exception of promotional and marketing pioneers such as Bill Veeck and Charlie Finley, it was until relatively recently considered distasteful, particularly to the more conservative and entrenched National League owners, to even promote ticket sales or fan loyalty. Merchandising of products bearing Major League logos was considered tasteless and sacrilegious. Accordingly, with the exception of television and ballpark promotions, which baseball's owners have finally accepted as resulting in increased revenues, Major League Baseball has remained largely regional and poorly promoted.

Major League stars such as Barry Bonds, Mark McGwire, Sammy Sosa, Alex Rodriguez, Ken Griffey, Jr., and Randy Johnson have enjoyed only a small fraction of the profile and exposure accorded to basketball giants such as Michael Jordan, Magic Johnson, and Shaquille O'Neal and football stars such as Steve Young, Dan Marino, Deion Sanders, and John Elway. It wasn't until athletic shoe manufacturers such as Nike and Reebok became the de facto marketing agencies for professional sports that baseball players started to achieve a portion of the commercial opportunities available to their basketball peers. Even then, it was a former football player, Bo Jackson, who became the most marketable face in baseball because of his skills in multiple sports.

If Major League Baseball's owners require a lesson in marketing or financial success in sports, they need to look no further than outside the windows of the commissioner's offices and across Park Avenue where another professional sports league adopted television as a means of promoting its game, earned vast revenues through television broadcasts and by merchandising products bearing team logos, and leveled its playing field in the process.[893] Back in the early 1960s, a young executive from the Los Angeles Rams was appointed commissioner of the then largely insignificant National Football League. Alvin "Pete" Rozelle saw the potential for growth in his league, particularly since the men who ran America's most successful sport, baseball, were provincial, ossified, and arrogant. Because the league was still young, regional, and lacking in direction, Rozelle was able to direct its future. Television coverage, television revenue, and logoed-product merchandising made the National Football League successful. Rozelle told professional football's owners that he would be negotiating all of the league's television and merchandising contracts and that the revenues from those contracts would be divided equally among all teams, irrespective of market share. The small market Green Bay Packers would receive the same share of television and merchandising revenues as the large market New York Giants and Chicago Bears. Revenue sharing would create parity, said Rozelle, and the league would only be as strong as its weakest team. Pete Rozelle was a pro-active visionary whose concept of "league-think" would have had little chance of succeeding in the National Football League if he had not secured the agreement of the powerful franchise owners in New York and Chicago. But Rozelle did convince all team owners great and small to agree and it was a tribute to his vision and leadership that the owners, except for the rare maverick such as Al Davis, followed his lead. The simple truth was that what was good for the National Football League was good for its teams and their owners.

Small wonder, then, that the financial condition of the National Football League, glutted with lucrative network television and licensing revenues, is far superior to that of Major League Baseball. Under the eight year, $17.6 billion contracts it signed in 1998, the National Football League's national television broadcasting revenues average $2.2 billion per year through 2005, four times that received under Major League Baseball's new national broadcasting contracts, and twice the total of Major League Baseball's national revenues and the combined "local" media revenues of all 30 Major League Baseball teams. According to *Forbes* magazine, the 31 National Football League franchises range in value from a high of $796 million (the Washington Redskins) to a low of $338 million (the Atlanta Falcons).[894] In Major League Baseball, only 40 percent of all teams are as valuable as the lowest-valued National Football League team. According to *Forbes*, the values of Major League Baseball's 30 franchises range from a high of $730 million (New York Yankees) to a low of $108 million (Montreal Expos).[895] The disparity in values of franchises in Major League Baseball is far greater than in the National Football League. In Major League Baseball, the most valuable team is worth nearly seven times as much as the least valuable team. In the National Football League, the most valuable team is worth less than two and one-half times as much as the least valuable team. Even the Green Bay Packers, a community-owned football team in a town with a population of 95,000, are valued at $392 million.[896]

The National Basketball Association, behind commissioner David Stern's progressive leadership, marketing, and merchandising, also has been immensely successful both in the United States and internationally. The National Basketball Association has actively promoted its stars, particularly to youth markets, and developed new ways to market its sport and merchandise. Baseball remains caught in a 19th century time warp in which baseball caps, which require little marketing, are the principal source of off-field revenue. Major League Baseball's large market owners cling to "me-think" which enables them to secure huge "local" revenues to the exclusion of their small-market counterparts and to use those revenues to build teams and telecommunications empires that ensure the gaps between the haves and have-nots will grow ever wider until audiences in distant locations refuse to either watch televised games that their home or regional teams have no chance of winning or attend games whose ticket prices multiply annually.

But Major League Baseball's owners don't need vision or league-think. They already have the Walter O'Malley pea pipe. You have a length of pipe full of peas, see. If you squeeze another pea in at one end, a pea is forced out the other. You put in the Yankees' payroll at $135 million here, and out there, at the other end, drop the Twins, Expos, A's, and Devil Rays at $35–40 million each. That, ladies and gentlemen, is Major League Baseball.

Chapter 15

REDEMPTION AND APOCALYPSE

The best place to catch a baseball hit by [Mark] McGwire is definitely not within the confines of the playing field, or sometimes even the ball park. Other players dial "1" for long distance. McGwire has to ask for an international operator.

—Thomas Boswell

Maybe the players are livelier now.

—Mickey Mantle in response to a comment that modern players' batting accomplishments were the product of a livelier baseball

I am the kind of fan who wants to get plenty of action for his money. I have some appreciation of a game [that features] a pitchers' duel and results in a score of one to nothing. But I must confess that I get the biggest kick out of the biggest score—a game in which the batters pole the ball into the far corners of the field, the outfielders scramble, and men run the bases. In short, my idea of the best game is one that guarantees the fans a combined score of not less than fifteen runs, divided about eight to seven.

President Franklin Delano Roosevelt

Why let people savor one of the best World Series ever? Let's have a labor mess! It really doesn't matter anyway.

You can imagine them saying, "When the dust settles, we can juice the ball up again and let Sammy Sosa take a crack at 80."

—Dan Patrick on the announcement by commissioner Bud Selig two days after the end of the 2001 World Series that Major League Baseball's owners had voted to eliminate two Major League teams

Major League Baseball was destined to end the 20th century on a sour note. Not since the Black Sox scandal of 1919, when gamblers paid eight members of the Chicago White Sox to throw the World Series, had the general public been so disillusioned and disinterested in baseball as it was by the mid–1990s. From 1972 to 1990, Major League Baseball had experienced seven work stoppages. Major League Baseball's owners had learned little from more than a century of mistakes. No longer were Major League Baseball's players criminally underpaid; by most reasonable standards, they were obscenely overpaid. And with their newfound affluence came a false sense of invincibility, as many players made as much news for their indiscretions off the field as their athletic prowess on it.

An already cynical public sighed when Commissioner Fay Vincent was forced to resign in September 1992. Vincent was replaced by an "interim" commissioner, the Milwaukee Brewers owner, Bud Selig. In spite of problems with the game's financial structure and labor relations, however, baseball began to build momentum in the early 1990s. The 1993 World Series ended dramatically when Joe Carter secured a second straight championship for the Toronto Blue Jays by hitting a ninth-inning home run to defeat the Philadelphia Phillies in six exciting games. For a change, action on the diamond was more newsworthy than that off the field.

The 1994 Major League Baseball season began in a portentous manner. The Major League Baseball Players Association was wary of the owners' reluctance to negotiate a new collective bargaining agreement. Warning shots were fired. If a new deal was not in place soon, the union would give serious consideration to a mid–season strike. The owners had suffered a series of labor setbacks over the preceding twenty years. Now under the stewardship of the interim commissioner, their own Bud Selig, they were in a public relations free-fall. Emboldened by the exhortations of a group of hawkish entrepreneurs, including Chicago White Sox owner Jerry Reinsdorf, Cincinnati Reds owner Marge Schott, and Texas Rangers owner Eddie Chiles, the owners were steadfast. They would take the game back from the players once and for all. The old days would return. After all, they did own the game. The Major League Baseball Players Association was as steadfast as Major League Baseball's owners. There would be no "give backs." Already exhausted by a number of work stoppages, baseball fans feigned indifference.

On the field, the 1994 season was shaping up as an exciting campaign. Players such as the San Francisco Giants' Matt Williams and the Houston Astros' Jeff Bagwell were off to torrid starts. Williams had hit 43 home runs by early August and was mounting a serious challenge to Roger Maris's 1961 single-season Major League record of 61 home runs. Bagwell's season was even more impressive. He was easily leading the National League in batting average and runs batted in and had hit 39 home runs. A National League "Triple Crown," a feat which had not been accomplished since Ducky Medwick of the Cardinals did so in 1937, was a distinct possibility.

The low-budget Montreal Expos were running away from the rest of the National League. The Expos fielded a team featuring seven home-grown starting players and an eighth, Manager Felipe Alou's son Moises, acquired by trade years earlier. Bereft of high-priced stars, the Expos were joyfully flying in the face of conventional success in the era of free agency. Moving from the decaying and cavernous Municipal Stadium into a new state of the art baseball-only facility proved to be the perfect tonic for a Cleveland Indians franchise that had not finished higher than third since 1959. Every game in the new Jacobs Field was a sellout and the Indians, featuring a team that had been built from shrewd draft choices and wise trades, were devastating their competition in the American League.

Major League Baseball's leagues had been realigned for the 1994 season. Each league now featured three divisions, East, Central, and West. All three division winners, as well as a wild card team, would now advance to the playoffs, doubling the number of post-season participants from four to eight. With the increase in playoff spots, optimism reigned in a number of previously disenfranchised cities. There was more to like about the 1994 baseball season than any in recent memory. Surely the men who played and owned the game would not permit stubbornness, greed, or stupidity to stop the action.

The owners' relentless effort to institute team salary caps, in effect a method of limiting the effects of free agency and preventing themselves from spending too much money, forced the players' hand. On August 12, 1994, this magical season was derailed as the players commenced a strike.[897] In early September, commissioner Selig cancelled the remainder of the season and all post-season play.[898] In taking their respective actions, the players and owners accomplished something two world wars and numerous other military campaigns and natural disasters had not. In a woefully embarrassing moment for Major League Baseball, America was deprived of one of its most cherished institutions as the World Series was cancelled. Neither the owners nor the players were free of blame and fans were disgusted by both.

Negotiations continued without progress during the offseason. With both sides remaining rigid in their respective positions, the owners decided to open spring training camps in 1995 with replacement players.[899] Tryouts were held throughout the country and a motley crew of has-beens and never-wases auditioned to pursue their big league dreams. On March 31, 1995, after a work stoppage of 232 days, including 920 missed games and no World Series, and a Federal Court ruling that the owners' use of replacement players and their failure to negotiate in good faith were unlawful, an accord was reached between the owners and the Players Association.[900] For better or worse, baseball was back.

A number of small market teams, shocked and disappointed with the judge's decision, immediately disposed of high-salaried players. After compiling the best record in the National League during the strike-shortened 1994 season, the Montreal Expos immediately dumped star outfielder Marquis Grissom and relief pitching ace John Wetteland at bargain prices. The Kansas City Royals unloaded Cy Young Award pitcher David Cone. If small market owners were forced to operate, it would be on their own terms and with no pretense of competitiveness. What resulted was a pitiful farce, even more insulting than using replacement players. Not surprisingly, the general public wanted little to do with baseball. Attendance fell and those who came to games booed long and loud.

The 1995 and 1996 seasons did little to remove the stench from the 1994 strike. A few warm moments were experienced, such as the night Cal Ripken surpassed Lou Gehrig's long-standing mark of 2,130 consecutive games played, but insufficient goodwill was generated to make fans forget the immediate past. As the 1995 season ended, the players and owners had yet to agree to the terms of a new collective bargaining agreement, casting even more uncertainty on the 1996 campaign. When a tentative deal was struck between the Major League Baseball Players Association and the owners' representatives, the owners, who were briefly practicing fiscal restraint, summarily rejected the pact. One week later, White Sox owner Jerry Reinsdorf signed Cleveland Indians slugger Albert Belle to a whopping five-year, $55 million contract.[901] The restraint Reinsdorf had been preaching to his counterparts was breached, ironically by himself. Feeling cheated and disillusioned, the owners took another vote to consider the labor package previously accepted by their representatives. This time, the deal was approved.[902] Major League Baseball now had a new five-year collective bargaining agreement which did not include salary limits. While the new collective bargaining agreement restored a semblance of labor peace to Major League Baseball, the game was still reeling. Interim Commissioner Bud Selig had accomplished little of substance in his three-year reign. The national pastime was lamented in *The Sporting News* as the "national past its time." Animosity between owners and players ran so deep that the owners felt compelled to undermine their principal resource, the players. Who could love a game that clearly did not love itself?

Major League Baseball's humiliation was complete with the 1997 World Series champion Florida Marlins. In their fifth year of existence, the Marlins defeated the Cleveland Indians in a seven-game World Series most memorable for having the then-lowest television ratings ever for a World Series. To add insult to ignominy, the television audience for the National Basketball Association finals, featuring Michael Jordan and his Chicago Bulls, surpassed the television audience of the World Series for the first time.

The Marlins were the logical result of Major League Baseball's lack of leadership, labor discord, and economic structure. Blockbuster Video and Waste Management mogul and Florida Marlins owner Wayne Huizenga decided, after four fruitless campaigns, to test whether south Florida would support a Major League Baseball franchise. Although he also owned the Miami Dolphins, an established and successful professional football franchise which was playing in new Joe Robbie Stadium, Huizenga was skeptical about the future of baseball in Miami without a new baseball stadium with enhanced revenue-generating capability. As co-tenants of Joe Robbie Stadium, the Marlins played their home games in a field lacking in both baseball character and aesthetics. Nevertheless, Huizenga was determined to build the best team money could buy for his great Miami baseball experiment.

Dave Dombrowski, the youthful architect of the surprising Montreal Expos teams of the early 1990s, was appointed as the Marlins' general manager. Dombrowski, long handcuffed by the Expos' budgetary constraints, was given a blank check and a mandate to build a winner immediately. Dombrowski quickly hired Jim Leyland as the Marlins' field manager. As manager of the Pittsburgh Pirates, Leyland had been an unwilling witness to the dismantling of one of the National League's best teams because of a lack of financial resources. In spite of losing star players such as three-time Most Valuable Player Barry Bonds, slugger Bobby Bonilla, and pitcher Doug Drabek to free agency, however, the Pirates managed to remain competitive. Much of the credit was owed to Leyland.

Dombrowski signed a bevy of high-priced free agents, including sluggers Bonilla and Moises Alou and pitchers Kevin Brown and Al Leiter. Dombrowski also acquired players who would soon be free agents and were too expensive for smaller market clubs to retain. Troubled, but immensely talented slugger Gary Sheffield was acquired from the San Diego Padres in a salary dump. The Marlins proceeded to sign Sheffield to a $65 million long-term contract, easily the most lucrative in the game. High priced, perhaps overpriced, veterans such as Devon White, Darren Daulton, and Jim Eisenreich were added to a team that included young homegrown standouts Charles Johnson, Edgar Renteria, and Livan Hernandez.

The Marlins were indeed formidable and finished with the National League's second best record. After dispatching the National League West champion San Francisco Giants and the National League East champion Atlanta Braves in the National League playoffs, the Marlins earned a berth in the World Series against the American League champion Cleveland Indians, which had defeated the defending World Series champion New York Yankees. The World Series, played in a combination of bitter cold in Cleveland and stifling heat in Miami, was an aesthetic fiasco. Baseball fans and the national media, disappointed that they had been deprived of a Yankees-Braves rematch, were appalled by the sloppy play. "It seems that the country wants Mike [Indians manager Hargrove] and myself to apologize for being in the World Series," observed Marlins manager Leyland. "But we have earned the right to represent our leagues here." Indeed they had. In fact, the Marlins were highly representative of what Major League Baseball had become. Florida finally overcame a Cleveland lead to win the series in the 11th inning of the seventh game. Baseball artistry had been at a minimum in the series, but fortunately not many people were watching.

Marlins owner Wayne Huizenga's $89 million free-agent spending spree allowed the Marlins to win the World Series in their fifth year, the fastest ever for an expansion team, easily surpassing the mark of the New York Mets, whose 1969 title came in their eighth year. "I've never been on a champion," gushed Darren Daulton, who had joined the Marlins in July. "All I know is it's over and we're on top. This has been a weird series, snow one day, 85 degrees the next. But it had a human element, and that's baseball." Unfortunately, Daulton was right. This was Major League Baseball. Venerable franchises such as the Boston Red Sox, Chicago Cubs, and Chicago White Sox, which had not won a World Series championship for a combined 250 years, were embarrassed by what the Marlins had accomplished in five short seasons. So was Major League Baseball. Although the

Marlins had played by the rules and committed no crimes, their guiltless spending had become the championship model. But worse was yet to come.

Huizenga, dissatisfied with the Marlins' attendance in their championship season and unsuccessful in securing support for building a new stadium, gave Dombrowski the order to begin dumping salary immediately after the World Series. Three days after sipping champagne, World Series hero Moises Alou was sent packing to Houston. High priced pitchers Kevin Brown, Al Leiter, and Robb Nen were quickly traded. Devon White, Bobby Bonilla, Gary Sheffield, and Charles Johnson soon followed. The Marlins were completely and swiftly gutted. Baseball, already reeling from adverse public relations, faced the daunting task of playing the 1998 season without a true defending champion. Major League Baseball had bottomed out. In 1998, the Marlins declined from 92 wins to 54, bringing to mind similar collapses by the Philadelphia Athletics in 1913 and 1932 when Connie Mack sold that team's star players. The public was disillusioned and disinterested. Baseball's owners and players had violated a sacred trust. What little integrity Major League Baseball had retained was now gone.

In 1920, following Major League Baseball's loss of fan confidence in the wake of the Black Sox scandal, baseball had been saved by Babe Ruth and his transformation of the game. Ruth's spectacular combination of charisma, bravado, and baseball skills caused fans to flock in droves to see the great man. Americans discovered that they enjoyed baseball again. Baseball endured. Seventy years later, Major League Baseball's owners were no more enlightened than their predecessors. The players, pampered and ridiculously wealthy, seemed incapable and unwilling to rescue the game. America's national pastime found itself in desperate need of an elixir. Baseball needed a savior, another Babe Ruth.

In 1998, baseball was blessed with a surfeit of riches. In an ironic twist of fate, baseball's inherent appeal and resilience resurfaced and the game returned to prominence without the aid of artificial stimuli. The game's most storied franchise, the New York Yankees, captured their 24th World Series championship. In winning 125 games, including games in the playoffs and the World Series, the Yankees had the most successful season in the history of Major League Baseball. Unlike earlier brash Yankees title teams, this juggernaut of a team seemed humble and earnest, and played a heady brand of fundamental baseball. Although their payroll was the second highest in the Major Leagues, these Yankees, led by understated manager Joe Torre, were difficult to dislike.

A number of other events helped to reaffirm baseball's magic in 1998.

Ironman Cal Ripken gracefully decided to end his streak of 2,581 consecutive games played because "it was time." Barry Bonds, a modern-day Willie Mays, became the first Major League player to both hit 400 home runs and steal 400 bases in a career. David Wells pitched a perfect game in Yankee Stadium, and *actually* knew that Don Larsen was the last Yankee to pitch a perfect game, in the 1956 World Series. Orlando "El Duque" Hernandez, a Cuban refugee, who several months earlier had risked his life by sailing across the choppy waters of the Caribbean, pitched in the World Series. Roger Clemens won an unprecedented fifth American League Cy Young Award. Chicago Cubs rookie pitching sensation Kerry Wood struck out a Major League record-tying 20 Houston Astros batters in a game without issuing a walk. The American League was blessed with three young shortstops for the ages, Alex Rodriguez, Nomar Garciaparra, and Derek Jeter, none of whom was anywhere near his prime. And with two full seasons remaining before the expiration of the collective bargaining agreement, there was no immediate threat of a players' strike or an owners' lockout. Peace, baby!

For Major League Baseball, 1998 was a summer of love. All right, Albert Belle and Barry Bonds were still surly, but even the losses suffered by baseball seemed to enrich it. Two of baseball's most cherished and revered broadcasters, Jack Brickhouse and Harry Caray, recorded their final outs. The passing of Brickhouse and Caray reinforced the sentimental and mystical aura surrounding baseball. Their last employers, the woeful Chicago Cubs, were so inspired they even made it into the post-season. Naturally they were summarily dispatched by the Atlanta Braves, but the Cubs in the playoffs? There must have been a lot of love out there.

The one factor that clearly served as the impetus for this surprising baseball renaissance in which more than 70 million spectators made 1998 a record attendance year was the season-long home run duel between brawny St. Louis Cardinals slugger Mark McGwire and Chicago Cubs star Sammy Sosa. In the magical 1998 season, the world sat transfixed while McGwire and Sosa pursued, and eventually passed, the most hallowed of Major League records, Roger Maris's single season home run total of 61. The captivating race, which saw McGwire peak at 70 and Sosa at 66, elevated the two to an international stardom that baseball players rarely achieve.[903]

After hitting 49 home runs as a rookie in 1987, Mark McGwire was hardly a neophyte in the game's power elite. But a series of nagging injuries and a lack of confidence had seen the big redhead's production slip so badly in 1991 that he posted a paltry and embarrassing .201 batting average with only 22 home runs. After two more years of injuries in which he managed a total of only 219 at bats, McGwire rediscovered his health, his confidence, and his swing. As his once mighty Oakland A's team unraveled, however, McGwire became the sole focus for the Bay Area's American League club. By hitting 52 home runs in 1996, McGwire caused America to realize that, if he was healthy, not a small order in McGwire's case, Roger Maris's single-season home run total of 61 was clearly within range. With 58 home runs in 1997, a late-season trade to the St. Louis Cardinals, and a reunion with former A's manager Tony Larussa, the spotlight intensified on Big Mac. But McGwire was also becoming loveable. Upon being traded to St. Louis, Larussa opined, "You have to realize with Mark that no matter how great a baseball player he is, he is a much, much better human being." During his first press conference in St. Louis, McGwire announced that he would be donating a sizable portion of his salary, $1 million per year, to a fund for abused children. Halfway through his announcement, the behemoth started to weep uncontrollably. "Being a father, knowing what children go through and thinking about all those helpless kids being abused, it makes me feel so helpless that I had to do something." Major League Baseball could not have planned a moment more heartening that the sight of this mighty man reduced to a blubbering mess on national television. McGwire had been quietly involved in a

Mark McGwire at bat.

number of charities in the past, but now it was official, he was a great guy. After pounding out 58 home runs in 1997, McGwire was also *the* story in baseball coming into the 1998 season.

The moment McGwire showed up in Florida for spring training in 1998, he was besieged. He was a traveling media show, the anointed one who would smash Maris's 37-year-old mark, which surprisingly had lasted longer than Babe Ruth's record of 60 home runs. How many will you hit in April, Mark? How about May? Do you think the record will fall before the All-Star Game? What's your favorite color? Do you see yourself as a transcendent figure, like Gandhi or Bob Dylan? Were you a caesarean birth? Obviously, it was also spring training for the media. McGwire knew that his assault on Maris's record would be conducted within a maelstrom of publicity the likes of which even the reclusive Maris and the gregarious Ruth had not experienced. The fish bowl was full and, for the big red guppy helplessly swimming around inside, fewer than 62 home runs would not be acceptable.

Four home runs in McGwire's first four games merely fanned the flames. At this rate, Maris's record would be eclipsed in mid–June. How about 100 homers, Mark? The Bunyanesque McGwire kept hitting them. By June 10, he had already pounded out 30 and the McGwire road show had become such a hit that even batting practice was a must-see event. From the moment McGwire emerged from the dugout during pre-game stretching, the media horde and waves of spectators surged forward. As the big redhead launched pitch after batting-practice pitch into the stands and beyond, it was like watching a fireworks display on the Fourth of July as choruses of breathless "ooh"s and "aah"s accompanied every rocket blast.

Controversy soon elevated McGwire's homer binge from the sports page to the front page. An intrepid reporter snooping in McGwire's locker discovered a bottle of androstenedione, a testosterone booster which is legal in baseball but banned in Olympic competition. It was true, said Big Mac, that he used the supplement to help him recover from intense workouts. But, as teammate Brian Jordan pointed out, he still had to hit the balls. Maybe McGwire's mammoth home runs would have only dented the lower part of the bleachers instead of the upper reaches, but it was folly to think that a drug propelled 70 home runs. Baseball has been becoming increasingly muscle-bound over recent years because big power numbers mean big money numbers. McGwire observed that, if androstenedione were banned by Major League Baseball, he would abide by the decision. But McGwire's drug controversy was now worldwide news. Pious poseurs, such as International Olympic Committee tyrant Juan Antonio Samaranch, urged baseball to ban the substance.

Members of the media seemed genuinely mystified that their constant hounding did not please the besieged, and clearly flustered, McGwire. The Cardinals took action and announced that the big man would only be available to the media for one-half hour before the start of each series. Obviously, Mac desperately needed some relief from the madness. He would get it, but from a most unlikely source.

"He showed progress the year before, but seemed to regress in 1997 when he set a team record with 174 strikeouts. He always has been an aggressive hitter with great raw power, and it was hoped that maturity would enable him to make the most of his considerable skills. Still, holes remain in his swing, both up and in, and down and away. Normally a high-percentage base stealer, he seemed to be running for his own numbers in 1997 and was thrown out quite a bit in the second half. He has the speed to steal, but chooses to run at odd times and sometimes betrays his intentions. Now going on 29, this may be as good as he gets."

According to Central Scouting, Sammy Sosa was an enigma and something of a disappointment coming into the 1998 season. While his numbers were very good, his dedication to the Cubs team had frequently been questioned. Sosa was known for wearing more gold than was on deposit in Fort Knox. When he was younger, Sammy wore a gold medallion the size of a hubcap around his neck. But it was difficult to deny Sosa his material indulgences. Growing up impoverished in the Dominican Republic, Sammy shined shoes for pennies to help his family eat. His athletic prowess was his ticket out and he knew it. Sammy didn't receive $10 million per year for hitting the cutoff man or perfectly executing the bunt or hit and run. He would swing for the fences, and regularly lead the league in strikeouts. But that was acceptable because balls in the bleachers meant dollars in his pocket. Defensively, Sammy had all the tools, a great throwing arm and speed to burn. But his frequent misplays in the outfield overshadowed his limitless potential. In many ways, Sammy Sosa was a mirror image of Major League Baseball. Too much money, too much ego, and absolutely no concern for fundamentals. Both were in need of a positive makeover.

On May 30, with Roger Maris's legacy dogging him, Mark McGwire had already hit 27 home runs. On the same date, Sammy Sosa had 13 home runs and seemed on his way to 40, with perhaps 100 runs batted in. Nice numbers, possibly not worth $10 million a year in this era of inflated batting statistics, but certainly upper echelon. By the time June ended, Mark McGwire had hit 37 home runs and was still on schedule to pass Maris. But by now Sammy Sosa had hit 33, including a remarkable 20 home runs

Sammy Sosa

in June. The New York Yankees, Atlanta Braves, San Diego Padres, Cleveland Indians, and Houston Astros had essentially clinched playoff spots. There was little drama on the scoreboard, but McGwire and Sosa provided unrivaled theater in the scorebook. Sosa was a polar opposite to McGwire. He had not been subjected to three years of inane home run questions. Most of the questions thrown at Sammy had centered on his selfishness. But with his Cubs winning, Sammy was a gracious competitor. "Mark McGwire is the man," Sammy said repeatedly; "it's his record to break. I just want to help my team win and represent my country and my team in the most positive way. I am not about personal stats, just about winning." True enough, Sosa's Cubs were embroiled in a wild card playoff race, while McGwire's Cardinals, with a decimated pitching staff, were woeful.

By the All Star break, McGwire had hit 37 home runs and Sosa 35. Both sluggers were now on pace to break Maris's legendary record. McGwire had repeatedly said that the single-season home run record was not at issue until someone hit number 50 before the beginning of September. But *Time*, *Newsweek*, ESPN, every television and radio network and station, Oprah, Letterman, Leno, and even President Clinton wanted a piece of McGwire and Sosa in this most mystical of baseball seasons. Big Mac was becoming irritable and losing popularity. Meanwhile, Sammy kept smiling.

On August 20, McGwire officially allowed the discussion about a new single-season home run record to begin. He had hit four home runs in the past two days and now had 51. A reflective McGwire allowed that he was actually in awe of himself. And rightly so. Over the next 10 games, Mark bashed nine more to catch Babe Ruth at 60. Every at-bat for Big Mac was a national media affair with prime time programming cutting away to live pictures of McGwire. Sammy was at 56 and gaining by the time McGwire tied Maris in a storybook scene that was so maudlin that even Hollywood wouldn't have touched it. With the Maris family in the stands at Busch Stadium and the rest of the country enjoying the Labor Day holiday, Big Mac hit number 61. McGwire did all the right things. He hugged the Maris family, paused dramatically to point skyward for acceptance from the Babe and Roger, and wished his dad a happy birthday, naturally his 61st. Sosa didn't need to send his best wishes. He was standing in left field watching and clapping because McGwire had tied Maris's record against the Cubs. What pie-eyed sentimentalist had written this script?

Commissioner Bud Selig, who was in attendance, was all smiles and pointed out how the pure, unabashed joy of baseball would heal the country. It was almost true. Baseball was everywhere. McGwire had piqued the interest of people from Glasgow to Guangzhou. The next day McGwire, with Sosa again afforded one of the best seats in the house, set the Major League record for home runs in a single season. Number 62 left the park and an excited McGwire had to run back and touch first base because he had gleefully vaulted over it. After crossing home plate, he lifted his son skyward and released his pressure, demons, and doubters. The single-season Major League home run record belonged to Mark McGwire, the Major Leagues' career leader in home runs per at-bat. Sammy even came in from the outfield for a hug and, if there was a dry eye in Busch Stadium, it probably belonged to Cubs pitcher Steve Trachsel, who wanted no part of this history and grumpily said so after the game. But for everyone else, it was love, love, love.

McGwire felt so good that he moved aside for a week and let Sosa catch up to him. Sammy had his own love fest a few days later at Wrigley Field when he slammed numbers 61 and 62 on a beautiful Sunday afternoon. When Sosa hit number 62, McGwire was still stuck at the same level. The two men went back and forth over the next couple of weeks and, although several teams were still vying for playoff positions, baseball and its fans focused on Mark and Sammy. Briefly, Sammy Sosa became the only player to have hit 66 home runs in a single Major League season when he took Jose Lima deep in Houston. Never mind Maris's record of 61, Sammy had broken Mark McGwire's record of 65. But, just as he had over the last month, Big Mac responded immediately and forcefully. Within 43 minutes after Sosa hit his 66th, McGwire tied Sammy. As Sosa was unable to improve on 66, McGwire hit numbers 67, 68, 69, and 70![904]

Major League Baseball's owners were indeed blessed. They had not one, but two leading men, diverse in both ancestry and temperament. One was a red-headed and bronzed California boy, the other a smiling native of the desperate Dominican Republic. The owners talked of healing, how the game had reclaimed its birthright in the country's heart. No gimmicks or meddling were necessary, baseball had reasserted itself without outside intervention. McGwire completely transformed the St. Louis Cardinals from a team of speed and defense to one of power. In ten of the 15 seasons immediately preceding the Cardinals' acquisition of McGwire, the team had hit the fewest home runs in the National League. In 1998, Big Mac's first full season as a Redbird, the Cardinals led the National League in home runs for the first time since 1944.[905] But if two guys can hit over 60 home runs and help set attendance records, what would happen if nine or 10 guys hit that many? Absurd as it may sound, one only has to look at some of the owners' more egregious mistakes of the past to realize that they are capable of such thoughts.

In 1999, Sosa and McGwire again engaged in a memorable home run duel, with Mac finishing at 65 and Sammy at 63. In spite of hitting 18 home runs more than any other player, however, there was hardly a repeat of the previous season's magic. Unlike Roger Maris's mark, McGwire's 1998 home run record was recent and hardly mystical. Still, there were only four players in Major League Baseball who had hit 60 home runs in a season and only two of them, McGwire and Sosa, had done it twice. In 2000, Sosa led all Major League sluggers with 50 home runs, as injuries limited McGwire to only 236 at-bats and 32 home runs. In 2001, Sosa blasted 64 more home runs while McGwire, again curtailed by injuries, could manage only 299 at-bats and 29 home runs. In 2001, the biggest story was that Barry Bonds hit 73 home runs, breaking McGwire's three-year-old record. But with Major League pitching generally acknowledged to be at its lowest level in decades, and several new stadiums making home runs commonplace even for middle infielders, the sight of Major League batters going deep has become decidedly routine. In 2000, 5,693 home runs were hit, more than in any season in Major League Baseball history. In 2001, largely because of a more pitcher-friendly strike zone, the total number of home runs fell to 5,458. In 2002, the number of home runs declined further to 5,059. But home runs have definitely become the largest attraction in the game, as historic records are increasingly being challenged by a combination of hitter-friendly stadiums, lively baseballs, more power-ful hitters, more effective bats, and increased *emphasis* on home runs.

Since 1998, baseball, most noticeably McGwire and Sosa, has been everywhere. McGwire and Sosa unwittingly became the perfect pair to revive baseball. Because of their diverse backgrounds and personalities, the game stretched boundaries with its appeal. Historically, in spite of fea-turing players from five continents, baseball was largely viewed as an American sport. While commissioner David Stern of the National Bas-ketball Association and Gary Bettman of the National Hockey League heartily embraced the international elements of their games, it was rumored that Bud Selig didn't even have a passport. Because of the 1998 home run duel between Sosa and McGwire, the personalities of interna-tional players such as Sammy Sosa and Ichiro Suzuki, and an extremely deep and talented pool of international stars, however, Major League Base-ball is finally attempting to go global. With a new emphasis on interna-tionalization in both commerce and culture, it is not a moment too soon.

After his breakthrough season in 1998, Sammy Sosa traveled to Japan with a Major League all-star team to play a series of eight exhibition games. Even with the Japanese propensity for suffocating the celebrated in idol-atry, it would have been difficult to have anticipated the magnitude of the reception Sosa received in baseball-mad Japan. From the moment his plane touched down in Tokyo, Sammy's visit to Japan consisted of an orgy of flashbulbs and screaming mobs of fans. After receiving a stand-ing ovation in his first at-bat in the first game of the exhibition series at the Tokyo Dome, Sosa hit a home run and, upon reaching home plate, respectfully bowed to the screaming throngs. Pure Hollywood perhaps, but there was little denying baseball's international appeal, particularly in Japan, a number of whose native pitchers were now plying their trade in America's Major Leagues.

Major League Baseball President Paul Beeston accompanied the Major League all stars on their tour of Japan. Beeston was naturally bull-ish on the international appeal of baseball. "A lot of people think I'm crazy, but I believe that baseball is poised to become the world's game," Beeston told *Time* magazine. "How many countries win in soccer? Maybe five or six. And in basketball the American Dream Team annihilates all comers. Twenty percent of the players in the big leagues are non–Amer-ican, and a World Cup format in baseball would see about nine or 10 teams with an opportunity to win. The market for baseball and the reserves of talent have hardly peaked. I firmly believe that baseball's popularity will soar because it really is the last civil game."

If 1998 saw the rebirth of Major League Baseball through the home run, the 1999, 2000, and 2001 seasons will be best remembered for the international players who left an indelible stamp on the game and a glimpse into the future. Major League rosters have featured Caribbean players for over three decades. Now, Japanese, Korean, and even Taiwanese players are also beginning to make their marks. In 1998, the Dominican Republic's Sammy Sosa was named Most Valuable Player in the National League and Puerto Rico's Juan Gonzales was named Most Valuable Player in the American League. In 1997, Dominican Pedro Martinez captured the National League's Cy Young Award and in 1999 and 2000, he won the American League's Cy Young Award. In 1999, the Texas Rangers' Puerto Rican–born catcher Ivan "Pudge" Rodriguez was named the American League's Most Valuable Player. In 2000, the Seattle Mariners' Japanese-born pitcher Kazuhiro Sasaki was named the American League's Rookie of the Year, becoming the second Japanese-born player, after Hideo Nomo in 1995, to win that award. In 2001, the St. Louis Cardinals Dominican-born Albert Pujols was named the National League's Rookie of the Year and the Seattle Mariners' Japanese-born Ichiro Suzuki was named the American League's Rookie of the Year and Most Valuable Player. In 2002, Oakland A's Dominican shortstop Miguel Tejada was named the American League's Most Valuable Player, Red Sox outfielder and designated hitter Manny Ramirez won the American League batting title, and Texas Rangers shortstop Alex Rodriguez led the Major Leagues in home runs and runs batted in.

Exciting Latin players (some of whom were born and raised in the United States), such as Rodriguez, Sosa, Gonzales, Martinez, Rodriguez, Tejada, Pujols, Toronto Blue Jays first baseman Carlos Delgado, Montreal Expos outfielder Vladimir Guerrero, Texas Rangers shortstop Alex Rodriguez, New York Yankees outfielder Bernie Williams, Boston Red Sox outfielder Manny Ramirez, Houston Astros outfielder Moises Alou, Seattle Mariners designated hitter Edgar Martinez, Texas Rangers first baseman Rafael Palmiero, Atlanta Braves outfielder Andruw Jones, and Boston Red Sox shortstop Nomar Garciaperra are now taking the spotlight. With basketball's popularity now attracting many of the best black American athletes, the number of black Americans in Major League Baseball is declining. But the number of Latin players is soaring. A release from commissioner Bud Selig's office highlighted that 178 of the 841 players (including those on the disabled list) on opening day rosters in 2000 were born in 17 countries outside the United States. Leading this group were 71 Major League players born in the Dominican Republic, including Sosa, Martinez, Guerrero, and Delgado. That over 20 percent of the current crop of Major League players are foreign-born confirms a trend that began in the 1960s with the first wave of Latin players.

And the Latin revolution has only begun. Of the nearly 6,600 players under contract to either Major League or minor league teams on opening day in 2000, more than 1,400 were from the Dominican Republic. In 1999, 860 foreign-born players were signed to professional contracts by Major League teams. Of these, 473 or 55 percent, hail from the Dominican Republic. Hundreds more come from Puerto Rico, Venezuela, Cuba, and Mexico. For many Americans, however, the phrase "Latin ballplayer" still conjures images not of Roberto Clemente or Juan Marichal, but of Chico Escuela, the pidgin-speaking player parodied on *Saturday Night Live*. "It was terrible—it infantilized Latin players," observed Roberto Gonzalez Echeverria, a Yale professor and author of *The Pride of Havana: A History of Cuban Baseball*.[906] While the Latin American ballplayer is no longer perceived as a stranger in a strange land, however, or a free-swinging, free-spirited, comic stereotype, some perceptions are difficult to erase.

Further expansion of the foreign influence in Major League Baseball came with the arrivals in Seattle Mariners uniforms of Kazuhiro Sasaki and Ichiro Suzuki, who were named the American League's Rookie of the Year in 2000 and 2001, respectively. Although a number of Asian-born pitchers had played in the Major Leagues, Suzuki, who had been a seven-time batting champion for the Orix Blue Wave in the Japanese Pacific League, became the Major Leagues' first Asian-born position player, along with Tsuyoshi Shinjo who broke in with the New York Mets in 2001. A cultural icon in his native Japan where Mariners games are broadcast in the middle of the night to millions of exultant viewers, Suzuki (who prefers to be called simply "Ichiro"—shades of Madonna, Prince, and Pele) thrilled his fans and Mariners management with a "rookie" season in which he led the Major Leagues in both batting average and stolen bases (the first player to lead in both categories since Jackie Robinson in 1949), won a Gold Glove, and was named both Rookie of the Year and Most Valuable Player in the American League (the only other player ever to do so was Fred Lynn in 1975), while leading his team to an American League Western Division championship and the American League Championship Series. The success of Kasuhiro and Suzuki will undoubtedly lead Major League Baseball's management to scout players with greater intensity in Japan, Korea, Taiwan, and other Asian nations.

The disparate elements of the great 1998 home run derby between Mark McGwire and Sammy Sosa proved irresistible to the media. Race had long been Major League Baseball's, and America's shame. The media now drew lines. Most of white America, we were told, was rooting for McGwire. People of color, the disenfranchised, and the immigrant sector were passionate for Sosa. During baseball's magical 1998 season, polls showed overwhelming white support for McGwire. Sports talk shows buzzed with calls from white fans wary of the upstart Sosa and the Latin threat to the great game. In predominantly ethnic urban areas, however, Sosa was the overwhelming choice to break Maris's home run mark. According to *Newsweek* magazine, "In politicized neighborhoods, like Harlem, it is difficult to find a McGwire supporter." When commissioner Bud Selig was present for McGwire's record-breaking home run in St. Louis, but absent later when Sosa broke Maris's and McGwire's marks, it only inflamed the debate. "What about Sammy Sosa? Why doesn't he get the same hurrahs?" A New Yorker observed in *Newsweek*. "I think it's racism. He's Dominican, he's dark. The icons of baseball have always been white." Writer Joseph Torres was infuriated by the notion that Houston Astros pitcher, and Dominican native, Jose Lima had served up easy pitches to his countryman Sosa to assist him to break Maris's record. "Those sort of attitudes make me want to vomit," said Torres. "Sometimes, it is just impossible for people to believe that Hispanics really can achieve greatness on their own merit."

The 2001 season witnessed the breaking of several of Major League Baseball's most hallowed career and single-season records, outstanding team and individual performances, the retirement of three future Hall of Fame players, the arrival of several exciting new stars, four tight playoff races in the National League, and a thrilling World Series which was delayed by the tragic events which occurred in New York City and Washington, D.C., on September 11, 2001.

In 2001, Barry Bonds recorded one of the greatest seasons in Major League history. In this titanic season, Bonds posted new single-season Major League records for home runs (73), bases-on-balls (177), slugging average (.863), and combined on-base percentage and slugging average (1.378). In doing so, Bonds broke Mark McGwire's three-year-old single season Major League home run record (70), Joe Bauman's long-standing "professional" record of 72 home runs hit in 1954 for the Roswell, New Mexico Rockets in the Longhorn League,[907] and Babe Ruth's longstanding single season Major League records for bases-on-balls (170), slugging average (.847), and combined on-base percentage and slugging average (1.377). Major League Baseball commissioner Bud Selig was present when Bonds broke McGwire's home run record. Bonds also recorded a batting average of .328, an on-base percentage of .515, 411 total bases, 107 extra-base hits, 129 runs scored, and 137 runs batted in. Yet, the combination of Bonds's long-established and well-deserved reputation for being arrogant, aloof, surly, and selfish; the American public's focus on the devastating events that occurred in New York City and Washington, D.C. on September 11, 2001; the fact that McGwire's single season home run record was only three years old; the lack of real competition in the 2001 home run race (Sammy Sosa's 64 home runs were the second-highest total in the Major Leagues); and Bonds's continuing inability to lead his team to post-season success conspired to somewhat tarnish the epic proportions of his feats in 2001.

In 1991, Rickey Henderson broke Lou Brock's career Major League record for stolen bases. In 2001, the much-traveled, 42-year-old Henderson also became the career Major League record holder for runs scored and bases-on-balls, breaking Ty Cobb's longstanding record for runs scored (2,245) and Babe Ruth's longstanding record for bases-on-balls (2,056). At the close of the 2002 season, Henderson had amassed Major League record career totals in stolen bases (1,403), runs scored (2,288), and bases on balls (2,179), as well as 3,040 hits, including 295 home runs. As with Barry Bonds, however, because of Henderson's much publicized arrogance and selfishness, he has not been accorded the acclaim for establishing these historic records that otherwise might have been expected. Nevertheless, Henderson also is assured of a place in Major League Baseball's Hall of Fame when he finally retires from the Major Leagues.

In 2001, Sammy Sosa became only the second player (with Mark McGwire) ever to have four seasons with at least 50 home runs and the only player to tally at least 60 home runs in three seasons. Sosa recorded his finest overall season in 2001, posting a .328 batting average, 64 home runs, a .737 slugging average, 425 total bases, 146 runs scored, and a Major League–leading 160 runs batted in. In 2001, Luis Gonzales recorded a .325 batting average, 57 home runs, 142 runs batted in, 128 runs scored, and 419 total bases, becoming only the fourth player (Babe Ruth, Roger Maris, and Mickey Mantle are the other three) to hit at least 50 home runs in a season for a World Series championship team and the first player since Steve Balboni in 1985 to hit at least 35 home runs for a World Series champion.

Alex Rodriguez, the Major Leagues' highest-paid, and possibly finest overall, player recorded another outstanding season in 2001 with 52 home runs, 135 runs batted in, 133 runs scored, and a .318 batting average, breaking Ernie Banks's single season Major League record for home runs by a shortstop and joining Babe Ruth, Jimmie Foxx, and Hack Wilson as the only players in Major League history to post at least 200 hits and 50 home runs in the same season. Other fine seasons were turned in by Jason Giambi (.342 batting average, 38 home runs, 109 runs scored, 120 runs batted in), Bret Boone (.331 batting average, 37 home runs, 141 runs batted in), Juan Gonzales (.325 batting average, 35 home runs, 140 runs batted in), Larry Walker (.350 batting average, 38 home runs, 123 runs batted in, and 107 runs scored), Shawn Green (.297 batting average, 49 home runs, 125 runs batted in, and 121 runs scored), and Todd Helton (.336 batting average, 49 home runs, 146 runs batted in, 132 runs scored, .685 slugging average, 105 extra-base hits, and 402 total bases).

In 2001, Helton became the first player in Major League history to record consecutive seasons with at least 100 extra-base hits. Only Lou Gehrig and Chuck Klein had previously posted at least 100 extra-base hits in more than one season, but those seasons were not consecutive. In 2001, Barry Bonds, Sammy Sosa, and Helton each collected at least 100 extra-base hits, the first season in which three players accomplished that feat. Four players, Bonds, Sosa, Helton, and Luis Gonzales, amassed at least 400 total bases in 2001. During the 2001 season, 21 players posted the offensive combination of a batting average of at least .300, at least 30 home runs, and at least 100 runs batted in, five fewer than the record 26 players who reached those levels in 2000. Of the 21 players who achieved this combination, fifteen played in the National League and only six played in the American League.

The 2001 season also featured a number of marvelous pitching performances. Randy Johnson posted 21 wins, 372 strikeouts (the fourth consecutive season in which Johnson has recorded more than 300 strikeouts), and a 2.49 earned run average, and won his third consecutive National League Cy Young Award after winning the American League Cy Young Award in 1995. Curt Schilling recorded 22 wins, 293 strikeouts, and a 2.98 earned run average. Roger Clemens won 20 games, posted a 3.51 earned run average, and won an unprecedented sixth American League Cy Young Award. Matt Morris won 22 games and recorded a 3.16 earned run average. Mariano Rivera saved 50 games and posted a 2.34 earned run average. Johnson and Schilling became the first teammates since Juan Marichal and Gaylord Perry in 1966 to each post at least 20 wins, 200 strikeouts, and earned run averages below 3.00. This level was reached on only seven occasions in the 1990s. In the American League, the youthful starting pitching corps of the Oakland A's, Mark Mulder, Tim Hudson, Barry Zito, and Corey Lidle (average age 25), combined for 69 wins.

The 2001 season marked the debut of two miraculous rookies. In the American League, the Rookie of the Year and Most Valuable Player was 27-year-old, Japanese-born Ichiro Suzuki, who joined the Seattle Mariners after nine seasons with the Orix Blue Wave in the Japanese Pacific League, in which he won seven Pacific League batting titles, seven Pacific League Gold Gloves, led the Pacific League in on-base percentage five times, and set the single-season Pacific League record for batting average. In his rookie season in the American League, Suzuki set American League records for singles (192) and hits by a rookie (242—also the most hits by any Major League player since Bill Terry's 254 hits in 1930). He also led the Major Leagues in batting average (.350—tied with Larry Walker) and stolen bases (56), the first time a player has led the Major Leagues in both categories since Jackie Robinson in 1949, won a Gold Glove, and led his Seattle Mariners team to the best record in Major League Baseball and an American League championship series showdown with the New York Yankees. In the National League, the St. Louis Cardinals' Dominican-born, 21-year-old Albert Pujols was named Rookie of the Year. Pujols, who played the 2000 season in Class A baseball, his only previous professional season, was not expected to make the Cardinals' 2001 regular-season roster. Pujols posted a .329 batting average, 37 home runs (narrowly missing the National League rookie record of 38 jointly held by Wally Berger and Frank Robinson), 130 runs batted in (breaking Berger's National League rookie record of 119), 112 runs scored, 47 doubles, a .610 slugging average, 88 extra-base hits (narrowly missing Hal Trotsky's Major League rookie record of 89), and 352 total bases (tying Dick Allen's Major League rookie record), in one of the greatest overall seasons ever recorded by a rookie.

The 2001 season also marked the retirement of three classic and classy Major League veterans. Baseball's iron-man, 41-year-old Cal Ripken, Jr., finally decided to retire after 21 seasons with the Baltimore Orioles, his only Major League team. Ripken played in more than 3,000 games and amassed 3,184 hits, 603 doubles, 431 home runs (including a record 345 as a shortstop), 1,695 runs batted in, and 1,647 runs scored, while being named the American League's Most Valuable Player twice and playing in a record 2,632 consecutive games. In the National League, 41-year-old Tony Gwynn called it quits after 20 seasons with the San Diego Padres, the only Major League team for which he played. Gwynn collected 3,141 hits, maintained a career .338 batting average, and won eight National League batting titles. Mark McGwire also announced his retirement on November 11, 2001, deciding to end a career that was defined by a unique ability to hit home runs and an unfortunate predilection for injuries. Regrettably for Major League Baseball fans, the big redhead's body simply refused to continue to support his efforts on the field. In his 16-year Major League career, Big Mac hit 583 home runs in only 6,187 at-bats, for a Major League career record one home run in every 10.6 at-bats. He also was the first major leaguer to hit 70 home runs, twice hit more than 60 home runs, and four times hit more than 50 home runs. Before the beginning of the 2001 season, St. Louis Cardinals management negotiated a two-year, $30 million extension of McGwire's contract for the 2002 and 2003 seasons. McGwire never signed the extension, preferring to wait to see if his performance in 2001 would justify two additional seasons. After a disappointing season in which he was unable to fully recover from the knee injury that also cut short his 2000 season, McGwire concluded that he was unable to continue playing at a level he considered appropriate and refused to accept the contract extension. In announcing his retirement, McGwire said, "I am unable to perform at a level equal to the salary the organization would be paying me. I believe I owe it to the Cardinals and the fans of St. Louis to step aside, so a talented free agent can be brought in as the final piece of what I expect can be a World Championship–caliber team." Ripken, Gwynn, and McGwire exhibited excellence on the field and class and dignity both on and off the field. Major League Baseball has no shortage of characters, whether in its ownership, in its management, or on the field, but it will surely miss the character of Cal Ripken, Jr., Tony Gwynn, and Mark McGwire.

Primarily as a result of an expanded strike zone, but also because of the emergence of several effective young pitchers, most Major League offensive statistics declined in 2001. Runs per game fell from 10.28 in 2000 to 9.55 in 2001, the lowest level since 1997. Home runs per game declined from 2.34 to 2.25, the lowest level since 1998. The Major Leagues' three leading home run hitters played in the National League, which averaged 2.28 home runs per game compared to 2.21 in the American League, the first season since 1972, the last year before the designated hitter rule was introduced in the American League, that more home runs per game were hit in the National League than in the American League. Over the same two-year period, overall Major League batting averages fell from .271 to .264, the lowest level since 1992; overall slugging averages dropped from .437 to .427, the lowest level since 1998; and overall on-base percentages declined from .345 to .332, the lowest level since 1993.

Several teams experienced unexpected success in 2001. In spite of losing future Hall of Famers Randy Johnson, Ken Griffey, Jr., and Alex Rodriguez in successive seasons, the Seattle Mariners won 116 games in the 2001 regular season, tying the record number of games won by the 1906 Chicago Cubs.[908] Also in the American League, the low-budget Oakland A's won 102 regular-season games and the New York Yankees won 95 regular-season games, while in the National League, the St. Louis Cardinals and Houston Astros each won 93 regular-season games.

Ichiro Suzuki

The record-setting events of 2001 and the devastating events of September 11, 2001, which had paralyzed a significant portion of American life, were followed by a thrilling World Series which displayed great drama as the four-time consecutive American League champion and three-time reigning World Series champion New York Yankees lost a seven-game endurance contest to the fourth-year Arizona Diamondbacks. The series, in which the home team won every game, began in Phoenix, where the Diamondbacks twice beat the Yankees convincingly (9–1 and 4–0) behind the flawless starting pitching of Curt Schilling and Randy Johnson. The series then moved to New York where the scrappy Yankees put together three consecutive come-from-behind one-run victories behind strong starting pitching and stronger relief pitching, twice producing game-tying home runs with two outs in the bottom of the ninth inning against Arizona's 22-year-old Korean-born relief pitcher Byung-Hyun Kim and each time winning in extra innings. In the series' sixth game, in Phoenix, the Diamondbacks crushed the Yankees 15–2 and set the stage for a dramatic seventh and deciding game. The game's two starting pitchers, Arizona's Curt Schilling and New York's Roger Clemens, pitched masterfully for 7⅓ and 6⅓ innings, respectively. The game entered the 8th inning tied 1–1, the Yankees scored a run in that inning, Arizona's left-handed starter Randy Johnson (who was the winning pitcher in game 6) pitched 1⅓ innings of perfect relief for the Diamondbacks, and the game proceeded into the bottom of the 9th inning with the Yankees' nonpareil relief pitcher Mariano Rivera protecting a narrow 2–1 lead. The setting seemed ripe for yet another celebration in Gotham. Fortunately for the Diamondbacks and unfortunately for George Steinbrenner's pin-striped crew, however, Rivera yielded three hits and made a costly throwing error, allowing the Diamondbacks to win 3–2 and dethrone the Yankees as World Champions after three consecutive World Series championships and four in the preceding five years. Schilling, who started games 1, 4, and 7, and National League Cy Young Award winner Johnson who recorded wins in games 2, 6, and 7, were joint recipients of the World Series Most Valuable Player award.

Nearly 40 million viewers watched game 7 of the 2001 World Series, the largest television audience for a baseball game in ten years and more than 25 percent larger than the number of viewers for the 2000 Subway Series between the Yankees and the New York Mets, which drew lukewarm interest outside New York. Game 1 of the 2001 World Series posted the lowest television ratings in World Series history, however, and overall only the 1998 World Series between the Yankees and the San Diego Padres drew lower television ratings than the 2001 World Series.

Offensive statistics continued to decline in 2002, as runs dropped from 9.55 per game in 2001 to 9.24 per game in 2002 and home runs fell from 2.25 per game in 2001 to 2.09 per game in 2002. Nevertheless, outstanding individual offensive performances were recorded in 2002 by Alex Rodriguez (57 home runs, 142 runs batted in, and 125 runs scored), Miguel Tejada (34 home runs, 131 runs batted in, 108 runs scored, and the American League's Most Valuable Player award), Manny Ramirez (.349 batting average, 33 home runs, and 107 runs batted in during an injury shortened season in which he had only 436 at-bats), Vladimir Guerrero (.336 batting average, 39 home runs, 111 runs batted in, and 106 runs scored), Magglio Ordonez (.320 batting average, 38 home runs, 135 runs batted in, and 116 runs scored), Jason Giambi (.314 batting average, 41 home runs, 122 runs batted in, 120 runs scored, and 109 bases on balls), and Jim Thome (.304 batting average, 52 home runs, 118 runs batted in, and 101 runs scored). Second year Major League players Alfonso Soriano (.300 batting average, 39 home runs, 102 runs batted in, 128 runs scored, and 41 stolen bases), Albert Pujols (.314 batting average, 34 home runs, 127 runs batted in, and 118 runs scored), and Ichiro Suzuki (.321 batting average, 208 hits, 31 stolen bases, and 111 runs scored) defied the "sophomore jinx" to post exceptional seasons. Outstanding pitching performances were recorded in 2002 by Randy Johnson (24 wins, 334 strikeouts, and a 2.32 earned run average to capture the National League pitching triple crown for the second consecutive year and the National League Cy Young Award for the fourth consecutive year), Pedro Martinez (20 wins and a 2.26 earned run average), Derek Lowe (21 wins and a 2.58 earned run average), Barry Zito (23 wins, a 2.75 earned run average, and the American League Cy Young Award), Curt Schilling (23 wins and a 3.23 earned run average), Bartolo Colon (20 wins and a 2.93 earned run average), John Smoltz (55 saves and a 3.25 earned run average after converting from a starting pitcher to a closer), and Eric Gagne (52 saves and a 1.97 earned run average).

Barry Bonds continued to wreak havoc on Major League Baseball's pitchers in 2002, winning his first batting title (.370), hitting 46 home runs, driving in 110 runs, scoring 117 runs, drawing a Major League record 198 bases-on-balls, and recording an on-base average of .582, a slugging average of .799, and a combined on-base percentage plus slugging average of 1.381, while leading his San Francisco Giants to the World Series. Possibly the least impressive aspect of Bond's fabulous 2001 and 2002 seasons, however, was his relatively low level of runs produced (combination of total runs scored plus total runs batted in minus home runs which appear in both totals), a statistic thought by many to be the most meaningful measure of an offensive player's performance and value to a team. In 2001, Bond's runs scored total of 129 was only the fourth highest total in the Major Leagues and his runs batted in total of 137 was only the sixth highest total in the Major Leagues. The resulting 193 runs produced ranked behind the runs produced in 2001 by Sammy Sosa (242), Todd Helton (229), Bret Boone (222), Alex Rodriguez (216), Luis Gonzalez (213), rookie Albert Pujols (205), and Juan Gonzalez (202) and *far* behind the 301 runs produced by Lou Gehrig in 1931 or any of the incredible *thirteen* seasons in which Gehrig produced at least 200 runs. Babe Ruth produced more than 200 runs in eleven seasons, including a high of 289 in 1921; Jimmie Foxx produced more than 200 runs in nine seasons, including a high of 262 in 1932; Joe DiMaggio produced more than 200 runs in eight seasons, with a high of 272 in 1937; Ted Williams posted runs produced totals in excess of 200 in eight seasons, with a high of 266 in 1949; and Hank Aaron and Stan Musial each produced more than 200 runs in six seasons. Moreover, most of those runs produced totals were amassed when a team's season included only 154 games. Although Monds hit more home runs in 2001 than any of those players ever hit in season, how meaningful were Bonds's clouts to the San Francisco Giants? Out of Bonds's total of 73 home runs in 2001, 46 were solo shots. He scored only 56 times in which he did not hit a home run and drove in only 29 runs other than by home runs. In 2002, the number of runs produced by Bonds declined to 181 (46 home runs, 110 runs batted in, and 117 runs scored). This ranked behind the runs produced in 2002 by Magglio Ordonez (213), Albert Pujols (211), Alex Rodriguez (210), Miguel Tejada (205), Jason Giambi (201), and seven other players.

In spite of relatively low run production in comparison to his enormous home run totals, reputation, and ego, Bonds is the Major Leagues' most feared and devastating hitter and has a powerful effect on his own team's lineup and opposing pitchers that is not limited to entries in box scores. Bonds was named the National League's Most Valuable Player for the fourth and fifth times in 2001 and 2002, respectively (no other player has been so honored more than three times), is generally regarded as the finest player of his era, and is a certain Hall of Fame inductee after his retirement. At the end of the 2002 season, Bonds had recorded 613 career home runs (behind only Hank Aaron [755], Babe Ruth [714], and his godfather Willie Mays [660] on the all time list), 514 career doubles, and 493 stolen bases. He is the only player to have collected career totals of at least 400 home runs and 400 stolen bases. Barring injury, Bonds could have at least two or three big seasons ahead of him. Yet, many fans find it exceedingly and increasingly difficult to admire Bonds's prowess on the field because of his egotistic, selfish, and sullen attitude.[909]

A number of Major League teams had successful 2002 campaigns. In the regular season, the New York Yankees, Atlanta Braves, and the low payroll Oakland A's each recorded over 100 victories to win their respective division championships. Tight pennant races occurred in the American League Western Division, the National League Central Division, and the National League Western Division. The Minnesota Twins, which had one of Major League Baseball's lowest payrolls in 2002 and had been threatened with extinction before the 2002 season began, surprisingly finished 13½ games ahead of their closest challenger in the American League Central Division.

In the American League Division Series, the Minnesota Twins surprised the Oakland A's to win their series in five games and, after losing their first game to the New York Yankees, the Anaheim Angels beat George Steinbrenner's highly compensated team in three consecutive games. In the National League Division Series, the St. Louis Cardinals swept the defending World Series champion Arizona Diamondbacks in three games and the San Francisco Giants dispatched the Atlanta Braves in five games. In the American League Championship Series, the Angels again lost the first game of the series, but then swept four straight games from the Twins. In the National League Championship Series, the Giants won four of five games from the Cardinals.

The 2002 World Series was generally expected to feature low scoring, defense, and solid pitching. Instead, the first World Series in which two wild card teams faced each other produced the most home runs (21) and runs scored (85) of any World Series in history. Barry Bonds erased his reputation as a poor postseason performer in a remarkable World Series in which he recorded a .471 batting average, four home runs, six runs batted in, eight runs scored, 13 bases on balls, a .700 on-base percentage, a 1.294 slugging average, and a 1.924 on-base percentage plus slugging average. Manager Mike Scioscia's plucky and resilient Angels, however, who trailed at some point in each of the seven exciting, high octane games of the series, survived three defeats by manager Dusty Baker's Giants, including a 16–4 thrashing in the fifth game, to prevail in the series' seventh game in which three rookie pitchers for the Angels allowed only one run over eight dramatic innings. The Angels' overall team effort, featuring the offensive and defensive play of Troy Glaus, Scott Spiezio, Darin Erstad, Garrett Anderson, Tim Salmon, and David Eckstein, and strong pitching performances by John Lackey, Francisco Rodriguez, Brendan Donnelly, and Troy Percival, ultimately overshadowed the single dimension offensive show provided by Barry Bonds and the Giants.

Television ratings for the all California 2002 World Series reflected the lowest percentage of total viewers in history, a decline of 24 percent from the New York Yankees and Arizona Diamondbacks World Series in 2001, 4 percent below the previous record low recorded in the Yankees' five game win over the New York Mets in the 2000 subway series, and 50 percent below the ratings for the Minnesota Twins' seven game victory over the Atlanta Braves in 1991. Television ratings for the 2002 World Series averaged only one-third of the ratings for the most recent National Football League Super Bowl and were lower than the ratings for the National Collegiate Athletic Association's 2002 basketball and football championship games.[910] ESPN and Fox also reported that television viewing of Major League Baseball's regular season games declined for the second consecutive year. Fox's parent, News Corporation, took a substantial charge against its earnings in 2002, announcing that it had overpaid for the rights to broadcast Major League Baseball. During 2002, live attendance at games also declined to 67.9 million, the first time total attendance had dipped below 70 million in five years.

Although Major League Baseball remains resilient and fans' interest in the game seems to have been rejuvenated since the 1998 season, one problem refuses to be resolved: the chaotic business of Major League Baseball. Alex Rodriguez's 10-year contract at an average annual salary of $25.2 million to play for the Texas Rangers exceeded the entire opening day payroll for the 2001 Minnesota Twins. "The disparities in team payrolls is a topic that is dominating almost all the others," admits Major League executive Sandy Alderson. "It's the one aspect of the game that permeates everyone's concerns outside of a handful of big-market franchises. We are at a dangerous stage, for all the positive things that are happening. What's happening is that a lot of small-market owners have figured out that it does them no good to have a $35 million payroll because they can't win. So they might as well have a $15 million or $20 million payroll and finish in the same place but with more money in their pockets."

Large payrolls certainly don't ensure success. The Baltimore Orioles and Los Angeles Dodgers of the last few seasons have demonstrated that. But a small payroll does guarantee failure. In spite of protests from the Major League Players Association, there is little hope for more than half the teams in baseball. Heralded home run tours by McGwire and Sosa in 1998 and 1999 played to full houses in Pittsburgh, Minnesota, Montreal, and Milwaukee. When Mark and Sammy left, however, those franchises experienced empty seats and empty hopes. Major League Baseball has become a six or seven team league in which the gulf between the haves and have-nots has never been wider. Every team that has played in the World Series in the last six years has had one of the eight highest payrolls in Major League Baseball and every World Series champion in the last six years has had one of the six highest payrolls in Major League Baseball.

In July 2000, the independent members of the "Blue Ribbon Panel on Baseball Economics" appointed by commissioner Selig to examine whether Major League Baseball's current economic system has created a problem of competitive balance in the game issued its report.[911] The Independent Members recommended "broad and sweeping changes to Major League Baseball's economic structure intended to close the gaping disparity between the game's 'haves and have-nots.'" The report recommended greater sharing of "local" revenues, a 50 percent competitive balance tax on team payrolls that exceed $84 million, a new "Commissioner's Pool" to assist low-revenue teams to meet club payrolls of at least $40 million, reforms of the existing amateur draft, the institution of an annual competitive balance draft to provide more talent to low-finishing clubs, and strategic franchise relocations to address competitive balance issues.

In issuing the report of the independent members, former United States Senator George Mitchell, their spokesman, announced, "The 18-month study left absolutely no doubt that large and growing revenue and payroll disparities exist in Major League Baseball, causing chronic problems of competitive imbalance. The economic data clearly substantiate the widespread notion that the problems have become much worse during the five seasons since the strike-shortened season of 1994 and seem likely to remain severe unless Major League Baseball undertakes remedial actions proportional to the problem." Mitchell went on to say, "The economic analysis set out in the report further indicates that the limited revenue sharing and payroll taxes approved as part of the 1996 Collective Bargaining Agreement with the Major League Baseball Players Association have produced neither the intended moderating of payroll disparities nor improved competitive balance." Mitchell concluded, "Baseball's current economic system has created a caste system in which only high revenue and high payroll clubs have a realistic opportunity to reach the post-season. That is not in the best interests of baseball fans, clubs or players." In addition to Senator Mitchell, the independent members included Yale University President Richard C. Levin, former Federal Reserve Chairman Paul A. Volcker, and conservative columnist George F. Will.

The report also alleged that, over the five-year period from 1995 through 1999, Major League Baseball owners had experienced an overall financial loss and that only three teams, the New York Yankees, Cleveland Indians, and Colorado Rockies, were profitable. Several economists have expressed skepticism at this aspect of the report, observing that the report was commissioned by Major League Baseball's owners for public relations purposes, that there are ample opportunities for manipulating the franchises' financial information, and that the "Independent Members" of the Blue Ribbon Panel are hardly independent. George Will, for example, is on the boards of directors of both the Baltimore Orioles and the San Diego Padres.

In hearings of the Senate Judiciary Committee Subcommittee on Antitrust, Business Rights, and Competition held in November 2000, Major League Baseball Commissioner Bud Selig announced, "it is time for sweeping changes in the economics of Major League Baseball." In December 2000, Selig proposed significant changes to the amateur draft system to include all international players in the draft and to institute a new "competitive balance draft." Under this latter proposal, each of the Major

League teams with the eight lowest winning percentages in the immediately preceding three years would be allowed to draft one player from a
pool of players currently under contract with the Major League teams
with the eight highest winning percentages over those years. Each of the
eight most successful teams would be able to protect 25 players in the
draft. This proposal was presented to the Major League owners for their
approval when they met in January 2001. Not surprisingly, the owners of
Major League Baseball's winningest teams viewed this proposal less favor-
ably than the owners of the game's less successful teams.

On October 6, 2001, only two days after the final game of the World
Series, Major League Baseball's owners voted 28–2 (Minnesota and Montreal dissenting) to reduce the number of Major League teams from 30 to
28 before the 2002 season. In announcing the proposed contraction, Major
League Baseball Commissioner Bud Selig noted that a significant number
of Major League owners, possibly a majority, favored eliminating four
teams. Details of this proposed contraction were never released, but speculation centered on the purchase by the Major League owners as a group
of the Montreal Expos and the Minnesota Twins, the disbanding of those
franchises, and a disbursal draft of the Expos and Twins players. Other
teams that have been mentioned as possible candidates for elimination
include the Florida Marlins, Tampa Bay Devil Rays, and Oakland A's.

Commissioner's Selig's announcement signaled a decision to reverse
over 40 years of Major League expansion during which the Major Leagues
grew from 16 teams in 1960 to 30 teams by 1998. No Major League has
contracted since 1900 when the 12-team National League dumped the Baltimore Orioles, Washington Senators, Cleveland Spiders, and Louisville
Colonels and became an 8-team league. One year later, the new American League fielded franchises in Washington (moved to Minnesota in 1961
to become the Twins), Baltimore (moved to New York in 1903 to become
the Yankees and in 1954 replaced by the St. Louis Browns which became
the Orioles), and Cleveland (where the Indians continue to play a century later). Only Louisville has not again become a Major League city. No
Major League team has moved since 1972 when the second Washington
Senators team became the Texas Rangers, two years after the Seattle Pilots
became the Milwaukee Brewers.

In announcing the proposed contraction, commissioner Selig stated
that "[i]t makes no sense for Major League Baseball to be in markets that
generate insufficient local revenues to justify the investment in the franchise." Selig also noted that the teams that would be eliminated "are teams
that we judge to be not capable, now or in the future, of generating enough
revenues to be a productive franchise. And by shifting teams, oftentimes

all you do is shift problems." These are interesting comments, whether the teams to be eliminated are Montreal and Minnesota or otherwise. Both Montreal and Minnesota have in previous years drawn well at the gate, with Minnesota being the first American League team to draw 3 million spectators in a season and Montreal drawing 1.7 million fans as recently as 1992. The fact that these teams currently produce relatively small revenues is largely the result of Major League Baseball's distorted "local" television revenue policies and those teams' inabilities to secure modern stadium facilities with executive suites, naming rights, and other revenue enhancement features. Because of such matters, the financial success of a franchise can be altered substantially in a short period of time. If the decision had been made to eliminate franchises in 1990 instead of 2001, the Pittsburgh Pirates, Seattle Mariners, and Cleveland Indians might have been eliminated. Today, those franchises are on firm financial bases and are playing in new ballparks. As for the economics of moving franchises, changing cities has proven to be enormously successful for the New York Yankees, Baltimore Orioles, San Francisco Giants, Los Angeles Dodgers, Atlanta Braves, Texas Rangers, and even Selig's own Milwaukee Brewers, if not as successful for the Oakland A's and Minnesota Twins. In any event, it is far from clear that moves of the Montreal Expos and Oakland A's franchises to new locations such as Northern Virginia/Washington, D.C. and San Jose, respectively, would not result in successful and productive long term financial situations for those franchises or that more visionary methods of revenue sharing would not increase the competitive balance throughout Major League Baseball.

Perhaps not coincidentally, Commissioner Selig's announcement of the proposed contraction came only one day before the expiration of the collective bargaining agreement between Major League Baseball's owners and the Major League Baseball Players Association. Commissioner Selig's contraction proposal was widely viewed as the first salvo in the negotiations for a new collective bargaining agreement and an attempt to place the blame for any work stoppage in 2002 on the players. After the 1990 owners' lockout, which occurred at a time of then record financial success for team owners, Marvin Miller observed, "the owners *never* seem to learn their lesson.... Labor disputes resulting in stoppages usually arise when an industry is in financial difficulty. Baseball has never been more prosperous. If you can have a dispute when profits are in the hundreds of millions of dollars and at an all-time high, you can have a dispute *anytime*. Such as when the basic agreement comes up for negotiation again."[912] Shortly after commissioner Selig's announcement, Donald Fehr, executive director of the Major League Baseball Players Association, called the announcement "most imprudent and unfortunate." Fehr observed, "[o]ver this last season, and, especially, over the last several weeks, we have been reminded, vividly, of the special place baseball holds in America. This makes it all the more unfortunate that the clubs would choose this moment to dash the hopes of so many of its fans. And, of course, this is the worst

Donald Fehr

manner in which to begin the process of negotiating a new collective bargaining agreement. We had hoped that we were in a new era, one that would see a much better relationship between players and owners. Today's announcement is a severe blow to such hopes." Fehr also noted, "[t]his decision has been made unilaterally, without any attempt to negotiate with the players, apparently without any serious consideration of other options, including relocation, and seemingly with little concern for the interests of the fans. We consider this action to be inconsistent with the law, our contract, and perhaps most important, the long-term welfare of the sport." One day after commissioner Selig's announcement, the Major League Baseball Players Association filed a grievance with Shyam Das, Major League Baseball's permanent arbitrator, claiming that the owners had violated Major League Baseball's collective bargaining agreement by unilaterally deciding to contract the number of Major League teams. Clearly, the Major League Baseball Players Association, one of America's most powerful unions and by far the most powerful union in sports, was not about to stand by idly while Major League Baseball's owners eliminate 50 Major League jobs, more than half of which are highly compensated starting player and starting pitcher positions, 80 total protected jobs on Major League rosters, and hundreds of minor league jobs.

Shortly after commissioner Selig's announcement of the proposed contraction, United States Senator Paul Wellstone of Minnesota and United States Representative John Conyers of Michigan jointly introduced legislation in the United States Congress to revoke baseball's judicially created antitrust exemption for issues relating to elimination or relocation of Major League Baseball franchises and asked President George W.

Bush, former managing partner of the Texas Rangers ownership group, to support that legislation. Several other members of the United States Senate and House of Representatives expressed concern regarding the proposed contraction and voiced support for the proposed legislation. Senate Majority Leader Tom Daschle asked commissioner Bud Selig to delay any decision regarding contraction for at least one year. In 1998, the antitrust exemption was revoked for labor matters, but remains in place for other matters including expansion, contraction, and relocation of franchises. Congressional hearings on this proposal were held in December 2001. At those hearings, Commissioner Selig presented evidence that purported to demonstrate that in 2001 Major League teams lost a total of over $500 million on revenues of $3.5 billion and that only seven of the 30 Major League teams made a profit. According to this information, Selig's Milwaukee Brewers were Major League Baseball's most profitable team in 2001, after taking into account revenue-sharing payments received from large-market teams. Several members of Congress, the Major League Baseball Players Association, a number of journalists, and various other commentators have expressed extreme skepticism about these figures, seeking clarification on the methodology used in calculating losses. In response to the owners' claims of financial distress, Donald Fehr, executive director of the Major League Baseball Players Association, has observed, "You go through *The Sporting News* for the last one hundred years, and you will find two things are always true. You never have enough pitching, and nobody ever made money." An article in *Forbes* magazine in April 2002 disputed Commissioner Selig's claims of financial woe and concluded that 20 of the 30 Major League Baseball franchises were profitable in 2001 and that, as a group, Major League Baseball's owners made $75 million in profits in 2001. Evidence has also been disclosed that Carl Pohlad, owner of the Minnesota Twins and reportedly Minnesota's wealthiest citizen, made indirect loans to Commissioner Selig's Milwaukee Brewers and Jerry McMorris's Colorado Rockies, in apparent violation of Major League Rule 20(c) which prohibits such loans without the consent of the other owners.

In addition to potential Congressional obstacles to contraction, legal challenges were mounted by concerned fans and cities in which teams that were possible candidates for contraction were located. A court in Hennepin County, Minnesota issued an injunction that required the Minnesota Twins to continue to play in Minnesota through the 2002 season and to satisfy their obligations under the lease of the Hubert H. Humphrey Metrodome. Subsequently, a settlement was reached between Major League Baseball and the Twins' landlord that requires the Twins to remain in Minnesota at least through the 2003 season.

Commissioner Selig also orchestrated a game of musical franchises in which the ownership of three Major League teams was changed. In this complicated set of interrelated transactions, John Henry, the former owner of the Florida Marlins, became the principal owner in the $660 million purchase of the Boston Red Sox and an 80 percent interest in New England Sports Network, the team's regional cable television network, from the Yawkey Trust; Jeffrey Loria, the former owner of the Montreal Expos, sold the Expos to the other 29 Major League owners for $120 million; and Loria purchased the Florida Marlins from Henry for $158.5 million. Major League Baseball has also announced that 22 of the Montreal Expos' games in 2003 will be played in San Juan, Puerto Rico. There is also considerable speculation that the Expos will be relocated to Washington, D.C. or its northern Virginia suburbs in 2003 or 2004. Other locations that have been discussed for relocation of the Expos include Charlotte, North Carolina and Portland, Oregon.

Negotiations for a new collective bargaining agreement between Major League Baseball's owners and the Major League Baseball Players Association began in earnest in early 2002. A number of important issues were discussed, including expansion of the amateur draft, a competitive balance draft, contraction of franchises, continuation of regular season inter-league play, drug testing, suspension of players, salary arbitration, minimum payrolls, the commissioner's discretionary fund, the expansion of revenue sharing, and an expansion of the luxury tax on teams with excessive payrolls. The owners proposed to extend the annual June draft, which was limited to players in the United States, Canada, and Puerto Rico, to players from around the world, to reduce the number of rounds in the draft, and permit teams to trade draft picks. The Players Association generally agreed with the owners' proposals, but proposed further reductions in the number of rounds of the draft and the ability to trade negotiating rights to players selected in the draft. The owners also proposed a competitive balance draft pursuant to which the eight teams with the highest winning percentages during the three previous years would be able to protect only 25 players. All other players in those teams' systems would be exposed to a draft in which each of the eight teams with the lowest winning percentages during the three previous years could select one player. The owners claimed they had the right to eliminate Major League teams without the approval of the Players Association, but were required to bargain on the effects of contraction such as the dispersal of players. The Players Association claimed that franchises could not be eliminated without its consent. The owners proposed mandatory random drug testing for illegal steroids, "nutritional supplements" such as creatine and androstenedione, and recreational drugs. The Players Association supported mandatory random testing for illegal steroids, but opposed testing for nutritional supplements and recreational drugs. The owners sought the right to suspend players without pay for on field misconduct; the Players Association, which had twice won grievances on this issue, opposed this proposal. The owners proposed to eliminate arbitration eligibility for the "Super Twos" (approximately 12 players per year who are eligible for arbitration after only two years of Major League service) and to have the ability to withdraw contract offers to players after salary arbitration amounts are exchanged. The Players Association opposed these proposals.

The remaining matters for negotiation involved two financial issues that have plagued Major League Baseball for generations: the owners' attempts to control player salaries and the division of revenues among owners. The owners sought to expand the gains that had been achieved in the 1995 collective bargaining agreement and to institute an interrelated web of arrangements that would address these two complicated issues. The owners proposal was to institute a minimum franchise payroll, including 40-man rosters and benefits, of $45 million per team (only the Montreal Expos and Tampa Bay Devil Rays were below that minimum in 2002); expand the revenue sharing that began in 1996, both from local revenue sources and from the commissioner's discretionary fund of national media and licensing revenues; and to expand the "luxury tax," which was imposed at rates of 34 to 35 percent in 1997, 1998, and 1999, to require payment of a 50 percent tax on the portions of team payrolls in excess of $98 million. The Players Association vigorously opposed these proposals, particularly the luxury tax, arguing that the arrangements were designed to limit player compensation by creating a disincentive for franchises to pay higher salaries. In April 2002, the Players Association's executive director Donald Fehr described the owners' economic proposals a "a wholesale attack on the salary structure."

After several months of negotiations that resulted in little progress, the Players Association set a strike date of August 30, 2002. If a new collective bargaining agreement were not concluded by that date, the players would strike and the remainder of the 2002 season and postseason (in which the owners make the largest portion of their revenues) would be cancelled. A number of hawkish owners expressed their willingness to endure a strike of one or more seasons if the Players Association did not accept their luxury tax and revenue sharing proposals. Fortunately for fans of Major League Baseball and those owners that did not have the financial ability to survive a lengthy strike, a compromise was reached on the important economic issues. With only a little more than three hours remaining before the strike was scheduled to take effect, representatives of the owners and the Players Association announced that they had reached agreement on the terms of a new collective bargaining agreement. Under the new agreement, the owners and the Players Association agreed to establish a committee to create rules for a new worldwide amateur draft, with the number of rounds of such draft, the ability of teams to trade draft picks and negotiating rights, and other details of the draft to be established by the committee. A competitive balance draft was not included in the agreement. The owners and Players Association agreed that no contraction of teams will occur before 2007, but that up to two teams can be eliminated in 2007 if the owners notify the Players Association of such proposed contraction by July 1, 2006. In 2003, all players will be randomly tested for illegal steroids as a survey. If at least five percent of all Major League players test positive in any survey year, mandatory random testing will occur during the following two years. If no more than two and one-half percent test positive in consecutive years, mandatory testing will cease. The first time a player tests positive, he will be placed in a treatment program. Subsequent positive tests will result in suspensions ranging from 30 days to two years. The Major League minimum annual salary was increased from $200,000 in 2002 to $300,000 for 2003 through 2006, with cost of living adjustments beginning in 2005. Inter-league play, which was included in the previous collective bargaining agreement on a test basis, was extended in the new agreement. Draft pick compensation for teams losing free agents was eliminated. The owners' contributions to players benefits were increased from $70 million to $115 million. To protect the solvency of suffering franchises, new rules were enacted to limit the amount of each team's debt. After a grace period, no team will be allowed to have debt more than ten times its EBITDA (earnings before interest, taxes, depreciation, and amortization), except that teams that have moved into newly constructed ballparks within the preceding ten years may have debt of up to 15 times their EBITDA.

On the principal financial issues, the Players Association made substantial concessions. The owners' split pool proposal was agreed for revenue sharing. Under this system, a base plan will be instituted in which each team will contribute 34 percent of its net local revenue after ballpark expenses to a pool that is redistributed equally to all 30 teams. In addition, a central fund plan will be instituted in which $72.2 million will be taken annually from those teams that are net payers in the base plan and redistributed to those teams that are net receivers in the base plan. The central fund plan will be phased in at 60 percent in 2003, 80 percent in

2004, and 100 percent thereafter. In addition, a total of $10 million annually will be taken from the owners' central fund for distribution at the discretion of the commissioner. Finally, the owners and Players Association agreed to impose a luxury tax on teams with total 40-man payrolls and player benefits in excess of $117 million in 2003, $120.5 million in 2004, $128 million in 2005, and $136.5 million in 2006. The rates of the luxury tax are 17.5 percent in 2003 and 22.5 percent in 2004 and 2005 for teams that exceed the threshold for the first time. The luxury tax rates increase to 30 percent for teams that exceed the threshold for a second time and 40 percent for teams that exceed the threshold more than twice. In short, the financial recommendations of the Blue Ribbon Panel on Baseball Economics have become enshrined in the new collective bargaining agreement. Interestingly, however, no minimum team payroll rule was included in the agreement. The agreement commences with the 2002 season and runs through December 19, 2006, but contains a "status-quo rollover" provision which permits the owners and players to conduct the 2007 season under the rules of this agreement if a new agreement has not yet been reached.

A players strike was averted and the remainder of the 2002 season and postseason was completed. Commissioner Selig and the owners have finally been able to claim a victory over the Players Association. Major League Players Association executive director Donald Fehr has been lauded by many for his flexibility in departing from the hard line, no give-backs negotiating policies historically employed by the Players Association and his willingness to adjust Major League Baseball's economics to help the game survive. Others, including Fehr's predecessor and Players Association icon Marvin Miller, have been harshly critical of the new agreement and the portions of the 1995 agreement in which revenue sharing and the luxury tax were introduced. Before the new collective bargaining agreement was negotiated, Fehr defended the luxury tax under the then existing collective bargaining agreement and the overall economic system under which Major League Baseball operates, observing, "it is not fair to judge things now because in a few years the provisions of the luxury tax will kick in and there will be some more equity. The players come to this process with the desire for a free market, no owner ever pays anybody more than he wants to or is willing to. And the owners entirely control who the other owners are going to be and what their operating costs are. Neither the players nor the owners have any interest in subsidizing bad management." With contraction possible in 2007, this is not exactly soothing tonic for teams and fans in Oakland, Minnesota, Miami, Tampa Bay, Montreal, Philadelphia, Kansas City, Pittsburgh, Milwaukee, and Detroit.

What lasting effect will the 2002 collective bargaining agreement

have? I suspect very little. Many of Major League Baseball's franchise owners are at least publicly committed to reducing their payrolls in 2003 and
beyond. If their actions are consistent with their public statements, which
has seldom been the case in the past, the luxury tax will be imposed on
few franchises. The new luxury tax and revenue sharing rules are expected
to have the greatest negative impact on George Steinbrenner's New York
Yankees and provide the most benefit to middle revenue teams with
medium payrolls. Other teams with high payrolls and media connections
such as the Red Sox, Mets, Dodgers, and Braves may also pay luxury tax.
But, with seemingly ever-increasing "local" media revenues now being
enhanced by the "YES" cable network, the Yankees will still be able to
outspend all other teams, other teams with media connections and revenues will be able to outspend teams without such links, and the teams
with media links will have the incentive to spend more because of the positive financial effects that greater success on the field is believed to have
on their media empires, even after the payment of luxury taxes. Moreover, without a competitive balance draft or a minimum team salary level,
the Yankees will still be able to stockpile players, owners like Carl Pohlad
who understand Major League Baseball's economics will be able to make
more money from revenue sharing and not be required to spend it on
player salaries, and many teams and their fans will remain condemned to
a mediocre existence. If the owners and the Players Association think that
all Major League Baseball needs is their new collective bargaining agreement and a little love to make things better, they better juice up the ball
some more, lower the pitcher's mound, shrink the strike zone, move in
the fences farther, and hope that Barry Bonds, Sammy Sosa, and Alex
Rodriguez each get about 3,000 at-bats every year.

The economics of Major League Baseball have changed dramatically
over the last quarter century. In 1975, the last season before the Messersmith-McNally arbitration decision created free agency, the average Major
League annual salary was $51,501 and the Major League annual minimum
salary was $13,500.[913] Except for Catfish Hunter who had been declared a
free agent the prior season because of a contractual breach, the highest
Major League salary was Dick Allen's $250,000.[914] Major League Baseball's
national television contract created a total of $17.5 million in revenue, to
be shared among its 24 teams, and total local television revenues, which
were not shared equally, totaled another $31 million.[915] Total attendance
was less than 30 million, only the Dodgers and Reds exceeded two million in attendance, average attendance was less than 1.25 million per team,
and seven teams drew fewer than one million spectators.[916] In 1978, total

Major League Baseball salaries were only $68.5 million, less than 25 percent of baseball's total revenues of $277.7 million.[917] In 2003, the average annual Major League salary will be approximately $2.5 million, the minimum annual salary will be $300,000, and the highest Major League annual salary will be in excess of $25 million.

National television revenues shared equally by Major League Baseball's 30 teams will total $570 million, an average of $19 million per team, more than the $17.5 million received by *all* Major League teams in 1975. In addition, "local" revenues, which are artificially low because of link-ups with media affiliates, will exceed $500 million for Major League Baseball's 30 teams. Total Major League attendance in 2002 was nearly 68 million, average team attendance was in excess of 2.26 million, six teams exceeded three million in attendance, 18 teams drew over two million fans, and only two teams failed to attract at least one million spectators. Yet, television viewing of Major League Baseball has declined. From 1996 to 2000, the number of viewers under 18 years of age watching the World Series declined by more than 30 percent.[918] Fox Broadcasting reports that it experienced a 20–25 percent drop in overall baseball ratings in 2001 and a further decline in viewing in 2002.

The business of Major League Baseball has never seen as much success, or been as great a failure, as in the last decade. Attendance, total revenues, and media revenues are at record high levels. In terms of percentage of revenues, player salaries, although high, are at acceptable levels. Until there is reasoned negotiation between the owners and the Players Association with the objective of forging a new business structure for Major League Baseball, however, the fiscal insanity and lack of competitiveness that now permeate and epitomize the Major Leagues will continue. In spite of Donald Fehr's protests to the contrary, as the independent members of Major League Baseball's Blue Ribbon Panel on Baseball Economics have clearly demonstrated, the luxury tax provisions of the previous collective bargaining agreement have not produced the desired effect of narrowing the gaps in revenues and payrolls between the haves and have-nots.

Neither will the increased revenue sharing and luxury tax provisions of the new collective bargaining agreement. If this gap is not narrowed, however, Major League Baseball is likely to experience a decline in popularity similar to that which occurred in the late 1950s and early 1960s when the New York Yankees were nearly perpetual World Series champions.

To retain a rooting interest, even a serious baseball fan must be able to convince himself in spring training that his team has at least a chance to compete for the World Series championship. For much of America, such self-delusion is increasingly impossible.

It is time now to repair the serious damage to the business of Major League Baseball before it does further harm to the game. But that damage cannot be repaired with a band-aid. Radical surgery is required.

Chapter 16

BASEBALL, INC.

Surely we are not so arrogant that we cannot learn from others. The NBA has evolved a formula. It may not be perfect, but it works. I beg you. Take that formula, refine that formula, share revenues with the players, and reward them handsomely on a basis that is economically fair to all—club, player, and public. There is so much more than economics to be considered. There is our society.

—Charles Bronfman

Ray, people will come, Ray. They'll come to Iowa for reasons they can't even fathom. They'll turn up your driveway not knowing for sure why they're doing it. They'll arrive at your door as innocent as children, longing for the past. "Of course we won't mind if you look around," you'll say. "It's only twenty dollars per person." They'll pass over the money without even thinking about it. For it is money they have and peace they lack. And they'll walk off to the bleachers and sit in their shirtsleeves on a perfect afternoon. They'll find they have reserved seats somewhere along one of the base lines where they sat when they were children and cheered their heroes and they'll watch the game and it'll be as if they dipped themselves in magic waters. Their memories will be so thick, they'll have to brush them away from their faces. People will come, Ray. The one constant through all the years, Ray, has been baseball. America has rolled by like an

army of steamrollers. It has been erased like a blackboard,
rebuilt, and erased again. But baseball has marked the
time. This field, this game, is a part of our past, Ray. It
reminds us of all that once was good and it could be
again. Oh, people will come, Ray. People will most
definitely come.

—James Earl Jones as Terrence
Mann in *Field of Dreams*

Over the preceding fifteen chapters, I have provided a brief history of both the sport and the business of Major League Baseball, recounting baseball's beauty and travails from the seemingly endless and perfect summers of our youth, to the disastrous strikes of the 1980s and 1990s, to the unrestrained joy of Mark McGwire and Sammy Sosa during the 1998 and 1999 seasons, to the somewhat more restrained events of the 2001 and 2002 seasons, to the recent economic and labor conflicts among Major League Baseball's owners and between the owners and the players. The inescapable message that filters through is simple. Except for minor bastardizations of recent decades, there is nothing wrong with the game of baseball, but there is plenty wrong with the business of Major League Baseball.

The game of baseball is as sublime as any game can be. It captures the imagination. It inspires and rewards heroic deeds. It encourages fan loyalty. It can be played at almost any skill or age level. It promotes intergenerational involvement, both as participants and as spectators. It can bind friends, families, cities, regions, and even countries. Unfortunately, the business of Major League Baseball regularly imperils these invaluable characteristics of the game.

As discussed in Chapter 14 of this book, the basic problems of Major League Baseball today can be encapsulated in one word. MONEY! There is too much of it, it is divided in an inefficient and unfair manner, and a lot more of it could be made if the owners and players weren't so selfish and intractable. As also discussed in Chapters 11, 14, and 15 of this book, the most significant problems facing Major League Baseball today are the vast disparity in revenues between the rich teams and the poor teams, the player salary structure, continuing hostilities between the owners and players primarily about money, eroding fan loyalty primarily related to owners and players squabbling about money and the fact that many teams now have absolutely no chance to be competitive because their payrolls are a small fraction of those of other teams, and excessive player movement primarily caused by differences in the abilities of teams to pay player salaries.

Over the last few years, a number of proposals have been made to address the issue of revenue and payroll imbalances between the haves and have nots. With the exception of the "competitive balance draft" proposed by the Blue Ribbon Panel on Baseball Economics in 2000, by commissioner Bud Selig in December 2000, and again by the owners during the negotiations for the 2002 collective bargaining agreement, and the proposed contraction of two Major League teams announced by commissioner Selig in November 2001, virtually all of these proposals focus on sharing of revenues among teams; *i.e.*, revenue transfers from higher revenue teams to lower revenue teams, and/or placing limitations or "caps" on individual or team salaries. Although increased revenue sharing and luxury taxes on excessive franchise payrolls are included in the new collective bargaining agreement, meaningful revenue transfers and franchise or player salary limits are anathema both to higher revenue owners and to players. Thus, in spite of the temporary compromise reached on these issues in the latest collective bargaining agreement, the vast disparity in revenues between Major League Baseball's higher revenue owners and lower revenue owners will continue to pit such owners against one another and cause disputes between the owners and the Players Association. The individuals who have fought baseball's wars over the last quarter of a century are not now going to become flexible. Instead of addressing these issues in the inefficient, confrontational, fractious, and destructive manner in which they have traditionally been addressed by Major League Baseball's owners and players, I propose a revolutionary revamping of Major League Baseball's business structure in a manner that will encourage cooperation of owners and players and the growth of both the sport and the business of baseball. At the same time, I propose that the game itself (as played in the National League) remain unchanged, except for a few minor adjustments to restore the historic integrity of the game.

Deng Xiao-Ping, the late chairman of the Communist Party of the People's Republic of China, contended that China needed to employ "socialism with Chinese tendencies" to reform its state-owned enterprises, encourage foreign investment, and develop its stock market, taxation system, and foreign trade. Chairman Deng's willingness to consider a radical departure from the strict economic dogma of his party saved his country from both economic and political collapse. If Major League Baseball's owners and players are willing to open their minds and consider another system of ownership and exploitation of the tools of Major League Baseball's production, their business and our national pastime can also be saved. What Major League Baseball needs today is enlightened capitalism with socialist tendencies.

As stated above, the principal problem with Major League Baseball is money. To be more specific, the principal problem is "local" revenues and particularly local media money. Before you conclude that I am a socialist or a religious fanatic who believes that money is the root of all evil, let me assure you that I have nothing against money. I like it. I would like to have more of it. I would like to see Major League Baseball's franchise owners and players have more of it. But money is at the root of most of Major League Baseball's evils. Not money itself, but the manner in which money is divided among the various providers of the tools of production of baseball's product. More than a decade ago, Major League Baseball Commissioner Bart Giamatti asked Major League Baseball's legal counsel Lou Hoynes what he saw as baseball's top business priority. "To more evenly distribute its revenues," Hoynes replied. "You don't need to be a genius to figure that out, but you do need to be a genius to figure out how." Little has changed since Hoynes's observation.[919]

If Major League Baseball is viewed strictly as a business, its products and sources of revenue are simple: baseball games and their exploitation at the ballpark and via media; ancillary merchandising and concessions; and promotional revenues including stadium naming rights, signage, and the like. The contributors of the tools of production of these products and revenues are equally simple: the players, the owners/operators of stadiums and franchises, and the fans who attend games and partake of media coverage. By their actions, Major League Baseball's selfish and stubborn owners and players have substantially curtailed the revenues that flow into their coffers and have created constant tension and conflict among one another. To eliminate such tension and conflict and its potentially disastrous effects on the game, I propose that the current ownership, management, and profit-sharing structure of Major League Baseball be supplanted by Baseball, Inc.

When the National League and the American League were formed, no franchise owner or player could have imagined the potential revenues that are being earned from the exploitation of baseball in the early 21st Century. Their attentions were focused on ballpark attendance and the modest concessions that could be earned at the ballpark. Today, those sources of revenue are still important, but they are far less meaningful than earnings from media coverage of baseball, merchandising revenues, and ancillary revenues. Media revenues are not only the most significant source of Major League Baseball's revenues, they are also the fastest growing, least efficiently exploited, and most inequitably distributed. The inefficient exploitation of this growing source of revenues and the unfair manner in which these revenues are distributed are responsible for baseball's distorted player salary structure, disparity in owner profitability, franchise shifts, declining fan loyalty, and labor unrest. When Major League Baseball's first franchises were awarded, no franchise owner imagined that one day he would be able to beam his team's games by satellite to distant corners of the earth and earn unbelievable revenues in doing so. This is exactly what occurs in baseball today for those few owners who have coupled their ownership of a Major League Baseball franchise with the ability to exploit that franchise's performances through electronic media. For teams such as the Los Angeles Dodgers, New York Yankees, New York Mets, Atlanta Braves, Chicago Cubs, and Boston Red Sox, this can mean well in excess of US$100 million in annual media revenues. For teams such as the Montreal Expos, Minnesota Twins, Kansas City Royals, Milwaukee Brewers, Pittsburgh Pirates, and Oakland Athletics, annual media revenues are less than US$25 million. This explains why Gary Sheffield's 1998 compensation from the Dodgers of nearly US$15 million was almost *twice* that of the entire 1998 Montreal Expos team. This also explains why in 1999 Kevin Brown, not Sheffield, was the Dodgers' most highly compensated player and why Kevin Brown's salary exceeded that of the entire 1999 Minnesota Twins team; why in 2000 neither Sheffield nor Brown, but Shawn Green, was the Dodgers' highest-paid player; why in 2001 Sheffield's annual salary of approximately $10 million was only 40 percent of the $25 million earned by Major League Baseball's current most highly compensated player, Alex Rodriguez; why the Yankees are perennially able to acquire critical depth at key positions in late-season salary dumps by non-contending franchises; and why, in spite of occasionally providing excitement to their fans, it is highly unlikely that the Expos, Twins, Royals, Brewers, Marlins, Devil Rays, Pirates, or A's will ever again be World Series champions.

The most important facet of my proposal for revamping Major League Baseball is that *all* of Major League Baseball's media and merchandising rights be owned by Baseball, Inc. Baseball, Inc. would exploit these revenues for the overall benefit of Major League Baseball and the contributors of its tools of production. You are probably now asking yourself, "What is this guy smoking? Astroturf? How is he going to get the large-market owners to agree to such a plan?" That is a good question. Fortunately, I have a good answer. "Make the large-market owners richer. And also the small-market owners. And also the players. And make the fans, the ultimate source of baseball's revenues, happier and eager to provide additional revenues to make the owners and players still richer." You ask, eloquently, "Huh? How could that work?" My answer is, "Revamp baseball. Increase its revenues. Control its costs. Distribute its profits efficiently and equitably among the contributors of the tools of its production. Encourage customer loyalty. Expand baseball's customer base. Operate the business of baseball like a business. Don't mess with the game."

We all can envision Rupert Murdoch, George Steinbrenner, and their large media-market brethren turning purple at the thought of losing their preferential media revenues. If Baseball, Inc. is properly organized and implemented, however, the income of even Major League Baseball's richest franchise owners would increase. You might ask, "How can that be? Surely if the small market owners and players receive a larger share of baseball's income, the major market owners will suffer." My response is, "That is not necessarily correct. The income of even the major market owners will increase." Again you might ask, "How can that be?" I reply, "Because the exploitation of baseball is not a zero sum game. Major market owners, small market owners, and players will make more money because revenues will increase and costs will decline. Revenues will increase because of a combination of an expanded and more receptive customer base and the coordinated professional exploitation of Major League Baseball's media and merchandising power. Costs will decline because Major League Baseball's most significant costs, player salaries, will be reduced." We also all can envision Marvin Miller, Donald Fehr, and Major League Baseball's players becoming apoplectic at the thought of reduced player salaries. If Baseball, Inc. is properly organized and implemented, however, the total income of players should grow and be more efficiently and fairly divided. In addition, the players will become indirect equity owners in the product of their efforts. Moreover, the game's most important asset, the fans, will be happier with the game and become even more loyal consumers of Major League Baseball's product.

Admit it. You're intrigued by Baseball, Inc., but confused about how it would work. To summarize, Baseball, Inc. would (i) overhaul Major League Baseball's management, (ii) restructure Major League Baseball's equity ownership, (iii) revamp the marketing of baseball's product, (iv) internationalize baseball, (v) realign the Major Leagues' divisions, scheduling, and the post-season playoff system, (vi) change the amateur player draft and institute a competitive balance draft for professional players, and (vii) introduce federal legislation to govern professional baseball.

(I)   *Baseball, Inc.'s Management Structure*. An important factor in the success of Baseball, Inc. will be the improvement of the business and profitability of Major League Baseball. For at least 30 years, the principal function of Major League Baseball's management, as exemplified by the Office of the commissioner, has been labor relations between the owners and the players and resolution of disputes between large-market and small-market owners. Management's focus in Baseball, Inc. would be changed to promoting the sport of baseball and increasing its profitability. Thus, the first important element of Baseball, Inc. is the complete overhaul of Major League Baseball's management structure to enable the business of baseball to be operated more efficiently and profitably. This revamping would involve the following:

(a) ***Incorporation***. Baseball, Inc. would be established as a corporation which would be governed by a board of directors. This board of directors would be comprised of an equal number of representatives of the franchise owners, the players, and the public. A distinguished chairman (*e.g.*, Hank Aaron, Stan Musial, or a retired president of the United States not currently under indictment) would preside over the board. Although the incorporation of Major League Baseball has very little to do with the *game* of baseball, it presents a vehicle and platform for accessing necessary capital and remedying many of the ills of the *business* of baseball. Participation in Major League Baseball's management by all of the principal contributors to the production of baseball's business is highly important to achieving this goal. I once thought that the idea of such a governing board was somewhat novel. As I learned in researching baseball's history for this book, however, there is little that has not been considered or implemented in baseball's long history. I learned that the short-lived Players' League (1890) was ruled by a senate of 16 members, two from each of its eight franchises, with eight selected by owners and eight selected by players. Each team was governed by an eight-man board comprised of four owners' representatives and four players' representatives.[920]

(b) ***Chief Executive***. A talented and capable chief executive officer with experience in finance, marketing, and labor relations would be appointed by Baseball, Inc.'s board of directors to replace the current role of commissioner. This chief executive would not be a mere figurehead. He would be an experienced and capable businessman who would be responsible for Baseball, Inc.'s day-to-day operations in accordance with guidelines established by its board of directors and would report to, and be a member of, the board.

(c) ***Operation of the Business of Baseball***. Baseball, Inc. would operate all aspects of Major League Baseball and would do so as a business. Baseball, Inc. would be organized as a business and the executives in charge of each of its significant divisions and enterprises would report to the chief executive. Interestingly, in researching baseball's history for this book I also found that the concept of all baseball being controlled by a single legal entity is not a novel concept. At the turn of the 20th century, the National League's stronger owners (today's equivalent of the large media market owners) forwarded the concept of a National Baseball Trust in which a single corporation would own all rights to baseball, including all player contracts. The stock of the corporation would have been owned by the holders of the eight existing franchises in proportion to the success of the franchises at the time of the creation of the corporation. The corporation would have been ruled by a five-member board elected by stockholders, with the top three franchise owners owning enough stock to constitute a majority. The board would have hired all team managers and would have licensed players to the teams. The board would have retained the power to move players among franchises at will to any locations in order to improve pennant races or otherwise generate the most revenue from gate attractions. Under the plan, the owners would have completely controlled the salaries and employment venues of all players in an infinitely adjustable system. Happily for the players and baseball's fans, the plan was, not surprisingly, favored by the three owners who would have owned the most stock in the corporation and opposed by the other five owners.[921] All teams in the short-lived Federal League (1913–1915) were owned by a single corporation, the shares of which were owned equally by the teams' operators.[922]

(d)   ***Minority Participation***. Baseball, Inc. would institute a meaningful program to encourage the hiring of minority individuals for top management and administrative positions in Baseball, Inc. and each of the Major League franchises. More than half a century after Jackie Robinson's integration of Major League Baseball's player ranks, no significant integration of its management and administrative positions has occurred. Even for Major League Baseball, this is a shocking and disgraceful record.

(II)   ***Baseball, Inc.'s Ownership Structure***. Perhaps the most significant problems with Major League Baseball today are the continuing conflicts among owners and between the owners and the players which result from the manner in which Major League Baseball's revenues and profits are divided. These conflicts will continue for as long as the owners' economic interests differ from one another and the owners' economic interests as a whole differ from those of the players. To resolve these conflicts, the next important element of Baseball, Inc. is the complete revamping of the ownership of Major League Baseball and the Major League players' salary structure to create a greater identity of economic interests among owners and between owners and players. This revamping would involve the following:

(a)   ***Multiple Ownership***. Baseball, Inc. would be equally owned by the providers of the important tools of Major League Baseball's production (*i.e.,* the franchise operators, the players, and the fans). Although at first you may think this sounds like some pseudo-intellectual, quasi-socialist plot to ruin our national game, I submit that it represents precisely the brand of enlightened capitalism that can save the game we love.

(b)   ***Public Ownership***. Baseball, Inc. would make an initial public offering of one-third of its share capital on the New York Stock Exchange or NASDAQ. Even with its historically weak business practices, Major League Baseball, especially after the principles of Baseball, Inc. are implemented, has far higher current and projected revenues, a better business plan, and greater growth

and profit potential than most of the dot.coms and
telecommunications enterprises that have effected initial public offerings in recent years. But why does baseball need all that money? The answer is simple: To
enable it to accomplish Baseball, Inc.'s objectives of
creating greater revenues and a revamped ownership
structure in which all parties receive increased financial returns.

(c) *Current Owners*. Baseball, Inc. would issue one-third
of its share capital to the current franchise owners as a
group. Each of Major League Baseball's franchise owners would receive an *equal* number of shares in Baseball, Inc. Although it seems impossible to believe that
Major League Baseball's current franchise owners would
accept only one-third of the action and share that one-
third equally, this split will seem more palatable after I
explain the other elements of Baseball, Inc.'s revamping of Major League Baseball's ownership structure.

(d) *Right to Operate Franchise*. Each current franchise
owner would be granted the right to operate a Major
League Baseball team in a specific metropolitan area
and would be entitled to retain 50 percent of the revenues from attendance at games, revenues relating to
stadium use including naming rights and signage fees,
revenues from parking, revenues from concessions and
merchandise sold and delivered at the games, and
other truly local non-media revenues. The franchisees
would be responsible for all costs of providing venues
for games and Baseball, Inc. would receive the remaining 50 percent of local non-media revenues. A logical
question might be that, if this tools of production
thing is so wise, why shouldn't all baseball revenue be
owned by Baseball, Inc.? The logically consistent
answer is that it should, but the current owners need
some incentives to accept Baseball, Inc. Although there
is probably no intellectually compelling reason for preserving the current treatment of even 50 percent of
local gate, stadium, and concession revenues, particularly in light of the disparities between the amounts
received by teams in the large population centers and

those in smaller markets, this precedent (with limited amounts of sharing for visiting teams) has existed throughout the history of organized baseball and, for a variety of reasons, including arrangements for ballpark usage that already have been made with municipalities and other third parties, probably should be allowed to continue with respect to a portion of such *truly* local income.

(e)   *Revenues*. All other forms of revenue generated by Major League Baseball, including 100 percent of media (current and future forms) and merchandising revenues, and the remaining 50 percent of local non-media revenues would belong to Baseball, Inc.

     Since baseball games began to be broadcast, owners have made their own deals for "local" radio and later television rights. Initially, media revenues from baseball were insignificant in comparison to revenues from ticket sales and concessions. Today, revenues at the ballpark pale in comparison to the enormous revenues realized by some owners from media exploitation and merchandising of baseball. Moreover, media revenues are inordinately concentrated in the hands of those few owners who have combined ownership of teams with control of media enterprises and are generated from broadcasting not only locally but also by transmission regionally, nationally, and throughout the world.

     This concentration of revenues permits the large media market teams (*e.g.*, the New York Yankees, the New York Mets, the Los Angeles Dodgers, the Boston Red Sox, the Atlanta Braves, the Chicago Cubs, and the Texas Rangers) to buy better players and field better teams. This encourages movement by established stars to teams that are able to pay them more. This also fosters a system in which smaller market teams serve as virtual farm clubs for larger market teams and encourages teams that will clearly not be participating in post-season play to dump the salaries of top players to richer teams during pennant races, thereby further concentrating top talent in the richer teams and diluting the talent and spectator appeal of the poorer teams.

Although limited sharing of revenues currently exists and the owners have recently voted to equally share future internet revenues, the disparity in revenues between the New York Yankees, Los Angeles Dodgers, and Atlanta Braves, on the one hand, and the Montreal Expos and Minnesota Twins, on the other hand, is increasing. This vast disparity should not be permitted to continue to grow.

Baseball's media revenues are not produced solely by the large media market teams. They are produced by a combination of resources provided by owners, players, and especially fans. Owners such as the Yankees' George Steinbrenner howl when revenue sharing is discussed, pointing out, "But I bought the New York Yankees, not the Montreal Expos!" True, George. But the Yankees, for all of their historic and current greatness, must play other teams to generate significant revenues. Even the most fanatic New York Yankees' supporters probably won't pay to see the Yankees play intra-squad games 162 or more times each year. As a general proposition, Baseball, Inc. should own *all* rights to current and future revenues from the exploitation of baseball and baseball merchandise, whether through local ticket sales, concessions, parking, naming rights, signage, advertising, and sales of merchandise or from local, regional, national, international, or intergalactic media, satellite, internet, or other forms of dissemination of baseball games or components thereof. Each franchise owner should be granted the perpetual right to retain 50 percent of all revenues from attendance at their teams' home games, stadium rights, parking, and concessions and merchandise sold at home games. *All* other revenues should belong to Baseball, Inc. In addition, the licensing revenues earned by players from baseball cards and other merchandise, which total in excess of $100 million annually and which currently are managed by the Major League Baseball Players Association, should be transferred to Baseball, Inc.

In his new book, Bill James reaches a similar conclusion regarding local broadcast revenues. James suggests that 50 percent of all such revenues should be retained by the team that sells the broadcasting rights and the remaining 50 percent should be shared equally by all teams.[923] Although I think that James's suggestion would be a significant improvement over the current treatment of "local" media revenues, it would still permit too large a share of overall revenues to be retained by teams in media centers or with media ownership. It also would encourage teams with media ownership to distort the revenues payable to other teams.

(f) ***Payments to Large Market Owners.*** To compensate the current large media market franchise owners (*e.g.,* Yankees, Mets, Braves, Dodgers, Cubs, Red Sox, Rangers) for their initial loss in preferential revenues from the changes resulting from Baseball, Inc., those owners would receive 50 percent of the proceeds of the Baseball, Inc. initial public offering. That's right. Half of the proceeds of the Baseball, Inc. initial public offering would be distributed to the current large media market owners as a one-time payment for giving up the current advantageous position they hold, but to which they should not be entitled. Although this may seem unfair to the small market owners, it is a necessary incentive to the current large media market owners to eliminate continuing inequity in the future.

(g) ***Players.*** Baseball, Inc. would issue one-third of its share capital to the players as a group, which shares would be held by players' trusts established for each team. Each such trust would own an equal number of shares in Baseball, Inc. The dividends earned annually from the Baseball, Inc. shares owned by the trust and the players' share of the team's bonus pool earnings (discussed below) would be divided by the trust according to its own rules which would be established by the players. For example, a trust might divide total income into separate components for long-term and single-season guaranteed compensation amounts, annual performance-based incentives, and post-season performance-based incentives. The players would determine their own compensation and would have nobody to blame but themselves if they make poor choices.

(h) **Retirement Fund**. A significant portion (*e.g.,* 10 percent) of Baseball Inc.'s annual profits would be allocated to a new players' retirement fund which would subsume the existing players pension plan and benefit the former players who helped to create the game and the business that will become Baseball, Inc.

(i) **Bonus Pool**. A significant portion (*e.g.,* 20–30 percent) of Baseball Inc.'s annual operating profits would be allocated to a bonus pool which would be distributed among the teams that reach the playoffs. This bonus pool would be distributed pursuant to a formula that would provide greater rewards for greater success (*i.e.,* the team that wins the World Series would receive the largest share of the pool, league pennant winners the second largest shares, and conference winners and division winners smaller shares), with such amounts being divided equally among the franchise operators (50 percent) and the players' trusts (50 percent) for such teams.

(j) **Operating Expenses**. Each franchise operator would have the obligation to pay player salaries, the cost of providing its team's stadium, and the other costs associated with operating the franchise. But why should the franchise operators pay the players' salaries if the players are going to own part of Baseball, Inc.? Because I'm not talking about the kind of salaries that are being paid today. I'm talking about normal (albeit somewhat high) wages being paid to the workers who are essential in producing the 50 percent of ticket, stadium, concession, merchandise, and parking revenues that would accrue entirely to the franchise operators.

(k) **Salaries**. Each franchise would have an identical overall salary level (which could not be exceeded and *must* be spent) and each player would have a maximum salary. For example, the annual overall players' salaries for each team might be US$12.5 million with each player earning a minimum of US$250,000 and a maximum annual salary of US$1 million. Under such a system, a team might have five $1 million players, ten $500,000 players, and ten $250,000 players, for example, or 25 players with $500,000 salaries each. Although you might think that the players would never agree to work for such low salaries, remember that this would be only a portion of the players' total compensation. They would end up making more in the long run from their shares of the profits of Baseball, Inc. *if* they remain productive players.

(III)   ***Marketing and Promoting Baseball***. The profitability of Major League Baseball could be greatly enhanced by improving its marketing and promotion. Thus, the third major element of Baseball, Inc. is the complete revamping of the marketing, promotion, and exploitation of Major League Baseball.

     (a)   ***Baseball World Broadcasting***. Baseball, Inc. would use one-third of the proceeds of the Baseball, Inc. initial public offering to establish "Baseball World Broadcasting," a 24 hour a day, 365 day a year telecommunications network, including television, internet, and other media forms, devoted *solely* to baseball. Baseball World would broadcast Major League, minor league, college, women's, and international games, documentaries, educational programs, baseball news programs, game shows, and merchandising programs. Baseball World would be financed by paid commercial advertisements. "You mean like ESPN or the Golf Channel?" you ask. "No, a lot better! No soccer, bowling, snooker, tractor pulls, ice skating, or X-Games. Just baseball, lots of baseball. Oh, and did I say, *no soccer!*"

     (b)   ***Licensing of Media Rights***. Baseball, Inc. would license the rights to broadcast or otherwise make media use of baseball's product to media providers other than Baseball World Broadcasting. These rights would be licensed on a collective basis with the purpose of furthering the joint short-term and long-term goals of increasing consumer interest and producing maximum levels of current and future revenues for Base-

ball, Inc. Current contractual obligations with broadcasters unaffiliated with current owners would be honored. Current contractual obligations with affiliates of
teams or their owners would be audited and, if necessary, cancelled or renegotiated to ensure Baseball, Inc.
receives full compensation for the use of its product.

(c) *Advertising and Promotion*. Baseball, Inc. would
finance the advertising and promotion of professional
baseball, including the expansion of Major League
Baseball's customer base. Major League Baseball has
historically done a pathetic job of promoting the
world's greatest game. Improving baseball's appeal,
especially to younger audiences, must be an important objective of Baseball Inc.'s chief executive officer.

(d) *Worldwide Media Dissemination*. Baseball World
Broadcasting would disseminate its product, in locally
adapted forms if appropriate, via satellite, internet, or
other media to large population centers around the
world. As anyone who has lived outside the United
States knows, it is difficult to remain an enthusiastic
baseball fan when few, if any, live games are telecast
in your home market. It is virtually impossible for a
foreign individual to become a fan under such conditions. Although worldwide dissemination of Baseball,
Inc.'s product by Baseball World Broadcasting may
not be immediately remunerative, this should be
viewed as a long-term investment by Baseball, Inc. To
develop new international markets, Baseball, Inc.
should initially provide its product at reduced or no
charge and make a concentrated effort to attract and
educate new viewers.

(e) *Marketing and Merchandising*. Baseball, Inc. would
completely overhaul the marketing of Major League
Baseball and its media and merchandising. Baseball,
Inc. would engage professional marketing personnel
and consultants to create various levels of marketing
focus (*e.g.*, youth, nostalgia, international, women,
fanatics) to engender loyalty and increase revenues.
Major League Baseball's marketing and merchandising has been woeful in comparison to that of the

National Basketball Association and the National Football League.

(f) ***Youth Appeal***. Baseball, Inc. would significantly expand its efforts to encourage the young, particularly inner-city youths, to become involved in baseball. In doing so, Major League Baseball would work with corporate sponsors and municipalities to make baseball more accessible and attractive to young people.

(IV) ***Internationalization***. The business of Major League Baseball and the size of its markets can be *dramatically* increased if the game can attract a worldwide audience. Thus, the fourth significant element in Baseball, Inc. is the internationalization of the game to expand existing markets and create new markets.

(a) ***Alliances and Establishment of Leagues***. Baseball, Inc. would seek to increase the internationalization of baseball. Baseball already has strong fan support in Japan, Korea, Taiwan, and the Caribbean. Some support is also found in the United Kingdom, Australia, and other countries. Baseball, Inc. would forge alliances with existing professional baseball leagues in these countries and finance the establishment of new professional leagues in other countries. Major League Baseball recently announced that the season opening series between the Seattle Mariners and the Oakland A's in 2003 will be played at the Tokyo Dome in Japan. Playing exhibition and season-opening series in Japan and Mexico is a small step in the right direction, but *much* more needs to be accomplished.

(b) ***Pan-American Baseball League***. As a prototype, Baseball, Inc. would finance the establishment of a new Pan-American Baseball League (the "PABL"). The PABL would initially have six teams: Mexico City, Havana, Santo Domingo, San Juan, Caracas, and Panama City. The PABL would have restrictions on sizes of rosters (*e.g.,* 20 players per team) and fixed annual overall team salaries (*e.g.,* US$3 million per team). Rosters could include up to three current Major League Baseball players with limited Major League experience (*e.g.,* less than two years). After that amount of Major League experience, a player could not play in both the PABL and Major League Baseball in the same calendar year. The PABL's season would run during Major League Baseball's off-season (*i.e.,* November through March). Each team would play 80 regular-season games per season (16 against each other team). All games would be played on weekends (one game on each Friday evening and Sunday afternoon or evening and a day-night doubleheader on each Saturday) and each team would visit each other team's city for two road trips during each season. The season would culminate in a PABL seven-game playoff series between the two teams with the best regular season records to be played as Friday and Saturday night games and a Sunday afternoon game on the home field of the team with the second-best regular-season record, and Friday and Saturday night games and a Sunday double header, if necessary, on the home field of the team with the best record on the following weekend. PABL games would receive television coverage, both locally, regionally, and on Baseball World Broadcasting. PABL teams would also receive sponsorship by major Latin American companies. Each team would be required to own or lease an inexpensive, but reliable aircraft to transport its players and would be required to provide suitable dormitory facilities for visiting teams' players. Baseball, Inc. would negotiate with, and provide reasonable compensation to, existing baseball leagues and authorities. Baseball, Inc. would help fund, and would own a 50 percent equity interest in, the PABL.

(c) ***Expansion of Leagues.*** Based on the example and lessons of the PABL, Baseball, Inc. would support the establishment of similar national or regional professional baseball leagues around the world. Possible early locations for establishment could include Australia, China, the Philippines, the United Kingdom, continental Europe, and South America.

(d) ***True World Series.*** Baseball, Inc. would begin preparations for the day when a true "World" Series can be held. After the game of baseball becomes sufficiently internationalized, a "World" Series championship could be held on a regular basis (perhaps every two years) to pit the North American champion against championship teams from other continents or regions.

(V)   ***Realignment of Divisions, Expansion, Scheduling, and Playoffs.*** The promotion of meaningful pennant races among natural rivals and the integrity and excitement of post-season action would increase the public's interest in Major League Baseball and increase Major League Baseball's profitability. Accordingly, another important component of Baseball, Inc. would be the realignment of the Major Leagues' divisions, scheduling, and playoff system.

    (a)   ***Rational Realignment of Divisions.*** The Major Leagues would be realigned (rationally *not* radically!) into two 16-team leagues with four four-team divisions each. The divisions would be organized in a manner that preserves the historical compositions of the American League and National League, recognizes historic rivalries and encourages new ones, and is broadly consistent with the historical Major League objective of having both American League and National League teams in each major demographic region. To achieve these objectives, I recommend the following realignment of Major League Baseball's leagues and divisions, movement of franchises, and expansion franchises, the costs of which would be financed by a combination of franchise fees to be paid for two expansion franchises and a portion of the proceeds of the Baseball, Inc. public offering. You might think that even considering expansion of Major League Baseball is foolish at a time when Major League owners are in favor of contraction. I disagree strongly. If Major League Baseball could overcome territorial squabbles to move two problem franchises to new locations in the United States, expand into two highly promising new locations outside the United States and one in the United States, and alter its current method of dividing "local" media revenues, the finances for all 32 Major League teams would be greatly improved.

AMERICAN LEAGUE

EASTERN CONFERENCE

ATLANTIC DIVISION

Boston Red Sox
New York Yankees
Florida Devil Rays*
Havana InFidels*

MIDWEST DIVISION

Baltimore Orioles
Toronto Blue Jays
Detroit Tigers
Cleveland Indians

WESTERN CONFERENCE

CENTRAL DIVISION

Chicago White Sox
Milwaukee Brewers***
Minnesota Twins
Kansas City Royals

PACIFIC DIVISION

Seattle Mariners
Anaheim Angels
San Jose Hackers****
Texas Rangers

NATIONAL LEAGUE

EASTERN CONFERENCE

ATLANTIC DIVISION

New York Mets
Philadelphia Phillies
Washington/Northern Virginia Senators*****
Atlanta Braves

MIDWEST DIVISION

Pittsburgh Pirates
Cincinnati Reds
Chicago Cubs
St. Louis Cardinals

WESTERN CONFERENCE
CENTRAL DIVISION

Colorado Rockies
Houston Astros
Las Vegas High Rollers**
Arizona Diamondbacks

PACIFIC DIVISION

San Francisco Giants
Los Angeles Dodgers
San Diego Padres
Mexico City Toros**

*Merger of Florida Marlins and Tampa Bay Devil Rays;
home games divided between Miami and Tampa
**Expansion team
***Change of Leagues
****Relocation of Oakland A's
*****Relocation of Montreal Expos

Obviously, my proposed realignment presents a number of anomalies. You are probably asking why the Baltimore Orioles, whose home city is on the Atlantic Ocean, would be in the Midwest Division of the American League. My answer is that I believe more interesting natural rivalries exist between Tampa Bay and Havana or New York and Havana than between Baltimore and any team in that division. You might also question a merger of the Florida Marlins and the Tampa Bay Devil Rays, but neither of these franchises has evidenced the ability to achieve sufficient attendance or financial success on its own and their consolidation and sharing of home games should improve their viability. You might also question the placement of Mexico City in the National League's Western Division. I believe time zones, demographics, and natural rivalries dictate Mexico City should be in the same division as the National League's California teams. You might also question the wisdom of expansion teams in Mexico City, Havana, and Las Vegas. The baseball history and fan support in Mexico City and Havana is deeper than in many current Major League cities. These cities represent by far the two most promising Major League expansion locations. Las Vegas has a dynamic, growing economy and is one of the world's leading tourist destinations. You also might wonder why I would move Milwaukee back to the American League. The answer is simple. That's where they belong. Although Commissioner Selig continues to insist that Milwaukee is a National League city, the Brewers spent more seasons in the American League (28) than the combination of years the Braves and the Brewers spent in the National League (18). Except for Selig's personal desires, there is no compelling reason for the Brewers to remain in the National League or to transfer the Arizona Diamondbacks to the American League, as Selig has proposed.

(b) *Scheduling.* To encourage divisional and conference rivalries, the regular season schedule for each team would be weighted in favor of conference and division competition. In a 162-game season, each team would play each team in its division 22 times (three three-game series and one two-game series in each city), each other team in its conference 12 times (two three-game series in each city), and each other team in its league six times (one three-game series in each city). It would be preferable, however, if the regular season were extended to either 164 or 168 games. In a 164-game regular season, each team would play each team in its division 20 times (one four-game series and two three-game series in each city), each other team in its conference 14 times (one four-game series and one three-game series in each city), and each other team in its league six times (one three-game series in each city). In a 168-game regular season, each team would play each team in its division 24 times (four three-game series in each city), each other team in its conference 12 times (two three-game series in each city), and each other team in its league six times (one three-game series in each city). Although the Major League Baseball Players Association has historically opposed lengthening the Major League season, that opposition would likely diminish under Baseball, Inc., because the players, as indirect owners of equity interests, would share in the additional revenues and profits of extra games.

(c) **No Regular Season Inter-League Play**. Inter-league play would be limited to spring training and the World Series. The current practice of regular season inter-league play cheapens the World Series, distorts league pennant races, and distorts league statistics.

(d) **Post-Season Play**. Two rounds of best-of-seven-games playoff series—*i.e.*, four conference championship series and two league championship series—would precede the World Series.

(VI) **Player Drafts**. The rules governing the drafting and roster protection of both amateur and professional players by Major League teams should be changed to limit the existing advantages of those Major League teams with the largest budgets to recruit and stockpile players.

(a) **International Amateur Player Draft**. The current amateur player draft should be extended to apply to players from throughout the world. The number of rounds of such draft should be decided by the Board of Directors of Baseball, Inc.

(b) **Competitive Balance Player Draft**. In addition to the amateur player draft, an annual competitive balance draft of professional players should be instituted along the lines of the proposal made in 2000 by the Blue Ribbon Panel on Baseball Economics, and made again by Commissioner Selig in December 2000 and by Major League Baseball's owners in the 2002 negotiations for the new collective bargaining agreement. Under this proposal, each of the eight franchises with the best overall records during the three immediately preceding years would be able to protect only 25 players on its roster, and all other players under contract to such franchises would be eligible to be drafted by the eight franchises with the worst overall records during such three year period, with each such franchise having the ability to select one (or perhaps more) of such unprotected player(s).

(c) ***Trading of Draft Picks and Players Selected in Drafts.***
Franchises should have the ability to trade the rights
to draft players in the amateur draft and the competitive balance draft and to trade the negotiating rights
to players that have been selected in those drafts.

(VII) ***Legislation.*** To ensure that Major League Baseball intro-
duces and adheres to the principles of Baseball, Inc., the
United States Congress would enact specific legislation to
govern our national pastime (the "Major League Baseball
Act"). At a minimum, the Major League Baseball Act would
(a) outlaw the designated hitter, the rabbit ball, Astroturf,
aluminum bats, orange or yellow baseballs, blue or red baseball gloves, symmetrical domed stadiums, inter-league play
(except during the World Series), radical realignment, and
all of the other foolish and short-sighted ideas introduced
to baseball since the 1960s; (b) require all current and future
Major League ballparks to comply with minimum standards
of professionalism. Although baseball parks should have
individual character and appeal on broad levels to different
groups, minimum standards of playability for all Major
League ballparks would be established. Many of the sillier
ideas of recently built parks which have an effect on the game
(*e.g.*, indoor or outdoor homer heavens, the center field hill
in Minute Maid Park) would be prohibited. Obviously,
spectators enjoy games in which runs are scored, particularly by home runs. Part of baseball's timeless appeal, however, is the fan's ability to make meaningful statistical
comparisons of players of different eras. All-time records
should not be challenged and regularly broken simply
because greedy owners believe more home runs will increase
attendance (*i.e.*, the homerfests in Coors Field would cease);
(c) establish and require enforcement of reasonable and
consistent strike zones and pitchers' mound heights; (d)
conform the rules of the two Major Leagues; (e) require
approval by 75 percent or more of the shareholders of Baseball, Inc. for the movement of any Major League team from
one metropolitan area to another; (f) provide a specific
exemption to the United States antitrust laws for baseball,
solely within the context of Baseball, Inc.; (g) provide for
Baseball, Inc. to be taxed as a partnership (*i.e.*, one tier of

taxation at the investor level); (h) exempt baseball from the sanctions of the Trading With the Enemy Act (better yet, make peace with Cuba!); and (i) require the consent of at least 75 percent of the shareholders of Baseball, Inc. and confirmation by the United States Congress for all significant future changes in the game of baseball.

That's it! That is my proposal for Baseball, Inc. and my plan for saving our national pastime. Of course, many of the elements of Baseball, Inc. require further refinement. The principles of Baseball, Inc. are, however, clear and reasonable. If Major League Baseball's current franchise owners and players do not accept the principles of Baseball Inc., the United States Congress should specifically legislate that Major League Baseball in its current form violates United States antitrust laws and should reform Major League Baseball pursuant to a system of its own creation. Based on recent congressional impeachment proceedings and leadership shifts and the presidential ballot recount debacle in Florida, I do not recommend that the franchise operators and players acquiesce in this.

Professional baseball has endured for one and one-third centuries, surviving more than half a century of blatant racism, nearly a century of virtual slavery for players, two World Wars, military conflicts in Mexico, Cuba, Vietnam, Korea, Eastern Europe, the Persian Gulf, and Afghanistan, and the malfeasance, misfeasance, and greed of its franchise owners, players union, and players. Baseball has survived because of the inherent beauty and perfection of the game. Yet this beauty and perfection continue to be eroded by the insatiable appetites of players and team owners, particularly major media market owners, for ever larger compensation and profits. A radically different business model should be instituted to supplant Major League Baseball's current business structure. Except for a few tweaks to restore some of baseball's important traditions that have been allowed to be diminished over the last quarter century, however, the game should be preserved.

If Baseball, Inc. is properly organized and implemented, Major League Baseball's major ills will be cured. The vast economic disparities between large and small media market teams will be minimized. Franchise shifts will be curtailed. Player movement will be reduced. Fan loyalty will increase. Baseball's fan base and sources of revenue will expand, both domestically and internationally. Baseball's appeal to the young and to women will grow. The quality of Major League players will improve. Major League Baseball's salary structure will stabilize. Labor strife will cease and strikes and lockouts will be prevented. Major League Baseball will have its first effective and professional management ever. Players and franchise operators alike will make more money. The game of baseball and the business of baseball will be separated. Lastly, but most importantly, we, the fans, will see more and better baseball. The kind of baseball played in our youths by Aaron, Williams, Mays, and Musial.

America has changed dramatically over the past one and one-third centuries. But baseball has endured. America needs baseball and baseball's traditions. Baseball is not only a link to our past, our ancestors, and a simpler time, it is part of the American heritage that has been passed down to us by our forefathers—a heritage as important in its way as our flag and our national anthem. It is also a link to our future and our descendants. Baseball is America's religion—our only common religion as a people.

... and may the sun never set on American baseball.
                    —President Harry S Truman

NOTES

Chapter 1

1. Will, George. *Men at Work: The Craft of Baseball*. New York: Macmillan, 1990.

2. Axthelm, Pete. *The City Game*. New York: Harper's Magazine Press, 1970.

3. Wolf, David. *Foul: The Connie Hawkins Story*. New York: Holt, Rinehart and Winston, 1972.

4. Chamberlain, Wilt. *A View from Above*. New York: Villard, 1991.

5. Jenkins, Dan. *Semi-Tough*. New York: Atheneum, 1972.

6. Jenkins, Dan. *Life Its Ownself*. New York: Simon & Schuster, 1984.

7. Giamatti, A. Bartlett. *A Great and Glorious Game*. Chapel Hill, N.C.: Algonquin, 1998.

8. Hemingway, Ernest. *The Old Man and the Sea*. New York: Charles Scribner's Sons, 1952, 22.

9. DeLillo, Don. *Underworld*. New York: Scribner, 1997, 17–43.

Chapter 2

10. *The National Advocate*, April 23, 1823.

11. Although several fine books chronicle baseball's early history, essential sources for anyone interested in this subject are Alexander, Charles. *Our Game: An American Baseball History*. New York: Henry Holt, 1991; Burk, Robert. *Never Just A Game: Players, Owners, and American Baseball to 1920*. Chapel Hill, N.C.: University of North Carolina Press, 1994; Koppett, Leonard. *Koppett's Concise History of Major League Baseball*. Philadelphia: Temple University Press, 1998; Levine, Peter. *A.G. Spalding and the Rise of Baseball: The Promise of American Sport*. New York: Oxford University Press, 1985; Melville, Tom. *Early Baseball and the Rise of the National League*. Jefferson, N.C.: McFarland, 2001; Rossi, John. *The National Game: Baseball and American Culture*. Chicago: Ivan R. Dee, 2000,

3–94; Seymour, Harold. *Baseball: The Early Years*. New York: Oxford University Press, 1960; Spalding, Albert G. *America's National Game*. Lincoln, Neb.: University of Nebraska Press, 1992 (Reprint of 1911 edition); Spink, Alfred H. *The National Game*, Carbondale, Ill.: Southern Illinois University Press, 2000 (Reprint of 1910 edition); Tygiel, Jules. *Past Time: Baseball As History*. New York: Oxford University Press, 2000, 1–34; and Voight, David and Nevins, Allan. *American Baseball: From Gentleman's Sport to Commissioner System*. State College, Pa.: Pennsylvania State University Press, 1983.

12. Alexander, *Our Game*, 4–5; Burk, *Never Just a Game*, 4–18; Seymour, *Baseball: The Early Years*, 15–17.

13. Burk, *Never Just a Game*, 4; DiSalvatore, Bryan. *A Clever Base-Ballist: The Life and Times of John Montgomery Ward*. Baltimore: The Johns Hopkins University Press, 1999, 76; Seymour, *Baseball: The Early Years*, 16–17.

14. Burk, *Never Just a Game*, 16–18; Seymour, *Baseball: The Early Years*, 35–36.

15. Burk, *Never Just a Game*, 5, 9–11; DiSalvatore, 77–80; Seymour, *Baseball: The Early Years*, 15–16, 23–34;

16. Alexander, *Our Game*, 11–16; Ryczek, William J. *When Johnny Came Sliding Home: The Post-Civil War Baseball Boom, 1965–1870*. Jefferson, N.C.: McFarland, 1998; Seymour, *Baseball: The Early Years*, 40–46.

17. Burk, *Never Just a Game*, 33; Ryczek, 251.

18. Guschov, Stephen. *The Red Stockings of Cincinnati: Base Ball's First All Professional Team and Its Historic 1869 and 1870 Seasons*. Jefferson, N.C.: McFarland, 1998; Koppett, 13; Melville, 32; Rossi, 15; Seymour, *Baseball: The Early Years*, 56.

19. Burk, *Never Just a Game*, 36–37; Rossi, 15; Seymour, *Baseball: The Early Years*, 56–57.

20. Guschov, 132; Koppet, 13–14; Seymour, *Baseball: The Early Years*, 57.

21. Alexander, *Our Game*, 21; Koppett, 14; Seymour, *Baseball: The Early Years*, 57.

22. Burk, *Never Just a Game*, 39; Seymour, *Baseball: The Early Years*, 56–58; Koppett, 13.

23. Melville, 42; Seymour, *Baseball: The Early Years*, 57.

24. Abrams, Roger I. *The Money Pitch: Baseball Free Agency and Salary Arbitration*. Philadelphia: Temple University Press, 2000; Guschov, 96; Melville, 39; Rossi, 20.

25. Melville, 41.

26. Alexander, *Our Game*, 22; Koppett, 17; Melville, 48; Rossi, 19; Ryczek, William J. *Blackguards and Red Stockings: A History of Baseball's National Association, 1871–1875*. Jefferson, N.C.: McFarland, 1992; Seymour, *Baseball: The Early Years*, 59.

27. Koppett, 17–18; Rossi, 19; Seymour, *Baseball: The Early Years*, 59–60.

28. Melville, 49.

29. Koppett, 18–19; Rossi, 21.

30. Thorn, et al., *Total Baseball*, 198.

31. Rossi, 21–22.

32. James, Bill. *The New Bill James Historical Baseball Abstract.* New York: Free Press, 2001, 28; Smith, Ron. *The Ballpark Book.* St. Louis: The Sporting News, 2000, 8, 11.

33. Thorn, et al., *Total Baseball,* 105.

34. Melville, 58.

35. Scully, Gerald W. *The Business of Major League Baseball.* Chicago: University of Chicago Press, 1989, 1.

36. Ibid.

37. Abrams, *The Money Pitch,* 8, 10.

38. Alexander, *Our Game,* 24; Rossi, 21–22; Ward, Geoffrey C. and Burns, Ken. *Baseball: An Illustrated History.* New York: Alfred A. Knopf, 1994, 26–29.

39. Koppett, 20; Seymour, *Baseball: The Early Years,* 60.

40. Alexander, *Our Game,* 26–27; Koppett, 20; Melvlle, 59–61; Rossi, 21–22; Seymour, *Baseball: The Early Years,* 69.

41. Abrams, *The Money Pitch,* 9; Alexander, *Our Game,* 26–27; Burk, *Never Just a Game,* 54; Koppett, 29; Rossi, 27; Seymour, *Baseball: The Early Years,* 80.

42. Burk, *Never Just a Game,* 51–58; Koppett, 25–29; Melville, 76–77; Rossi, 26–33; Seymour, *Baseball: The Early Years,* 75–85.

43. DiSalvatore, 89–90; Koppett, 28; Rossi, 28; Seymour, *Baseball: The Early Years,* 80–83.

44. Burk, *Never Just a Game,* 54; Koppett 29; Rossi, 27.

45. Abrams, *The Money Pitch,* 11; Rossi, 28.

46. Alexander, *Our Game,* 28; Burk, *Never Just a Game,* 56–57; DiSalvatore, 90; Koppett, 30–31; Melville, 84–85; Rossi, 29.

47. Alexander, *Our Game,* 29–30; Burk, *Never Just a Game,* 60–61; DiSalvatore, 90; James, *The New Bill James Historical Baseball Abstract,* 18; Koppett, 32; Melville, 90–95; Seymour, *Baseball: The Early Years,* 87–88.

48. Alexander, *Our Game,* 33–34; Melville, 113–114.

49. Burk, *Never Just a Game,* 56–65; Koppett, 32–34; Melville, 97–100.

50. Koppett, 31–35; Rossi, 29.

51. Alexander, *Our Game,* 31–33; DiSalvatore, 145.

52. Abrams, *The Money Pitch,* 10; Burk, *Never Just a Game,* 62–64; DiSalvatore, 158–159; Koppett, 34–35; Melville, 115; Rossi, 31–32; Seymour, *Baseball: The Early Years,* 104–115.

53. Burk, *Never Just a Game,* 58–62; Melville, 103–111.

54. Burk, *Never Just a Game,* 69–70; Koppett, 40–41; Melville, 131; Nemec, David. *The Beer and Whiskey League: The Illustrated History of the American Association.* New York: Lyons & Burford, 1994; Rossi, 29–30; Seymour, *Baseball: The Early Years,* 135–147.

55. Alexander, *Our Game,* 35; Koppett, 40–41; Melville, 131.

56. Alexander, *Our Game,* 36; Koppett, 40–41; Melville, 131.

57. Koppett, 41; Melville, 133; Thorn, et al., *Total Baseball,* 105.

58. Melville, 133–134.

59. Burk, *Never Just a Game*, 70; Koppett, 40–41; Melville, 130; Seymour, *Baseball: The Early Years*, 139–142.

60. Burk, *Never Just a Game*, 73; Koppett, 41; Melville, 137; Rossi, 31; Seymour, *Baseball: The Early Years*, 144–147.

61. Thorn, et al., *Total Baseball*, 105.

62. Alexander, *Our Game*, 38–40; Burk, *Never Just a Game*, 74–75; Koppett, 45–46; Rossi, 30; Seymour, *Baseball: The Early Years*, 148–161.

63. Burk, *Never Just a Game*, 76; Koppett, 47–48; Seymour, *Baseball: The Early Years*, 154–155.

64. Burk, *Never Just a Game*, 76.

65. Burk, *Never Just a Game*, 85; Seymour, *Baseball: The Early Years*, 169.

66. Alexander, *Our Game*, 48–49; James, *The New Bill James Historical Baseball Abstract*, 49; Rossi, 41; Smith, *The Ballpark Book*, 11–12.

67. Burk, *Never Just a Game*, 86; DiSalvatore, 175.

68. Burk, *Never Just a Game*, 92.

69. Alexander, *Our Game*, 39; Koppett, 51.

70. Abrams, *The Money Pitch*, 14; Alexander, *Our Game*, 53; Burk, *Never Just a Game*, 94–98; DiSalvatore, 175–178; Koppett, 55–56; Rossi, 44; Seymour, *Baseball: The Early Years*, 221–222.

71. DiSalvatore, 178.

72. Abrams, *The Money Pitch*, 13; Burk, *Never Just a Game*, 88.

73. Abrams, *The Money Pitch*, 14; Burk, *Never Just a Game*, 101; DiSalvatore, 245; Koppett, 58; Rossi, 45.

74. Abrams, *The Money Pitch*, 14; Burk, *Never Just a Game*, 104–106; DiSalvatore, 269–321; Koppett, 59; Lowenfish, Lee. *The Imperfect Diamond: A History of Baseball's Labor Wars*. New York: Da Capo, 1991 (Revised Edition), 35; Rossi, 45–46; Seymour, *Baseball: The Early Years*, 222–239.

75. Burk, *Never Just a Game*, 106; Abrams, Roger I. *Legal Bases: Baseball and the Law*. Philadelphia: Temple University Press, 1998, 18.

76. Koppett, 59; Seymour, *Baseball: The Early Years*, 228.

77. Burk, *Never Just a Game*, 105–110; Koppett, 59–60; Seymour, *Baseball: The Early Years*, 221–239.

78. Alexander, *Our Game*, 55; Lowenfish, 36.

79. Abrams, *Legal Bases*, 19–20; Seymour, *Baseball: The Early Years*, 236.

80. Abrams, *Legal Bases*, 20; Seymour, *Baseball: The Early Years*, 236–237.

81. Alexander, *Our Game*, 55; Koppett, 60; Seymour, *Baseball: The Early Years*, 233.

82. Alexander, *Our Game*, 57–58; Seymour, *Baseball: The Early Years*, 238–239.

83. Seymour, *Baseball: The Early Years*, 240–248.

84. Burk, *Never Just a Game*, 121–124; Koppett, 63–66; Rossi, 50–52.

85. Seymour, *Baseball: The Early Years*, 265–274, 293–306.

86. Burk, *Never Just a Game*, 125; Koppett, 68–73; Rossi, 57.

87. Rossi, 52.

88. Thorn, et al., *Total Baseball*, 105–106; Rossi, 53.

89. Thorn, et al., *Total Baseball*, 106.

90. Koppett, 74–75; Smith, *The Ballpark Book*, 11.

91. Rossi, 55.

92. Burk, *Never Just a Game*, 140; Koppett, 83–84.

93. All player statistics in this book have been taken from James, Bill. *The Bill James Historical Baseball Abstract*. New York: Villard, 1986; James, Bill (ed.), *All-Time Baseball Source Book*. Skokie, Ill.: Stats. Inc., 1998; Reichler, Joseph L. (ed.), *The Baseball Encyclopedia: The Complete and Official Record of Major League Baseball* (9th ed.). New York: Macmillan, 1993; and Thorn, John, and Palmer, Pete (eds.). *Total Baseball* (6th ed.). New York: Total Sports, 1999. An excellent chronicle of early baseball players can be found in Faber, Charles F. *Baseball Pioneers: Ratings of Nineteenth Century Players*. Jefferson, N.C.: McFarland, 1997. See also Rossi, 34–38.

94. Abrams, *The Money Pitch*, 16; Seymour, *Baseball: The Early Years*, 107.

95. Abrams, *The Money Pitch*, 12; Rossi, 44; Ward, et al., 29–30.

96. Ward, et al., 29.

97. Alexander, *Our Game*, 52; DiSalvatore, 247–250.

98. Abrams, *The Money Pitch*, 12; Ward, et al., 31.

99. Abrams, *The Money Pitch*, 18; Alexander, *Our Game*, 94; Koppett, 103; Lowenfish, 71; Ward, et al., 75.

100. Abrams, *The Money Pitch*, 18; Alexander, *Our Game*, 94–95; Koppett, 102–103; Lowenfish, 71; Ward, et al., 75.

101. Abrams, *The Money Pitch*, 17; Alexander, *Our Game*, 76–77; Burk, *Never Just a Game*, 142; Koppett, 87–91; Rossi, 59–62; Seymour, *Baseball: The Early Years*, 307–324.

102. Abrams, *The Money Pitch*, 17; Alexander, *Our Game*, 78; Burk, *Never Just a Game*, 150; Koppett, 89; Rossi, 62–63.

103. Abrams, *The Money Pitch*, 17.

104. Rossi, 63–64.

105. Lowenfish, 68–69.

106. Abrams, *Legal Bases*, 29–34; Burk, *Never Just a Game*, 153.

107. Abrams, *Legal Bases*, 34–38; Burk, *Never Just a Game*, 153–154.

108. Abrams, *Legal Bases*, 40; Burk, *Never Just a Game*, 153–154; Lowenfish, 69; Rossi, 64.

109. Thorn, et al., *Total Baseball*, 106; Rossi, 65.

110. Alexander, *Our Game*, 82–83; Burk, *Never Just a Game*, 157; Lowenfish, 70; Rossi, 65; Seymour, *Baseball: The Early Years*, 323–324.

111. Alexander, *Our Game*, 86; Burk, *Never Just a Game*, 157; Lowenfish, 70; Rossi, 66.

112. Burk, *Never Just a Game*, 156–157; Koppett, 97–98; Lowenfish, 70–71; Rossi, 65–66.

113. Murdock, Eugene C. *Ban Johnson: Czar of Baseball*. Westport, Ct.: Greenwood Press, 1982.

114. White, G. Edward. *Creating the National Game: Baseball Transforms Itself, 1903–1953*. Princeton, N.J.: Princeton University Press, 1996.

115. Rossi, 75–77; Thorn, et al., *Total Baseball,* 106.

116. Helyar, John. *Lords of The Realm: The Real History of Baseball.* New York: Villard Books, 1994, 5–6; Seymour, *Baseball: The Golden Age,* 344; United States Census Bureau, Population Estimates Program, Population Division, Historical Population Estimates: July 1, 1900 to July 1, 1999.

117. Alexander, *Our Game,* 92; Burk, *Never Just a Game,* 178–179; James, *The New Bill James Historical Baseball Abstract,* 90, 113–114; Koppett, 100–101, 116, 160; Lowenfish, 71; Rossi, 76–79; Seymour, *Baseball: The Golden Age,* 49–53; Smith, *The Ballpark Book,* 11–14.

118. Rossi, 76; Seymour, *Baseball: The Golden Age,* 53; Smith, *The Ballpark Book,* 11–14.

119. Koppett, 127–128; Rossi, 77; Seymour, *Baseball: The Golden Age,* 72.

120. Alexander, *Our Game,* 92.

121. Seymour, *Baseball: The Golden Age,* 122–127.

122. Ibid., 123.

123. Ibid., 122.

124. Probably the most complete and balanced biography of Cobb is Alexander, Charles C. *Ty Cobb.* New York: Oxford University Press, 1984. A more biased, but nevertheless fascinating, view of Cobb's career and life is Cobb, Ty and Stump, Al. *My Life in Baseball: The True Record.* Garden City, NY: Doubleday, 1961.

125. Alexander, *Ty Cobb,* 50, 68, 80–81, 105.

126. Rossi, 79–83; Tygiel, *Past Time,* 35–63.

127. Kashatus, William C. *Connie Mack's '29 Triumph.* Jefferson, N.C.: McFarland, 1999; Lieb, Frederick G. *Connie Mack: Grand Old Man of Baseball.* New York: G.P. Putnam's Sons, 1945; Tygiel, *Past Time,* 35–63.

128. Alexander, Charles C. *John McGraw.* New York: Viking Penguin, 1988; Durso, Joseph. *The Days of Mr. McGraw.* Englewood Cliffs, N.J.: Prentice-Hall, 1969; Tygiel, *Past Time,* 35–63.

129. Burk, *Never Just a Game,* 188; James, *The New Bill James Historical Baseball Abstract,* 114–115; Koppett, 104.

130. Burk, *Never Just a Game,* 194–197; James, *The New Bill James Historical Baseball Abstract,* 105; Koppett, 115–121; Rossi, 84–91; Seymour, *Baseball: The Golden Age,* 199–213.

131. Abrams, *Legal Bases,* 54; Lowenfish, 86; Seymour, *Baseball: The Golden Age,* 200–201.

132. Lowenfish, 86; Rossi, 86; Seymour, *Baseball: The Golden Age,* 201.

133. Alexander, *Our Game,* 103; Rossi, 86.

134. Alexander, *Our Game,* 103; Burk, *Never Just a Game,* 201; Lowenfish, 82–83.

135. Abrams, *The Money Pitch,* 19; Alexander, *Our Game,* 128; Lowenfish, 87; Rossi, 87; Seymour, *Baseball: The Golden Age,* 205–207.

136. Burk, *Never Just a Game,* 206; Rossi, 87; Thorn, et al., *Total Baseball,* 106.

137. Abrams, *Legal Bases,* 55; Burk, *Never Just a Game,* 207–208; Lowenfish, 88–89; Seymour, *Baseball: The Golden Age,* 212–213.

138. Abrams, *Legal Bases,* 55; Lowenfish, 89–90; Seymour, *Baseball: The Golden Age,* 212.

139. Abrams, *Legal Bases,* 55; Burk, *Never Just a Game,* 201–207; Koppett, 117; Seymour, *Baseball: The Golden Age,* 212; Ward, et al., 123.

140. Abrams, *Legal Bases,* 56; Alexander, *Our Game,* 104; Burk, *Never Just a Game,* 208–209; Koppett, 117–118; Lowenfish, 91; Ward, et al., 123; Rossi, 89–91.

141. Lowenfish, 91.

142. Abrams, *Legal Bases,* 56; Koppett, 118–119; Seymour, *Baseball: The Golden Age,* 241–244.

143. Abrams, *Legal Bases,* 57; Lowenfish, 105.

144. Abrams, *Legal Bases,* 57–58; Lowenfish, 105–107; Rossi, 90–91.

145. *Federal Baseball Club of Baltimore, Inc. v. National League of Professional Clubs,* 259 U.S. 200 (1922).

146. *Toolson v. New York Yankees,* 346 U.S. 356 (1953); *Flood v. Kuhn,* 407 U.S. 258 (1972).

147. Burk, *Never Just a Game,* 211; Creamer, Robert W. *Babe: The Legend Comes to Life.* New York: Simon & Schuster, 1974, 119–120; Rossi, 91.

148. Creamer, *Babe,* 158–170; Koppett, 126–129; Rossi, 91–94;

149. Thorn, et al., *Total Baseball,* 106.

150. Alexander, *Our Game,* 106; Burk, *Never Just a Game,* 211; Lowenfish, 92–94; Rossi, 91–92.

151. Alexander, *Our Game,* 114.

152. Thorn, et al., *Total Baseball,* 106.

153. Alexander, *Our Game,* 115–116; Burk, *Never Just a Game,* 232–234; Seymour, *Baseball: The Golden Age,* 294–310.

154. Asinof, Elliot. *Eight Men Out: The Black Sox and the 1919 World Series.* New York: Holt, Rinehart & Winston, 1963; Burk, *Never Just a Game,* 232–234; Koppett, 135–143; Rossi, 100–103; Ward, et al., 133–145.

Chapter 3

155. Alexander, *Our Game,* 115–116; Burk, *Never Just a Game,* 232–234; Rossi, 97–103; Seymour, *Baseball: The Golden Age,* 294–310.

156. Rossi, 103; Ward, et al., 155.

157. Babe Ruth's life and career have been chronicled by a number of writers. The first book I read about Ruth, over 40 years ago, is Van Riper, Guernsey, Jr. *Babe Ruth: Baseball Boy.* New York: Bobbs-Merrill, 1954. This book was published as part of "The Childhood of Famous Americans Series" which included youth-oriented biographies of approximately 100 Americans, including Thomas Edison, Meriwether Lewis, Franklin Delano Roosevelt, Pocahontas, and Babe Ruth. An account of Ruth's early life for more mature readers is Gilbert, Brother C.F.X. *Young Babe Ruth: His Early Life and Baseball Career, from the Memoirs of a Xaverian Brother.* Jefferson, NC: McFarland, 1999. The most complete, and I believe best, biography of baseball's greatest and most celebrated player is

Creamer, Robert W. *Babe: The Legend Comes to Life.* New York: Simon & Schuster, 1974.

158. James, *The Bill James Historical Baseball Abstract,* 125.

159. James, *The New Bill James Historical Baseball Abstract,* 121.

160. Creamer, *Babe,* 186–188.

161. Ibid., 205.

162. Alexander, *Our Game,* 120; Creamer, *Babe,* 207–209; Okrent, Daniel et al. (eds.). *The Ultimate Baseball Book.* Boston: Houghton Mifflin, 1979, 338.

163. Creamer, *Babe,* 212.

164. Alexander, *Our Game,* 141; Ward, et al., 155.

165. Shaughnessy, Dan. *The Curse of the Bambino.* New York: Penguin, 1991.

166. Alexander, *Our Game,* 120; James, *The Bill James Historical Baseball Abstract,* 125; James, *The New Bill James Historical Baseball Abstract,* 120–122; Rossi, 104, 112–113; Seymour, *Baseball: The Golden Age,* 423–426.; Ward, et al., 153.

167. Creamer, *Babe,* 217–218; Seymour, *Baseball: The Golden Age,* 425.

168. Ritter, Lawrence, *Lost Ballparks: A Celebration of Baseball's Legendary Fields.* New York: Penguin, 1992, 162; Smith, *The Ballpark Book,* 254.

169. An excellent account of American sporting heroes in the 1920s can be found in Kahn, Roger. *A Flame of Pure Fire: Jack Dempsey and the Roaring '20s.* New York: Harcourt, 1999.

170. Rossi, 103–105; Seymour, *Baseball: The Golden Age,* 427; Tygiel, *Past Time,* 73–86.

171. Thorn, et al., *Total Baseball,* 106.

172. Alexander, *Our Game,* 122–129; Rossi, 106.

173. Rossi, 106.

174. Alexander, *Our Game,* 125–126; Seymour, *Baseball: The Golden Age,* 311–313.

175. Alexander, *Our Game,* 125–126; Seymour, *Baseball: The Golden Age,* 311–312.

176. Koppett, 137; Lowenfish, 98.

177. Rossi, 106.

178. Holtzman, Jerome. *The Commissioners: Baseball's Midlife Crisis.* New York: Total Sports, 1998, 26–27.

179. Holtzman, 22–23; Rossi, 106–107; Seymour, *Baseball: The Golden Age,* 322–323.

180. Holtzman, 15, 28; Seymour, *Baseball: The Golden Age,* 324.

181. Holtzman, 29–34; Rossi, 108–109.

182. Alexander, *Our Game,* 130–132; Lowenfish, 104; White, 105.

183. Alexander, *Our Game,* 133–134; White, 111.

184. Thorn, et al., *Total Baseball,* 106.

185. Creamer, *Babe,* 254.

186. Ibid.

187. Ibid.

188. Ibid., 244–245.

189. Burk, Robert F. *Much More Than a Game*. Chapel Hill, N.C.: University of North Carolina Press, 2001, 18; Creamer, *Babe*, 244–256; Holtzman, 36–37; Koppett, 165–166; Seymour, *Baseball: The Golden Age*, 392–393.

190. Creamer, *Babe*, 276; Smith, *The Ballpark Book*, 38–45; White, 39–45.

191. Smith, *The Baseball Book*, 42.

192. James, Bill. *Universal Stats Calendar*, November 18, 2000.

193. A detailed discussion of baseball and its business during the 1920s is provided in Burk, Robert F., *Much More Than a Game*, 3–39.

194. Alexander, *Our Game*, 137; Curran, William. *Big Sticks: The Batting Revolution of the '20s*. New York: William Morrow, 1990; James, *The Bill James Historical Baseball Abstract*, 405; Rossi, 104–105, 112–114; Seymour, *Baseball: The Golden Age*, 425–427.

195. Seymour, *Baseball: The Golden Age*, 425; Thorn, et al., *Total Baseball*, 645–646.

196. Alexander, *Our Game*, 137; Thorn, et al., *Total Baseball*, 650.

197. Creamer, *Babe*, 218; Rossi, 113.

198. Thorn, et al., *Total Baseball*, 650.

199. Alexander, *Our Game*, 146.

200. Alexander, Charles C. *Rogers Hornsby*. New York: Owl Books, 1995; Seymour, *Baseball: The Golden Age*, 393–395.

201. Seymour, *Baseball: The Golden Age*, 393–395.

202. Alexander, *Our Game*, 146–148; Lowenfish, 116; Seymour, *Baseball: The Golden Age*, 400–422.

203. Alexander, *Our Game*, 146–147; Seymour, *Baseball: The Golden Age*, 413–419.

204. Alexander, *Our Game*, 147.

205. Lipman, David. *Mr. Rickey: The Story of Branch Rickey*. New York: 1966; Polner, Murray. *Branch Rickey: A Biography*. New York: Atheneum, 1982.

206. James, *The New Bill James Historical Baseball Abstract*, 486.

207. Seymour, *Baseball: The Golden Age*, 343–344; Thorn, et al., *Total Baseball*, 106–107.

208. Seymour, *Baseball: The Golden Age*, 344.

209. Light, Jonathan Fraser. *The Cultural Encyclopedia of Baseball*. Jefferson, N.C.: McFarland, 1997, 642.

210. Creamer, *Babe*, 346.

211. Ibid., 351.

212. Seymour, *Baseball: The Golden Age*, 345–346.

Chapter 4

213. Bardo, Michael D. (ed.), *The Defining Moment: The Great Depression and the American Economy in the Twentieth Century*. Chicago: University of Chicago Press, 1998; McElvaine, Robert S. *The Depression: America, 1929–1941*. New York: Times Books, 1981, 38–39.

214. Ibid.

215. Ibid., 41.

216. DeLong, J. Bradford. *Slouching Towards Utopia: The Economic History of the Twentieth Century*. Berkeley, Cal.: University of California Press, 2000; McElvaine, 40.

217. Samuelson, Paul A. *Economics* (8th Ed.). New York: McGraw-Hill, 1970, 73–75.

218. Samuelson, 189.

219. McElvaine, 45.

220. Alexander, *Our Game,* 159; Samuelson, 189.

221. Samuelson, 189.

222. For more detailed discussions of baseball during the Great Depression, see Burk, *Much More Than a Game,* 40–68; Gregory, Robert. *Diz: Dizzy Dean and Baseball During the Great Depression*. New York: Villard, 1992; Honig, Donald. *Baseball in the '30s: A Decade of Survival*. New York: Crown, 1989; Honig, Donald. *Baseball: When the Grass Was Real*. Lincoln, Neb.: University of Nebraska Press, 1975; Rossi, 121–141; Tygiel, *Past Time,* 87–115.

223. Thorn, et al., *Total Baseball,* 107.

224. Alexander, *Our Game,* 161–164; Burk, *Much More Than a Game,* 43.

225. Barber, Red. *1947: When All Hell Broke Loose in Baseball*. Garden City, N.Y.: Doubleday, 1982; 7–8; Burk, *Much More Than a Game,* 33–38; Koppett, 175–177; Light, 247; Tygiel, *Past Time,* 91–96; Ward, et al., 179, 182; White, 115–117, 285–292.

226. Thorn, et al., *Total Baseball,* 107.

227. Light, 642.

228. Helyar, 422; Lowenfish, 119; Miller, Marvin. *A Whole Different Ball Game: The Inside Story of Baseball's New Deal*. New York: Simon & Schuster, 1991, 361.

229. Creamer, *Babe,* 350.

230. Burk, *Much More Than a Game,* 42; Creamer, *Babe,* 350, 356, 371, 375.

231. Creamer, *Babe,* 375.

232. Ibid., 383–402.

233. Light, 315.

234. Kashatus, William C. *Connie Mack's '29 Triumph*; Koppett, 177–178; Rossi, 116–117; Ward, et al., 207–208.

235. Daniel, W. Harrison. *Jimmie Foxx: Baseball Hall of Famer, 1907–1967*. Jefferson, N.C.: McFarland, 1996.

236. James, *The Bill James Historical Baseball Abstract,* 424.

237. Alexander, *Our Game,* 164–165; Burk, *Much More Than a Game,* 44; Rossi, 124; Ward, et al., 260–261.

238. Koppett, 178.

239. Alexander, *Our Game,* 157; Koppett, 179.

240. Parker, Clifton Blue. *Fouled Away: The Baseball Tragedy of Hack Wilson*. Jefferson, N.C.: McFarland, 2000.

241. Alexander, *Our Game,* 157.

242. Lieb, Frederick G. *The St. Louis Cardinals: The Story of a Great Baseball Club*. Carbondale, Ill.: Southern Illinois University Press, 2001 (reprint of 1949 edition), 154–170.

243. Feldmann, Doug. *Dizzy and the Gashouse Gang*. Jefferson, N.C.: McFarland, 2000; Gregory, Okrent, et al., 153–170.

244. Tygiel, Jules. *Baseball's Great Experiment: Jackie Robinson and His Legacy*. New York: Oxford University Press, 1983, 53.

245. Rossi, 128–131.

246. Koppett, 190–191; Rossi, 140–141; Tygiel, *Past Time*, 97–101. For a detailed discussion of night baseball and the early use of lights in baseball, see White, 160–189.

247. Helyar, 40.

248. Koppett, 190; Rossi, 140.

249. Ibid.

250. Rossi, 140; Thorn, et al., *Total Baseball*, 107.

251. Warfield, Don. *The Roaring Red Head: Larry McPhail—Baseball's Great Innovator*. South Bend, In.: Diamond Communications, 1987; Tygiel, *Past Time*, 95–115.

252. Koppett, 189–190; Tygiel, *Past Time*, 64–73, 89. For a detailed discussion of radio and baseball, see White, 206–244.

253. Helyar, 365.

254. Ibid.

Chapter 5

255. Creamer, Robert. *Baseball in '41: A Celebration of the Best Baseball Season Ever—In the Year America Went to War*. New York: Penguin, 1991.

256. For detailed chronicles of DiMaggio's life and career, the interested fan should read Allen, Maury. *Where Have You Gone Joe DiMaggio? The Story of America's Last Hero*. New York: E.P. Dutton, 1975; Creamer, Richard Ben. *Joe DiMaggio: The Hero's Life*. New York: Simon & Schuster, 2000; and Schoor, Gene. *Joe DiMaggio: A Biography*. New York: Doubleday, 1980.

257. Hemingway, Ernest. *The Old Man and The Sea*. New York: Charles Scribner's Sons, 1952, 22.

258. Miller, 154.

259. Silverman, Al. *Joe DiMaggio: The Golden Year, 1941*. Englewood Cliffs, N.J.: Prentice-Hall, 1969.

260. For detailed chronicles of the life and baseball career of Ted Williams, the interested fan should read Linn, Ed. *Hitter: The Life and Turmoils of Ted Williams*. New York: Harcourt Brace, 1993; Seidel, Michael. *Ted Williams: A Baseball Life*. Chicago: Contemporary Books, 1991; and Williams, Ted with Underwood, John. *My Turn at Bat: The Story of My Life*. New York: Simon & Schuster, 1969.

261. Linn, 160; Williams, 87.

262. Linn, 161–162.

263. For more extensive coverage of Musial's life and career, the interested fan should read Giglio, James N. *Musial: From Stash to Stan the Man*. Columbia, Mo.: University of Missouri Press, 2001; Lansche, Jerry. *Stan the Man Musial: Born to Be a Ballplayer*. Dallas: Taylor Publishing, 1994; and Musial, Stan with Broeg, Bob. *Stan Musial: "The Man's" Own Story*. New York: Doubleday, 1964.

264. Giglio, 127–134.

265. Ibid., 145.

266. Ibid.

267. Ibid., 188, 205.

268. James, *The Bill James Historical Baseball Abstract*, 384.

269. Ritter, Lawrence S. *Lost Ballparks: A Celebration of Baseball's Legendary Fields*. New York: Penguin Books, 1992, 162; Smith, *The Ballpark Book*, 256.

270. Ritter, 188–189; Smith, *The Ballpark Book*, 289–290.

271. Ibid., 22–29.

272. Burk, *Much More Than a Game*, 69–74; Gilbert, Bill. *They Also Served: Baseball and the Home Front, 1941–1945*. New York: Crown, 1992; Kashatus, William C. *One-Armed Wonder Pete Gray: Wartime Baseball and the American Dream*. Jefferson, N.C.: McFarland, 1995; Okrent, et al., 216–221; Rossi, 142–143; Ward, et al., 275–279, 283–284.

Chapter 6

273. In recent years, a number of excellent books have been published about black baseball and the Negro Leagues, including Bruce, Janet. *The Kansas City Monarchs: Champions of Black Baseball*. Lawrence, Kan.: University of Kansas Press, 1985; Debono, Paul. *The Indianapolis ABCs*. Jefferson, N.C.: McFarland, 1997; Holway, John B. *Blackball Stars: Negro League Pioneers*. Westport, Ct.: Meckler Books, 1988; Holway, John B. *Black Diamonds: Life in the Negro Leagues from the Men Who Lived It*. Westport, Ct.: Meckler Books, 1989; Holway, John B. *Josh and Satch: The Life and Times of Josh Gibson and Satchel Paige*. Westport, Ct.: Meckler Books, 1991; Holway, John B. *The Complete Book of Baseball's Negro Leagues: The Other Half of Baseball History*. Fern Park, Fl.: Hastings House, 2001; Kelley, Brent. *The Negro Leagues Revisited: Conversations with 66 More Baseball Heroes*. Jefferson, N.C.: McFarland, 2000; Kelley, Brent. *Voices from the Negro Leagues: Conversations with 52 Baseball Standouts of the Period 1924–1960*. Jefferson, N.C.: McFarland, 1998; Paige, Leroy "Satchel" as told to Lebovitz, Hal. *Satchel Paige's Own Story*. Westport, Ct.: Meckler Books, 1948; Peterson, Robert. *Only the Ball Was White: A History of Legendary Black Players and All-Black Professional Teams*. New York: Oxford University Press, 1970; Ribowsky, Mark. *A Complete History of the Negro Leagues: 1884 to 1955*. Secaucus, N.J.: Citadel Press, 1995; Rogosin, Donn. *Invisible Men: Life in Baseball's Negro Leagues*. New York: Atheneum, 1983; Tygiel, *Past Time*, 116–143.

274. Holway, *The Complete Book of Baseball's Negro Leagues*, 16; Ribowsky,

12–15.; Ward, et al., 40. Detailed discussions of early black baseball can be found in Peterson, 16–72; Ribowsky, 10–40; and Seymour, *Baseball: The People's Game,* 531–609.

275. Holway, *Blackball* Stars, 1–2; Holway, *The Complete Book of Baseball's Negro Leagues,* 16; Peterson, 18; Tygiel, Jules. *Baseball's Great Experiment: Jackie Robinson and His Legacy.* New York: Oxford University Press, 1983, 10–12.

276. Holway, *The Complete Book of Baseball's Negro Leagues,* 17; Peterson, 22; Tygiel, *Baseball's Great Experiment,* 13; Ribowsky, 18–19.

277. Holway, *The Complete Book of Baseball's Negro Leagues,* 22–25.

278. Holway, *The Complete Book of Baseball's Negro Leagues,* 23; Peterson, 28; Ribowsky, 32; Tygiel, *Baseball's Great Experiment,* 14.

279. Holway, *The Complete Book of Baseball's Negro Leagues,* 18.

280. Ibid., 26–136.

281. Ibid., 104.

282. Ibid., 21.

283. Ibid.

284. Ibid., 29–31.

285. Whitehead, Charles E. *A Man and His Diamonds: A Story of the Great Andrew (Rube) Foster, the Outstanding Team He Owned and Managed and the Superb League He Founded and Commissioned.* New York: Vantage, 1980.

286. Alexander, *Our Game,* 153–154; James, *The New Bill James Historical Baseball Abstract,* 166–167; Holway, *Blackball Stars,* 8–35; Peterson, 103–115; Ribowsky, 50–60.

287. Holway, *The Complete Book of Baseball's Negro Leagues,* 153; Ribowsky 66–67; Rogosin, 80, 83.

288. Alexander, *Our Game,* 154; Holway, *Blackball Stars,* 21; Holway, *The Complete Book of Baseball's Negro Leagues,* 139; Ribowsky, 100–106; Tygiel, *Baseball's Great Experiment,* 16–17.

289. Holway, *Blackball Stars,* 21; Holway, *The Complete Book of Baseball's Negro Leagues,* 139; Peterson, 103–115; Ribowsky, 50–60; Rossi, 109–143; Tygiel, *Past Time,* 116–143; White, 127–159.

290. Alexander, *Our Game,* 154–155; Holway, *The Complete Book of Baseball's Negro Leagues,* 175, 215.

291. Holway, *The Complete Book of Baseball's Negro Leagues,* 271–272.

292. Holway, *The Complete Book of Baseball's Negro Leagues,* 258; Ribowsky, 120–130.

293. Alexander, *Our Game,* 178–186; James, *The New Bill James Historical Baseball Abstract,* 167–168.

294. Holway, *The Complete Book of Baseball's Negro Leagues,* 257–258.

295. Holway, *The Complete Book of Baseball's Negro Leagues,* 276; Holway, *Blackball Stars,* 299–326; Ribowsky, 157–171; Rogosin, 14–17.

296. Holway, *The Complete Book of Baseball's Negro Leagues,* 299; Ribowsky, 157–171; Rogosin, 104–109.

297. Peterson, 80–102; Ribowsky, 172–204.

298. Rogosin, 25–26.

299. Rogosin, 118–151.

300. Ibid., 86–91.

301. The statistics used in this chapter are taken from the Statistical Appendix to Holway, *The Complete Book of Baseball's Negro Leagues.*

302. James, *The New Bill James Historical Baseball Abstract,* 189; Holway, *Blackball Stars,* 96–124; Peterson, 241–243.

303. Brashler, William. *Josh Gibson: A Life In the Negro Leagues.* Chicago: Ivan R. Dee, 1978; Holway, *Josh and Satch,* 190–191; Peterson, 158–170.

304. Peterson, 225–226.

305. Holway, *Blackball Stars,* 36–49; Peterson, 74–79.

306. James, *The New Bill James Historical Baseball Abstract,* 186; Holway, *Blackball Stars,* 36–49.

307. James, *The New Bill James Historical Baseball Abstract,* 180–191; Holway, *Blackball Stars;* Peterson, 207–250.

308. Holway, *Josh and Satch;* Paige.

309. Holway, *Blackball Stars;* Peterson, 209–221.

310. *The Sporting News,* March 3, 1948.

311. Koppett, 222; Veeck, Bill with Linn, Ed. *Veeck—As in Wreck: The Autobiography of Bill Veeck.* Evanston, Ill.: Holtzman Press, 1962, 170–171.

312. Ward, et al., 283.

313. Ibid.

314. Holtzman, 67–79; Ward, et al., 284.

315. Burk, *Much More Than a Game,* 75–104.

Chapter 7

316. A number of books provide a detailed analysis of Jackie Robinson's integration of Major League Baseball. The interested fan should read Barber, Red. *1947: When All Hell Broke Loose in Baseball.* Garden City, N.Y.: Doubleday, 1982; Falkner, David. *Great Time Coming: The Life of Jackie Robinson from Baseball to Birmingham.* New York: Simon & Schuster, 1995; Frommer, Harvey. *Rickey and Robinson: The Men Who Broke Baseball's Color Barrier.* New York: Macmillan, 1982; Lipman, David. *Mr. Baseball: The Story of Branch Rickey.* New York: 1966; Marvin, Arthur. *Branch Rickey: American in Action.* Boston: 1957; Polner, Murray. *Branch Rickey: A Biography.* New York: Atheneum, 1982; Robinson, Jackie and Duckett, Alfred. *I Never Had It Made.* New York: G.P. Putnam's, 1972; Tygiel, Jules. *Baseball's Great Experiment: Jackie Robinson and His Legacy.* New York: Oxford University Press, 1983.

317. Tygiel, *Baseball's Great Experiment,* 52; Ward, et al., 129.

318. Tygiel, *Baseball's Great Experiment,* 48.

319. Alexander, *Our Game,* 198; Tygiel, *Baseball's Great Experiment,* 47, 56–59, 68–70.

320. Tygiel, *Baseball's Great Experiment,* 48, 54–59.

321. Ibid., 58.

322. Ibid., 58–59.
323. Falkner, 106–108, 110–112; Tygiel, *Baseball's Great Experiment*, 65–67.
324. Falkner, 112–113; Tygiel, *Baseball's Great Experiment*, 69.
325. Falkner, 112–113; Tygiel, *Baseball's Great Experiment*, 57–58.
326. Falkner, 115; Tygiel, *Baseball's Great Experiment*, 69–72.
327. Tygiel, *Baseball's Great Experiment*, 120–143.
328. Ibid., 80–81.
329. Giglio, 152–153; Koppett, 223.
330. Giglio, 149; Koppett, 223.
331. Ibid.
332. Koppett, 223; Tygiel, *Baseball's Great Experiment*, 168–176.
333. *New York Times*, April 16, 1947.
334. Koppett, 223; Tygiel, *Baseball's Great Experiment*, 186.
335. Giglio, 150–159; Tygiel, *Baseball's Great Experiment*, 185–188.
336. Robinson, 64; Tygiel, *Baseball's Great Experiment*, 184.
337. Tygiel, *Baseball's Great Experiment*, 322.
338. Ibid., 322–323.
339. Burk, *Much More Than a Game*, 130.
340. Ibid., 131.
341. For chronicles of Latin influences in Major League Baseball, read Bjarkman, Peter C. *Baseball With a Latin Beat*. Jefferson, N.C.: McFarland, 1994; Regalado, Samuel O. *Viva Baseball!: Latin Major Leaguers and Their Special Hunger.* Urbana, Ill.: University of Illinois Press, 1998.
342. Alexander, *Our Game*, 235; Burk, *Much More Than a Game*, 131.
343. Ibid., 132.
344. Undated *Sporting News* clipping in Tygiel, *Baseball's Great Experiment*, 344.

Chapter 8

345. McCullough, David. *Truman*. New York: Simon & Schuster, 1992, 468–476, 531–532.
346. Ibid., 473–476, 532.
347. Ibid., 586–588, 642–643.
348. Ibid., 587, 639, 631, 667.
349. Thorn, et al., *Total Baseball*, 107.
350. Ibid.
351. Ibid.
352. Burk, *Much More Than a Game*, 108–109; Thorn, et al., *Total Baseball*, 107.
353. Thorn, et al., *Total Baseball*, 107–108.
354. Alexander, *Our Game*, 203–204; Burk, *Much More Than a Game*, 85–86, 104–106; Giglio, 127–134; Koppett, 226–227; Rossi, 150–152.
355. Giglio, 128; Lowenfish, 140.

356. Alexander, *Our Game,* 204.

357. Burk, *Much More Than a Game,* 105–106; Rossi, 151–152; White, 292–295.

358. Abrams, *Legal Bases,* 60–61; Alexander, *Our Game,* 204; Lowenfish, 153–168.

359. 346 U.S. 356 (1953).

360. 259 U.S. 200 (1922).

361. Lowenfish, 186–187; White, 295–299.

362. Abrams, *Legal Bases,* 61–62; Lowenfish, 186.

363. Holtzman, 43–84; Koppett, 224–226.

364. Holtzman, 85–120; Koppett, 229–230.

365. Alexander, *Our Game,* 203; Burk, *Much More Than a Game,* 87–95; Helyar, 10–11; Koppett, 229; Lowenfish, 140–147; Rossi, 152–153.

366. Lowenfish, 141.

367. Lowenfish, 146, 150.

368. Alexander, *Our Game,* 203; Helyar, 11; Koppett, 229; Lowenfish, 149.

369. For excellent accounts of the life and career of Stengel, the interested fan should read Allen, Maury. *You Could Look It Up: The Life of Casey Stengel.* New York: Times Books, 1979; Creamer, Robert W. *Stengel: His Life and Times.* New York: Simon & Schuster, 1984; and Durso, Joseph. *Casey: The Life and Legend of Charles Dillon Stengel.* Englewood Cliffs, N.J.: Prentice-Hall, 1967.

370. For detailed accounts of Major League Baseball in New York during this period, the interested fan should read Allen, Lee. *The Giants and the Dodgers: The Fabulous Story of Baseball's Fiercest Period.* New York: G.P. Putnam's, 1964; Allen, Maury. *The Yankees: Four Fabulous Eras of Baseball's Most Famous Team.* New York: Random House, 1980; Ford, Whitey, Mantle, Mickey, and Durso, Joseph. *Whitey and Mickey: An Autobiography of the Yankee Years.* New York: Viking, 1977; Frommer, Harvey. *New York City Baseball: The Last Golden Age, 1947–1957.* New York: Macmillan, 1980; Golenbock, Peter. *Bums: An Oral History of the Brooklyn Dodgers.* New York: G.P. Putnam's, 1984; Golenbock, Peter. *Dynasty: The New York Yankees, 1949–1964.* Englewood Cliffs, N.J.: Prentice-Hall, 1975; Halberstam, David. *The Summer of '49.* New York: William Morrow, 1989; Halberstam, David. *October 1964.* New York: Villard, 1994; Honig, Donald. *Baseball in the '50s: A Decade of Transition.* New York: Macmillan, 1987; Kahn, Roger. *The Era: 1947–1957— When the Yankees, the Giants and the Dodgers Ruled the World.* New York: Ticknor & Fields, 1993; Oakley, J. Ronald. *Baseball's Last Golden Age, 1946–1960.* Jefferson, N.C.: McFarland, 1994; Prince, Carl. *Brooklyn's Dodgers: The Bums, the Borough, and the Best of Baseball, 1947–1957.* New York: Oxford University Press, 1996; Rosenthal, Harold. *The Ten Best Years of Baseball: An Informal History of the Fifties.* Chicago: Contemporary Books, 1979; Tygiel, *Past Time,* 144–164.

371. Thorn, et al., *Total Baseball,* 107.

372. Ibid.

373. Rossi, 159–160; Smith, *The Ballpark Book,* 17.

374. Thorn, et al., *Total Baseball,* 107.

375. Helyar, 233–235; Thorn, et al., *Total Baseball*, 107; Veeck, *Veeck—As in Wreck*, 83–196.

376. Alexander, *Our Game*, 226–227; Koppett, 233–235.

377. White, 303–315; Tygiel, *Past Time*, 165–181.

378. Alexander, *Our Game*, 227–228.

379. Rossi, 160–161; Thorn, et al., *Total Baseball*, 107; Tygiel, *Past Time*, 165–174; White, 311–312.

380. Thorn, et al., *Total Baseball*, 107.

381. Alexander, *Our Game*, 227.

382. Alexander, *Our Game*, 228; Holtzman, 114; Veeck, 213–229.

383. Helyar, 235; Rossi, 161; Thorn, et al., *Total Baseball*, 107; Tygiel, *Past Time*, 175–177; White, 311–312.

384. Rossi, 161–162; Thorn, et al., *Total Baseball*, 108; Tygiel, *Past Time*, 177–178; White, 311–314.

385. Tygiel, *Past Time*, 178; White, 313–314.

386. Alexander, *Our Game*, 231; Tygiel, *Past Time*, 178–180.

387. Helyar, 53; Tygiel, *Past Time*, 178–180.

388. Helyar, 53–59; Rossi, 162–165; White, 314–315.

389. Tygiel, *Past Time*, 167–170.

390. Alexander, *Our Game*, 238–239; Helyar, 57–59; Rossi, 164–165.

391. Helyar, 58.

392. Thorn, et al., *Total Baseball*, 107; Tygiel, *Past Time*, 178–186.

393. Alexander, *Our Game*, 242–243.

394. Thorn, et al., *Total Baseball*, 107.

395. Ibid.

396. United States Census Bureau, Population Estimates Program, Population Division, Historical Population Estimates: July 1, 1900 to July 1, 1999; United States Census Bureau, Population Division, Population of the 100 Largest Cities and Other Urban Places in the United States: 1790 to 1990.

397. Ibid.

398. Lowenfish, 171–181; 189–190; White, 295–308.

399. For a complete account of Stengel's 45-minute rambling and contorted congressional testimony, *see* Einstein, Charles (ed.), *The Baseball Reader: Favorites from the Fireside Book of Baseball*. New York: McGraw-Hill, 1986. For an abbreviated version, *see* Holtzman, 108–112.

400. Koppett, 272; Tygiel, *Past Time*, 186..

401. Alexander, *Our Game*, 246–247; Tygiel, *Past Time*, 186–187.

402. Koppett, 274–275.

403. Rossi, 170; Tygiel, *Past Time*, 187–189.

404. Tygiel, *Past Time*, 189–194.

405. Alexander, *Our Game*, 266; Koppett, 296; Tygiel, *Past Time*, 190.

406. Thorn, et al., *Total Baseball*, 107.

407. Alexander, *Our Game*, 266.

408. Koppett, 297–300; Tygiel, *Past Time*, 190.

409. Alexander, *Our Game*, 266; Koppett, 277–280; Tygiel, *Past Time*, 193.

410. Koppett, 300.

411. Koppett, 300; Tygiel, *Past Time,* 194–197.

412. Ibid.

413. Thorn, et al., *Total Baseball,* 107–108.

414. Mays, Willie with Einstein, Charles. *Born to Play Ball.* New York: G.P. Putnam's, 1955; Mays, Willie with Sahadi, Lou. *Say Hey: The Autobiography of Willie Mays.* New York: Simon & Schuster, 1988.

415. Aaron, Hank with Wheeler, Lonnie. *I Had Hammer: The Hank Aaron Story.* New York: Harper Collins, 1991.

416. Campanella, Roy. *It's Good to Be Alive.* Boston: Little, Brown, 1959.

417. Ford, Whitey, Mantle, Mickey, and Durso, Joseph. *Whitey and Mickey: An Autobiography of the Yankee Years.* New York: Viking, 1977; Gluck, Herb. *The Mick, an American Hero: The Legend and the Glory.* New York: Jove, 1985; Mantle, Merlyn, Mantle, Mickey Jr., Mantle, David, and Mantle, Dan. *A Hero All His Life.* New York: Harper Collins, 1996; Mantle, Mickey and Pepe, Phil. *My Favorite Summer: 1956.* New York, Doubleday, 1991.

418. Gruver, Edward. *Koufax.* New York: Taylor Publishing, 2000.

419. Gibson, Bob with Pepe, Phil. *From Ghetto to Glory: The Story of Bob Gibson.* Englewood Cliffs, N.J.: Prentice-Hall, 1968; Gibson, Bob with Wheeler, Lonnie. *Stranger to the Game: The Autobiography of Bob Gibson.* New York: Penguin, 1994.

420. Scully, Gerald W. *The Business of Major League Baseball.* Chicago: University of Chicago Press, 1898, 44–97; Wright, Russell O. *A Tale of Two Leagues. How Baseball Changed as the Rules, Ball, Franchises, Stadiums and Players Changed, 1900–1998.* Jefferson, N.C.: McFarland, 1999, 9.

421. Helyar, 78.

422. Scully, *The Business of Major League Baseball,* 54–56.

423. Thorn, *Total Baseball,* 107.

424. Alexander, *Our Game,* 264; Burk, *Much More Than a Game,* 139; Thorn, et al., *Total Baseball,* 108.

425. Alexander, *Our Game,* 270; Burk, *Much More Than a Game,* 139.

426. Thorn, et al., *Total Baseball,* 107–108.

427. Burk, *Much More Than a Game,* 139; Rossi, 181.

428. Burk, *Much More Than a Game,* 109.

429. Ibid.

430. Burk, *Much More Than a Game,* 117–119; Lowenfish, 183–184.

431. Burk, *Much More Than a Game,* 119; Lowenfish, 184.

432. Burk, *Much More Than a Game,* 121; Helyar, 14; Lowenfish, 188.

433. Burk, *Much More Than a Game,* 120; Lowenfish, 188.

434. Helyar, 14; Lowenfish, 190.

435. Light, 639–640.

436. Light, 639–640; Scully, *The Business of Major League Baseball,* 152.

437. Koppett, 310

438. Alexander, *Our Game,* 261; Burk, *Much More Than a Game,* 149; Helyar, 24; Lowenfish, 197–199.

439. Lowenfish, 198.

440. Helyar, 24.

441. Helyar, 24; Lowenfish, 198.

442. 347 U.S. 483 (1954).

443. 163 U.S. 537 (1896).

444. Ambrose, Stephen E. *Eisenhower: The President.* New York: Simon & Schuster, 1984, 497–499; Caro, Robert A. *The Years of Lyndon Johnson: The Means of Ascent.* New York: Alfred A. Knopf, 1990, xvi–xxxiv, 125, 196; Dalek, Robert. *Flawed Giant: Lyndon Johnson and His Times: 1961–1973.* Oxford University Press, 1998, 25–38, 111–121, 203–211, 221–226, 323–328, 517–533.

445. Karnow, Stanley. *Vietnam: A History: The First Complete Account of Vietnam at War.* New York: Viking Press, 1983, 682.

446. United States National Park Service. Vietnam Veterans Memorial.

447. Karnow, 654, 684.

Chapter 9

448. Gruver, *Koufax,* 212.

449. Allen, Dick and Whitaker, Tim. *Crash: The Life and Times of Dick Allen.* New York: Ticknor & Fields, 1989, 185.

450. Allen, *Crash,* 48.

451. Ibid., 12.

452. Ibid., 17.

453. Ibid., 2.

454. Ibid., 38.

455. Ibid., 69.

456. Ibid., 6–8.

457. Ibid., 64–66.

458. Ibid., 74.

459. Ibid., 187.

460. *Los Angeles Times,* October 11, 1969.

461. Allen, *Crash,* 119.

462. Flood, Curt and Cater, Richard. *Curt Flood: The Way It Is.* New York: Trident Press, 1970, 38.

463. Helyar, 97.

464. Flood, 139, 172; Helyar, 102–103; Miller, 172.

465. Flood, 172–175, 228–236; Helyar, 99–101; Lowenfish, 208.

466. Flood, 185; Helyar, 103.

467. Flood, 194–195.

468. Burk, *Much More Than a Game,* 162–163; Flood, 17, 190–191, 193; Helyar, 103.

469. Flood, 17; Miller, 185.

470. Miller, 185–186.

471. Ibid., 180–184.

472. Flood, 194; Helyar, 103; Miller, 187–189.

473. Ward, et al., 411.

474. Flood, 18.

475. Kuhn, Bowie. *Hardball: The Education of a Baseball Commissioner.* Lincoln, Neb.: University of Nebraska Press, 1987, 37.

476. Flood, 16–17.

477. Report of Independent Members, Blue Ribbon Panel on Baseball Economics, July 2000.

478. Miller, 197.

479. Ibid., 200.

480. Ward, et al., 250.

481. Ibid., 423.

482. Miller, 239.

483. Flood, 16.

484. Bouton, Jim. *Ball Four.* New York: Macmillan, 1970.

485. Flood, 143.

486. 15 U.S.C. §§ 1–6.

487. 15 U.S.C. §§ 15–16.

488. 259 U.S. 200 (1922).

489. 346 U.S. 356 (1953).

490. Burk, *Much More Than a Game,* 177–179.

491. *Flood v. Kuhn,* 407 U.S. 258 (1972).

492. Ibid.

493. 347 U.S. 483 (1954).

494. 407 U.S. 258 (1972).

495. 15 U.S.C. § 27a (1998).

496. 15 U.S.C. §§ 12–27 (1994); 29 U.S.C. § 52 (1994).

497. Flood, 208–210.

498. Flood, 210–215; Lowenfish, 213; Miller, 200–202.

499. Allen, *Crash,* 186.

500. James, *The New Bill James Historical Baseball Abstract,* 438.

501. Miller, 103.

502. *Los Angeles Times,* October 11, 1969.

503. Ibid.

504. *San Francisco Examiner,* October 5, 1974.

505. *Los Angeles Herald-Examiner,* August 5, 1977.

Chapter 10

506. Abrams, *The Money Pitch,* 14; Alexander, *Our Game,* 53; Burk, *Never Just a Game,* 94–98; DiSalvatore, 175–178; Koppett, 55–56; Rossi, 44; Seymour, *Baseball: The Early Years,* 221–222.

507. A brief history of the reserve system can be found in Seymour, *Baseball: The Early Years,* 104–115.

508. Abrams, *The Money Pitch,* 14; Burk, *Never Just a Game,* 104–106; DiSalvatore, 269–321; Koppett, 59; Lowenfish, 35; Rossi, 45–46; Seymour, *Baseball: The Early Years,* 222–239.

509. Seymour, *Baseball: The Golden Years,* 169–195.

510. Burk, *Much More Than a Game,* 117–121; Lowenfish, 183–188.

511. Burk, *Much More Than a Game,* 121; Lowenfish, 188; Miller, 8.

512. Burk, *Much More Than a Game,* 112; Helyar, 15; Miller, 8.

513. Burk, *Much More Than a Game,* 146.

514. Rossi, 185.

515. Burk, *Much More Than a Game,* 128.

516. Burk, *Much More Than a Game,* 146; Helyar, 21–22; Lowenfish, 195–196; Miller, 3–10.

517. Burk, *Much More Than a Game,* 147–148; Helyar, 18–22; Miller, 19–32.

518. Burk, *Much More Than a Game,* 148–151; Helyar, 25; Miller, 4–10, 33–61.

519. Helyar, 27.

520. Burk, *Much More Than a Game,* 151–152; Helyar, 25; Lowenfish, 191–192; Miller, 91–92, 143.

521. Miller, 92.

522. Burk, *Much More Than a Game,* 152; Miller, 92, 143, 147.

523. Helyar, 26; Lowenfish, 200–201; Miller, 69, 91.

524. Lowenfish, 199; Miller, 154.

525. Helyar, 32; Burk, *Much More Than a Game,* 151; Lowenfish, 201; Miller, 53.

526. Burk, *Much More Than a Game,* 154; Helyar, 28–29; Lowenfish, 199.

527. Helyar, 29; Miller, 156–157.

528. Helyar, 29; Miller, 157.

529. Helyar, 29.

530. Ibid., 80.

531. Burk, *Much More Than a Game,* 156; Helyar, 30–31.

532. Miller, 80.

533. Burk, *Much More Than a Game,* 157; Helyar, 38.

534. Helyar, 84, 86–87; 91–95.

535. Burk, *Much More Than a Game,* 157–158; Helyar, 27, 84; Koppett, 314.

536. Helyar, 107–109; Koppett, 335; Lowenfish, 211; Miller, 206, 213–215.

537. Burk, *Much More Than a Game,* 165.

538. Alexander, *Our Game,* 280; Burk, *Much More Than a Game,* 173–175; Helyar, 112; Miller, 210–212.

539. Burk, *Much More Than a Game,* 174; Helyar, 113; Miller, 205.

540. Burk, *Much More Than a Game,* 175–177; Helyar, 114–122; Koppett, 336–337; Lowenfish, 215–217.

541. Alexander, *Our Game,* 280–281; Burk, *Much More Than a Game,* 177; Helyar, 122; Koppett, 337; Miller, 221.

542. Helyar, 119.

543. Burk, *Much More Than a Game,* 183–187; Helyar, 132.

544. Alexander, *Our Game,* 281; Lowenfish, 217–218; Miller, 109.

545. Helyar, 151; Koppett, 357.

546. Helyar, 173; Holtzman, 164–167.

547. Alexander, *Our Game,* 281; Koppett, 357; Miller, 109.

548. Helyar, 152.

549. Ibid.

550. Helyar, 173, 197; Miller, 370.

551. Alexander, *Our Game,* 281; Koppett, 338.

552. Koppett, 358.

553. Helyar, 124, 161; Holtzman, 157.

554. Burk, *Much More Than a Game,* 180; Helyar, 123; Holtzman, 157–158; Lowenfish, 219; Miller, 240.

555. Burk, *Much More Than a Game,* 180; Helyar, 124–126; Holtzman, 157–158; Koppett, 359; Lowenfish, 219; Miller, 240.

556. Burk, *Much More Than a Game,* 188; Helyar, 123–126; Holtzman, 158; Koppett, 359; Miller, 240.

557. Burk, *Much More Than a Game,* 188; Helyar, 128; Koppett, 359; Miller, 240–241.

558. Burk, *Much More Than a Game,* 188; Helyar, 128–129; Holtzman, 158.

559. Burk, *Much More Than a Game,* 188–189; Helyar, 137; Miller, 227–230.

560. Burk, *Much More Than a Game,* 188–190; Helyar, 137–138; Miller, 111–114, 227–230.

561. Koppett, 359.

562. Burk, *Much More Than a Game,* 191; Helyar, 140.

563. Burk, *Much More Than a Game,* 191–193; Helyar, 140–150.

564. Alexander, *Our Game,* 296; Burk, *Much More Than a Game,* 192; Helyar, 148.

565. Helyar, 149.

566. Burk, *Much More Than a Game,* 193; Helyar, 154–155; Holtzman, 158–159.

567. Helyar, 155.

568. Burk, *Much More Than a Game,* 193; Helyar, 159; Koppett, 361.

569. Helyar, 159; Burk, *Much More Than a Game,* 193–195; Holtzman, 159; Lowenfish, 15–20; Miller, 114–116, 245.

570. Burk, *Much More Than a Game,* 195; Helyar, 158–160. Holtzman, 160; Miller, 245.

571. Burk, *Much More Than a Game,* 196; Holtzman, 159; Koppett, 361; Miller, 244.

572. Helyar, 124; Miller, 246.

573. Helyar, 166–167; Miller, 247, 249.

574. Burk, *Much More Than a Game,* 198; Helyar, 167; Koppett, 362.

575. Alexander, *Our Game,* 297; Burk, *Much More Than a Game,* 199; Helyar, 169; Koppett, 362; Miller, 250.

576. Burk, *Much More Than a Game,* 199; Helyar, 169; Miller, 250.

577. Burk, *Much More Than a Game,* 198; Miller, 255.

578. Burk, *Much More Than a Game,* 199; Holtzman, 161; Miller, 251, 254.

579. Holtzman, 161; Miller, 251.

580. Alexander, *Our Game,* 297; Burk, *Much More Than a Game,* 200.

581. Helyar, 171; Holtzman, 162; Miller, 259.

582. Helyar, 173; Holtzman, 162; Miller, 259.

583. Helyar, 171–173; Holtzman, 162; Miller, 259.

584. Alexander, *Our Game,* 297; Helyar, 173–174; Holtzman, 162–173; Miller, 258–264.

585. Alexander, *Our Game,* 297–298; Burk, *Much More Than a Game,* 202–203.

586. Burk, *Much More Than a Game,* 205–206; Holtzman, 164; Koppett, 368–369; Miller, 267.

587. Abrams, *The Money Pitch,* 29; Burk, *Much More Than a Game,* 206; Helyar, 337; Holtzman, 225; Koppett, 414.

588. Abrams, *The Money Pitch,* 29; Holtzman, 225.

589. Lowenfish, 263.

590. Helyar, 198–215.

591. Burk, *Much More Than a Game,* 208; Holtzman, 224.

592. Burk, *Much More Than a Game,* 208; Helyar, 221; Holtzman, 224; Miller, 286, 290.

593. Helyar, 217–219.

594. Helyar, 221; Holtzman, 224.

595. Helyar, 221; Miller, 287–288.

596. Burk, *Much More Than a Game,* 208.

597. Alexander, *Our Game,* 313.

598. Burk, *Much More Than a Game,* 223; Koppett, 370; Miller, 296.

599. Koppett, 370; Miller, 297.

600. Holtzman, 224.

601. Burk, *Much More Than a Game,* 224; Helyar, 224–225; Miller, 120.

602. Burk, *Much More Than a Game,* 224.

603. Burk, *Much More Than a Game,* 226; Lowenfish, 230–231.

604. Burk, *Much More Than a Game,* 226–227; Lowenfish, 230; Miller, 290–291.

605. Helyar, 228; Lowenfish, 230–231.

606. Burk, *Much More Than a Game,* 228; Helyar, 261; Lowenfish, 239–240; Miller, 295.

607. Koppett, 371.

608. Alexander, *Our Game,* 313–314; Koppett, 386–387.

609. Koppett, 386.

610. Miller, 311.

611. Helyar, 262.

612. Burk, *Much More Than a Game,* 229; Helyar, 263; Koppett, 387; Miller, 288.

613. Koppett, 388; Miller, 288.

614. Koppett, 388; Miller, 298.

615. Burke, *Much More Than a Game,* 229–230; Helyar, 263; Koppett, 388; Miller, 288–290.

616. Koppett, 388; Miller, 298.

617. Miller, 299.

618. Helyar, 262.

619. Helyar, 286; Koppett, 391–392.

620. Miller, 313–314.

621. Koppett, 392.

622. Burk, *Much More Than a Game*, 234; Helyar, 288; Miller, 318.

623. Light, 642; Miller, 318.

624. Thorn, et al., *Total Baseball*, 108–109.

625. Helyar, 325; Koppett, 413.

626. Burk, *Much More Than a Game*, 235–236; Helyar, 322–323; Koppett, 412–413.

627. Burk, *Much More Than a Game*, 235–237; Helyar, 323–324; Koppett, 413; Miller, 320–335.

628. Miller, 335.

629. Helyar, 327–328; Koppett, 414.

630. Helyar, 327; Koppett, 414.

631. Helyar, 327–329; Koppett, 414.

632. Helyar, 329; Koppett, 414; Lowenfish, 258–259.

633. Lowenfish, 263; Koppett, 414–415.

634. Abrams, *The Money Pitch*, 143.

635. Light, 642.

636. Helyar, 299.

637. Abrams, *The Money Pitch*, 154; Burk, *Much More Than a Game*, 241; Helyar, 303–304.

638. Helyar, 305.

639. Ibid., 337.

640. Ibid., 318–319.

641. Helyar, 331; Holtzman, 222.

642. Helyar, 333; Holtzman, 221.

643. Helyar, 334–363; Holtzman, 226–228.

644. Sands, Jack and Gammons, Peter. *Coming Apart at the Seams. How Baseball Owners, Players & Television Executives Have Led Our National Pastime to the Brink of Disaster.* New York: Macmillan, 1993, 64–82.

645. Helyar, 337; Holtzman, 225; Koppett, 414–415; Lowenfish, 263.

646. Burk, *Much More Than a Game*, 250–258; Holtzman, 229; Koppett, 415.

647. Helyar, 360; Holtzman, 229; Koppett, 415.

648. Helyar, 346–347, 360–361; Koppett, 416; Sands, 64–82.

649. Helyar, 363; Holtzman, 229.

650. Lowenfish, 268–269; Koppett, 416.

651. Burk, *Much More Than a Game*, 260; Holtzman, 229; Koppett, 416.

652. Koppett, 416.

653. Helyar, 414; Holtzman, 263; Koppett, 416.

654. Alexander, *Our Game*, 359; Helyar, 416; Koppett, 417; Lowenfish, 274.

655. Alexander, *Our Game*, 359; Helyar, 416–424; Holtzman, 264–265; Koppett, 417; Lowenfish, 276.

656. Koppett, 417.

657. Helyar, 413; Light, 640.

658. Light, 640.

659. Helyar, 455.

660. Ibid., 458–461, 491.

661. Ibid.

662. Helyar, 461, 491; Light, 642.

663. Helyar, 455, 493–498, 506–517; Koppett, 418.

664. Helyar, 527–534; Koppett, 418.

665. Helyar, 541–545.

666. Ibid., 546.

667. Holtzman, 274; Koppett, 419.

668. Koppett, 419.

669. Ibid.

670. Burk, *More Than Just a Game*, 288; Holtzman, 274; Koppett, 419.

671. Koppett, 419.

672. Burk, *More Than Just a Game*, 288; Koppett, 420.

673. Burk, *Much More Than a Game*, 290; Holtzman, 275; Koppett, 420.

674. Koppett, 420.

675. Ibid.

676. Burk, *Much More Than a Game*, 291; Holtzman, 279; Koppett, 421.

677. Holtzman, 279; Koppett, 421.

678. Burk, *Much More Than a Game*, 292; Holtzman, 280; Koppett, 463.

679. Holtzman, 279; Koppett, 463.

680. Ibid.

681. Holtzman, 279, 282; Koppett, 464–465.

682. Holtzman, 282; Koppett, 467.

683. Burk, *Much More Than a Game*, 295–298; Holtzman, 283; Koppett, 467.

684. In the Curt Flood Act of 1998, the United States Congress repealed the judicially created antitrust exemption for baseball, but only with respect to labor relations "directly relating to or affecting major league baseball players." 15 U.S.C. § 27a (1998); amending 15 U.S.C. §§ 12–27 (1994) and 29 U.S.C. § 52 (1994). The Curt Flood Act specifically excludes from its coverage minor league baseball, the amateur draft, relations between the major and minor leagues, franchise relocations, intellectual property, broadcasting rights, and major league umpires, all of which continue to be exempted from the application of the federal antitrust laws.

Chapter 11

685. Thorn, et al., *Total Baseball*, 108.

686. Ibid.

687. Ibid., 109.

688. Ibid.

689. Ibid.

690. Helyar, 328; Miller, 318; Light, 641–642.
691. Helyar, 461, 491; Light, 641–642.
692. Miller, 62.

Chapter 12

693. Smith, *The Ballpark Book*, 8, 11.
694. Rossi, 41; Smith, *The Ballpark Book*, 11–12.
695. Koppett, 100–101, 116, 160; Rossi, 76–77; Smith, *The Ballpark Book*, 11–14.
696. Rossi, 159–160; White, 307.
697. Helyar, 67–71; Ward, et al., 386.
698. Helyar, 71; Ward, et al., 386.
699. Rossi, 172–173.
700. Helyar, 75. Yellow baseballs actually were used on an experimental basis in several Major League games in the late 1930s.
701. Helyar, 74–75.
702. Alexander, *Our Game*, 332.
703. Helyar, 75.
704. Ibid.
705. Alexander, *Our Game*, 289.
706. Ibid., 290.
707. *Sports Illustrated*, December 24, 2001.
708. Bouton, Jim. *Ball Four*. New York: Macmillan, 1970.
709. Flood, Curt and Carter, Richard. *Curt Flood: The Way It Is*. New York: Trident Press, 1970.
710. Alexander, *Our Game*, 353.
711. Alexander, *Our Game*, 327–328; Helyar, 342.
712. Alexander, *Our Game*, 326–327.
713. Alexander, *Our Game*, 329; Helyar, 342.
714. Melville, 59–61.
715. Melville, 92–94; Koppett, 32.
716. Koppett, 75, 101–102, 143, 154; Seymour, *Baseball: The Golden Age*, 274–293; Ward, et al., 8–9, 61.
717. Burk, *Much More Than a Game*, 13; Seymour, *Baseball: The Golden Age*, 324–330.
718. Burk, *Much More Than a Game*, 13; Seymour, *Baseball: The Golden Age*, 330.
719. Alexander, *Our Game*, 143–145; Burk, *Never Just a Game*, 231; Holtzman, 37–40; Koppett, 164; Seymour, *Baseball: The Golden Age*, 382–384; Ward, et al., 182–184.
720. A more extensive discussion of commissioner Giamatti's banishment of Pete Rose can be found in Chapter 13 of this book.

Chapter 13

721. Holtzman, 9.

722. Burk, *Never Just a Game,* 142, 150; Koppett, 88–93; Rossi, 59–63. Seymour, *Baseball: The Early Years,* 307–324.

723. Holtzman, 22–23.

724. Seymour, *Baseball: The Golden Age,* 311–314.

725. Burk, *Much More Than a Game,* 10; Burk, *Never Just a Game,* 207; Holtzman, 15; Koppett, 117; Rossi, 107; White, 106.

726. Burk, *Much More Than a Game,* 10; White, 106.

727. Burk, *Never Just a Game,* 207–209; Holtzman, 20–21; Koppett, 117; Seymour, *Baseball: The Golden Age,* 212–213; Ward, et al., 123.

728. Holtzman, 22, 26–27; Seymour, *Baseball: The Golden Age,* 320.

729. Burk, *Never Just a Game,* 236; Holtzman, 28; Seymour, *Baseball: The Golden Age,* 320.

730. Holtzman, 22–27; Koppett, 141; Seymour, *Baseball: The Golden Age,* 322.

731. Burk, *Much More Than a Game,* 13; Seymour, *Baseball: The Golden Age,* 324–330.

732. Seymour, *Baseball: The Golden Age,* 330; Ward, et al., 144.

733. Burk, *Much More Than a Game,* 13; Seymour, *Baseball: The Golden Age,* 330.

734. Burk, *Much More Than a Game,* 14; Seymour, *Baseball: The Golden Age,* 389.

735. Holtzman, 35–40.

736. Melville, 92–94; Koppett, 32.

737. Koppett, 75, 101–102, 143, 154; Seymour, *Baseball: The Golden Age,* 274–293; Ward, et al., 8–9, 61.

738. Alexander, *Our Game,* 143–145; Burk, *Never Just a Game,* 231; Holtzman, 37–40; Koppett, 164; Seymour, *Baseball: The Golden Age,* 382–384; Ward, et al., 182–184.

739. Lowenfish, 110–111.

740. Burk, *Much More Than a Game,* 18; Creamer, *Babe,* 244–256; Holtzman, 36–37; Koppett, 165–166; Seymour, *Baseball: The Golden Age,* 392–393.

741. Holtzman, 41–42; Koppett, 175–177, 193; Lowenfish, 118, 121–123.

742. Burk, *Much More Than a Game,* 80; Veeck, *Veeck—As in Wreck,* 171–172.

743. Holtzman, 42; Lowenfish, 123.

744. Holtzman, 42; Koppett, 213.

745. Holtzman, 45.

746. Ibid., 46.

747. Holtzman, 45; Koppett, 213; Lowenfish, 124.

748. Lowenfish, 123–124.

749. Holtzman, 45.

750. Chandler, Albert B. *Heroes, Plain Folks and Skunks: The Life and Times of Happy Chandler.* Chicago: Bonus Books, 1989; Holtzman, 44.

751. Burk, *Much More Than a Game,* 45–46; Holtzman, 48–52; Koppett, 226–227.

752. Burk, *Much More Than a Game,* 104–107; Holtzman, 50–52; Koppett, 228.

753. Holtzman, 54.

754. Ibid., 58.

755. Holtzman, 58–66; Koppett, 225.

756. Holtzman, 53.

757. Ibid., 63.

758. Holtzman, 69; Tygiel, *Baseball's Great Experiment,* 81.

759. Holtzman, 71.

760. Ibid., 72–73.

761. Ibid., 44.

762. Ibid., 79–81.

763. Ibid., 82.

764. Ibid., 83.

765. Ibid., 86.

766. Holtzman, 87; Lowenfish, 172–173.

767. Sands, 41.

768. Holtzman, 91; Ruth, George Herman. *Babe Ruth's Own Book of Baseball.* Lincoln, Neb.: University of Nebraska Press, 1992. Reprint of 1928 edition.

769. Ibid., 98.

770. Ibid., 116–117.

771. Ibid.

772. *Veeck,* 360.

773. Ibid., 367.

774. Ibid., 367.

775. Holtzman, 118.

776. Ibid., 119.

777. Lowenfish, 199.

778. Holtzman, 125.

779. Ibid., 125.

780. Holtzman, 129.

781. Ibid., 131.

782. Ibid.

783. Burk, *Much More Than a Game,* 159; Helyar, 93.

784. Helyar, 93–94; Holtzman, 134.

785. Holtzman, 138.

786. Helyar, 105; Holtzman, 138–141, 147–150, 168, 191–194, 196–199.

787. Holtzman, 145.

788. Ibid., 153.

789. Miller, 214–215.

790. Holtzman, 153–154; Miller, 215.

791. Ibid., 160–161.

792. Helyar, 183–184; Holtzman, 171; Koppett, 373.

793. Helyar, 185–187; Holtzman, 171; Koppett, 373.
794. Helyar, 183–188; Holtzman, 171.
795. Burk, *Much More Than a Game,* 204; Helyar, 192–194; Miller, 377–378.
796. Holtzman, 170.
797. Ibid., 183.
798. Miller, 378.
799. Holtzman, 188–190.
800. Ibid., 190.
801. Ibid., 199–207.
802. Ibid., 202–206.
803. Helyar, 288.
804. Holtzman, 206.
805. Ibid., 206.
806. Ibid., 209.
807. Burk, *Much More Than a Game,* 244; Helyar, 312; Holtzman, 209.
808. Helyar, 312; Holtzman, 209.
809. Holtzman, 209; Miller, 385.
810. Helyar, 315–317.
811. Burk, *Much More Than a Game,* 254; Holtzman, 209.
812. Helyar, 321.
813. Holtzman, 212; Sands, 42.
814. Helyar, 312; Holtzman, 212–213.
815. Burk, *Much More Than a Game,* 248; Holtzman, 213–217.
816. Holtzman, 217; Sands, 81.
817. Helyar, 333; Holtzman, 221.
818. Burk, *Much More Than a Game,* 250–253; Holtzman, 220–229; Sands, 64–82.
819. Article XVIII(h) of the Major League Baseball Basic Agreement (1981).
820. Holtzman, 226; Sands, 81.
821. Helyar, 360; Holtzman, 229; Lowenfish, 268–269; Koppett, 415–416.
822. Helyar, 363; Holtzman, 230.
823. Helyar, 364; Holtzman, 231; Sands, 81.
824. Burk, *Much More Than a Game,* 260; Helyar, 382–388; Lowenfish, 270; Miller, 390; Sands, 81–91.
825. Burk, *Much More Than a Game,* 262; Helyar, 389.
826. Helyar, 390; Holtzman, 236.
827. Helyar, 389.
828. Holtzman, 242.
829. Helyar, 397–399; Holtzman, 260.
830. Helyar, 401–404; Holtzman, 247–254; Miller, 395–396.
831. Helyar, 404–405; Holtzman, 254.
832. Helyar, 405; Holtzman, 254; Miller, 397.
833. Holtzman, 256.
834. Helyar, 405; Holtzman, 255.
835. Helyar, 406; Holtzman, 255; Miller, 402.

836. Miller, 394–402.

837. Ibid., 393–394.

838. Holtzman, 257–270.

839. Burk, *Much More Than a Game,* 285–290; Holtzman, 272, 274–276; Koppett, 419–420, 456–460.

840. Burk, *Much More Than a Game,* 292; Holtzman, 280–281; Koppett, 462–463.

841. Holtzman, 282; Koppett, 464.

842. Holtzman, 274, 284.

843. Holtzman, 285; Miller, 400–411.

Chapter 14

844. Helyar, 39.

845. Ibid., 47.

846. Ibid., 48.

847. Ibid., 49.

848. Ibid.

849. Ibid., 53.

850. Ibid., 52–60.

851. Ibid., 58.

852. Ibid., 60.

853. Ibid., 58–59.

854. Ibid., 24.

855. Ibid., 61.

856. Ibid., 61.

857. Ibid., 43.

858. Ibid., 66, 364.

859. Ibid.

860. Ibid., 364.

861. Alexander, *Our Game,* 222.

862. Burk, *Much More Than a Game,* 109.

863. Helyar, 47.

864. Ibid., 47.

865. Burk, *Much More Than a Game,* 110; Helyar, 76; Lowenfish, 183.

866. Burk, *Much More Than a Game,* 110; Helyar, 76–77; Lowenfish, 183.

867. Alexander, *Our Game,* 222; Helyar, 66, 366.

868. Alexander, *Our Game,* 222; Burk, *Much More Than a Game,* 139; Helyar, 66.

869. Helyar, 66.

870. Burk, *Much More Than a Game,* 139; Helyar, 66; Koppett, 297–298.

871. Helyar, 16, 66, 366.

872. Ibid., 66, 366.

873. Ibid., 366.

874. Ibid.

875. Ibid.

876. Ibid., 367.

877. Helyar, 372; Holtzman, 207.

878. Helyar, 387; Sands, 90.

879. Koppett, 458–459.

880. Ibid., 483.

881. *Associated Press* syndicated story, September 26, 2000.

882. For detailed chronicles of television and its financial impact on baseball, read Klatell, David and Marcus, Norm. *Sports for Sale: Television, Money, and the Fans.* New York: Oxford University Press, 1989; Rader, Benjamin G. *In Its Own Image: How Television Has Transformed Sports.* New York: Free Press, 1984; Sands, Jack and Gammons, Peter. *Coming Apart at the Seams: How Baseball Owners, Players, and Television Executives Have Led Our National Past Time to the Brink of Disaster.* New York: Macmillan, 1993.

883. Helyar, 372.

884. Ibid., 372–381.

885. *SportsLine.com,* July 10, 2001.

886. Helyar, 177–183.

887. Noll, Roger G. and Zimbalist, Andrew (eds.) *Sports, Jobs & Taxes: The Economic Impact of Sports Teams and Stadiums.* Washington, D.C.: Brookings Institution Press, 1997, 30–36.

888. Helyar, 58–59.

889. Noll, et al.

890. Noll, et al., 9–11.

891. This debate is clearly beyond the scope of this book. For a thorough analysis of the economics of professional sports and publicly financed stadiums, I recommend Cagan, Joanna and de Mause, Neil. *Field of Schemes: How the Great Stadium Swindle Turns Public Money Into Private Profit.* Monroe, ME: Common Courage Press, 1998; Gorman, Jerry and Calhoun, Kirk. *The Name of the Game: The Business of Sports.* New York: John Wiley & Sons, 1994; Noll, et al.; Quirk, James and Fort, Rodney. *Pay Dirt: The Business of Professional Team Sports.* Princeton, N.J.: Princeton University Press, 1992; Quirk, James and Fort, Rodney. *Hard Ball: The Abuse of Power in Pro Team Sports.* Princeton, N.J.: Princeton University Press, 1999; Rosentraub, Mark S. *Major League Lo$ers: The Real Cost of Sports and Who's Paying for It.* New York: Basic Books, 1999; Sherman, Len. *Big League, Big Time: The Birth of the Arizona Diamondbacks, the Billion-dollar Business of Sports, and the Power of the Media in America.* New York: Pocket Books, 1998; Sommers, Paul M. (ed.). *Diamonds Are Forever: The Business of Baseball.* Washington, D.C.: Brookings Institution Press, 1992; Weiner, Jay. *Stadium Games: Fifty Years of Big League Greed and Bush League Boondoggles.* Minneapolis: University of Minnesota Press, 2000; Zimbalist, Andrew. *Baseball and Billions: A Probing Look Inside the Big Business of Our National Pastime.* New York: Basic Books, 1992.

892. Noll, et al., 494.

893. Helyar, 315–316.

894. *Forbes,* January 8, 2002.

895. Ibid.

896. Ibid.

Chapter 15

897. Burk, *Much More Than a Game,* 288; Koppett, 456–457.

898. Burk, *Much More Than a Game,* 290; Koppett, 457.

899. Burk, *Much More Than a Game,* 292; Holtzman, 280–281; Koppett, 462–463.

900. Abrams, *Legal Bases,* 194–195; Burk, *Much More Than a Game,* 292; Holtzman, 282; Koppett, 463–464.

901. Burk, *Much More Than a Game,* 295.

902. Ibid., 296.

903. A moving account of the 1998 season is provided in Lupica, Mike. *Summer of '98: When Homers Flew, Records Fell, and Baseball Reclaimed America.* New York: G.P. Putnam's Sons, 1999.

904. An account of each of McGwire's 70 home runs during the 1998 season is provided in *The Sporting News. Celebrating 70: Mark McGwire's Historic Season.* St. Louis: The Sporting News, 1998.

905. James, Bill. *Bill James Baseball Stats Calendar.* November 10, 2000.

906. Gonzalez Echeverria, Roberto. *The Pride of Havana: A History of Cuban Baseball.* New York: Oxford University Press, 1999.

907. Josh Gibson reportedly hit 75 home runs in various Negro League and barnstorming games in 1931. Holway, *Josh and Satch,* 39.

908. The 1906 Cubs played a 154-game schedule and the 2001 Mariners played a 162-game schedule.

909. I share David Halberstam's inability to enjoy the majesty of Barry Bonds's career, the reasons for which were set forth in two frank articles in *ESPN Page 2* on October 29, 2002, and July 19, 2001.

910. *Slam Sports,* October 28, 2002.

911. Report of the Independent Members of the Commissioner's Blue Ribbon Panel on Baseball Economics (July 2000).

912. Miller, 362.

913. *Forbes,* April 15, 2002.

914. Burk, *Much More Than a Game,* 208; Holtzman, 224; Light, 642.

915. Burk, *Much More Than a Game,* 205–206; Holtzman, 164; Koppett, 368–369; Miller, 267; Light, 641.

916. Koppett, 483.

917. Thorn, et al., *Total Baseball,* 108.

918. Miller, 285.

919. *SportsLine.com,* July 10, 2001.

Chapter 16

920. Helyar, 523.

921. Burk, *Never Just a Game,* 105–106; Koppett, 59; Seymour, *Baseball: The Early Years,* 228–229.

922. Burk, *Never Just a Game,* 152–153; Koppett, 90; Seymour, *Baseball: The Early Years,* 317–320.

923. Burk, *Never Just a Game,* 195; Seymour, *Baseball: The Golden Age,* 199.

924. James, *The New Bill James Historical Baseball Abstract,* 327–328.

BIBLIOGRAPHY

This book is not intended as an academic resource or an exhaustive treatment of the various topics that it discusses. Obviously a writer is influenced by, and draws from, a multitude of sources in writing a book such as this. In my case, during nearly fifty years as a baseball fan, I have attended thousands of baseball games, watched and listened to tens of thousands more on television and radio, read thousands of newspaper and magazine articles on baseball in hundreds of publications—many of which are no longer in existence—and read hundreds of baseball books— some magnificent and others execrable. All of these sources have provided important background information and helped me to form my views. I cannot personally—or even here in print—thank all of the players, announcers, journalists, and authors to whom I owe a debt, but I do wish to cite the following books which contain material relevant to various topics discussed in this book and which can provide more detailed analysis of those topics to the interested reader.

Aaron, Hank with Wheeler, Lonnie. *I Had a Hammer: The Hank Aaron Story.* New York: Harper Collins, 1991.

Abrams, Roger I. *Legal Basis: Baseball and the Law.* Philadelphia: Temple University Press, 1998.

_____. *The Money Pitch: Baseball Free Agency and Salary Arbitration.* Philadelphia: Temple University Press, 2000.

Alexander, Charles C. *John McGraw.* New York: Viking Penguin, 1988.

_____. *Our Game: An American Baseball History.* New York: Henry Holt, 1991.

_____. *Rogers Hornsby.* New York: Owl Books, 1995.

_____. *Ty Cobb.* New York: Oxford University Press, 1984.

Allen, Dick and Whitaker, Tim. *Crash: The Life and Times of Dick Allen.* New York: Ticknor & Fields, 1989.

Allen, Lee. *100 Years of Baseball.* New York: Bartholomew House, 1950.

_____. *The Cincinnati Reds.* New York: G.P. Putnam's, 1948.

_____. *The Giants and the Dodgers: The Fabulous Story of Baseball's Fiercest Feud.* New York: G.P. Putnam's, 1964.

Allen, Lee and Meany, Tom. *Kings of the Diamond: The Immortals in Baseball's Hall of Fame.* New York: G.P. Putnam's, 1965.

Allen, Maury. *All Roads Lead to October! Boss Steinbrenner's 25-Year Reign Over the New York Yankees.* New York: St. Martin's Press, 2000.

_____. *Baseball's 100: A Personal Ranking of the Best Players in Baseball History.* New York: A & W Visual Library, 1981.

_____. *Jackie Robinson: A Life Remembered.* New York: Franklin Watts, 1987.

_____. *Roger Maris: A Man for All Seasons.* New York: Donald Fine, 1986.

_____. *Where Have You Gone, Joe DiMaggio? The Story of America's Last Hero.* New York: E.P. Dutton, 1975.

_____. *You Could Look It Up: The Life of Casey Stengel.* New York: Times Books, 1979.

Ambrose, Stephen E. *Eisenhower: The President.* New York: Simon & Schuster, 1984.

Anderson, Dave. *Pennant Races: Baseball at Its Best.* New York: Doubleday, 1994.

_____. *The Yankees: Four Fabulous Eras of Baseball's Most Famous Team.* New York: Random House, 1980.

Angell, Roger. *Five Seasons.* New York: Simon & Schuster, 1977.

_____. *Late Innings.* New York: Simon & Schuster, 1982.

_____. *Season Ticket.* Boston: Houghton-Mifflin, 1988.

_____. *The Summer Game.* New York: Viking Press, 1972.

Asinof, Elliott. *Eight Men Out: The Black Sox and the 1919 World Series.* New York: Holt, Rinehart, and Winston, 1963.

Axthelm, Pete. *The City Game.* New York: Harper's Magazine Books, 1970.

Barber, Red. *1947: When All Hell Broke Loose in Baseball.* Garden City, N.Y.: Doubleday, 1982.

Bardo, Michael D. (ed). *The Defining Moment: The Great Depression and The American Economy in the Twentieth Century.* Chicago: University of Chicago Press, 1998.

Barzun, Jacques. *God's Country and Mine: A Declaration of Love Spiced with a Few Harsh Words.* Boston: Little, Brown and Company, 1954.

Benson, Michael. *Ballparks of North America: A Comprehensive Historical Reference to Baseball Grounds, Yards, and Stadiums, 1845 to the Present.* Jefferson, N.C.: McFarland, 1989.

Berra, Yogi with Horton, Tom. *Yogi: It Ain't Over ....* New York: Harper, 1989.

Bjarkman, Peter C. *Baseball with a Latin Beat.* Jefferson, N.C.: McFarland, 1994.

Bjarkman, Peter C. (ed.). *Baseball and The Game of Ideas: Essays for the Serious Fan.* Delhi, N.Y.: Birch, 1993.

Boswell, Thomas. *The Heart of the Order*. New York: Penguin, 1989.

Bouton, Jim. *Ball Four*. New York: Macmillan, 1970.

Brashler, William. *Josh Gibson: A Life in the Negro Leagues*. Chicago: Ivan R. Dee, 1978.

Brosnan, Jim. *The Long Season*. New York: Grosset & Dunlap, 1960.

Bruce, Janet. *The Kansas City Monarchs: Champions of Black Baseball*. Lawrence, Kan.: University of Kansas Press, 1985.

Burk, Robert F. *Much More Than A Game: Players, Owners, and American Baseball Since 1921*. Chapel Hill, N.C.: University of North Carolina Press, 2001.

_____. *Never Just A Game: Players, Owners, and American Baseball to 1920*. Chapel Hill, N.C.: University of North Carolina Press, 1994.

Cagan, Joanna and de Mause, Neil. *Field of Schemes: How the Great Stadium Swindle Turns Public Money into Private Profit*. Monroe, Me.: Common Courage Press, 1998.

Campanella, Roy. *It's Good to Be Alive*. Boston: Little, Brown, 1959.

Caray, Harry with Berdi, Bob. *Holy Cow*. New York: Villard, 1989.

Caro, Robert A. *The Years of Lyndon Johnson: The Means of Ascent*. New York: Alfred A. Knopf, 1990.

Chadwick, Bruce. *When the Game Was Black and White: The Illustrated History of the Negro Leagues*. New York: Abbeville Press, 1992.

Chamberlain, Wilt. *A View from Above*. New York: Villard, 1991.

Chandler, Albert B. *Heroes, Plain Folks and Skunks: The Life and Times of Happy Chandler*. Chicago: Bonus Books, 1989.

Charlton, James (ed.). *The Baseball Chronology: The Complete History of the Most Important Events in the Game of Baseball*. New York: Macmillan, 1991.

Cobb, Ty with Stump, Al. *My Life in Baseball: The True Record*. Garden City, N.Y.: Doubleday, 1961.

Cohen, Stanley. *A Magic Summer: The '69 Mets*. New York: Harcourt Brace Jovanovich, 1989.

Colangelo, Jerry. *How You Play the Game: Lessons for Life from the Billion-Dollar Business of Sports*. New York: American Management Association, 1999.

Costas, Bob. *Fair Ball: A Fan's Case for Baseball*. New York: Broadway Books, 2000.

Craft, David and Owens, Tom. *Redbirds Revisited: Great Memories and Stories from St. Louis Cardinals*. Chicago: Bonus Books, 1990.

Cramer, Richard Ben. *Joe DiMaggio: The Hero's Life*. New York: Simon & Schuster, 2000.

Creamer, Robert W. *Babe: The Legend Comes to Life*. New York: Simon & Schuster, 1974.

_____. *Baseball in '41: A Celebration of the Best Baseball Season Ever in the Year America Went to War*. New York: Penguin, 1991.

_____. *Stengel: His Life and Times*. New York: Simon & Schuster, 1984.

Curran, William. *Big Sticks: The Batting Revolution of the 20's*. New York: William Morrow, 1990.

Daley, Arthur. *All the Home Run Kings*. New York: G.P. Putnam's, 1972.

Daniel, W. Harrison. *Jimmie Foxx: Baseball Hall of Famer, 1907–1967*. Jefferson, N.C.: McFarland, 1996.

Debono, Paul. *The Indianapolis ABCs: History of a Premier Team in the Negro Leagues*. Jefferson, N.C.: McFarland, 1997.

DeLillo, Don. *Underworld*. New York: Scribner, 1997.

DeLong, J. Bradford. *Slouching Towards Utopia: The Economic History of the Twentieth Century*. Berkeley, Cal.: University of California Press, 2000.

Dickson, Paul (ed.). *Baseball's Greatest Quotations*. New York: Harper Collins, 1991.

DiSalvatore, Bryan. *A Clever Base-Ballist: The Life and Times of John Montgomery Ward*. Baltimore: The Johns Hopkins University Press, 1999.

Durocher, Leo with Linn, Ed. *Nice Guys Finish Last*. New York: Simon & Schuster, 1975.

Durso, Joseph. *Baseball and the American Dream*. St. Louis: The Sporting News, 1986.

_____. *Casey: The Life and Legend of Charles Dillon Stengel*. Englewood Cliffs, N.J.: Prentice-Hall, 1967.

_____. *The Days of Mr. McGraw*. Englewood Cliffs, N.J.: Prentice-Hall, 1969.

Dworkin, James B. *Owners Versus Players: Baseball and Collective Bargaining*. Boston: Auburn House, 1981.

Einstein, Charles. *Willie's Time: A Memoir*. Philadelphia: J.B. Lippincott, 1979.

_____ (ed.). *The Baseball Reader: Favorites from the Fireside Book of Baseball*. New York: McGraw-Hill, 1986.

Eskenazi, Gerald. *Veeck: A Baseball Legend*. New York: McGraw-Hill, 1988.

Faber, Charles F. *Baseball Pioneers: Ratings of 19th Century Players*. Jefferson, N.C.: McFarland, 1997.

_____. *Baseball Ratings: The All-Time Best Players at Each Position*. Jefferson, N.C.: McFarland, 1995.

Falkner, David. *Great Time Coming; The Life of Jackie Robinson from Baseball to Birmingham*. New York: Simon & Schuster, 1995.

Feldmann, Doug. *Dizzy and the Gashouse Gang: The 1934 St. Louis Cardinals and Depression-Era Baseball*. Jefferson, N.C.: McFarland, 2000.

Feller, Bob. *Strikeout Story*. New York: Grosset & Dunlap, 1947.

Fizel, John, Gustafson, Elizabeth, and Hadley, Lawrence (eds.). *Sports Economics: Current Research*. New York: Praeger, 1999.

Fleming, G.H. *Murderer's Row: The 1927 New York Yankees*. New York: William Morrow, 1985.

Flood, Curt and Carter, Richard. *Curt Flood: The Way It Is*. New York: Trident Press, 1970.

Ford, Whitey with Pepe, Phil. *Slick: My Life In and Around Baseball*. New York: William Morrow, 1987.

Ford, Whitey, Mantle, Mickey, and Durso, Joseph. *Whitey and Mickey: An Autobiography of the Yankee Years*. New York: Viking, 1977.

Frick, Ford. *Games, Asterisks and People: Memoirs of a Lucky Fan*. New York: Crown, 1973.

Frommer, Harvey. *New York City Baseball: The Last Golden Age, 1947–1957*. New York: Macmillan, 1980.

_____. *Rickey and Robinson: The Men Who Broke Baseball's Color Barrier*. New York: Macmillan, 1982.

Giamatti, A. Bartlett. *A Great and Glorious Game*. Chapel Hill, N.C.: Algonquin, 1998.

Gibson, Bob with Pepe, Phil. *From Ghetto to Glory: The Story of Bob Gibson*. Englewood Cliffs, N.J.: Prentice-Hall, 1968.

Gibson, Bob with Wheeler, Lonnie. *Stranger to the Game: The Autobiography of Bob Gibson*. New York: Penguin, 1994.

Giglio, James N. *Musial: From Stash to Stan the Man*. Columbia, Mo.: University of Missouri Press, 2001.

Gilbert, Bill. *They Also Served: Baseball and the Home Front, 1941–1945*. New York: Crown, 1992.

Gilbert, Brother C.F.X. (Ed. Harry Rothgerber). *Young Babe Ruth: His Early Life and Baseball Career, from the Memoirs of a Xaverian Brother*. Jefferson, N.C.: McFarland, 1999.

Gluck, Herb. *The Mick, An American Hero: The Legend and the Glory*. New York: Jove, 1985.

Goldstein, Richard. *Spartan Seasons: How Baseball Survived the Second World War*. New York: Macmillan, 1980.

Goldstein, Warren. *Playing for Keeps: A History of Early Baseball*. Ithaca, N.Y.: Cornell University Press, 1989.

Golenbock, Peter. *Bums: An Oral History of the Brooklyn Dodgers*. New York: G.P. Putnam's, 1984.

_____. *Dynasty: The New York Yankees, 1949–1964*. Englewood Cliffs, N.J.: Prentice-Hall, 1975.

_____. *The Spirit of St. Louis: A History of the St. Louis Cardinals and Browns*. New York: Avon, 2000.

Gonzalez Echeverria, Roberto. *The Pride of Havana: A History of Cuban Baseball*. New York: Oxford University Press, 1999.

Gorman, Bob. *Double X: Jimmie Foxx, Baseball's Forgotten Slugger*. New York: Bill Goff, 1990.

Gorman, Jerry and Calhoun, Kirk. *The Name of the Game: The Business of Sports*. New York: John Wiley, 1994.

Graham, Frank. *Lou Gehrig: A Quiet Hero*. New York: G.P. Putnam's, 1942.

Greenberg, Hank. *The Story of My Life*. New York: Times Books, 1989.

Gregory, Robert. *Diz: Dizzy Dean and Baseball During the Great Depression.* New York: Viking, 1992.

Gruver, Edward. *Koufax.* New York: Taylor Publishing, 2000.

Guschov, Stephen. *The Red Stockings of Cincinnati: Base Ball's First All Professional Team and Its Historic 1869 and 1870 Seasons.* Jefferson, N.C.: McFarland, 1998.

Gutman, Dan. *Baseball Babylon: From the Black Sox to Pete Rose, the Real Stories Behind the Scandals that Rocked the Game.* New York: Penguin, 1992.

Halberstam, David. *October 1964.* New York: Villard, 1994.

_____. *Summer of '49.* New York: William Morrow, 1989.

Hall, Donald. *Fathers Playing Catch with Sons.* New York: North Point, 1985.

Helyar, John. *Lords of the Realm: The Real History of Baseball.* New York, Villard: 1994.

Hemingway, Ernest. *The Old Man and the Sea.* New York: Charles Scribner's & Sons, 1952.

Henrich, Tommy with Gilbert, Bill. *Five O'Clock Lightning: Ruth, Gehrig, DiMaggio, Mantle and the Glory Years of the New York Yankees.* New York: Carol Publishing, 1992.

Herzog, Whitey with Pitts, Jonathan. *You're Missin' a Great Game: From Casey to Ozzie, the Magic of Baseball and How to Get It Back.* New York: Simon & Schuster, 1999.

Hoban, Michael. *Baseball's Complete Players: Ratings of Total-Season Performance for the Greatest Players of the 20th Century.* Jefferson, N.C.: McFarland, 2000.

Holtzman, Jerome. *No Cheering in the Press Box.* New York: Holt, Rinehart and Winston, 1973.

_____. *The Commissioners: Baseball's Mid–Life Crisis.* New York: Total Sports, 1998.

Holway, John B. *Blackball Stars: Negro League Pioneers.* Westport, Ct.: Meckler Books, 1988.

_____. *Black Diamonds: Life in the Negro Leagues from the Men Who Lived It.* Westport, Ct.: Meckler Books, 1989.

_____. *Josh and Satch: The Life and Times of Josh Gibson and Satchel Paige.* Westport, Ct.: Meckler Books, 1991.

_____. *Josh Gibson, Negro Great.* New York: Chelsea House Publishers, 1995.

_____. *The Complete Book of Baseball's Negro Leagues: The Other Half of Baseball History.* Fern Park, Fl.: Hastings House, 2001.

Honig, Donald. *Baseball America: The Heroes of the Game and the Times of Their Glory.* New York: Macmillan, 1985.

_____. *Baseball Between the Lines: Baseball in the '40s and '50s as Told by the Men Who Played It.* New York: Coward, McCann, and Geoghegan, 1976.

_____. *Baseball in the '50s. A Decade of Transition.* New York: Macmillan, 1987.

_____. *Baseball in the '30s: A Decade of Survival.* New York: Crown, 1989.

_____. *Mays, Mantle, Snider: A Celebration.* New York: Macmillan, 1988.

_____. *The Power Hitters.* St. Louis: The Sporting News, 1989.

James, Bill. *Stats All-Time Major League Handbook.* Skokie, Ill.: Stats, Inc., 2000.

_____. *The Bill James Historical Baseball Abstract.* New York: Villard, 1986.

_____. *The Great American Baseball Stat Book.* New York: Ballantine, 1987.

_____. *The New Bill James Historical Baseball Abstract.* New York: Free Press, 2001.

James, Bill (ed.). *All-Time Baseball Source Book.* Skokie, Ill.: Stats, Inc., 1998.

Jenkins, Dan. *Life Its Ownself.* New York: Simon & Schuster, 1984.

_____. *Semi-Tough.* New York: Atheneum, 1972.

Johnson, Dick and Spout, Glenn. *Ted Williams: A Portrait in Words and Pictures.* New York: Walker, 1991.

Kahn, Roger. *A Flame of Pure Fire: Jack Dempsey and the Roaring '20s.* New York: Harcourt, 1999.

_____. *Memories of Summer: When Baseball Was an Art, and Writing About It a Game.* New York: Hyperion, 1997.

_____. *The Boys of Summer.* New York: Harper & Row, 1971.

_____. *The Era: 1947–1957—When the Yankees, the Giants and the Dodgers Ruled the World.* New York: Ticknor & Fields, 1993.

_____. *The Head Game: Baseball Seen from the Pitcher's Mound.* New York: Harcourt, 2000.

Karnow, Stanley. *Vietnam: A History: The First Complete Account of Vietnam at War.* New York: Viking Press, 1983.

Kashatus, William C. *Connie Mack's '29 Triumph: The Rise and Fall of the Philadelphia Athletics Dynasty.* Jefferson, N.C.: McFarland, 1999.

_____. *One-Armed Wonder Pete Gray, Wartime Baseball and the American Dream.* Jefferson, N.C.: McFarland, 1995.

Kelly, Brent. *In the Shadow of the Babe: Interviews with Baseball Players Who Played with or against Babe Ruth.* Jefferson, N.C.: McFarland, 1995.

_____. *The Early All Stars: Conversations with Standout Baseball Players of the 1930s and 1940s.* Jefferson, N.C.: McFarland, 1997.

_____. *The Negro Leagues Revisited: Conversations with 66 More Baseball Heroes.* Jefferson, N.C.: McFarland, 2000.

_____. *Voices from the Negro Leagues: Conversations with 52 Baseball Standouts of the Period 1924–1960.* Jefferson, N.C.: McFarland, 1998.

Klatell, David and Marcus, Norman. *Sports for Sale: Television, Money, and the Fans.* New York: Oxford University Press, 1989.

Koppett, Leonard. *Koppett's Concise History of Major League Baseball.* Philadelphia: Temple University Press, 1998.

Kuhn, Bowie. *Hardball: The Education of a Baseball Commissioner.* Lincoln, Neb.: University of Nebraska Press, 1987.

Lansche, Jerry. *Stan the Man Musial: Born to Be a Ballplayer*. Dallas: Taylor Publishing, 1994.

Levine, Peter. *A.G. Spalding and the Rise of Baseball: The Promise of American Sport*. New York: Oxford University Press, 1985.

Lieb, Frederick G. *Connie Mack: Grand Old Man of Baseball*. Carbondale, IL: Southern Illinois University Press, 2001 (reprint of 1944 edition).

_____. *The St. Louis Cardinals: The Story of a Great Baseball Club*. Carbondale, IL: Southern Illinois University Press, 2001 (reprint of 1944 edition).

Light, Jonathan Fraser. *The Cultural Encyclopedia of Baseball*. Jefferson, N.C.: McFarland, 1997.

Linn, Ed. *Hitter: The Life and Turmoils of Ted Williams*. New York: Harcourt Brace, 1993.

Lipman, David. *Mr. Baseball: The Story of Branch Rickey*. New York: 1966.

Lipsyte, Robert and Levine, Peter. *Idols of the Game: A Sporting History of the American Century*. Atlanta: Turner Publishing, 1995.

Lowenfish, Lee. *The Imperfect Diamond: A History of Baseball's Labor Wars*. New York: Da Capo, 1991.

Lowenfish, Lee and Loupien, Tony. *The Imperfect Diamond: The Story of Baseball's Reserve System and the Men Who Fought to Change It*. New York: Stein & Day, 1980.

Lowry, Philip. *Green Cathedrals*. Cooperstown, N.Y.: Society for American Baseball Research, 1986.

Lupica, Mike. *Summer of 1998: When Homers Flew, Records Fell, and Baseball Reclaimed America*. New York: NTC/Contemporary Publishing Co., 2000.

Mann, Arthur. *Branch Rickey: American in Action*. Boston: 1957.

Mantle, Merlyn, Mantle, Mickey Jr., Mantle, Donald, and Mantle, Dan. *A Hero All His Life*. New York: Harper Collins, 1996.

Mantle, Mickey and Pepe, Phil. *My Favorite Summer: 1956*. New York: Doubleday, 1991.

Mays, Willie with Einstein, Charles. *Born to Play Ball*. New York: G.P. Putnam's, 1955.

Mays, Willie with Sahadi, Lou. *Say Hey: The Autobiography of Willie Mays*. New York: Simon & Schuster, 1988.

McCarver, Tim with Robinson, Ray. *Oh, Baby I Love It!* New York: Dell Books, 1987.

McCullough, David. *Truman*. New York: Simon & Schuster, 1992.

McElvaine, Robert S. *The Great Depression: America 1929–1941*. New York: Times Books, 1981.

McGuire, Mark and Gormley, Michael Sean. *The 100 Greatest Baseball Players of the 20th Century Ranked*. Jefferson, N.C.: McFarland, 2000.

McNeil, William F. *Ruth, Maris, McGwire, and Sosa*. Jefferson, N.C.: McFarland, 1999.

Mead, William. *Baseball Goes to War*. Washington, D.C.: Farragut Publishing, 1985.

Melville, Tom. *Early Baseball and the Rise of the National League*. Jefferson, N.C.: McFarland, 2001.

Miller, James Edward. *The Baseball Business: Pursuing Pennants and Profits in Baltimore*. Chapel Hill, N.C.: University of North Carolina Press, 1990.

Miller, Jon with Hyman, Mark. *Confessions of a Baseball Purist: What's Right— and Wrong—with Baseball, as Seen from the Best Seat in the House*. New York: Simon & Schuster, 1998.

Miller, Marvin. *A Whole Different Ball Game: The Inside Story of Baseball's New Deal*. New York: Simon & Schuster, 1991.

Minks, Benton. *100 Greatest Hitters*. Greenwich, Ct.: Bison Books, 1988.

Moffi, Larry and Kronstadt, Jonathan. *Crossing the Line. Black Major Leaguers, 1947–1959*. Jefferson, N.C.: McFarland, 1994.

Monteleone, John J. *Branch Rickey's Little Blue Book*. New York: Macmillan, 1995.

Moore, Jack B. *Joe DiMaggio: Baseball's Yankee Clipper*. New York: Greenwood Press, 1986.

Morgan, Joe with Lally, Richard. *Long Balls, No Strikes: What Baseball Must Do to Keep the Good Times Rolling*. New York: Crown, 1999.

Murdock, Eugene C. *Ban Johnson: Czar of Baseball*. Westport, Ct.: Greenwood Press, 1982.

Musial, Stan with Broeg, Bob. *Stan Musial: "The Man's" Own Story*. New York: Doubleday, 1964.

Nathan, David H. *The McFarland Baseball Quotations Dictionary*. Jefferson, N.C.: McFarland, 2000.

Nathan, David H. (ed). *Baseball Quotations*. New York: Ballantine, 1991.

Nelson, Kevin (ed.). *Baseball's Greatest Quotes: The Wit, Wisdom, and Wisecracks of America's National Pastime*. New York: Simon & Schuster, 1982.

Nemec, David. *The Beer and Whiskey League: The Illustrated History of the American Association*. New York: Lyons & Burford, 1994.

Noll, Roger G. and Zimbalist, Andrew (ed.). *Sports, Jobs & Taxes: The Economic Impact of Sports Teams and Stadiums*. Washington, D.C.: Brookings Institution, 1997.

Oakley, J. Ronald. *Baseball's Last Golden Age, 1946–1960*. Jefferson, N.C.: McFarland, 1994.

Okrent, Daniel and Levine, Harris (eds.) *The Ultimate Baseball Book*. Boston: Houghton Mifflin, 1979.

Paige, Leroy Satchel and Lebovitz, Hal. *Pitchin' Man: Satchel Paige's Own Story*. Westport, Ct.: Meckler, 1948.

Parker, Clifton Blue. *Fouled Away: The Baseball Tragedy of Hack Wilson*. Jefferson, N.C.: McFarland, 2000.

Parrott, Harold. *The Lords of Baseball*. New York: Praeger, 1976.

Pepe, Phil. *Talkin' Baseball: An Oral History of Baseball in the 1970s.* New York: Ballantine, 1998.

_____. *The Wit and Wisdom of Yogi Berra.* New York: Hawthorn, 1974.

Peterson, Robert. *Only the Ball Was White: A History of Legendary Black Players and All-Black Professional Teams.* Englewood Cliffs, N.J.: Prentice-Hall, 1970.

Pietrusza, David, Silverman, Matthew, and Girshman, Michael. *Baseball: The Biographical Encyclopedia.* Kingston, N.Y.: Total/Sports Illustrated, 2000.

Polner, Murray. *Branch Rickey: A Biography.* New York: Atheneum, 1982.

Prince, Carl. *Brooklyn's Dodgers: The Bums, the Borough, and the Best of Baseball, 1947–1957.* New York: Oxford University Press, 1996.

Quirk, James, and Fort, Rodney. *Hard Ball: The Abuse of Power in Pro Team Sports.* Princeton, N.J.: Princeton University Press, 1999.

_____. *Pay Dirt: The Business of Professional Team Sports.* Princeton, N.J.: Princeton University Press, 1992.

Rader, Benjamin G. *Baseball: A History of America's Game.* Urbana, Ill.: University of Illinois Press, 1992.

_____. *In Its Own Image: How Television Has Transformed Sports.* New York: Free Press, 1984.

Rains, Rob. *The St. Louis Cardinals.* New York: St. Martin's Press, 1992.

Regalado, Samuel O. *Viva Baseball! Latin Major Leaguers and Their Special Hunger.* Urbana, Ill.: University of Illinois Press, 1998.

Reichler, Joseph L. (ed.). *The Baseball Encyclopedia: The Complete and Official Record of Major League Baseball* (9th ed.). New York: Macmillan, 1993.

Reidenbaugh, Lowell. *The Sporting News Selects Baseball's 25 Greatest Teams.* St. Louis: The Sporting News, 1988.

Reston, James, Jr. *Collision at Home Plate: The Lives of Pete Rose and Bart Giamatti.* Edward Burlingame Books, 1991.

Ritter, Lawrence. *Lost Ballparks. A Celebration of Baseball's Legendary Fields.* New York: Penguin Books, 1992.

_____. *The Glory of Their Times: The Story of the Early Days of Baseball Told by the Men Who Played It.* New York: William Morrow, 1966.

Robinson, Jackie with Duckett, Alfred. *I Never Had It Made.* New York: G.P. Putnam's, 1972.

Rogosin, Donn. *Invisible Men: Life in Baseball's Negro Leagues.* New York: Atheneum, 1983.

Rose, Pete with Kahn, Roger. *Pete Rose: My Story.* New York: Macmillan, 1989.

Rosenthal, Harold. *The Ten Best Years of Baseball: An Informal History of the Fifties.* Chicago: Contemporary Books, 1979.

Rosentraub, Mark S. *Major League Lo$ers: The Real Cost of Sports and Who's Paying for It.* New York: Basic Books, 1999.

Rossi, John P. *A Whole New Game: Off the Field Changes in Baseball, 1946–1960.* Jefferson, N.C.: McFarland, 1999.

_____. *The National Game: Baseball and American Culture*. Chicago: Ivan R. Dee, 2000.

Rowan, Carl T., with Jackie Robinson. *Wait Till Next Year: The Life Story of Jackie Robinson*. New York: Random House, 1960.

Ruth, George Herman. *Babe Ruth's Own Book of Baseball*. Lincoln, Neb.: University of Nebraska Press, 1992. Reprint of 1928 edition.

Ruth, George Herman and Considine, Bob. *The Babe Ruth Story*. New York: E.P. Dutton, 1948.

Ryczek, William J. *Blackguards and Red Stockings: A History of Baseball's National Association, 1871–1875*. Jefferson, N.C.: McFarland, 1992.

_____. *When Johnny Came Sliding Home: The Post–Civil War Baseball Boom, 1865–1870*. Jefferson, N.C.: McFarland, 1998.

Samuelson, Paul A. *Economics* (8th Ed.). New York: McGraw-Hill, 1970.

Sands, Jack and Gammons, Peter. *Coming Apart at the Seams: How Baseball Owners, Players, and Television Executives Have Led Our National Pastime to the Brink of Disaster*. New York: Macmillan, 1993.

Schoor, Gene. *Joe DiMaggio: A Biography*. New York: Doubleday, 1980.

Scully, Gerald W. *The Business of Major League Baseball*. Chicago: University of Chicago Press, 1989.

_____. *The Market Structure of Sports*. Chicago: University of Chicago Press, 1995.

Seidel, Michael. *Ted Williams: A Baseball Life*. Chicago: Contemporary Books, 1991.

Senzell, Howard. *Baseball and the Cold War*. New York: Harcourt Brace Jovanovich, 1977.

Seymour, Harold. *Baseball: The Early Years*. New York: Oxford University Press, 1990.

_____. *Baseball: The Golden Age*. New York: Oxford University Press, 1971.

_____. *Baseball: The People's Game*. New York: Oxford University Press, 2001.

Shaughnessy, Dan. *The Curse of the Bambino*. New York: Penguin, 1991.

Sherman, Len. *Big League, Big Time: The Birth of the Arizona Diamondbacks, the Billion-dollar Business of Sports, and the Power of the Media in America*. New York: Pocket Books, 1998.

Shouler, Ken. *The Real 100 Best Baseball Players of All Time ... and Why!* Lenaxa, Kan.: Addax Publishing, 1998.

Silverman, Al. *Joe DiMaggio: The Golden Year, 1941*. Englewood Cliffs, N.J.: Prentice-Hall, 1969.

Silverman, Brian (ed.). *Going, Going, Gone....: The History, Lore, and Mystique of the Home Run*. New York: Harper Collins, 2000.

Smelser, Marshall. *The Life That Ruth Built: A Biography*. New York: Quadrangle/New York Times Book Company, 1975.

Smith, Red. *Red Smith on Baseball*. Chicago: Ivan R. Dee, 2000.

Smith, Ron. *The Ballpark Book: A Journey Through the Fields of Baseball Magic.* St. Louis: The Sporting News, 2000.

Sobol, Ken. *Babe Ruth and the American Dream.* New York: Random House, 1974.

Sommers, Paul M. *Diamonds Are Forever. The Business of Baseball.* Washington, D.C.: The Brookings Institution, 1992.

Spalding, Albert G. *America's National Game.* Lincoln, Neb.: University of Nebraska Press, 1992 (reprint of 1911 edition).

Sporting News, The. *Baseball: 100 Years of the Modern Era: 1901–2000.* St. Louis: The Sporting News, 2001.

_____. *Baseball's Greatest Players: A Celebration of the 20th Century's Best.* St. Louis: The Sporting News, 1998.

_____. *Celebrating 70: Mark McGwire's Historic Season.* St. Louis: The Sporting News, 1998.

_____. *The Sporting News Baseball Guide: The Ultimate 2001 Season Reference.* St. Louis: The Sporting News, NTC/Contemporary Publishing, 2001

_____. *The Sporting News Baseball Register: 2001 Edition.* St. Louis: The Sporting News NTC/Contemporary Publishing, 2001.

_____. *The Sporting News Complete Baseball Record Book: 2001 Edition.* St. Louis: The Sporting News NTC/Contemporary Publishing, 2001.

Stats, Inc. *Bill James Presents .... Stats Major League Handbook 2001.* Skokie, Ill.: Stats, Inc. 2001.

Sullivan, Neil J. *The Dodgers Move West.* New York: Oxford University Press, 1987.

Sywoff, Seymour, Hirdt, Steve, Hirdt, Tom, and Hirdt, Peter. *The Elias Baseball Analyst.* New York: Macmillan, 2000.

Thorn, John. *A Century of Baseball Lore.* New York: Galahad Books, 1976.

Thorn, John (ed.). *The Arm Chair Book of Baseball.* New York: Collier, 1985.

Thorn, John and Palmer, Pete (eds.) *Total Baseball* (6th ed.). New York: Total Sports, 1999.

Torrez, Andrew. *Off Base: New Insights into an Old Game.* New York: Woodford Publishing, 1999.

Tygiel, Jules. *Baseball's Great Experiment: Jackie Robinson and His Legacy.* New York: Oxford University Press, 1983.

_____. *Past Time: Baseball as History.* New York: Oxford University Press, 2000.

Van Riper, Jr., Guernsey. *Babe Ruth: Baseball Boy.* New York: Bobbs-Merrill, 1954.

Veeck, Bill. *The Hustler's Handbook.* New York: Fireside Sports Classics, 1985.

Veeck, Bill and Linn, Ed. *Veeck—As in Wreck.* Evanston, Ill.: Holtzman Press, 1962.

Voight, David and Kachline, Clifford. *American Baseball: From Postwar Expansion to the Electronic Age.* State College, Pa.: Pennsylvania State University Press, 1983.